Sharing the Legacy and Narrative Leadership Experiences of Black Women in Education

Ashley N. Storman
The Storman Group LLC, USA

Destiny Reddick
Redefine the Pipeline LLC, USA

A volume in the Advances in Educational Marketing, Administration, and Leadership (AEMAL) Book Series

Published in the United States of America by
    IGI Global
    Information Science Reference (an imprint of IGI Global)
    701 E. Chocolate Avenue
    Hershey PA, USA 17033
    Tel: 717-533-8845
    Fax: 717-533-8661
    E-mail: cust@igi-global.com
    Web site: http://www.igi-global.com

Copyright © 2024 by IGI Global. All rights reserved. No part of this publication may be reproduced, stored or distributed in any form or by any means, electronic or mechanical, including photocopying, without written permission from the publisher.
Product or company names used in this set are for identification purposes only. Inclusion of the names of the products or companies does not indicate a claim of ownership by IGI Global of the trademark or registered trademark.

Library of Congress Cataloging-in-Publication Data

CIP DATA PENDING

ISBN: 9798369306987
isbn: 9798369306994
eISBN: 9798369307007

British Cataloguing in Publication Data
A Cataloguing in Publication record for this book is available from the British Library.

All work contributed to this book is new, previously-unpublished material.
The views expressed in this book are those of the authors, but not necessarily of the publisher.

For electronic access to this publication, please contact: eresources@igi-global.com.

Table of Contents

Preface.. xii

Section 1
Stories of Self

Chapter 1
Too Bold, Black, and Brilliant: Navigating the Leadership Tightrope of
Assimilation vs. Authenticity.. 1
Destiny Reddick, Redefine the Pipeline LLC, USA

Chapter 2
It's Not Me I See 63
Taylor C. J. Wynne, The Ohio State University, USA

Chapter 3
Life, Family, and Academia: Navigating the Superwoman Schema.................... 81
Chenell C. Loudermill, Independent Researcher, USA

Chapter 4
Navigating Academia the Ultimate Set-Up: I Knew It Was a Set Up, Because
It Was Too Easy!.. 91
Andrea "Andi" Toliver-Smith, Howard University, USA

Chapter 5
Leading and Surviving With Aftershocks 105
Bri'Yana Nicole Merrill, George Mason University, USA

Section 2
Stories of Us

Chapter 6
That's the Way Love Goes: On Black Women Leaders, Family Stories, and
Higher Education 125
Eboni L. Sterling, House Esther LLC, USA

Chapter 7
Reclaiming the Mainstream Depiction of Black Women: The Modern-Day
Representation of Black Women in Academia 159
   Lovis M. Nelson-Williams, Baylor University, USA

Chapter 8
From Mammy to Matriarch 177
   DeNiece Kemp, Confluence Academies-South City, USA

Chapter 9
Too Much of My Rhythm Causing Them So Much Blues 197
   Asueleni E. Deloney, Hand 'N Hand Coaching, USA

Section 3
Stories of Now

Chapter 10
The Price of a Token: The Effects of Tokenism on Black Women in Higher
Education 217
   Chinyere Turner, Partners in Justice LLC, USA

Chapter 11
Who Said I Can't Lead: The Journey to Leadership in Higher Education as a
Black Female... 235
   Ty Jiles, Prairie State College, USA
   Megan N. Lyons, North Carolina Central University, USA

Chapter 12
Crowned in Authenticity: Black Women Redefining Leadership by Leading
With Value and Purpose.. 251
   Ashley N. Storman, The Storman Group LLC, USA

Compilation of References 275

About the Contributors 299

Index.. 307

Detailed Table of Contents

Preface.. xii

Section 1
Stories of Self

Chapter 1
Too Bold, Black, and Brilliant: Navigating the Leadership Tightrope of
Assimilation vs. Authenticity... 1
Destiny Reddick, Redefine the Pipeline LLC, USA

This chapter uses a tightrope analogy to illustrate how Black women in educational leadership balance assimilating into white professional norms while staying true to themselves. It examines this balance's psychological and professional challenges, including identity negotiation, cultural betrayal, and transitioning from "work pet" to "work threat." Drawing on Black feminist theory and Patricia Hill Collins' Matrix of Domination, the chapter provides a detailed analysis of these experiences. Results reveal strong correlations between identity affirmation and increased psychological workplace abuse. The EmpowH.E.R. Leadership Blueprint offers strategies to address these challenges, aiming to empower Black women to maintain their authentic identities in professional environments.

Chapter 2
It's Not Me I See 63
Taylor C. J. Wynne, The Ohio State University, USA

This chapter explores the context and lived experiences of four Black women graduate students at The University of Florida and how the lack of Black women represented in institutional leadership roles and faulty roles have impacted their matriculation throughout graduate school. Topics within this chapter closely examine categories including the systemic scarcity of Black women working in higher education, culturally responsive mentorship, three semi-structured interviews of current Black women graduate students, and implications for future consideration. This chapter will identify oppressive institutional assumptions about Black women in the academy that has contributed to an educational culture of disinvestment for Black women graduate students, faculty, staff, and senior-level leadership. The purpose of this chapter is to interrogate a system that has intentionally lessened the number of representation amongst Black women working in higher education due to factors relating to burnout, isolation, insufficient pay, racial battle fatigue, and chronic stress.

Chapter 3
Life, Family, and Academia: Navigating the Superwoman Schema................... 81
  Chenell C. Loudermill, Independent Researcher, USA

Women began to establish themselves in the workforce during the 1960s and have since entered various professions. Today, Black women make up 65% of all African Americans enrolled in higher education and account for nearly three percent of academic faculty at degree serving institutions. Black women work fervently to find work-life balance but lack the necessary supports to do so. In this chapter, the author details her experiences of battling the Strong Black Woman Phenomenon and her quest for work-life balance. She discusses experiences, lessons learned along the way, and finding the power to resist the demands to exude perfection and wield the double-edge sword of being a superwoman.

Chapter 4
Navigating Academia the Ultimate Set-Up: I Knew It Was a Set Up, Because
It Was Too Easy!.. 91
  Andrea "Andi" Toliver-Smith, Howard University, USA

This chapter illustrates the academic journey of a Black woman in the field of communication sciences and disorders. Dr. Andi Toliver-Smith started her journey at a Historically Black College or University (HBCU) and transferred to a Predominately White Institution (PWI). She was encouraged by her instructors to continue her education and to obtain her PhD in the field. When seeking out a master's program, she experienced microaggressions for the first time when visiting universities. She completed her master's degree at an HBCU and her PhD at her former PWI university. Her experiences compelled her to develop a support group for BIPOC students. She realized that it was imperative to keep the students in the program in order to expand the field. However, there has been little support for the BIPOC faculty. These experiences led Dr. Toliver-Smith to the forefront of the movement to expand the field of CSD through attraction and retention of BIPOC students and faculty. She has also noted responsibility for faculty of color to maintain a presence in higher education settings.

Chapter 5
Leading and Surviving With Aftershocks 105
  Bri'Yana Nicole Merrill, George Mason University, USA

In this chapter there will be a closer examination into the emotional tax that is experienced by young, Black student leaders within institutions of higher education. The emotional taxes are amplified feelings of isolation and otherness within the workplace due to gender, race, and/or ethnicity. As a result, the person is left with the arduous task of flourishing at work. While this term was originally coined to explain the experiences of marginalized professionals in the workplace, it can also be explained in the context of student leaders in colleges and universities. Throughout this chapter, the author will highlight the impact of racial trauma on Black students and propose strategies for self-care. Through these techniques and self-reflection there is an emphasis on the importance of being bold in one's self-identity and authenticity.

Section 2
Stories of Us

Chapter 6
That's the Way Love Goes: On Black Women Leaders, Family Stories, and
Higher Education 125
  Eboni L. Sterling, House Esther LLC, USA

Black women leaders are daring to reimagine higher education. Infusing love in their leadership practices, they embark on unconventional journeys. Repurposing family stories, these leaders consider love and apply the elusive concept to leadership. The utility of retrospective family storytelling fortifies Black women leaders in this quest. In the challenging realm of academia, Black women battle to survive professionally and personally. Arguably, retrospective family storytelling is a determinant of Black women leaders' survival and sustenance at predominately white institutions of higher education. A complex relationship remains between Black women in academia and the metanarratives manufactured by the dominant group. Even when Black women reach the pinnacle of success, the threat of exclusion and marginalization looms. Often, racial and gender-related stressors are backdrops. Despite these challenges, Black women employ progressive strategies, such as love, as a means of resistance, a tactical force to reconfigure the anatomy of higher education.

Chapter 7
Reclaiming the Mainstream Depiction of Black Women: The Modern-Day
Representation of Black Women in Academia 159
    Lovis M. Nelson-Williams, Baylor University, USA

Black women faculty in academia face unique challenges in the workplace, some
of which stem from the historical marginalization of Black women in mainstream
media. These challenges manifest as tokenism and lack of equal pay. Even in the
face of these complexities, Black women have been able to permeate the bounds
of the professional workspace by acquiring professional degrees at high rates at
the turn of the 21st century. Black women faculty in academia are, unfortunately,
negatively impacted by the unwelcoming environments of their academic institutions.
The depiction of Black women in mainstream outlets acts as a barrier to workplace
achievement for Black women professionals. For example, representations include the
mammy, the asexual house servant, or Jezebel, the hypersexual Black woman. This
chapter examines the history of controlling images of Black women in mainstream
portrayals, the challenges faced by Black women faculty in academia, and the
modern-day media representations of Black women faculty that aid in normalizing
their presence in higher education institutions.

Chapter 8
From Mammy to Matriarch 177
    DeNiece Kemp, Confluence Academies-South City, USA

This chapter provides an insightful perspective on two stereotypes unique to Black
women, the mammy and the sapphire, and how they contribute to the formation
of the matriarchal model in Black women educators. It offers an understanding of
how these experiences can be shaped to positively impact all students, especially
African American students and their families. Interwoven throughout the chapter
are personal narratives from five African American women who work in education
in varying roles to further illustrate how these stereotypes manifest in their work.
This chapter also includes the author's personal narrative of her experiences with
two students and their mothers, providing a powerful testament to the multifaceted
impact of Black women embracing the matriarchal model. The narratives provide
a framework for understanding the importance of the matriarchal model and the
mentorship and community that are associated with it. In this chapter, stereotypes
about Black women are challenged, and Black women are encouraged to take
ownership for their identity.

Chapter 9
Too Much of My Rhythm Causing Them So Much Blues 197
  Asueleni E. Deloney, Hand 'N Hand Coaching, USA

In this chapter, the author examines the manifestations of workplace discrimination in educational settings and other industries where Black women hold leadership positions. This analysis includes an exploration of equity vs. equality, psychological safety, and the concept of diversity dishonesty, among other relevant topics. The discussion is supported by various research methodologies, including focus groups and auto-ethnography. The chapter aims to raise awareness of these discriminatory practices and their persistent impact on Black women's professional advancement which ties directly with this book, Sharing the Legacy and Narrative Leadership Experiences of Black Women in Education. It highlights the psychological burden Black women often bear as they navigate the complexities of workplace presentation and behavior to avoid conflict, jeopardizing career progression or facing wrongful termination. The author contends that confronting these discriminatory environments directly is essential for mitigating their detrimental effects on Black women's professional experiences.

Section 3
Stories of Now

Chapter 10
The Price of a Token: The Effects of Tokenism on Black Women in Higher Education 217
  Chinyere Turner, Partners in Justice LLC, USA

Tokenism is the practice of making only a perfunctory or symbolic effort to do a particular thing, especially by recruiting a small number of people from underrepresented groups to give the appearance of equality within a workforce. Tokenism has always been a point of contention in diversity and inclusion conversations, mainly because tokenism can affect those of any marginalized community. However, tokenism through the lenses of professional Black women has not been explored as thoroughly. "The Price of a Token" will analyze the various factors of tokenism that Black women experience in professional settings and the price they unwillingly must pay in being assigned a token.

Chapter 11
Who Said I Can't Lead: The Journey to Leadership in Higher Education as a
Black Female.. 235

Ty Jiles, Prairie State College, USA
Megan N. Lyons, North Carolina Central University, USA

This chapter provides a personal account of the author's journey toward achieving
a leadership role in higher education as a young black female. By sharing these
experiences and insights, the authors hope to shed light on the importance of
representation and why it is crucial for minorities and females in higher education.
Throughout the chapter, the authors address four major concerns that make the
path to leadership particularly challenging for women. These concerns encompass
various aspects, such as societal biases, gender stereotypes, limited opportunities for
advancement, and lack of support systems. By examining these challenges in detail,
readers can better understand women's unique obstacles on their journey toward
leadership positions. Furthermore, the chapter will provide strategies for retaining
and supporting women in leadership roles within higher education settings. These
strategies will focus on creating inclusive environments, providing mentorship
opportunities, advocating for equal opportunities, and fostering a supportive network.

Chapter 12
Crowned in Authenticity: Black Women Redefining Leadership by Leading
With Value and Purpose.. 251
  Ashley N. Storman, The Storman Group LLC, USA

Authentic leadership is the cornerstone of the leadership style adopted by Black
women educators. Grounded in Patricia Hill Collins's Black feminist thought theory,
this research explores the lived experiences of Black women leaders in education.
Through a qualitative focus group of K-12 and higher education leaders, participants
share their narratives. The researcher addresses key inquiries: What is the current
leadership experience, how is it evolving, and what is the future of leadership for Black
women? From the findings, the author developed a framework titled "Managing the
Consciousness of Oppression" to help Black women proactively equip themselves
with strategies to resist and challenge discriminatory practices in their professional
journeys. It is crucial that stakeholders, including administrators, supervisors, and
mentors, recognize and incorporate the indispensable leadership style of Black
women leaders. Failing to do so may result in these women forging their own path
toward equity, fairness, and inclusivity.

Compilation of References 275

About the Contributors 299

Index.. 307

Preface

A TOAST TO TRANSFORMATION: IT ALL STARTED OVER MARGARITAS

About sixteen months ago, we, the co-editors, Dr. Ashley Storman and Dr. Destiny Reddick—met at a Mexican restaurant for happy hour (*and dinner*), primarily to catch up with one another as Black professional women and mothers. We had previously worked together in higher education at a private, midwest, predominantly white institution (PWI), Storman as the Director of Diversity, Equity, and Inclusion and Reddick as the Assistant Dean of the School of Education.

DRIVEN BY THE SAME FRUSTRATIONS AND CHALLENGES THAT MANY BLACK WOMEN FACE IN ACADEMIA, WE HAD BOTH DEPARTED FROM THIS INSTITUTION FOR NEW ROLES

At that moment, over chips and salsa, we swapped stories about our new workplaces, discussing the familiar themes we were encountering. We laughed and vented, and somewhere in between the first and second rounds of margaritas, it hit us:

IF WE WERE BOTH FACING THE SAME CHALLENGES IN DIFFERENT SPACES, THERE *MUST* BE COUNTLESS OTHER BLACK WOMEN IN EDUCATION EXPERIENCING SIMILAR STRUGGLES

It was not until this pivotal meeting that the idea for this book took shape. Considering our expertise on the topic, and with us both running consulting firms specializing in diversity, equity, and inclusion, we recognized a critical need to document and share the experiences of Black women leaders in education. This idea quickly evolved into action. As we reached out for chapter proposals, we were overwhelmed by the response, confirming the urgent need for this work. Our goal became clear: to create a comprehensive volume that would catalyze change and empowerment for readers. The purpose is to document the invaluable contributions and legacy of Black women in education, and to inspire and guide future leaders.

Black women in education represent diverse impactful leadership experiences, spanning historically black colleges and universities (HBCUs), predominantly white institutions (PWIs), and other educational settings. They face multifaceted challenges, including systemic racism, gender discrimination, and cultural biases. Despite these obstacles, their journeys are marked by extraordinary achievements, an unwavering commitment to equity, and a profound influence on the communities they serve. However, their legacies are often underrepresented in historical accounts and academic discourse.

Therefore, the stories collected in this volume—comprising narratives, theory, and research—seek to amplify the intersectional lived experiences of Black women in education, serving as leaders in diverse sectors, from PK-12 and higher education to student affairs, academia and beyond. This collection also offers strategies to empower black women and organizations to reshape the professional landscape into psychologically safe spaces for all future leaders.

THE URGENCY OF NOW

The urgency of our work is marked by the tragic loss of Dr. Antoinette "Bonnie" Candia-Bailey, a beloved alumna and Vice President of Student Affairs at Lincoln University. Dr. Candia-Bailey, a trailblazer and advocate for HBCUs, tragically took her own life after enduring severe mistreatment and bullying in her leadership role.

Her story is a stark reminder of the psychological and emotional abuse Black women face in academia, often exacerbated by their Blackness, boldness, and brilliance.

Her death calls us to prioritize our mental health, challenge systemic injustices, and create supportive networks for Black women in education. We must continue research-driven work, foster safe spaces, and advocate for equitable treatment. Dr. Candia-Bailey's story fuels our determination to push for change, ensuring that the weight of systemic oppression silences no more voices.

Research consistently highlights that Black women are among the most educated populations in the United States, yet they remain underrepresented in leadership roles (American Association of University Women, n.d.; Brookings Institution, 2017; Center for American Progress, n.d.; NewsOne, 2021; ThoughtCo, 2020). Despite meeting and often exceeding societal expectations in terms of work experience and advanced degrees, Black women still face significant barriers to leadership positions. This discrepancy underscores a systemic issue that this book aims to address. By highlighting our lived experiences, we aim to pave the way for a more diverse and inclusive academic landscape. This is not just a testament to the contributions of Black women in education; it is a roadmap for future leaders to push boundaries and break barriers. The time to act is now, and we must do so collectively.

AN INCLUSIVE INVITATION: WHO SHOULD READ THIS

This book is designed for professionals and researchers from various backgrounds and disciplines, including education, psychology, sociology, human resources, business, gender studies, African American studies, leadership development, law, healthcare, and more. It is a vital resource for those in leadership positions seeking to foster equitable workplaces and develop culturally competent leaders.

Topics covered include recruitment and retention, identity negotiation, tokenism, representation, mid-level management, affinity circles, mentoring, stereotypes, diversity, equity, inclusion, belonging, and psychologically safe workspaces.

NARRATIVES THAT EMPOWER: THE STORY OF SELF, THE STORY OF US, THE STORY OF NOW

As co-editors, we intentionally leaned into the powerful approach of leveraging Black women's narratives and lived experiences in education. Drawing on the groundbreaking research of Marshall Ganz (2023), Senior Lecturer in Leadership, Organizing, and Civil Society at the Kennedy School of Government, we emphasize the transformative power of storytelling. As Ganz highlights, compelling storytelling is a tool for understanding and mobilization, allowing diverse groups to articulate shared values, confront systemic injustices, and envision a future where equity and inclusion are paramount. This approach leveraging the telling of stories and narratives is deeply rooted in the Black literary tradition as recently illuminated by education scholars such as Dr. Gholnecsar (Gholdy) Muhammad, whose recent works, "Cultivating Genius" (2020) and "Unearthing Joy" (2023) highlight the historical significance of black literary societies, emphasizing storytelling in Black communities as catalysts for social change (Muhammad, 2020, 2023).

Ganz's framework of public narrative—comprising the *Story of Self*, the *Story of Us*, and the *Story of Now*—emphasizes the transformative power of narratives in connecting across differences, fostering empathy, and embracing vulnerability and emotion and demonstrates how personal stories can inspire collective action and drive social change. Through the Story of Self, the Story of Us, and the Story of Now, we illustrate how personal stories can ignite collective action and drive social change.

Weaving this perspective into our book helps frame important narratives that honor the legacy of Black women in education leadership and creates a common thread that binds our experiences, challenges, and triumphs. Embracing this framework, we aim to inspire and move readers into action as they engage with the chapters of our book. Through these narratives, we invite you to join us in celebrating Black women's legacy and continued impact in education.

The following chapters delve into the Stories of Self, Us, and Now, illustrating the profound impact of Black women's leadership in education.

Through the *Stories of Self*, we explore personal journeys and the unique experiences that shape individual leaders.

Chapter 1: Too Bold, Too Black, Too Brilliant: A Psychologically Hazardous Journey Navigating the Tightrope of Assimilation vs. Authenticity in Leadership – Implications for Fostering Workspaces that EmpowHER Unapologetic Excellence

Using the tightrope analogy, she highlights the delicate balance these women must maintain between assimilating into white professional norms and remaining authentically themselves. This chapter explores psychological and professional risks, such as identity negotiation, cultural betrayal, and the transition from "work pet" to "work threat." The EmpowHER blueprint introduced here serves as a strategic guide to empower Black women to advocate for their strengths and foster supportive, equitable work environments. By focusing on personal journeys and identity struggles, Reddick's narrative aligns with Ganz's concept of sharing those moments that shape one's calling and values.

Chapter 2: It's Not Me I See

This chapter examines the lack of representation in leadership roles and the oppressive institutional assumptions that impact the educational culture. Addressing issues such as burnout, isolation, insufficient pay, racial battle fatigue, and chronic stress, this chapter highlights shared challenges and communal resilience. By focusing on the collective identity and experiences, Wynne's narrative fits within Ganz's framework of fostering solidarity and shared purpose among readers.

Chapter 3: Life, Family, and Academia: Navigating the Superwoman Schema

The researcher explores the demands of being a superwoman and finding power in resisting perfection. This narrative aligns with Ganz's framework by sharing personal struggles and growth, thus enabling others to resonate with her experiences and find inspiration in her journey toward balance and self-empowerment.

Chapter 4: Navigating Academia the Ultimate Set-Up: I Knew it was a Set Up Because It Was Too Easy!

The author's personal journey from an HBCU to a PWI is a quintessential "Story of Self." She shares her experiences with microaggressions and her efforts to develop a support group for BIPOC students. This chapter highlights the need for support for BIPOC faculty and the movement to expand the field of Communication Sciences and Disorders through attraction and retention of diverse students and faculty. By focusing on her individual experiences and the personal challenges she faced, Toliver-Smith's narrative encapsulates the essence of Ganz's concept of storytelling that conveys deep personal meaning and calling.

Chapter 5: Leading and Surviving With Aftershocks

This chapter examines the emotional tax experienced by young Black student leaders in higher education. By exploring feelings of isolation and otherness due to gender, race, and ethnicity, Merrill highlights the personal impact of racial trauma. The chapter proposes strategies for self-care, emphasizing the importance of bold self-identity and authenticity. In line with Ganz's framework, this narrative shares personal moments of struggle and resilience, allowing readers to connect with the author's experiences and draw parallels with their own.

The *Stories of Us* highlight the collective challenges and triumphs of Black women in educational leadership, emphasizing shared values and community.

Chapter 6: That's the Way Love Goes: On Black Women Leaders, Family Stories, and Higher Education

Reimagine higher education through the collective lens of Black women leaders who infuse love into their leadership practices. By repurposing family stories and considering love as a leadership concept, this chapter explores how retrospective family storytelling fortifies Black women leaders in academia, aligning with the "Story of Us" by emphasizing shared cultural values and experiences, aligning with Ganz's framework by highlighting the importance of collective identity and communal resilience.

Chapter 7: Reclaiming the Mainstream Depiction of Black Women: The Modern-Day Representation of Black Women in Academia

Nelson-Williams' chapter is a "Story of Us" that examines historical and modern-day representations of Black women in mainstream media and academia. Discussing challenges like tokenism and unequal pay, it highlights how these depictions impact Black women faculty and calls for a reevaluation of these narratives. By addressing shared cultural challenges and the collective impact on Black women, this chapter aligns with Ganz's framework by emphasizing the importance of communal identity and shared values.

Chapter 8: From Mammy to Matriarch

By using personal narratives to illustrate how stereotypes like the mammy and sapphire contribute to the matriarchal model in Black women educators, Kemp's chapter provides a "Story of Us" by emphasizes community, mentorship, and challenging stereotypes, showcasing the positive impacts of embracing this model. This narrative fits within Ganz's framework by highlighting the shared experiences and values that bind Black women educators together, fostering a sense of collective identity and purpose.

Chapter 9: Too Much of My Rhythm Causing Them So Much Blues

In this chapter, Deloney examines the various forms of workplace discrimination faced by Black women in leadership roles within educational settings and other industries. Through an exploration of equity versus equality, psychological safety, and diversity dishonesty, supported by focus groups and auto-ethnography, the chapter highlights the ongoing impact of these discriminatory practices on Black women's career advancement. The discussion aims to raise awareness of the psychological burden these women bear while navigating complex workplace dynamics.

Finally, the *Stories of Now* address the urgent challenges we face today and the actions we must take to create a more equitable future.

Chapter 10: The Price of a Token: The Effects of Tokenism on Black Women in Higher Education

Turner presents a "Story of Now," analyzing the effects of tokenism on Black women in higher education. It explores the significant personal and professional costs involved in symbolic diversity and inclusion efforts. By addressing urgent contemporary issues and calling for immediate action and change, this narrative aligns with Ganz's framework of motivating readers to confront and address present-day challenges.

Chapter 11: Who Said I Can't Lead: The Journey to Leadership in Higher Education as a Black Female

This chapter by Jiles and Lyons offers a "Story of Now," providing a personal account of their journey to leadership in higher education and highlighting current challenges faced by young Black females. It provides strategies for retaining and supporting women in leadership roles, addressing present-day issues and solutions. This narrative aligns with Ganz's framework by focusing on contemporary challenges and the need for immediate action to create a more equitable future.

Chapter 12: Crowned in Authenticity: Black Women Redefining Leadership by Leading With Value and Purpose

Finally, Storman's chapter explores the current leadership experiences of Black women educators through a qualitative focus group, fitting the "Story of Now." It addresses how leadership is evolving and the future trajectory of Black women educators. By focusing on contemporary challenges and forward-looking solutions, this narrative aligns with Ganz's framework by motivating readers to take immediate action to foster equity and inclusion in education.

We invite you to sit back, relax, grab your favorite beverage, and get ready to dive into these powerful narratives. Join us on this journey, engage with these stories, and contribute to the ongoing work of fostering an inclusive and equitable educational landscape—because sometimes, the best ideas are born over margaritas.

REFERENCES

Brookings Institution. (2017, December 4). *Black women are earning more college degrees, but that alone won't close race gaps*. Retrieved from https://www.brookings.edu/research/black-women-are-earning-more-college-degrees-but-that-alone-wont-close-race-gaps/

Section 1
Stories of Self

Chapter 1
Too Bold, Black, and Brilliant:
Navigating the Leadership Tightrope of Assimilation vs. Authenticity

Destiny Reddick
https://orcid.org/0009-0001-6627-814X
Redefine the Pipeline LLC, USA

ABSTRACT

This chapter uses a tightrope analogy to illustrate how Black women in educational leadership balance assimilating into white professional norms while staying true to themselves. It examines this balance's psychological and professional challenges, including identity negotiation, cultural betrayal, and transitioning from "work pet" to "work threat." Drawing on Black feminist theory and Patricia Hill Collins' Matrix of Domination, the chapter provides a detailed analysis of these experiences. Results reveal strong correlations between identity affirmation and increased psychological workplace abuse. The EmpowH.E.R. Leadership Blueprint offers strategies to address these challenges, aiming to empower Black women to maintain their authentic identities in professional environments.

DOI: 10.4018/979-8-3693-0698-7.ch001

Copyright © 2024, IGI Global. Copying or distributing in print or electronic forms without written permission of IGI Global is prohibited.

INTRODUCTION

Underrepresented employees are publicly encouraged to behave in ways that bring about private criticism: Use your voice- but not too loudly. Be bold- but not too bold. Pursue excellence- but not beyond existing markers. (Frank, 2022)

STORY OF SELF: ONE BLACK WOMAN'S PATH TO EDUCATION LEADERSHIP

Picture it. It was a clear and crisp morning in September of 2012. At 28 years old, I had just been appointed as an Instructional Specialist at an elementary school covering Kindergarten through Grade Five in suburban America. I was heavily pregnant with my first child, eight months along, when I found myself on the floor of my mother's bathroom in a prayer position. My large belly pressed firmly against my legs, and my face was wet with tears. I sobbed intensely yet quietly as my first-born daughter, Zuri Raye, now eleven years old, swam inside my belly without a care in the world. I will never forget my desperate plea to God that morning.

Dear God,
Thank you for allowing me to get pregnant- finally!
Forgive me, God, but I do have one final request...
Please know, I am not ready...
I ask that you spare me this first time, God.
I am going through enough in my new leadership role.
Entering my teaching career with a master's degree didn't help.
They still question. They still wait. For me to fail.
This could be my only chance.
I CAN do this. I know it.
Nevertheless, I can NOT and will NOT be able to focus
if you choose me...
...to be a mother of a black boy in America.

My prayer that day was that the first child I was carrying inside me was not born a black male living in America. To contextualize my feelings as a 28-year-old brand new mommy, not that fearing being a mother of a black boy in America needs much additional context, earlier in 2012, the tragic death of Trayvon Martin had rocked the nation and the world, quite frankly. Trayvon Martin, a 17-year-old

Black boy, was killed earlier that year in Sanford, Florida while returning home from a convenience store after a purchase of iced tea and Skittles. Trayvon's murder was racially polarizing. The Black community, all too familiar with the policing of Black bodies, was outraged. Media outlets villainized this baby-faced 17-year-old Black child as a delinquent, a drug user. One of our generation's most significant movements, B.L.M. (*Black Lives Matter*), arose from this tragedy. However, what became evident to me was that Black children, especially Black boys, were seen as a threat in the United States.

Many say that this traumatic, violent, politically polarizing event rooted in racism caused the Trayvon Martin generation, a "group of people who were moved into action because of it," and I must admit my black education colleagues and I were hyped. We were ready for anything. It was this exact backdrop of the racial reality of violence and injustice that fueled my first-time motherhood fears. Visualizing Trayvon Martin's babyface, with that bag of Skittles and a bottle of iced tea as his only items as he lay on the ground, dead, bleeding out, with NO gun, NO knife, and NO anything, coined as some possible "suspicious person" made it terrifying to think of possibly carrying a black boy in my belly as a first-time mother and bringing a Black boy into a world where his life could be cut short simply because of the color of his skin- smooth, chocolate, baby skin, or not. That day in 2012, I became part of the "Trayvon Martin generation" (Hajela, 2022). In October 2012, I gave birth to a healthy daughter, Zuri Raye. In 2017, I gave birth to my second child, a son, Zane.

The year 2012 was significant because I was pregnant with my first child and had just stepped into my first educational leadership position. Plagued with anxiety about my new role, I did not feel I could also shoulder the responsibility of keeping a Black son safe in a society that justified the murder of an innocent child as "standing your ground." The doubts and fears I was experiencing as a Black woman in a leadership role were overwhelming. These doubts and fears have been described as the psychological concept of imposter syndrome. The term "imposter phenomenon" was introduced in 1978 by clinical psychologists Pauline Clance and Suzanne Imes, who defined the term as "an internal experience of intellectual phoniness" (Cockley, 2024, para. 5). Eventually, an alternative perspective was developed, prompting many to cease using the term.

In her 2021 book, *I'm Not Yelling: A Black Woman's Guide to Navigating the Workplace*, Leiba insightfully highlighted that women tended to use the term "imposter syndrome" to refer to something within them, or internal, as the research suggested the root cause was internal; however, most people who have been documented to experience imposter syndrome are women or members of historically marginalized groups. This infers an alternative viewpoint that imposter syndrome, as most understand it, may stem from external forces, in some cases, such as gender or racial oppression and inequities. Cockley (2024) suggested redefining imposter syndrome for racially minoritized individuals, "persistent beliefs or actions of intellectual and professional self-doubt among racially minoritized people due to experiences, systems, or principles of racial oppression and inequity," an external perspective that does not place the blame on women and people of color but instead focuses on environmental causes (Cockley, 2024, para. 5).

In my case, I had been promoted to a leadership role after only six years of elementary classroom teaching. Initially, I was thrilled, but eventually, I began questioning my skills, knowledge, and abilities. I was one of only three Black educators in the school. White coworkers had already challenged me regarding my level of education. Now, as an educational leader, I hoped I had earned the confidence of my white colleagues. I was wrong. My new leadership role began what can only be described as a horror show.

A FAILED BALANCING ACT: NAVIGATING THE TIGHTROPE OF ASSIMILATION AND AUTHENTICITY

Being a Black woman in the workplace can feel like starring in "Thriller," a horror show where the fright never ends. Hampton (2021) highlights recent novels such as *The Other Black Girl* and *All Her Little Secrets* that capture the "justified paranoia and hypervigilance" black women experience in the workplace (Hampton, 2021). These narratives reveal the chilling reality of systemic racism and psychological abuse that Black women endure daily in professional settings, turning their careers into a continuous battle for survival and recognition. As a result, and out of desperation for psychological safety, some Black women choose to assimilate.

Black women in educational leadership are forced to navigate the complex and impossible balance between assimilation and authenticity, facing unique psychological and professional challenges due to systemic racial and gender biases. Assimilation refers to how individuals or groups adopt another group's cultural traits or social patterns. As reported by Hirsch, according to Park and Burgess, assimilation involves a series of processes through which individuals become community members by adopting similar attitudes and behaviors (Hirsch, 1942).

This chapter will detail my research study, which explores the phenomenon of assimilation versus authenticity for black women in education leadership through the lens of a concept called identity negotiation and argues for creating psychologically safe work environments using the *EmpowH.E.R. Leadership Blueprint*. Drawing directly from the experiences and narratives informed by black women in education leadership, the *EmpowH.E.R. Leadership Blueprint* provides practical strategies to support and retain Black women as educational leaders, enabling them to thrive authentically and without fear of retribution.

PROBLEM STATEMENT

The balance between authenticity and assimilation is like walking on a tightrope. When walking a tightrope, one must tread lightly to satisfy two opposing forces. Assimilation refers to how individuals or groups adopt another group's cultural traits or social patterns. This process often involves gradually losing one's original cultural identity to take on the traits of the dominant culture (Pauls, 2024, para. 1), whereas authenticity in leadership allows for embracing the true self into one's leadership style and interactions, freely expressing identities without fear of marginalization. Black women in educational leadership must engage in a constant back-and-forth performance between assimilating into white, patriarchal professional norms and staying true to their intersectional identities as Black women who face both race and gender-based oppression. This intersectionality poses unique challenges for black women in educational leadership, which white men dominate. Successfully walking this tightrope is crucial for Black women in leadership roles who wish to be successful, considered skilled, and respected in their professional networks.

The pressure to assimilate is not unique to Black women, but the impacts can be particularly severe for this group. A study commissioned and reported by Essence (2020) found that scores of Black women felt pressured to assimilate by hiding their authentic selves at work to conform to the predominant workplace culture. This included toning down their appearance, softening their demeanor, and holding back in conversations (Holmes, 2020, para. 3). The same study found that more than 70% of the 650 Black women studied feared being labeled the "angry Black woman (Holmes, 2020, para. 3). As a result, 50% of Black women millennials, 42% of Gen Xers, and 30% of Baby Boomers strived to be seen as the "Acculturated Girl Next Door," a professional who is unthreatening and willing to conform (Lewis, 2020, para. 3, 4). Consequently, 80% of Black women surveyed felt they needed to adjust their personalities to succeed at work, compared to just 62% of non-Hispanic White women. Additionally, 57% of Black women felt they must physically appear a certain way (e.g., straightened hair or a specific style of dress) to receive a promotion (Lewis, 2020, para. 3, 4).

However, assimilating often fails to yield the desired results. Despite their efforts, many Black women still face significant barriers to career advancement. The perceived positive impact of assimilation includes reduced overt discrimination and increased opportunities for career advancement. It can lead to a loss of self-identity and increased stress levels that are psychologically damaging due to the constant need to monitor personal behavior and appearance (Holmes, 2020, par. 2). Assimilation can be both psychologically damaging and professionally ineffective. Furthermore, assimilation perpetuates systemic issues within the workplace. When Black women feel compelled to conform, it reinforces the notion that the dominant culture is the norm and discourages diversity and inclusion. This affects the individual and hampers the organization's ability to benefit from diverse perspectives and talents (Purdie-Vaughns et al., 2008).

Black women in educational leadership roles often find themselves walking a tightrope, balancing the demands of conformity to dominant professional norms with the desire to remain faithful to cultural and personal identities." Black women often face stereotypes and biases that undermine their leadership abilities, making it essential to create supportive and inclusive work environments" (Travis & Thorpe-Moscon, 2020, p. 3). This delicate balance is the foundation of identity negotiation, a concept directly related to assimilation and authenticity that references this balancing act of adapting behavior and presentation to align with societal and organizational norms while maintaining authenticity and integrity. Both assimilation and authenticity, including shifting back and forth between the three, harm black women professionally, socially, and psychologically. "Psychological safety describes a team climate characterized by interpersonal trust and mutual respect in which people are comfortable being themselves" (Edmondson, 1999, p. 354).

Research on creating psychologically safe workplaces for Black women in leadership and related concepts is gradually emerging. However, actionable frameworks providing specific, immediately implementable strategies are scarce. Therefore, this study also aims to develop an actionable framework, *EmpowH.E.R. Leadership Blueprint*, that can be used by organizations and Black women alike to support psychologically safe workspaces where Black women in leadership feel recognized for their contributions, appreciated for their authentic selves, and protected from the mental and emotional toll of navigating hostile or indifferent work environments arising from negative stereotypes related to their identities as Black women. Informed by the direct narratives and advice of Black women in education leadership, providing specific guidance to help organizations implement significant changes to ensure that Black women can thrive in their professional environments, express their true identities without fear of retribution or marginalization, and foster a sense of belonging and empowerment that helps retain black women in education leadership; this study aims to make a substantial impact.

CONCEPTUAL FRAMEWORK

The main concept explored is how identity negotiation impacts black women's leadership and workplace environment in education. To investigate the phenomenon of identity negotiation related to assimilation and authenticity, this study employed a framework based on three main catalysts of psychological workplace abuse experienced by Black women. The categories "Too Bold," "Too Black," and "Too Brilliant" represent common negative stereotypes that adversely impact their professional reach and well-being. These catalysts were used to analyze Black women's experiences and self-perceptions in educational leadership. By examining the relationship between these negative stereotypes about black women and their impact, the study aimed to explore how these dynamics affect Black women psychologically, physically, mentally, socially, and professionally. Additionally, a correlational quantitative research design and thematic analysis of qualitative data provided deeper insights into Black women's lived experiences and identity negotiation processes, offering a comprehensive understanding of how these dynamics operate in educational leadership contexts and identifying recommendations to create psychologically safe work environments.

The researcher developed the *Too Bold, Too Black, Too Brilliant* conceptual framework following an extensive literature review. It serves as the strategic classification of common negative societal stereotypes about Black women to explore the concept of identity negotiation. Two models emerged from the literature review as most relevant in highlighting the structural power perpetuating negative stereotypes about black women that may correlate with them experiencing psychological workplace abuse: Patricia Hill Collins's *Matrix of Domination* and Kecia M. Thomas's research on black women in leadership transitioning from *work pet to work threat*.

The four domains of Collins' *Matrix of Domination—structural, disciplinary, hegemonic, and interpersonal*—offer a comprehensive lens to understand how Black women in educational leadership negotiate their identities.

1. *Structural Domain* refers to the large-scale social structures, such as laws, policies, and institutions, that systematically oppress Black women.
2. *Disciplinary Domain:* manages oppression through organizational practices and rules that maintain control over Black women.
3. *Hegemonic Domain:* propagating ideologies and cultural norms that justify the status quo.
4. *Interpersonal Domain:* encompasses everyday interactions and personal relationships that perpetuate systemic oppression. Microaggressions, subtle insults, and daily acts of discrimination uphold the subordinate status of Black women (Black Feminisms, 2019).

Thomas et al. (2013) conducted a study that explored how Black women transition from being well-liked and valued for their diversity to facing hostility and resistance when they assert their professional influence and seek leadership opportunities. She coined this troubling pattern as the *Work Pet to Work Threat* phenomenon. Thomas et al. identified several themes within this phenomenon:

1. *Tokenism*: when Black women are the only representative of their race or gender in their workplace or team, and their presence is merely for diversity or to create the appearance of inclusivity rather than being valued for their skills, expertise, and unique perspectives.
2. *Invisibility*: contributions, achievements, and talents are consistently overlooked or undervalued, and ideas are dismissed or ignored despite their accomplishments
3. *Pressure to Assimilate:* pressure to conform to dominant cultural norms and expectations in the workplace, often to the detriment of their identities and unique experiences.
4. *Mistreatment:* microaggressions, bias, prejudice, or even overt discrimination; experience explicit forms of racism, such as being subjected to derogatory comments, stereotyping, or being denied opportunities for career advancement.
5. *Overprotection:* when colleagues are overprotective of Black women, this can manifest as excessive scrutiny, skepticism, or an unwillingness to entrust them with significant responsibilities. It stems from assumptions that they are not as competent as their peers, and it can undermine their confidence and professional growth.

Building on Collins's *Matrix of Domination*, which explored the principles of dominance and privilege to identify specific catalysts that could amplify negative stereotypes about Black women, and Thomas's *Work Pet to Work Threat* phenomenon, which contextualizes how negative stereotypes specifically manifest for Black women in the workplace, fifteen negative stereotypes related to Black women were identified in the literature. These stereotypes were all connected to three categories or catalysts.

The first catalyst, *Too Bold*, focused on Black women's demeanor or personality traits. The second catalyst, *Too Black*, related to Black women's cultural attributes, mainly physical appearance. The third catalyst, *Too Brilliant*, was related to the perception of intelligence assigned to black women.

A more detailed analysis of the three catalysts related to common stereotypes about black women is below:

Catalyst # 1 - Too Bold: Assertiveness Misinterpreted

Related Stereotypes

Angry Black Woman: portrays Black women as perpetually angry, aggressive, and hostile, dismissing their legitimate concerns and emotions (Harris-Perry, 2011).

Strong Black Woman: suggests that Black women are inherently resilient and self-sufficient, often leading to their emotional and physical needs being overlooked or minimized (Abrams, Maxwell, Pope, & Belgrave, 2014).

Unprofessional: assumes that Black women lack the decorum, behavior, or appearance deemed appropriate for professional settings (Harris-Perry, 2011).

Aunt Jemima: portrays Black women as subservient and cheerful domestic workers who exist to serve others (Collins, 2000).

Theoretical Insights

Collins' Hegemonic Domain of Power: highlights how the "angry Black woman" stereotype underpins frequent microaggressions, misinterpreting assertiveness as aggression (Collins, 2000).

Collins' Disciplinary Domain of Power: illustrates the pressure on Black women to suppress their assertiveness to avoid negative stereotypes, aligning with Thomas's Work Pet to Work Threat phenomenon (Thomas et al., 2013).

Figure 1. "Too bold" catalyst: Common stereotypes about black women that relate to "boldness"

Impact of the Black Women's Common Identity Negotiation Responses

Stereotype & Workplace Abuse Catalyst #1:   "TOO BOLD"

**Catalyst #1:
TOO
BOLD**
<u>Stereotypes</u>

**Angry Black Woman:
Aggressive, confrontational**

Overly Emotional

Unprofessional

Note. This figure was created by the author and illustrates common stereotypes about Black women being "Too Bold," such as the Angry Black Woman, Strong Black Woman, Unprofessional, and Aunt Jemima.

Catalyst # 2 - Too Black: Cultural Identity and Tokenization

Related Stereotypes

Sapphire: characterizes Black women as sassy, loud, and domineering, often seen as emasculating to men (West, 1995).

The Token: positions Black women as diversity hires, undermining their qualifications and contributions (Collins, 2000).

The Outsider/Cultural Deviant: views Black women as inherently different and unable to conform to dominant cultural norms, leading to marginalization and exclusion (Collins, 2000).

Jezebel: sexualizes Black women, viewing them as promiscuous and morally loose, often leading to their exploitation and objectification (West, 1995).

Mammy: stereotypes Black women as nurturing, self-sacrificing caretakers, often erasing their own personal aspirations and needs (West, 1995).

Modern-Day Prostitute: links Black women to prostitution, criminalizing their sexuality and portraying them as morally bankrupt (West, 1995).

Breeder of Slavery: historically cast Black women as mere child-bearers, reducing them to their reproductive capabilities (Collins, 2000).

Theoretical Insights

Collins' Structural Domain of Power: explains how societal structures tokenize Black women, leading to undervaluation and increased pressure to assimilate (Collins, 2000).

Collins' Disciplinary Domain of Power: describes the intense pressure to conform to white, patriarchal norms, exacerbated by intersectionality (Collins, 2000).

Collins' Hegemonic Domain of Power: demonstrates how cultural and ideological means perpetuate negative stereotypes, undervaluing Black women's contributions (Collins, 2000).

Figure 2. "Too black" catalyst: Common stereotypes about black women that relate to "blackness"

Note. This figure was created by the author and represents common stereotypes about Black women being "Too Black," including Sapphire, The Token, The Outsider/Cultural Deviant, Jezebel, Mammy, Modern-Day Prostitute, and Breeder of Slavery.

Catalyst # 3 - Too Brilliant: Perception of Intelligence and Undervaluation

Related Stereotypes

Overreaching Ambition: depicts Black women as overly ambitious, perceived as threatening or overly competitive (Givens, 2021).

Minimized Value of Skills and Intellectual Contributions: Black women are assumed to lack the necessary skills for high-level professional roles, thereby undervaluing their intellectual contributions and overall impact. This bias often leads to them being overlooked for promotions and hiring opportunities, further perpetuating their underrepresentation in leadership positions (Givens, 2021).

Intellectual Inferiority: stereotypes Black women as less intelligent and capable of intellectual achievement (Collins, 2000).

Theoretical Insights

Collins' Interpersonal Domain of Power: reveals how daily interactions can trivialize Black women's intellectual contributions, aligning with the "Too Brilliant" catalyst (Collins, 2000). ● Collins'

Structural Domain of Power: shows how Black women are often underestimated and forced into roles beneath their capabilities, reflecting the pet-to-threat phenomenon identified by Thomas (Thomas et al., 2013).

Collins' Disciplinary Domain of Power: provides insight into how Black women strategically temper their brilliance to align with organizational expectations (Collins, 2000).

These three catalysts not only reflect the negative stereotypes about Black women but also act as triggers, or catalysts, for workplace abuse events that Black women endure when their overall presence and behaviors challenge the existing status quo of dominance, power, and privilege.

Figure 3. "Too brilliant" catalyst: Common stereotypes about black women that relate to "brilliance"

Note. This figure was created by the author and depicts common stereotypes about Black women being "Too Brilliant," such as Overreaching Ambition, Minimized Value of Skills and Intellectual Contributions, and Intellectual Inferiority.

PURPOSE OF THE STUDY

This research study aims to illuminate the unique challenges Black women face in educational leadership roles within the pre-kindergarten to grade 12 and higher education sectors, focusing on the balance between assimilation and authenticity, commonly referred to as identity negotiation or identity shifting, and the impacts of psychological workplace abuse. The core research questions driving the exploration of identity negotiation for Black women in educational leadership were:

PRIMARY RESEARCH QUESTION

- *How do Black women in educational leadership navigate the challenges of maintaining their authentic identities while facing psychological workplace abuse, and what are the correlations between their self-perception related to Blackness, Boldness, and Brilliance and their experiences of such abuse?*

Secondary Research Questions

- *How does the self-perception of Black women in educational leadership correlate with their experiences of psychological workplace abuse, considering variables such as age and leadership experience?*
- *What common themes of psychological workplace abuse are reported by Black women in educational leadership, and how do these experiences reflect negative societal stereotypes about Black women?*
- *How do Black women's lived experiences and personal narratives in educational leadership inform the development of the EmpowH.E.R. Leadership Blueprint?*

Based on the insights gained from this study, the *EmpowH.E.R. Leadership Blueprint* was designed to address and mitigate the impact of negative stereotypes on Black women in educational leadership.

REVIEW OF THE LITERATURE

Black women in leadership positions often face unique challenges that require them to navigate a tightrope between assimilating in predominantly white professional environments and maintaining their authenticity. This balancing act, or tightrope, is a complex process of identity negotiation that impacts their psychological well-being, professional experiences, and leadership effectiveness (Jones & Shorter-Gooden, 2003). The adjustment of Black women's self-presentation to fit into dominant cultural norms while striving to remain faithful to cultural and personal identities has been explored in books such as "Shifting: The Double Lies of Black Women in America" (Jones & Shorter-Gooden, 2003). This process is described as particularly complex because of the constant balance of the pressures of assimilation with the need to remain authentic. The tightrope analogy vividly illustrates this struggle, highlighting the precariousness and psychological toll of such a balancing act. This construct is most effective when explored using gendered racism and Black feminist methodologies.

GENDERED RACISM AND BLACK FEMINIST METHODOLOGIES

Gendered racism consists of race-based prejudice, harassment, and violence experienced by Black American women (Szymanski & Stewart, 2010). These intersecting oppressive actions create chronic psychological stress, which leads to adverse mental health outcomes, such as depressive symptoms and anxiety (Williams & Lewis, 2019). Davis (1983) added that while many women face gender oppression in the home, Black American women face household concerns alongside gender oppression in the workplace, a space they occupied long before the women's liberation movement. As such, social issues that are specific to Black American women must be studied using Black feminist theory and Black feminist methodologies.

According to Black feminist theory, Black American womanhood involves navigating a racist, sexist society, which results in lived experiences that are distinct from the men of their race group and the white Americans of their sex category (Collins, 1990, 1999). Black Feminist Theory (BFT) refers to a standpoint epistemology in which Black women are empowered to recover their subjugated knowledge and use it to study how matrices of oppression (race, gender, class) reinforce each other in varying contexts (Collins, 1990). Black feminist scholars explained that theory is developed from experiential knowledge and daily lived experience. BFT challenged traditional notions of research, including the language of validity, rigor, and reliability that contribute to preserving the status quo and safeguarding social order (Collins, 2016) and yielded a specific kind of knowledge in which multiple truths coexist (McCall, 2005).

Collins (1990) offered a literary contribution to the Black feminist discourse that furthered the energy ignited by older Black feminists. Specifically, Collins introduced Black feminist thought, which differed from Black feminist theory because it indicated an action component. Collins (1990) framed Black feminist thought as an oppositional action that countered the negation and exclusion of Black women's experiences and, thus, their knowledge. Her work emphasized key actionable goals for Black women: to define themselves, establish positive, multiple representations of themselves, use their cultural heritage as energy to resist daily discrimination, and confront interlocking structures of domination, such as race, gender, and class oppression.

Around the same time Black feminist thought entered the BFT discourse, Crenshaw (1989) introduced the concept of intersectionality. Intersectionality refers to a survival theory that intentionally attends to the various ways race and gender interact to form the multiple dimensions of Black women's experiences, especially in employment. Because Black feminists have "long theorized the mutually constitutive nature of race and gender by describing black women's 'double' jeopardy... and by analyzing the metalanguage of race..." (Nash, 2011, p. 451), Crenshaw's intersectionality framework became a preferred lens for Black feminists to identify how race and gender collided under particular conditions.

A few years ago, I vowed to avoid desperately seeking the attention of non-Black women on issues unique to Black women. However, understanding intersectionality is crucial, as it highlights why this leadership topic is critical. According to Collins in "Intersectionality as Critical Theory," "as subordinated groups such as Indigenous peoples, African Americans, women, LGBTQ people, and Latinos/as began challenging both the substance of knowledge about their experiences and the power arrangements within society, oppositional or resistant knowledge was produced." This marked the conceptualization of intersectionality.

THE URGENCY OF INTERSECTIONALITY (CRENSHAW, 2016)

Imagine a large auditorium filled with eager faces, the hum of conversation slowly dying down as a powerful woman takes the stage. Kimberlé Crenshaw, a scholar, writer, and civil rights activist, stands poised and ready to engage the audience. Her eyes scan the crowd, and a hush falls over the room as she begins to speak.

"I'd like to try something new," Crenshaw announces, her voice both calm and commanding. "Those of you who are able, please stand up".

Curious and a bit uncertain, people around the room rise from their seats, glancing at one another. Crenshaw continues, "I'm going to name some names. When you hear a name that you don't recognize, you can't tell me anything about them, I'd like you to take a seat and stay seated. The last person standing, we're going to see what they know".

A ripple of laughter and murmurs spreads through the crowd as they prepare to engage in the exercise. "Eric Garner. Mike Brown. Tamir Rice. Freddie Gray", Crenshaw calmly but loudly announces.

As expected, many in the audience remain standing, familiar with these names. Crenshaw pauses, allowing the recognition to sink in before she resumes, "Michelle Cusseaux. Tanisha Anderson. Aura Rosser. Meagan Hockaday".

Gradually, more people take their seats. Some look puzzled, others thoughtful, as they realize the unfamiliarity of these names. Crenshaw surveys the room again. So, if we look around, there are about four people still standing," she notes, a gentle smile tugging at her lips. "Actually, I'm not going to put you on the spot. I just say that to encourage transparency so you can be seated".

Laughter and relief ripple through the audience as the remaining few take their seats. Crenshaw transitions,

So those of you who recognized the first group of names know that these were African-Americans who have been killed by the police over the last two and a half years," Crenshaw explains. "What you may not know is that the other list is also African-Americans who have been killed within the last two years. Only one thing distinguishes the names that you know from the names that you don't know: gender.

The room falls into a heavy silence as the weight of her words sinks in. Crenshaw's tone is both somber and resolute as she continues,

Now, it is surprising, isn't it, that this would be the case? I mean, there are two issues involved here. There's police violence against African-Americans, and there's violence against women, two issues that have been talked about a lot lately. But when we think about who is implicated by these problems, when we think about who is victimized by these problems, the names of these Black women never come to mind.

Crenshaw pauses to let the gravity of this revelation resonate with the audience, Why does a frame matter? Well, an issue that affects Black people and an issue that affects women, wouldn't that necessarily include Black people who are women and women who are Black people? The simple answer is that this is a trickle-down approach to social justice, and many times it just doesn't work.

Crenshaw's voice rises with urgency, "Without frames that allow us to see how social problems impact all the members of a targeted group, many will fall through the cracks of our movements, left to suffer in virtual isolation. But it doesn't have to be this way".

As the audience reflects on these powerful words, the significance of intersectionality becomes clear. Figure 4 displays the actual image that Crenshaw projects on the screen during the opening of her famous TED talk, documented above, as she goes deeper into the concept of intersectionality (Crenshaw, 2016).

Figure 4. Crenshaw's concept of intersectionality

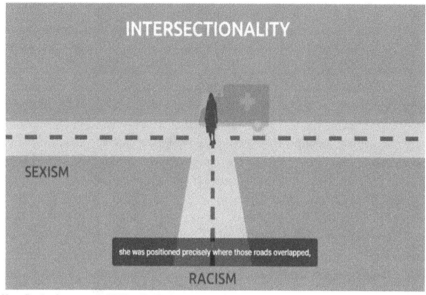

Note. During her renowned TED talk, Kimberlé Crenshaw displayed this image, represented by Figure 4 above, to illustrate the concept of intersectionality. The image of a woman standing at a street intersection powerfully conveys the overlapping and intersecting social identities and related systems of oppression and discrimination faced by Black women.

By the late 1990s, Kimberle' Crenshaw, the thought leader who gave the preceding speech about intersectionality, recognized the need for a new frame to critique unique socio-political problems through her analysis of legal cases and social issues where traditional views of discrimination failed to capture the complexities of individuals belonging to multiple marginalized groups. Crenshaw's "framing problem" resulted from a legal case involving a Black woman suing for workplace discrimination. The judge in the case claimed that legally acknowledging the Black woman's dual discrimination complaint would give her "preferential treatment" and a "double advantage," a flawed line of thinking that overlooked the compounded nature of her experience (Crenshaw, 2016). The legal system's framework for understanding discrimination was partial and distorted, focusing on race or gender independently but not the intersection of the two. Crenshaw famously argued, "When you can't see a problem, you pretty much can't solve it" (Crenshaw, 2016). This case illustrated the critical need for a framework that acknowledged and addressed the overlapping forms of discrimination that Black women encounter, a recognition that is essential to foster work environments that support and empower Black women, allowing them an escape from navigating the tightrope of assimilation versus authenticity. Understanding Crenshaw's development of intersectionality underscores the necessity of addressing the unique challenges Black women face in leadership.

INTERSECTIONAL OPPRESSION IN ACTION

Recently, Dr. Claudine Gay stepped down from Harvard University's presidency as the first Black woman President of an Ivy League university after only nine months. Despite Dr. Gay's extensive qualifications and achievements, which included a Ph.D. in Government from Harvard, a distinguished career as a professor of African and African American Studies, and service as the Dean of the Faculty of Arts and Sciences, Dr. Gay was subjected to a level of scrutiny far beyond other university presidents who participated in congressional hearings.

During her tenure, Dr. Gay was involved in specific congressional hearings about freedom of speech and antisemitism on Ivy League campuses. These hearings scrutinized how universities handle controversial speakers, student protests, and incidents of antisemitism, placing additional pressure on Dr. Gay as she navigated these complex and highly charged issues. The intense questioning and public scrutiny she faced were disproportionate compared to her peers, highlighting the additional burdens placed on Black women in leadership positions.

In her resignation statement, Dr. Gay poignantly remarked, "It has been distressing to have doubt cast on my commitments to confronting hate and to upholding scholarly rigor—two bedrock values that are fundamental to who I am—and frightening to be subjected to personal attacks and threats fueled by racial animus" (CNN Staff, 2024). Dr. Gay's departure underscores the extreme challenges Black women face in high-profile leadership roles, where their qualifications are often overshadowed by undue scrutiny and relentless bias and reflects a broader trend where Black women in leadership are subjected to undue stress and obstacles that make their professional environments psychologically hazardous.

To illustrate yet another example of how the intersection of oppressed identities such as race and gender causes unique issues for black women in the workplace, consider the CROWN Act. The CROWN Act stands for "Create a Respectful and Open World for Natural Hair" and ensures employers cannot discriminate against Black women for wearing their hair naturally. The sheer fact that in the year 2024, Black women even needed state legislation to protect them from discrimination based on their natural hair texture speaks volumes, and sadly, as of June of 2024, the CROWN Act has only been passed in 26 out of the 50 U.S. states, after being federally filibustered by Republicans in 2022. The CROWN Act filibuster was led by Senator Rand Paul (R-KY), who argued that existing federal laws already provide the protections the act seeks to enforce.

The resistance to the CROWN Act underscores the privilege within the legislative process, where those not directly affected by racial discrimination can obstruct measures designed to protect marginalized groups. Despite clear testimonies and evidence showing the necessity of such legislation, the filibuster led by Senator Rand Paul prevented the bill from moving forward.

Hair discrimination, which is somehow not considered race-based discrimination in the United States of America, has been impacting black women in the workplace for years. Dove's CROWN research study in 2019 found that African American women face the highest instances of hair discrimination and are more likely to be sent home from the workplace because of their hair. The study also uncovered that 80 percent of African American women felt they needed to switch their hairstyle to align with more conservative standards to fit in at work. Hair discrimination occurs not only in the workplace but in schools as well.

STORY OF SELF: KIANNA'S 'HAIRY', INTERSECTIONAL DILEMMA

Below, I describe an incident at a university where I was employed as a professor, which we will call "Stanton University," a predominantly white institution. A young Black woman, whom we will call Kianna, was studying to become a schoolteacher in the education program there.

One day, Kianna reached out to me, visibly disturbed. She had just encountered a white woman in leadership within the university's educator preparation program. Upon seeing Kianna with her hair no longer in "ethnic" braids, the white woman had told her, "You look so much more professional with your hair like that."

This incident starkly highlighted the implicit and explicit racism Black women face daily, even in institutions of learning. To put the situation into perspective, there were significantly fewer Black students in the program compared to white students—I had never encountered a single Black male education undergraduate at the university.

The white woman in leadership, who was supposed to promote equity and inclusion, made this comment to Kianna without any awareness of its impact on a future Black teacher. I recall carefully planning how to address this incident with her, knowing I had to avoid her playing the victim and prevent the situation from being turned around on me as being aggressive or mean. When I finally brought it to her attention, she was completely unaware of the offensiveness of her comment until I explained it to her. I think I do recall this grown white woman in leadership having tears over the situation that had offended Kianna.

Turns out, this event was just the tip of the iceberg. On another occasion, while I was standing in the doorway of my office, this same white woman touched my hair without asking and then asked me if I could explain wigs and weaves to her because of something her white daughter was involved in at school. I wasn't even wearing a wig or weave at the time. I remember trying my hardest to smile and pretend it didn't bother me because I didn't know what else to do, caught off guard like that, and because I had already endured so many racist incidents during my tenure at that university.

This was the same white leader who once asked me why "black men like white women" and, when I responded, debated my response, bringing up a personal example that refuted my theory. She said directly to me, "You know that's why 'we' don't like you guys, because you don't like yourselves." I specifically remember her using the word "we" because I had to ask her then, "Who?" before she quickly clarified that she meant some white people. This conversation occurred when she and I discussed colorism within the Black community. It was exhausting and racially fatiguing.

These behaviors from a leader in the university's educator preparation program at a university that preaches diversity, inclusion, and equity were disheartening and sent a message to Black students about their place and value in such an environment. The psychological toll of witnessing such invisibility to the unique perspectives of Black women is profound.

Sharing narratives of lived experiences that document the nature of the discrimination Black women, and even black female students, face in the workplace and schools, such as issues with sporting their natural hair, which can be perceived as unprofessional by white leadership, becomes essential to intentionally display how black women's lives are impacted psychologically, socially, and professionally through discriminatory and unfair workplace treatments, to rally for change.

The extreme scrutiny and pressure that black women experience relating to their natural hair cause some black women in leadership to resort to chemical straightening, and what Dr. Gay experienced is part of a broader pattern where Black women in leadership roles often feel compelled to conform to dominant cultural norms in their professional environments. This phenomenon is known as assimilation.

THE COSTS AND CONSEQUENCES ASSOCIATED WITH ASSIMILATION

Assimilation refers to how individuals or groups adopt another group's cultural traits or social patterns. This process often involves gradually losing one's original cultural identity to blend in with the dominant culture. According to Park and Burgess, as reported by Hirsch, assimilation involves a series of processes through which individuals become community members by adopting similar attitudes and behaviors (Hirsch, 1942). Specifically in the context of this study, assimilation refers to the process by which Black women in educational leadership adapt or conform to the predominant cultural norms and expectations of their professional environments. This often involves downplaying or altering aspects of their cultural identity, behaviors, and expressions to align with the dominant group's standards. Assimilation can manifest in various ways, such as modifying speech, appearance, or leadership styles, to be perceived as more acceptable or less threatening by colleagues and superiors. Black women use identity shifting, also known as identity negotiation, as a coping strategy to manage workplace discrimination and stereotypes. This can help reduce overt discrimination and potentially increase opportunities for career advancement. However, the psychological effects of assimilation can be significant, leading to stress, feelings of inauthenticity, and the erasure of one's cultural heritage (Collins, 2000; Jones & Shorter-Gooden, 2003).

IDENTITY NEGOTIATION

Identity negotiation, or shifting, refers to the ongoing process through which a person's identity can be negotiated through choices made in cultural interactions and can refer specifically to an individual with a minoritized identity who may alter their behavior to either assimilate into the dominant group or to protect their personal sense of self (Ting-Toomey, 2005). This process requires Black women in leadership positions to reconcile their personal, cultural, and professional identities amidst external pressures and expectations and adapt their behavior and presentation to align with societal and organizational norms while maintaining authenticity and integrity. According to Jones and Shorter-Gooden (2004), Black women frequently engaged in "shifting," a form of identity negotiation that involves an adjustment of self-presentation and behavior to traverse the complexities of race and gender in predominantly white environments.

PERCEIVED BENEFITS OF ASSIMILATION

While there are various costs associated with Black women's identity negotiation/shifting practices, there are numerous advantages to shifting one's identity in the workplace. Some Black women perceived identity shifting to be positive as they hoped to be "the model Black citizen" to represent their Black family well and leave a positive legacy for future Black women in a professional environment (Dickens & Chavez, 2018). Career-oriented Black women grew to use their place in the workforce to create new images of Black womanhood, causing racist and sexist images and barriers to weaken (Bell, 1990). One primary example is how Black women shifted their speech patterns to combat stereotypes in the workplace. Black women acknowledged shifting speech patterns to combat stereotypical beliefs from their supervisors and colleagues (Ting-Toomey, 1999). They also used role flexing/shifting as a means of "proving them wrong" by justifying themselves by highlighting their strengths and disproving stereotypes by speaking better or hiding one's true feelings, such as anger in the workplace (Jones & Shorter-Gooden, 2003). Some Black women viewed shifting as an asset and a coping mechanism for their workplace survival through this lens. Jones and Shorter-Gooden (2003) defined role flexing/shifting as an adaptive survival mechanism when there is no option to fix or untangle discrimination in the workplace. Also, biculturality is an asset that causes divergent thinking, creativity, risk-taking, and boundary-spanning amongst Black women (Bell, 1990).

THE RISKS OF AUTHENTICITY

On the other hand, authenticity, in this research study, is defined as the ability of Black women in educational leadership to fully and freely express their cultural identities, values, and beliefs in their professional roles without fear of retribution or marginalization. It involves embracing and integrating one's true self into one's leadership style and professional interactions. Authenticity means being able to assert one's opinions, showcase cultural heritage, and lead with confidence in one's intellectual abilities and insights. Achieving authenticity in the workplace fosters a sense of empowerment, belonging, and psychological safety, allowing individuals to thrive and contribute meaningfully to their organizations. According to Jones and Shorter-Gooden (2003), some Black women choose to resist the oppressive realities that cause them to negotiate their identity in the workplace. However, being authentic can also lead to heightened scrutiny, bias, and potential career risks, such as being denied promotions or facing marginalization (Dickens & Womack, 2020).

Authenticity in leadership allows Black women to challenge and change the workplace culture. As more individuals embrace their true selves, others will be encouraged to do the same, leading to a more diverse and accepting workplace. This shift can ultimately benefit the organization by leveraging all its employees' unique perspectives and strengths. Despite the advantages, many Black women choose not to be authentic at work. The fear of being perceived as less competent or too aggressive remains a significant deterrent. Essence (2021) stated, "Scores of us are so worried about being perceived negatively that we hide our authentic selves in the workplace, choosing instead to tone down our appearance, soften our demeanor, and hold back in our conversations"). There is a risk with authenticity; Black women can face heightened scrutiny and bias when deciding to embrace their authentic selves, a complex balancing act. Black women, especially those in leadership positions, must carefully balance the pressures of conformity with the desire for genuine self-expression while striving to maintain professional integrity and obtain career advancement. Constantly navigating assimilation and authenticity in the workplace is a tricky and never-ending balancing act for Black women. As Jones and Shorter-Gooden (2003) describe, many Black women choose to resist the oppressive realities that pressure them to negotiate their identity in the workplace. The balancing act of navigating when to assimilate versus remain authentic can cause mental anguish for many Black women serving in education leadership roles.

A BALANCING ACT: THE PSYCHOLOGICAL TOLL OF IDENTITY NEGOTIATION

Assimilation and authenticity in leadership harm Black women in leadership roles, not just psychologically but also socially, professionally, and even physically. It is assumed that authenticity in leadership leads to negative outcomes, but assimilation can also have detrimental effects and outcomes for Black women in leadership. Research has shown that assimilation is associated with increased stress levels, decreased job satisfaction, persistent self-doubt, hindered career advancement, and loss of cultural identity. Conversely, authenticity has been associated with retaliation and marginalization, isolation and lack of social support, increased workplace conflicts, heightened scrutiny and criticism, microaggressions, barriers to career advancement, and burnout (Jones & Shorter-Gooden, 2003; Holder et al., 2015; Jean-Marie & Brooks, 2019; Lewis et al., 2017; McCluney & Rabelo, 2020; Roberts et al., 2019; West et al., 2020).While many organizations may have a generally healthy work culture, they can still fail to ensure psychological safety for their employees and leaders. Tulshyan (2022) identified four critical warning signs that indicate a lack of psychological safety for women of color in the workplace. These warning signs, listed below, highlight areas where improvement is essential, even in well-meaning organizations.

1. *Lack of Safe Mechanisms to Report Bias:* Mechanisms to report bias and harassment are either nonexistent or ineffective.
2. *Women of Color Are Penalized for Speaking Up:* Psychological safety is often compromised for women of color who speak up about issues.
3. *White Comfort Is Prioritized:* Double standards exist for white employees and employees of color, with employees of color being required to police their tone.

4. *Lack of Advocacy for Women of Color:* There is a lack of advocacy and allyship from peers and managers. Despite good intentions, many managers do not have the tools to recognize or address everyday bias. This gap in support can lead to exclusion and isolation for women of color.

These warning signs are especially important because Black women, due to a combination of historical, cultural, and social factors, experience and show signs of mental health challenges in unique ways. Historically, Black women have often felt disrespected, unprotected, and neglected, causing their mental health symptoms to differ from those typically associated with mental illness. This difference in experience can lead to underdiagnosis and undertreatment, further exacerbating mental health issues (Watson & Hunter, 2015).

Black women often reported symptoms such as persistent sadness, loss of interest in once-loved activities, changes in appetite and sleep patterns, and a heightened sense of worthlessness and hopelessness (Leiba, 2024). Shipp (2023) examined depressive symptoms among Black women and found that they more frequently reported sleep disturbance, self-criticism, and irritability, as opposed to more typical symptoms like a depressed mood. Because Black women's symptoms present differently, they run the risk of misdiagnosis and undertreatment. Williams and Mohammed (2009) emphasized the need for more research on historically understudied and minoritized populations to identify symptoms better and reduce health disparities.

METHODOLOGY AND RESEARCH DESIGN

This mixed-methods research employed phenomenological and correlational approaches to explore identity negotiation among Black women in education leadership roles. The study focused on the preference for assimilation versus authenticity in the lived experiences of these women. Specifically, it examined how Black females in education leadership experience the psychological climate of their workplace environments and its correlation with variables such as age, professional education leadership experience, and perceptions of mistreatment rooted in societal stereotypes about Black women.

Participants

Participants were recruited through the researcher's and book publisher's professional networks. The researcher, a Black woman with 18 years of experience in education leadership, used her connections to ensure a diverse and representative sample. All participants identified as Black women working in PK-12 and/or higher education leadership roles.

Participant Information

- Total Number of Participants: 22 (13 for the survey, 9 for the focus group, with some overlap).
- All participants identified as black women currently serving in education leadership roles.
- Age Range: 25-60 years.
- Professional Experience: Ranging from 5 to 30 years in education leadership.
- Educational Background: Various degrees, including Bachelor's, Master's, and Doctorates'.
- Geographical Location: Participants from multiple regions across the United States.

DATA COLLECTION METHODS AND ANALYSIS

Quantitative Collection Methods: Online Survey Design and Administration

The researcher designed an online survey based on insights gathered about identity negotiation and stereotypes about black women from the comprehensive literature review. Thirteen pre-approved online survey participants provided data aligning with their self-perception of their intersectional identities as black women, their cumulative professional education leadership experience, their age, and their experiences with psychological workplace abuse. Verification was ensured through participants' official Google accounts and their school institution's email addresses. The online survey, administered via Google Forms, included approximately twenty-five questions, most requiring five-point Likert-scale responses. A Likert-scale sample online survey question and an open-ended sample online survey question is included below:

Sample Online Survey Question (Likert Scale)

Using the grid below, please indicate the frequency with which you feel that your professional demeanor is misinterpreted as fitting the "bold and expressive" stereotype in your leadership role. Then, in the same row as your selected frequency, choose the column that best represents the level of impact this misinterpretation has on your leadership and professional identity.

1. Frequency Choices:
    1. I have never experienced this dynamic in my workplace setting.
    2. I sometimes experience this dynamic in my workplace.
    3. I regularly encounter situations relating to this dynamic in my workplace.
    4. I very frequently or always encounter situations relating to this dynamic in my workplace.
2. Impact Choices:
    1. This frequency has no negative impact on me professionally or as a leader in my workplace.
    2. This frequency has minimal negative impact on me professionally or as a leader in my workplace.
    3. This frequency sometimes negatively impacts me professionally or as a leader in my workplace.
    4. This frequency often negatively impacts me professionally or as a leader in my workplace.
    5. This frequency significantly impacts me negatively professionally or as a leader in my workplace.

SAMPLE ONLINE SURVEY QUESTION (OPEN-ENDED)

Black Female Stereotypes Impact

If applicable, reflect on specific instances where you've encountered negative stereotypes as a Black female leader. Describe the nature of these stereotypes and how they've impacted your professional interactions and credibility.

Qualitative Collection Methods: Online Live Focus Group

In addition to the survey, an online live focus group was conducted via Zoom with nine participants, some of whom had also completed the survey. This approach facilitated the collection of richer, more detailed qualitative data by allowing for real-time interaction and deeper discussion. The live focus group provided a platform for participants to share their experiences and perspectives to add depth to the findings. As mentioned previously, some of the qualitative data were also derived from open-ended questions from the online survey, allowing for richer, more layered perspectives.

Sample Focus Group Topics Related to Identity Negotiation and Career Milestones

- *Discussion on pivotal leadership moments*
- *Experiences of identity negotiation choices (assimilation vs. authenticity)*
- *Strategies for coping with professional challenges*
- *Detailed narratives on career milestones*
- *Questions about initial leadership roles and experiences*
- *Items on professional recognition and advancement*
- *Queries about encountering psychological workplace abuse and managing stereotypes*
- *Questions on mentorship and influence on policy*

DATA ANALYSIS

This study's data was analyzed using quantitative and qualitative methods to provide a comprehensive understanding of the research questions. The primary data sources included responses from an online survey and a live focus group via Zoom.

Quantitative Data Analysis

The online survey facilitated through Google Forms was the survey tool used to collect quantitative data. Thirteen participants successfully completed the survey.

Likert Scale: Responses to Likert scale online survey questions were assigned numerical values ranging from 1 (Strongly Disagree) to 5 (Strongly Agree). This allowed for measuring and statistically analyzing participants' attitudes and perceptions across various dimensions. Some open-ended questions contributed to the qualitative data, but most online survey questions were measured using a five-point Likert scale (i.e. Strongly Disagree, Disagree, Neutral, Agree, Strongly Agree).

Quantitative Data Measurement

To systematically assess the variables in this study, a series of five-point Likert scales was used for quantitative data collection. This section explains how each attribute was measured before ranking the data and applying statistical formulas to measure correlations. Refer to Table 1 for a detailed breakdown of the scoring system used for each attribute.

Identity Index

The Identity Index measures the participants' self-perception and identity as Black women in leadership roles. This index includes multiple dimensions such as cultural identity, professional identity, and personal experiences. Each dimension was assessed using specific survey questions, and responses were assigned numerical values on a five-point Likert scale, where:

- 1 Point: Strongly Disagree
- 2 Points: Disagree
- 3 Points: Neutral
- 4 Points: Agree
- 5 Points: Strongly Agree

Psychological Workplace Abuse

Psychological Workplace Abuse was measured using multiple indicators such as perceived frequency of microaggressions, workplace discrimination, emotional exhaustion, and psychological distress. Each of these indicators was assessed through specific survey questions, and responses were assigned numerical values on a five-point Likert scale. The categories and their Likert scale scores are as follows:

Perceived Frequency of Microaggressions

- 1 Point: No experience of microaggressions
- 2 Points: Minimal experience of microaggressions
- 3 Points: Moderate experience of microaggressions
- 4 Points: Frequent experience of microaggressions
- 5 Points: Chronic experience of microaggressions

Workplace Discrimination

- 1 Point: No experience of workplace discrimination
- 2 Points: Minimal experience of workplace discrimination
- 3 Points: Moderate experience of workplace discrimination
- 4 Points: Frequent experience of workplace discrimination
- 5 Points: Chronic experience of workplace discrimination

Emotional Exhaustion

- 1 Point: No emotional exhaustion
- 2 Points: Minimal emotional exhaustion
- 3 Points: Moderate emotional exhaustion
- 4 Points: Frequent emotional exhaustion
- 5 Points: Chronic emotional exhaustion

Psychological Distress

- 1 Point: No psychological distress
- 2 Points: Minimal psychological distress
- 3 Points: Moderate psychological distress
- 4 Points: Frequent psychological distress
- 5 Points: Chronic psychological distress

Age

Participants' ages were collected as part of the demographic section of the online survey and were categorized into distinct career stages based on a five-point Likert scale, acknowledging that age often correlates with experience and leadership maturity. The scoring system used is as follows:

- 1 Point: 26-30 years (Early career leaders)
- 2 Points: 31-35 years (Developing leaders)
- 3 Points: 36-45 years (Mid-career leaders)
- 4 Points: 46-55 years (Experienced leaders)
- 5 Points: 56+ years (Veteran leaders)

Professional Leadership Experience

Professional Leadership Experience was assessed through questions focusing on the participants' duration in their current leadership roles, their total leadership experience in education, and the description of their past leadership roles. The scoring system for each aspect is detailed below:

Current Full-Time Leadership Role Duration (Q5)

- 1 Point: 0-1 year (Entry-level experience)
- 2 Points: 1-3 years (Early experience)

- 3 Points: 3-5 years (Mid-level experience)
- 4 Points: 5-10 years (Advanced experience)
- 5 Points: 10+ years (Expert level)

Total Leadership Experience in Education (Q6)

- 1 Point: 0-3 years (Limited overall experience)
- 2 Points: 3-7 years (Early significant experience)
- 3 Points: 7-12 years (Mid-career level)
- 4 Points: 12-20 years (Advanced experience)
- 5 Points: 20+ years (Highly seasoned leader)

Description of Past Leadership Roles (Q7)

- 1 Point: Limited roles with minimal responsibility
- 2 Points: Some leadership roles with moderate responsibility
- 3 Points: Several significant leadership roles
- 4 Points: Numerous substantial roles with high responsibility
- 5 Points: Extensive and prestigious leadership roles

QUANTITATIVE ANALYSIS: MEASURING FOR CORRELATION

Correlation Calculation: Statistical techniques were used to analyze the relationships between identity index scores and other variables such as age and professional education leadership experience and participants' experiences of psychological workplace abuse.

Kendall's Tau was used to calculate correlations between ranked attributes such as participant's age, professional education, leadership experience, and overall connectedness to the Too Bold, Black, and Brilliant societal stereotypes about black women and their experience with psychological abuse in the workplace. This non-parametric statistic was chosen to examine correlations between these attributes for its suitability in handling ordinal data and ties, ensuring robust and accurate correlation measures, making it suitable for tied Likert scale responses. The raw scores for each attribute were ranked to account for duplicate responses, ensuring a more accurate correlation analysis. Kendall's Tau was used to analyze relationships to allow for a robust and accurate measure of these relationships, ensuring the findings reflected the participants' experiences. Ties were handled by assigning the average rank to tied scores.

Identity Index: The Identity Index score was calculated by aggregating scores from multiple survey items related to each participant's self-perception of their alignment with stereotypes associated with black women relating to their Blackness, Boldness, and Brilliance. Each item contributed equally to the overall index. The identity index score served as the independent variable in the correlational analysis. It represented how connected each participant felt to their overall Blackness, Boldness, and Brilliance as related to societal stereotypes about black women using Likert scale responses. This independent variable focused on observing correlations between the participant's connection to their intersectional identity and their lived experiences as a leader in the workplace, especially as it relates to psychological workplace abuse. Some sample questions used to measure each participant's self-perception of their own Blackness, Boldness, and Brilliance which are included below:

> How comfortable are you with asserting your opinions in professional settings (1= Never comfortable; 2= Hardly ever comfortable; 3= Moderately comfortable; 4=Nearly Always comfortable; 5 = Always comfortable)?
> How important is expressing your heritage/community and identity as a black woman in your daily life; please consider both professional and personal aspects of your life. (1= Not at all important; 2=Marginally important; 3= Important; 4=Quite important; 5 =Extremely important)?

Quantitative Data Measurement of Focus Attributes

To systematically assess the variables in this study, a series of five-point Likert scales was used for quantitative data collection. This section explains how each attribute was measured before ranking the data and applying statistical formulas to measure correlations. Refer to Table 1 for a detailed breakdown of the scoring system used for each attribute.

Identity Index

The Identity Index measures the participants' self-perception and identity as Black women in leadership roles. This index includes multiple dimensions such as cultural identity, professional identity, and personal experiences. Each dimension was assessed using specific survey questions, and responses were assigned numerical values on a five-point Likert scale, where:

- 1 Point: Strongly Disagree
- 2 Points: Disagree

- 3 Points: Neutral
- 4 Points: Agree
- 5 Points: Strongly Agree

Psychological Workplace Abuse

Psychological Workplace Abuse was measured using multiple indicators such as perceived frequency of microaggressions, workplace discrimination, emotional exhaustion, and psychological distress. Each of these indicators was assessed through specific survey questions, and responses were assigned numerical values on a five-point Likert scale. The categories and their Likert scale scores are as follows:

Perceived Frequency of Microaggressions

- 1 Point: No experience of microaggressions
- 2 Points: Minimal experience of microaggressions
- 3 Points: Moderate experience of microaggressions
- 4 Points: Frequent experience of microaggressions
- 5 Points: Chronic experience of microaggressions

Workplace Discrimination

- 1 Point: No experience of workplace discrimination
- 2 Points: Minimal experience of workplace discrimination
- 3 Points: Moderate experience of workplace discrimination
- 4 Points: Frequent experience of workplace discrimination
- 5 Points: Chronic experience of workplace discrimination

Emotional Exhaustion

- 1 Point: No emotional exhaustion
- 2 Points: Minimal emotional exhaustion
- 3 Points: Moderate emotional exhaustion
- 4 Points: Frequent emotional exhaustion
- 5 Points: Chronic emotional exhaustion

Psychological Distress

- 1 Point: No psychological distress
- 2 Points: Minimal psychological distress

- 3 Points: Moderate psychological distress
- 4 Points: Frequent psychological distress
- 5 Points: Chronic psychological distress

Age

Participants' ages were collected as part of the demographic section of the online survey and were categorized into distinct career stages based on a five-point Likert scale, acknowledging that age often correlates with experience and leadership maturity. The scoring system used is as follows:

- 1 Point: 26-30 years (Early career leaders)
- 2 Points: 31-35 years (Developing leaders)
- 3 Points: 36-45 years (Mid-career leaders)
- 4 Points: 46-55 years (Experienced leaders)
- 5 Points: 56+ years (Veteran leaders)

Professional Leadership Experience

Professional Leadership Experience was assessed through questions focusing on the participants' duration in their current leadership roles, their total leadership experience in education, and the description of their past leadership roles. The scoring system for each aspect is detailed below:

Current Full-Time Leadership Role Duration (Q5)

- 1 Point: 0-1 year (Entry-level experience)
- 2 Points: 1-3 years (Early experience)
- 3 Points: 3-5 years (Mid-level experience)
- 4 Points: 5-10 years (Advanced experience)
- 5 Points: 10+ years (Expert level)

Total Leadership Experience in Education (Q6)

- 1 Point: 0-3 years (Limited overall experience)
- 2 Points: 3-7 years (Early significant experience)
- 3 Points: 7-12 years (Mid-career level)
- 4 Points: 12-20 years (Advanced experience)
- 5 Points: 20+ years (Highly seasoned leader)

Description of Past Leadership Roles (Q7)

- 1 Point: Limited roles with minimal responsibility
- 2 Points: Some leadership roles with moderate responsibility
- 3 Points: Several significant leadership roles
- 4 Points: Numerous substantial roles with high responsibility
- 5 Points: Extensive and prestigious leadership roles

Table 1. Scoring attributes summary

Attribute	1 Point	2 Points	3 Points	4 Points	5 Points
Current Full-Time Leadership Role Duration	0-1 year (Entry-level experience)	1-3 years (Early experience)	3-5 years (Mid-level experience)	5-10 years (Advanced experience)	10+ years (Expert level)
Total Leadership Experience in Education	0-3 years (Limited overall experience)	3-7 years (Early significant experience)	7-12 years (Mid-career level)	12-20 years (Advanced experience)	20+ years (Highly seasoned leader)
Description of Past Leadership Roles	Limited roles with minimal responsibility	Some leadership roles with moderate responsibility	Several significant leadership roles	Numerous substantial roles with high responsibility	Extensive and prestigious leadership roles
Perceived Frequency of Microaggressions	No experience of microaggressions	Minimal experience of microaggressions	Moderate experience of microaggressions	Frequent experience of microaggressions	Chronic experience of microaggressions
Workplace Discrimination	No experience of workplace discrimination	Minimal experience of workplace discrimination	Moderate experience of workplace discrimination	Frequent experience of workplace discrimination	Chronic experience of workplace discrimination
Emotional Exhaustion	No emotional exhaustion	Minimal emotional exhaustion	Moderate emotional exhaustion	Frequent emotional exhaustion	Chronic emotional exhaustion
Psychological Distress	No psychological distress	Minimal psychological distress	Moderate psychological distress	Frequent psychological distress	Chronic psychological distress

QUALITATIVE DATA ANALYSIS

Qualitative data was collected from the online live focus group transcripts and the open-ended online survey question responses. The focus group was conducted via Zoom with nine participants, some of whom had also completed the survey.

The qualitative data analysis in this study followed a systematic thematic analysis process to explore the lived experiences of Black women in educational leadership. This method was informed by the step-by-step process described by Naeem, Ozuem,

Howell, and Ranfagni (2023) in their article published in the International Journal of Qualitative Methods.

The thematic analysis process included six key steps: transcription, familiarization with the data, selection of keywords, coding, theme development, conceptualization, and conceptual model development. These steps ensured a thorough and systematic examination of the data, leading to the identification of key themes and the development of a conceptual model.

Thematic Analysis Six-Step Process

1. *Transcription and Familiarization:* Transcribing the focus group discussions and online survey responses to immerse in the data and identify initial themes.
2. *Selection of Keywords:* Identifying recurring patterns and terms using the 6Rs criteria: realness, richness, repetition, rationale, repartee, and regal.
3. *Coding:* Assigning codes to segments of data to capture their core message, significance, or theme. This step simplifies complex textual data by transforming it into a theoretical form.
4. *Theme Development:* Organizing codes into meaningful groups to identify patterns and relationships, offering insights into the research question.
5. *Conceptualization:* Defining concepts emerging from the data and understanding their relationships using tools like diagrams or models.
6. *Development of Conceptual Model:* Creating a conceptual model to encapsulate all findings and insights grounded in theoretical frameworks.

RESULTS

A framework based on three catalysts—*Too Bold, Too Black, Too Brilliant*—was employed to investigate the phenomenon of identity negotiation for Black women in educational leadership based on common societal stereotypes relating to black women that potentially impact them in their leadership roles. The *Too Bold, Too Black, Too Brilliant* conceptual framework was used as an anchor to analyze Black women's lived experiences and self-perceptions in educational leadership, providing a lens through which the nuances of identity negotiation can be better understood.

This study aimed to reveal the intricate balance Black women leaders must maintain between authenticity and assimilation by navigating and responding to stereotypes of being *Too Bold* (misinterpreted assertiveness), *Too Black* (explicit stereotypes about physical attributes and cultural expressions), and *Too Brilliant* (undervaluation of intellectual contributions). This study also examined the extent to which Black women negotiated their identities based on contextual factors and explored changes in their experiences of identity negotiation and psychological abuse after obtaining leadership roles.

The findings, derived from a combination of focus group discussions and online survey responses with open-ended questions and Likert scale items, illuminated Black women's strategies and coping mechanisms to manage their professional identities amidst these pervasive stereotypes. Additionally, the study explored the correlation between Black Women's approaches to identity negotiation and their experiences of psychological workplace abuse, offering insights into how these dynamics evolved with their professional advancement.

PRIMARY RESEARCH QUESTION

How do Black women in educational leadership navigate the challenges of maintaining their authentic identities while facing psychological workplace abuse, and what are the correlations between their self-perception related to Blackness, Boldness, and Brilliance andtheir experiences of such abuse?

Secondary Research Questions

How does the self-perception of Black women in educational leadership correlate with their experiences of psychological workplace abuse, considering variables such as age and leadership experience?

What common themes of psychological workplace abuse are reported by Black women in educational leadership, and how do these experiences reflect negative societal stereotypes about Black women?

How do Black women's lived experiences and personal narratives in educational leadership inform the development of the EmpowH.E.R. Leadership Blueprint?

Qualitative Results: Themes and Sub-Themes: Navigating Identity in Leadership

Participants described the tension between maintaining their cultural identity and assimilating to fit professional norms.

Significant Quotations

- Participant #2: "I felt strongly connected to my cultural identity within my leadership role. It manifested in my decision-making and interactions with colleagues, but sometimes I felt pressured to assimilate to fit in."
- Participant #6: "As an undergraduate student, I was often asked to take photos and be in marketing campaigns as a student leader. However, I was not paid or compensated for the time or the usage of my image/likeness."

Experiences of Tokenism

Participants frequently felt tokenized, leading to feelings of being valued for diversity rather than their skills.

Significant Quotations

- Participant #2: "Sometimes I felt tokenized in my role. It felt like I was there to meet a diversity quota rather than for my skills and contributions."

Impact of Negative Stereotypes

Negative stereotypes such as being seen as "too aggressive" or "too bold" were common, impacting professional interactions and self-perception.

Significant Quotations

- Participant #6: "Negative stereotypes about Black women impacted my professional life. I was labeled 'too aggressive' or 'too bold' simply for expressing my opinions."

Relevant Patterns and Themes Relating to the Perception of Catalyst Stereotypes in the Workplace

The research study revealed significant themes and patterns in the experiences of Black women in educational leadership, particularly concerning the three catalysts: *Too Bold, Too Black, and Too Brilliant.* The qualitative data from focus group interviews and open-ended survey questions highlighted participants' different responses and outcomes when negotiating their identities through assimilation or authenticity as they relate specifically to the negative stereotypes about black women associated with each catalyst. To visually represent these findings, Figures 5, 6, and 7 below display the most relevant responses and themes that participants noted concerning each catalyst: *Too Bold, Too Black, and Too Brilliant.*

Figure 5. Common responses to black women being "too bold" in educational leadership

Note. This figure illustrates the frequent responses and themes experienced by Black women leaders when their assertiveness is misinterpreted as aggressiveness, highlighting the stereotypes of the Angry Black Woman and the Strong Black Woman.

Figure 6. Common responses to black women being "too black" in educational leadership

Note. This figure depicts the common responses and themes associated with Black women embracing their cultural identity, often leading to perceptions of being unprofessional or "ghetto."

Figure 7. Common responses to black women being "too brilliant" in educational leadership

Note. This figure shows the typical responses and themes encountered by Black women who showcase their intellectual brilliance, frequently resulting in being perceived as overly ambitious or intimidating.

TOO BOLD: ASSERTIVENESS MISINTERPRETED

Assimilation: Participants often felt compelled to suppress their assertiveness to avoid the "Angry Black Woman" stereotype. This included downplaying their boldness in voice, opinions, and leadership styles to fit in with their colleagues.

- Participant A: "I found myself constantly biting my tongue in meetings. Speaking up was just not worth the risk of being labeled as aggressive."
- Participant B: "I had to soften my approach and be less direct, which sometimes meant my ideas weren't taken seriously."

Impact: While this strategy helped avoid immediate conflict, it often led to limited career growth and professional recognition due to the perception of being passive or less competent.

Authenticity: Those who chose to be authentic faced stereotypes such as the "Strong Black Woman" and were often misjudged as confrontational or aggressive.

- Participant C: "Whenever I spoke my mind, I was seen as too confrontational. It didn't matter that my male colleagues did the same and were praised for it."
- Participant D: "Being bold and assertive meant my emotional and physical needs were often overlooked. They just assumed I could handle anything."

Impact: This authenticity often resulted in their needs being overlooked and their boldness being perceived negatively, impacting their professional relationships and advancement.

Too Black: **Cultural Identity and Tokenization**

Assimilation: Participants frequently downplayed their cultural expressions and conformed to dominant norms to blend in. This included altering their appearance, speech, and behavior to avoid being tokenized or stereotyped.

- Participant E: "I stopped wearing my natural hair and switched to more conservative styles to avoid standing out."
- Participant F: "I felt the need to tone down my cultural expressions to fit in with the predominantly white leadership team."

Impact: This often led to feelings of inauthenticity and isolation but helped avoid the negative perceptions associated with being "too Black."

Authenticity: When participants embraced their cultural identity, they were often perceived as unprofessional or "ghetto," their cultural heritage was seen as inappropriate for professional settings.

- Participant G: "Wearing traditional attire or speaking in my natural dialect was seen as unprofessional, which was disheartening."
- Participant H: "Displaying my cultural heritage made me feel more connected to my roots, but it also came with the cost of being judged and marginalized."

Impact: Despite the personal satisfaction and authenticity, this often resulted in their professionalism being questioned and increased scrutiny from colleagues.

Too Brilliant: **Perception of Intelligence and Undervaluation**

Assimilation: Participants who underplayed their intellectual achievements did so to fit in, often resulting in missed opportunities and others taking credit for their work.

- Participant I: "I had to downplay my qualifications to avoid intimidating my peers. It was frustrating to see less qualified individuals being promoted."
- Participant J: "Often, my contributions were overlooked, and others took credit for my ideas without repercussions."

Impact: This led to significant professional dissatisfaction and hindered career advancement despite their high qualifications.

Authenticity: Those who showcased their brilliance faced stereotypes such as being perceived as "know-it-alls" or overly ambitious, which intimidated colleagues.

- Participant K: "Exhibiting my full potential often resulted in being seen as a threat rather than an asset."
- Participant L: "Despite my qualifications, I was frequently underestimated and had to work twice as hard to prove myself."

Impact: While authenticity brought a sense of personal fulfillment, it also led to increased scrutiny, resistance, and a challenging work environment.

STRATEGIES FOR COPING AND RESILIENCE

Participants used various strategies to cope with challenges, including adjusting communication and seeking support.

Significant Quotations

- Participant #7: "I learned to adjust my communication style to avoid being perceived as aggressive, and I sought support from mentors who understood my experiences."

Common Milestones in Leadership

Common milestones in the careers of Black women in educational leadership included initial leadership roles, professional recognition, encountering stereotypes, advancing in leadership, seeking and providing mentorship, and influencing policy.

Significant Quotations

- Participant #3: "My journey started with an initial leadership role where I faced significant stereotypes. With time, I advanced in my career, sought mentorship, and eventually provided mentorship to others."

Quantitative Results: Correlational Analysis

The identity index score served as the independent variable in the correlational analysis. It represented how connected each participant felt to their overall Blackness, Boldness, and Brilliance as related to societal stereotypes about black women based on Likert scale responses.

As previously mentioned, statistical techniques were used to analyze the relationships between identity index scores and other variables such as age and professional education leadership experience and participants' experiences of psychological workplace abuse.

This study used Kendall's Tau (τ) to measure the correlation between different variables. Kendall's Tau ranges from -1 to 1 and indicates both the strength and direction of a relationship between two variables. A positive correlation ($\tau > 0$) means that as one variable increases, the other also tends to increase. Conversely, a negative correlation ($\tau < 0$) means that the other tends to decrease as one variable increases. A τ value close to 1 or -1 indicates a strong relationship, while a value close to 0 indicates a weak relationship. The p-value associated with each correlation indicates the statistical significance; a p-value less than 0.05 suggests the correlation is statistically significant. For example, a strong positive correlation ($\tau = 0.990$, $p < 0.001$) between the Identity Index and psychological workplace abuse means that a stronger identification with Blackness, Brilliance, and Boldness is strongly associated with higher levels of workplace abuse, and this relationship is highly significant statistically.

IDENTITY INDEX AND PSYCHOLOGICAL WORKPLACE ABUSE

After making the correlation calculations, the following was noted:

A strong positive correlation was observed between the participant's Identity Index and their experiences of psychological workplace abuse ($\tau = 0.990$, $p < 0.001$). This indicates that participants who strongly identified with their Blackness, Brilliance, and Boldness tended to report higher levels of psychological workplace abuse. This finding supports the primary research question by demonstrating that stronger identity connections associated with common stereotypes about Black women being "Too Bold, Too Black, and Too Brilliant" correlate with more frequent and severe experiences of psychological workplace abuse for Black women in education leadership participating in the study. In everyday terms, this suggests that the more a Black woman in educational leadership embraces and identifies with her cultural and personal strengths, the more she might encounter negative psychological experiences at work. This supports the main research question, showing that embracing these identities, which are often stereotyped, is associated with increased workplace abuse.

Age and Psychological Workplace Abuse

A medium-strong correlation was identified between age and psychological workplace abuse ($\tau = 0.546$, $p = 0.007$), indicating that older participants tended to report higher levels of psychological workplace abuse while working in their education leadership roles. This finding provides insight into how age might influence Black women in education leadership's vulnerability to psychological workplace abuse, with older Black female participants experiencing more psychological distress.

Professional Education Leadership Experience and Psychological Workplace Abuse

The strongest positive correlation within the study was found between professional leadership experience and psychological workplace abuse ($\tau = 1.0$, $p < 0.001$). This suggests that participants with more extensive leadership experience reported higher levels of psychological workplace abuse. This supports the secondary research question by showing that higher professional standing and responsibilities might expose Black females in educational leadership to more psychological abuse.

Identity Index and Age

A moderate positive correlation was observed between the Identity Index and Age ($\tau = 0.377$, $p = 0.027$). This indicates that older participants tend to have a stronger connection to their Blackness, Brilliance, and Boldness as these concepts relate to stereotypes about Black women in education. This finding enriches the study by linking identity development with age, suggesting that identity perceptions might deepen over time.

Interpretation of Findings

The findings were interpreted to conclude how Black women in educational leadership navigate the balance between assimilation and authenticity. The results informed strategies for creating psychologically safe work environments that allow Black women to thrive authentically.

Possible Obstacles to the Research

- Recruitment challenges in obtaining a diverse and representative sample of Black women in educational leadership.
- Ensuring participant anonymity and confidentiality in sensitive discussions about workplace abuse.
- Balancing the integration of quantitative and qualitative data to provide comprehensive insights.

Settings

The research was conducted online, utilizing surveys and virtual focus groups to gather data from participants across various educational institutions.

Time

The research was cross-sectional, capturing data at one specific time to understand Black women's current experiences in educational leadership. However, participants were asked to reflect on their past experiences to provide a broader context for the study's findings.

CONCLUSION

This research analysis underscored Black women's significant challenges in balancing assimilation and authenticity in professional settings. The integration of quantitative scores and qualitative narratives revealed clear patterns of psychological abuse and professional barriers, emphasizing the systemic issues within organizations that perpetuate stereotypes and discrimination. The findings also highlighted the complex interplay between a Black woman in education leadership's personal identity, professional experience, age, and experiences of psychological workplace abuse.

Several positive correlations suggest that black women in education leadership who identified more strongly with their racial and gender identity and those with more leadership experience may face higher levels of psychological workplace abuse. Additionally, older participants tended to have stronger connections to their identity and experience more psychological workplace abuse. These insights underscore the need for targeted interventions and a clear blueprint of applicable support systems to address Black women's unique challenges in education leadership roles.

By understanding these dynamics and outlining actionable guidance, stakeholders can implement more effective strategies to support Black women in educational leadership, fostering environments where they can thrive without facing disproportionate psychological abuse. Using Kendall's Tau in this study provided a robust and accurate measure of these relationships, ensuring the findings are reliable and reflect the participants' experiences.

This study's insights contributed to the development of the *EmpowH.E.R. Leadership Blueprint*, designed to address and mitigate the impact of negative stereotypes on Black women in educational leadership. By addressing these challenges, the blueprint aims to empower Black women to maintain their authentic identities while navigating the complexities of their professional environments and provide targeted guidance to organizations on how they can provide psychologically safe spaces where black women in education leadership can lead as their authentic selves. The *EmpowH.E.R. Leadership Blueprint* aims to provide this guidance so that Black women in education leadership and beyond can express their true identities in their workspaces without fear of retribution while receiving the support and recognition they deserve.

THE *EMPOWH.E.R. LEADERSHIP BLUEPRINT: SUPPORTING BLACK WOMEN IN LEADERSHIP*

The *EmpowH.E.R. Leadership Blueprint* is an actionable framework designed to give organizations the blueprint to address and mitigate the impact of negative stereotypes on Black women in leadership. Although it is designed to be applied to any leadership field, a specific focus of the study and narratives that informed this framework stems from education leadership. It aims to create psychologically safe workspaces where these women can thrive unapologetically, express their authentic identities without fear of retribution, and foster a climate of belonging and empowerment. The blueprint guides organizations and Black women alike, ensuring that their unique perspectives are recognized, their contributions are appreciated, and they are protected from the mental and emotional toll of navigating hostile or indifferent work environments.

Drawing on insights from the lived experiences of the black women and education leaders who participated in this study, the *EmpowH.E.R. Leadership Blueprint* emphasizes healing, humanity, excellence, and resilience, guiding Black women in advocating for themselves while identifying conditions necessary for employers to support these efforts. Additionally, the framework outlines the risks organizations face if they fail to implement these non-negotiables, especially concerning diversity, equity, inclusion, belonging, and the psychological safety of Black and other intersectional women. By addressing these critical issues and fostering empowerment, the *EmpowH.E.R. Leadership Blueprint* ensures that Black women are retained in leadership roles and empowered to bring their whole, authentic selves to their work.

The *EmpowH.E.R.* framework is grounded in theory, specifically Patricia Collins' *Matrix of Domination*, which highlights how Black women resist multiple levels of domination—personal, community, and systemic. Its core principles align with the H.E.R. acronym and represent 1. Healing and holism, 2. Empowerment and excellence, and 3. Recognition and resilience.

HEALING AND HOLISM

Healing and holism require organizations to address personal and systemic barriers by integrating healing practices, including mental health resources, from culturally competent professionals into the institution's mental health programs. Leaders at all levels, especially senior executives, must endorse, actively promote, and participate in these programs to demonstrate the organization's commitment to mental health and wellness.

Actionable Examples of Healing and Holism Initiatives Include

- Develop and maintain a resource directory of mental health professionals specializing in the needs of Black and intersectional women (personal).
- Develop mental health programs that include healing practices from Black and intersectional cultural backgrounds (community).
- Regularly consult with Black mental health professionals to update and refine healing practices (community).
- Enact flexible scheduling policies to accommodate attendance at wellness programs (systemic).
- Develop and enforce anti-retaliation protocols for employees seeking mental health support (systemic).

EMPOWERMENT AND EXCELLENCE

Empowerment and excellence require fostering an environment that actively supports cultural initiatives and counters systemic biases by creating spaces that honor and uplift Black women's and other intersectional women's voices in leadership. Opportunities for Black and other intersectional women in leadership to share their experiences and challenges in a supporting environment are integral to these populations feeling included and valued. Additionally, an investment in events and educational workshops highlighting these shared experiences and challenges must be promoted and supported with a top-down commitment to equity and inclusion, especially from white male leaders.

Actionable examples of empowerment and excellence initiatives include:

- Regularly review and update policies to ensure they counteract systemic biases (systemic).
- Establish regular forums and platforms for sharing experiences and challenges (community).
- Implement feedback mechanisms to act on the insights provided by Black and intersectional women (personal).
- Allocate budget and resources for continuous educational programs on diversity and inclusion (systemic).
- Ensure widespread participation through mandatory attendance policies (systemic).
- Implement mentorship programs pairing senior leaders with Black and intersectional women (community).
- Train all leaders on non-racist systemic practices and the importance of mentorship (systemic).

RECOGNITION AND RESILIENCE

Recognition and resilience require the creation of supportive networks, which enhance community resilience against exclusion. Affinity groups and cultural initiatives ensure that Black and intersectional women have a community within the network. Access to resources and funding for personal and professional development can further enhance inclusion and belonging within the institution.

Actionable examples of recognition and resilience include:

- Provide consistent funding and resources for affinity groups (systemic).

- Designate physical and virtual spaces for these groups to meet and collaborate (community).
- Develop formalized programs and regular meetings for sharing experiences and feedback (community).
- Ensure representation of Black and intersectional women in leadership decision-making processes (systemic).
- Guarantee funding and organizational support for ongoing development programs (systemic).
- Enforce mandatory participation to ensure widespread impact and awareness (systemic).
- Implement structured mentorship programs with clear goals and accountability (personal).
- Regularly communicate and demonstrate executive commitment to equity and inclusion initiatives (systemic).

By leveraging Collins' framework, Black and intersectional women can effectively support and enhance the implementation of the *EmpowH.E.R. Leadership Blueprint*, ensuring organizational commitments to diversity, equity, and inclusion are met and sustained. It is essential to remember that the organization and its leaders are ultimately responsible for creating a just and inclusive workplace.

EMPOWH.E.R. CAREER JOURNEY: APPLYING THE LEADERSHIP BLUEPRINT

This final section gives a concrete example of how to apply the *EmpowH.E.R. Leadership Blueprint* using the career journey moments that were most relevant and common as told from the participants' lived experiences. This example weaves in actual moments black women in education report occur during their careers as educational leaders while providing practical guidance for how Black women navigating their leadership journeys in education can be supported.

Common Career Events, Phases, and Milestones for Black Women in Education Leadership

Relevant Career Theme #1 That Emerged From the Research: High Stakes Leadership Moment

- **Description**: Black women often face critical junctures where their capabilities, identity, or leadership style are tested, such as taking on new leadership roles or being promoted.
- **Example**: Facing scrutiny and stereotypes (e.g., being seen as "Too Bold," "Too Black," or "Too Brilliant").
- *EmpowH.E.R.* **Application**: Healing & Holism
- *Advocate for Culturally Competent Mental Health Resources*: When taking on a new role, Black women should have access to mental health professionals who understand their unique experiences. This ensures they have the support needed to manage the additional stress and scrutiny.
- *Wellness Workshops:* Organize and participate in wellness workshops that focus on stress management, mindfulness, and self-care specifically tailored to Black women in leadership.
- *Rationale:* These initiatives help mitigate the psychological toll of high-stakes leadership moments by providing culturally relevant support, promoting resilience, and fostering a sense of community and understanding within the organization.

Relevant Career Theme #2 that Emerged from the Research: Negotiating Personal and Professional Identities

- **Description**: Black women must decide how to navigate stereotypes and biases, choosing between assimilation (conforming) and authenticity (being true to oneself).
- **Example**: Deciding whether to downplay achievements to fit in or to embrace and showcase them.
- *EmpowH.E.R.* **Application: Empowerment & Excellence**
- Engage in Leadership Development Programs: Participate in programs that enhance visibility and influence within the organization. These programs should be designed to celebrate and leverage the unique perspectives and strengths of Black women.

- Form Alliances for Inclusive Policies: Build coalitions with other minority groups to advocate for policies that promote diversity and inclusion, ensuring that Black women can be authentic without facing retaliation.
- Participate in Policy Review Committees: Join committees that review and implement policies to safeguard against systemic biases, ensuring that the workplace culture supports authenticity.
- *Rationale:* These actions empower Black women to advocate for systemic changes that create an inclusive environment, allowing them to be authentic while reducing the risk of negative repercussions.

Relevant Career Theme #3 That Emerged From the Research: Navigating Assimilation vs. Authenticity

- **Assimilation (Strategic Conformity)**:
- **Description**: Adapting to dominant norms and suppressing aspects of identity.
- **Impact**: This can lead to career growth but also feelings of disconnection and loss of cultural identity.
- **Authenticity (Authentic Leadership)**:
- **Description**: Embracing true self despite potential backlash.
- **Impact**: Can inspire others but often involves facing resistance and increased scrutiny.
- *EmpowH.E.R.* **Application**: **Recognition & Resilience**
- Participate in Affinity Groups: Join or establish groups that provide support and solidarity among Black women and other marginalized groups within the organization. These groups can serve as safe spaces for sharing experiences and strategies for resilience.
- Mentor Others: Actively mentor junior Black women and other intersectional colleagues, sharing strategies for navigating authenticity and assimilation.
- Advocate for Institutional Support for Professional Development: Push for organizational policies that fund and support continuous professional development specifically geared toward Black and intersectional women.
- Rationale: These measures create a supportive community that recognizes the unique challenges faced by Black women, promoting resilience and providing a network

Relevant Career Theme #4 That Emerged From the Research: Feedback Loops: Cycles of Identity and Leadership

- **Description**: Identity negotiation creates two feedback loops: Assimilation (leading to loss of identity) and Authenticity (leading to ongoing scrutiny).
- **Example**: Leaders continually choose between fitting in and being true to themselves.
- *EmpowH.E.R.* **Application**: <u>**Healing & Holism**</u>
- Regularly Consult with Mental Health Professionals: Ensure ongoing access to culturally competent mental health services to address the emotional toll of identity negotiation.
- Build Support Networks: Foster relationships with colleagues who understand and support the challenges of being authentic in the workplace.
- Advocate for Systemic Mental Health Policy Changes: Work with leadership to implement policies that prioritize mental health and provide necessary resources for all employees.
- *Rationale:* These initiatives provide continuous support, helping Black women manage the emotional challenges of navigating identity in leadership roles.

Relevant Career Theme #5 that Emerged from the Research: FLEE Pathways: Escaping Feedback Loops

- **Creating Your Own Space**:
- **Description**: Leaving the system to start new ventures (e.g., consulting firms).
- **Challenges**: Requires resources not all Black women possess.
- **Coping Within the System**:
- **Description**: Remaining in the system while enduring systemic abuse and using various coping strategies.
- **Impact**: Often leads to chronic stress and mental health issues.
- *EmpowH.E.R.* **Application**: <u>**Empowerment & Excellence**</u>
- **Enhance Organizational Visibility and Influence**: Leverage existing platforms to highlight the contributions and challenges of Black women in leadership, promoting a culture of recognition and respect.
- **Form Alliances**: Collaborate with other marginalized groups to strengthen collective advocacy efforts, ensuring policies reflect diverse perspectives.
- **Ensure Policies Counteract Systemic Biases**: Regularly review and revise organizational policies to eliminate systemic barriers and promote equity.

- **Rationale**: These actions empower Black women to either create their own spaces where they can thrive or improve existing systems to reduce stress and promote mental health.

FROM LEADERSHIP TO LEGACY: PASSING THE TORCH TO *EMPOWH.E.R.* FUTURE LEADERS

Reflecting on the tightrope analogy introduced at the beginning of this chapter, the journey of Black women in educational leadership is a precarious balance between assimilating into dominant cultural norms and staying true to their authentic selves. My personal story from September 2012, as I knelt in prayer, pregnant with my first child and stepping into my first leadership role, underscores the immense psychological and professional challenges faced by Black women. The fear I felt for my unborn child's future in a society marred by racial violence and the doubts I harbored about my own capabilities as a leader were not unique to me; they are emblematic of the broader struggles that many Black women encounter.

The results of this study reveal the harsh realities of identity negotiation for Black women in educational leadership, encapsulated by the catalysts of being "Too Bold," "Too Black," and "Too Brilliant." These catalysts reflect not only the stereotypes that Black women must navigate but also the significant impact on their professional and psychological well-being. The *EmpowH.E.R. Leadership Blueprint,* proposed in this chapter, aims to offer strategies to address these challenges and empower Black women to maintain their authentic identities within professional environments.

As this chapter draws to a close, it is essential to revisit the powerful imagery and narratives that have guided our understanding of these complex dynamics. This brings the story back to my daughter, Zuri, the child I was pregnant with during those challenging early days of my leadership journey. Now, at eleven years old and preparing to enter middle school, Zuri has already begun to navigate her own experiences of assimilation and authenticity. She has volunteered to author a poem about her experiences and share her short narrative, which poignantly captures this research's ongoing relevance and importance.

My name is Zuri Raye Reddick. I am eleven years old. I am a black girl headed to middle school this coming school year.

When my mom, one of this book's co-editors, first told me about this book, "Sharing the Legacy and Narrative Leadership Experiences of Black Women in Education," that she and her friend, Dr. Storman, were planning to co-edit together, it made me think of a poem that my mom hung in my room when I was younger called "Too Black".

~Too Black~
LaTasha Williams

I am defiant if I SEPARATE.
I am fake if I ASSIMILATE.
They consider my uniqueness STRANGE.
They call my language SLANG.
They see my confidence as CONCEIT.
They see my mistakes as DEFEAT.
My questions make me UNAWARE.
My advancement is somehow UNFAIR.
To voice concern is DISCONTENTMENT.
If I don't trust them, I'm too APPREHENSIVE.
They consider my success ACCIDENTAL.
They minimize my intelligence to POTENTIAL.
They take my kindness for WEAKNESS.
They take my silence for SPEECHLESSNESS.
My character is constantly UNDER ATTACK.
Pride for my race makes me "TOO BLACK".

Ever since I was younger, this poem stared back at me from my bedroom wall, and as soon as I learned to read, I started figuring out how to read some of the words. It was exciting to be able to read, but I still didn't quite "get it". All I ever thought was, "Oh, that girl next to the poem's words is pretty! She looks just like me!" I asked my mom, "But why is she so mad?"

Once I began attending school, after a few years, not only did I start to "get" the poem, but it became my reality, even at a young age! So, when my mother told me about this book project about one year ago, I knew I had to find a way to be involved.

I decided to attend the kickoff for "Sharing the Legacy and Narrative Leadership Experiences of Black Women in Education," where all the interested authors met to discuss ideas.

I was quiet at first because all these educated, brilliant black women spoke in a circle. Then, I got brave enough to share one of my stories and another. Before I knew it, it was like all the air getting sucked out of a balloon, except I didn't feel deflated. I felt encouraged! That day, the contributing authors said I was doing the right thing by discussing my experiences as a black girl attending a mostly non-black school. I learned that it was okay to tell my stories. It was okay to have feelings and emotions. And it was okay to be mad about it all, sometimes.

After we left, I thought long and hard about how I wanted this book to help younger black girls, not just black women, because how black women are treated now started when they were little black girls in school, just like me.

Even at school, I am treated differently or unfairly just because of the color of my skin, the curls in my hair, the movement of my hips, or the shape of my lips.

The preceding line comes from a poem I wrote called "Too Different", based on my perspective of the "Too Black" poem that hung in my room as a little girl. It is inspired by the message of this book- to tell our stories and to celebrate and empower one another while being ourselves and knowing that is okay.

It's not us. We can be black. We can be bold. We can be brilliant. And we can be different. That makes us who we are; we have influence and are strong leaders because of it.

So, below is my poem, "Too Different," an important reminder that every black girl needs to be proud of their culture and who they are and take that freedom with them as they grow into black, bold, and brilliant leaders of the future!

~Too Different~

By Zuri Raye Reddick

If a Black woman has a dream,
It's considered unreachable.
To fit into the world's society,
means lighter skin.
They Can Attack.
But when I fight back, I'm too "AGGRESSIVE"!
Society wants me to change how I Talk, Laugh, and Look.
But they took away these parts of me for themselves.
Society wants to make me a "BETTER" version of myself, which means...
WHITE!
But when I Assimilate,
Now, I'm too FAKE!
I am treated differently or unfairly just because of the
color of my skin,
and the curls in my hair,
and the movement of my hips,
and the shape of my lips.
I guess...No... I *am* PROUD to be "Too Different".
Too Bold. Too Black. And Too Brilliant.

At only eleven years old, Zuri's words bring to life the critical need for research, knowledge, and changed practices related to the challenges of identity negotiation faced by Black women and girls. Creating supportive environments where they can thrive without compromising their authenticity is essential. By addressing these issues today, the groundwork is laid for the next generation of Black female leaders to navigate their paths with confidence, resilience, and a sense of belonging. This chapter is dedicated to them and to the ongoing fight for equity and inclusion in educational leadership.

REFERENCES

Abrams, J. A., Maxwell, M., Pope, M., & Belgrave, F. Z. (2014). Carrying the World With the Grace of a Lady and the Grit of a Warrior: Deepening Our Understanding of the "Strong Black Woman" Schema. *Psychology of Women Quarterly*, 38(4), 503–518. 10.1177/0361684314541418

Bell, E. L. J. E. (1990). The Bicultural Life Experience of Career-Oriented Black Women. *Journal of Organizational Behavior*, 11(6), 459–477. 10.1002/job.4030110607

Black Feminisms. (2019, July 16). The Matrix of Domination and the Four Domains of Power. Black Feminisms. Retrieved from https://blackfeminisms.com/matrix/

Cockley, K. (2024, March 14). It's time to reconceptualize what imposter syndrome means for people of color. *Harvard Business Review*. https://hbr.org/2024/03/its-time-to-reconceptualize-what-imposter-syndrome-means-for-people-of-color

Collins, P. H. (1990). *Black feminist thought: Knowledge, consciousness, and the politics of empowerment*. Routledge.

Collins, P. H. (1999). *Black feminist thought: Knowledge, consciousness, and the politics of empowerment* (2nd ed.). Routledge.

Collins, P. H. (2000). *Black feminist thought: Knowledge, consciousness, and the politics of empowerment* (2nd ed.). Routledge.

Collins, P. H., & Bilge, S. (2016). *Intersectionality*. Polity Press.

Crenshaw, K. (2016, October). The urgency of intersectionality [Video]. TED Conferences. https://www.ted.com/talks/kimberle_crenshaw_the_urgency_of__intersectionality

Davis, A. Y. (1983). *Women, Race & Class*. Random House.

Dickens, D. D., & Chavez, E. L. (2018). Navigating the Workplace: The Costs and Benefits of Shifting Identities at Work among Early Career U.S. Black Women. *Sex Roles*, 78(11-12), 760–774. 10.1007/s11199-017-0844-x

Frank, T. J. (2022). *The waymakers: Clearing the path to workplace equity with competence and confidence*. Berrett-Koehler Publishers.

Givens, S. M. (2021). Black Women and Stereotypes: Implications for the Education and Socialization of African American Children. *The Journal of Black Psychology*, 47(6), 399–417.

Hajela, D. (2022, February 24). Trayvon Martin's death 10 years later: A family's pain, a community's push for change. *AP News*. https://apnews.com/article/trayvon -martin-death-10-years-later-c68f12130b2992d9c1ba31ec1a398cdd

Hall, E. J., Everett, J. E., & Hamilton-Mason, J. (2012). Black Women Talk About Workplace Stress and How They Cope. *Journal of Black Studies*, 43(2), 207–226. 10.1177/0021934711413272222457894

Hampton, R. (2021, November 8). Being a Black woman in the workplace can be like starring in a thriller. *SLATE News & Politics*. https://slate.com/culture/2021/ 11/other-black-girl-all-her-little-secrets-review-work-horror.html

Harris-Perry, M. V. (2011). *Sister Citizen: Shame, Stereotypes, and Black Women in America*. Yale University Press.

Hirsch, W. (1942). Assimilation as concept and as process. *Social Forces*, 21(1), 35–39. 10.2307/2570428

Holmes, T. E. (2020, October 27). Black women at work: How we shape our identities on the job. *Essence*. https://www.essence.com/news/money-career/black-women -work-how-we-shape-our-identities-job/

Jean-Marie, G., & Brooks, J. S. (2019). *Black women scholars in educational leadership: Critical perspectives on race, gender, and social justice*. Peter Lang Publishing.

Jones, C., & Shorter-Gooden, K. (2003). *Shifting: The double lives of Black women in America*. HarperCollins.

Jones, M. K., Lee, L. H., Gaskin-Wasson, A. L., & McKee, A. D. (2021). The psychological impact of racism: Emotional stress among African American women. *The Journal of Black Psychology*, 47(3), 170–193. 10.1177/00957984211007339

Lewis, J. A., Mendenhall, R., Harwood, S. A., & Browne Huntt, M. (2017). Coping with gendered racial microaggressions among Black women college students. *Journal of African American Studies*, 21(1), 32–48. 10.1007/s12111-017-9342-0

Lewis, T. (2020, October 27). New ESSENCE study: Hiding your authentic self at work can damage your career. *Essence*. Retrieved from https://www.essence.com/ news/money-career/essence-study-hiding-authentic-personality-work-damaging/

McCall, L. (2005). The complexity of intersectionality. *Signs (Chicago, Ill.)*, 30(3), 1771–1800. 10.1086/426800

McCluney, C. L., & Rabelo, V. C. (2020). Conditions of visibility: An intersectional examination of Black women's belongingness and distinctiveness at work. *Journal of Vocational Behavior*, 118, 103373. 10.1016/j.jvb.2020.103373

Naeem, M., Ozuem, W., Howell, K., & Ranfagni, S. (2023). A step-by-step process of thematic analysis to develop a conceptual model in qualitative research. *International Journal of Qualitative Methods*, 22(11), 16094069231205789. Advance online publication. 10.1177/16094069231205789

Pauls, E. (2024, June 12). Assimilation. *Encyclopedia Britannica*. https://www.britannica.com/topic/assimilation-society

Purdie-Vaughns, V., Steele, C. M., Davies, P. G., Ditlmann, R., & Crosby, J. R. (2008). Social identity contingencies: How diversity cues signal threat or safety for African Americans in mainstream institutions. *Journal of Personality and Social Psychology*, 94(4), 615–630. 10.1037/0022-3514.94.4.61518361675

Roberts, L. M., Mayo, A. J., & Thomas, D. A. (Eds.). (2019). *Race, work, and leadership: New perspectives on the Black experience*. Harvard Business Review Press.

Shipp, K. (2023). Mental health looks different for everyone: The Black female perspective. *The Red & Black*. Retrieved from https://www.redandblack.com/

Shorter-Gooden, K. (2004). Shifting: The Double Lives of Black Women in America. *The Journal of Black Psychology*, 30(3), 333–335.

Spates, K., Evans, N. L., & Jackson, C. E. (2020). Gendered racism and mental health among young adult US Black women: The moderating roles of gender identity and Africentric worldview. *Sex Roles*, 83(1-2), 47–57. 10.1007/s11199-019-01081-2

Szymanski, D. M., & Stewart, D. N. (2010). Racism and sexism as correlates of African American women's psychological distress. *Sex Roles*, 63(3-4), 226–238. 10.1007/s11199-010-9788-020352053

Thomas, K. M., Johnson-Bailey, J., Phelps, R. E., Tran, N. M., & Johnson, L. N. (2013). Women of color at midcareer: Going from pet to threat. In Comas-Díaz, L., & Greene, B. (Eds.), *Psychological health of women of color: Intersections, challenges, and opportunities* (pp. 275–290). Praeger. 10.5040/9798216002536.ch-014

Travis, D. J., & Thorpe-Moscon, J. (2020). Day-to-day experiences of emotional tax among women and men of color in the workplace. *Catalyst : Feminism, Theory, Technoscience*.

Tulshyan, R. (2022). *Inclusion on purpose: An intersectional approach to creating a culture of belonging at work*. MIT Press. 10.7551/mitpress/14004.001.0001

Watson, N. N., & Hunter, C. D. (2015). Anxiety and depression among African American women: The costs of strength and negative attitudes toward psychological help-seeking. *Cultural Diversity & Ethnic Minority Psychology*, 21(4), 604–612. 10.1037/cdp000001525602466

West, C., Donovan, R. A., & Daniel, B. (2020). The price of opportunity: Coping with gendered racial microaggressions as a Black woman senior leader. *Equality, Diversity and Inclusion*, 39(2), 175–194. 10.1108/EDI-11-2018-0218

West, C. M. (1995). Mammy, Sapphire, and Jezebel: Historical images of Black women and their implications for psychotherapy. *Psychotherapy (Chicago, Ill.)*, 32(3), 458–466. 10.1037/0033-3204.32.3.458

Williams, D. R., & Mohammed, S. A. (2009). Discrimination and racial disparities in health: Evidence and needed research. *Journal of Behavioral Medicine*, 32(1), 20–47. 10.1007/s10865-008-9185-019030981

Williams, M. T., & Lewis, J. A. (2019). Gendered racial microaggressions, trauma, and mental health in African American women. *Journal of Feminist Family Therapy*, 31(3-4), 129–151. 10.1080/08952833.2019.1651090

Chapter 2
It's Not Me I See

Taylor C. J. Wynne
The Ohio State University, USA

ABSTRACT

This chapter explores the context and lived experiences of four Black women graduate students at The University of Florida and how the lack of Black women represented in institutional leadership roles and faulty roles have impacted their matriculation throughout graduate school. Topics within this chapter closely examine categories including the systemic scarcity of Black women working in higher education, culturally responsive mentorship, three semi-structured interviews of current Black women graduate students, and implications for future consideration. This chapter will identify oppressive institutional assumptions about Black women in the academy that has contributed to an educational culture of disinvestment for Black women graduate students, faculty, staff, and senior-level leadership. The purpose of this chapter is to interrogate a system that has intentionally lessened the number of representation amongst Black women working in higher education due to factors relating to burnout, isolation, insufficient pay, racial battle fatigue, and chronic stress.

EVERY GHETTO, EVERY CITY

"I can make a career out of this?" This was my first reaction after speaking with my mentor at the University of Toledo (UT) when finding out, for the first time, about the field of Higher Education as an occupation. Before attending UT, whenever I thought about the work of an educator, I instinctively regarded the K-12 educational setting. I knew about the professoriate by default of being a college student, but I didn't know the steps one took to become a professor. A graduate degree in Higher Education – Student Affairs was a foreign concept to me. Partially due to the lack

DOI: 10.4018/979-8-3693-0698-7.ch002

Copyright © 2024, IGI Global. Copying or distributing in print or electronic forms without written permission of IGI Global is prohibited.

of Black women I saw in faculty roles, but also due to the minimal information I received about careers in higher education overall.

Data collected from the National Center for Education Statistics (2021) reveal that Black women tenured faculty makeup 2% of all tenured faculty in the American higher education system (NCES, 2021). While Black women are tremendously under-represented in higher education faculty roles, there was not an urgency to introduce undergraduate Black women to this career path. Once I initiated deeper research into the work of higher education, I quickly concluded that the professoriate was gatekept from Black women, and the hidden curriculum on how to thrive in the Ivory Tower was often only shared with White men. I would find myself asking, "How can an institution originally funded by slavery and built by the hands of my enslaved Black ancestors deny me access to this space?" At that time, I hadn't known about the systematic reasons that contributed to the lack of Black women faculty. I hadn't known about Black feminist epistemologies that centered work around these issues, and, at the time, I hadn't known any of the Black women theorists who were doing work to bring light to this issue. What I did know as a sophomore in college was that I didn't see many versions of myself teaching on the college level. Despite coming to this conclusion, I maintained an eagerness to learn more about higher education and absorb as much knowledge as I could about the field – both the good and bad.

After attending conferences and perceiving different expressions of research methodologies and topics, I realized that addressing the forgotten stories and expe-riences of Black women college students could be turned into a career. In college, I introduced myself to four Black feminist trailblazers - bell hooks, Audre Lorde, Roxane Gay, and Patricia Hill Collins. I studied their work and fell in love with how seen, validated, and understood I felt after reading their books. I find comfort in knowing that I'll always have their literature to reference and find answers in. Despite this newfound understanding, the reality of my educational setting would resurface when I attended my predominantly white classes. Class was led by non-Black professors with viewpoints heavily saturated in whiteness coursework was deeply rooted in Eurocentric teachings with linear cultural perspectives. To me, the classroom wasn't a space where disruptive thinking was encouraged; it was a siloed place, where I was expected to conform to the norms of my environment. My cre-ative freedom, joy, and diversity of thought were fostered outside of the classroom through participation in service-learning trips over spring break, community-centered research and outreach, and identity-based affinity groups on campus. Like many of the Black students at my undergraduate institution, the academic classroom felt limiting, and assignments appeared irrelevant due to the cultural disconnect from our lived experiences. I began inquiring more about this feeling of classroom dis-connect during my undergraduate years at UT. My experience at UT was unique because of the above-average percentage of Black students that attended UT during my undergraduate career. I had impactful mentorship, nurturing administrators, and an extremely close and supportive group of friends. As an executive board member of the National Pan-Hellenic Council on my campus, my connection to the Black community at UT bolstered both on campus and throughout the community, refining my Black experience at UT. What made my time at UT particularly special is the intentional mentorship that I received from the Black women around me. I'm grateful for my "OG" mentor, and countless other Black women in the community who contributed to my growth and development as I emerged into young womanhood while in college. They corrected me with love, comforted me at my lowest, and never withdrew from having the hard conversations about my life trajectory. My mentors created a space on campus for me to just be a Black girl. A space to unclench and exist without stereotype threat. A space where I felt invested in and safe. A space where I was understood and seen. While none of these Black women faculty ever served as my professor, I knew that my Black peers who took their class enjoyed their classroom experience and made sure never to miss that specific class. It didn't necessarily matter what class subject was being taught. What made the difference was that their professor was Black – in this case, a Black woman. That's when I knew that faculty representation in the classroom on the collegiate level was critical and lacking. The Black women faculty at UT that I looked up to were often the only Black women represented in their departments. I saw that they were overworked and fatigued, but I didn't have the vocabulary, that I have now, to interpret what exactly I was witnessing. I saw that Black women faculty at UT were drastically underrepresented; however, I didn't feel the true impact of this underrepresentation until I began my graduate program. After noticing this trend of underrepresentation in grad school, I decided to take a closer look into how the lack of representation of Black women faculty in higher education impacts the graduate school experience for Black women who desire space in the professoriate.

THE MISEDUCATION

Out of an eagerness to explore life outside of Ohio, I selected the University of Florida (UF) as my next steppingstone. When I arrived at the University of Florida in the fall of 2022, I was ready to embark on an exciting journey within the academy that would consist of transformative research and molding young minds to change the world. I truly believed that the world of higher education was at my fingertips and that I would bring about change in a matter of two years. I had no idea of what I was walking into. During my first year of grad school at UF, I was confronted with countless racialized and sexist experiences that left me with an adverse awareness of the realities of existing in academia as a Black woman. As I began navigating the systematic and structural racism woven within the foundation of my Historically White Institution (HWI), I realized a noticeable pattern of inertia in the academy and how Black women in these spaces suffered the most. Through my exposure as a Graduate Assistant across two drastically different departments, I was offered a unique insight into the academy that's often hidden from students. I witnessed and experienced the hegemonic politics, sexism, ageism, and racism that are embedded in the fabric of higher education. I witnessed how Black women were burned out and stretched thin across university obligations. I witnessed how the Black women around me could not always practice wellness and rest in the ways that their non-Black colleagues could. I witnessed the fatigue that Black women in higher education carried with them. I witnessed how the experiences of Black women were gaslit, and their concerns placed on the backburner. I saw all of the burdens that Black women in the academy shouldered, the lack of institutional support to address their needs, and the invisibility/hyper-visibility that many of them faced. These are all factors that can be attributed to the lack of representation and institutional urgency to rectify this trend. As a young Black woman in my early twenties who's in the beginning stages of learning this work, the trend of mistreatment toward Black across the academy is extremely concerning. Hearing about the premature deaths of Dr. JoAnne Epps, Dr. Orinthia Montague, and Dr. Antoinette Candia-Bailey, passing away within months of each other was disconcerting to me. During my moments of reflection, I continuously find myself reflecting on what can I do to ensure that my time and work in this field isn't cut short due to burnout. What intentional self-care and wellness practices do I need to adopt, and what are the Black women faculty around me doing to thrive, experience freedom, and find enjoyment in the academy? To equip myself better for what higher education had in store for me, I began attending more conferences, networked with like-minded peers, and familiarized myself with the culture of the academy and how Black women faculty are navigating this space. As a byproduct, I was introduced to the world of Black Feminist Epistemology and Endarkened Feminist Epistemology (Collins, 1990; Dillard, 2000). Every feeling that accompanied my concerns within higher education had a name to it. By aligning my observations with theory, I was able to make sense of what was happening to and around me. In *Teaching to Transgress* (hooks, 1994), bell hooks notes that she came to theory "to make the pain go away. I saw in theory a location for healing." Similar to hooks, I began leaning heavily into theory as a guidebook to understand my experiences and serve as a navigational tool for my success in higher education. From there, I began theorizing my lived experiences for myself, and finding healing within this mapping.

KILLING ME SOFTLY

My initial realization within the academic setting regarding the underrepresentation of Black women was the absence of culturally responsive mentorship for Black girls and women in higher education, specifically for those interested in pursuing a career as faculty. While in undergrad and grad school, I saw countless organized mentorship programs for Black women and girls in educational or neighborhood spaces; however, the same cannot be said for Black girls – to the magnitude that we see for Black boys. Dr. Monique Morris, author of *Pushout* (2015), addresses how the preconceived stereotypes and tropes placed on Black girls and women in education negatively impact their socialization in educational spaces as they develop. The assumption is that, because of their academic success, Black women and girls don't need the same amount of mentorship and support as Black boys and young men. Nevertheless, research by the National Institute of Health indicates that Black girls and young women are battling serious unmet mental health struggles. The suicide rate for Black girls ages 13-19 increased by 182% from 2001 to 2017 (Price, 2019). The miseducation and disinvestment, coupled with the lack of representation, results in countless Black girls being left to figure out their experiences on their own. For me and other Black women graduate students (BWGS), finding Black women who could serve as mentors to prepare us for future faculty roles presented a challenge because of the way the system is set up – leaving many BWGS to navigate the road to the professoriate on their own. Research from the National Institutes of Health indicates that junior and early-career faculty members who received faculty mentors are 25% more likely to have top-tier publications than faculty without mentors. This is especially critical for women and minority faculty (Blau et al., 2020). However, when there is an intentional systematic scarcity of Black women in faculty roles, I begin to interrogate the system that has created this challenge, and not the women within it. While I desired the mentorship of a Black woman throughout grad school and eventually found one, I became increasingly interested in identifying the systematic reasons that prevent accessible mentorship between BWGS and Black women faculty from transpiring. I saw an inconsistency between hearing about the importance of mentorship and retrospectively seeing how many of my BWGS peers could not find a Black woman to mentor and guide them throughout their doctoral journey. While research has supported how instrumental culturally responsive mentorship is, I noticed a lack of research that identified why specific populations have a hard time locating culturally responsive mentorship relationships – especially within BWGS at predominantly white institutions. As I began to observe collegiate academic spaces, I developed an interest in seeing how colleges and universities create space for culturally responsive mentorship among Black women faculty and BWGS. I also began to evaluate institutional cultures around wellness, support, and mentorship for BWGS and the lack thereof. Support for BWGS and Black women faculty is often overlooked due to higher education's perception of strength within this demographic. There is a tendency in higher education to misappropriate the concept of #BlackGirlMagic to justify their lack of support to Black women faculty specifically. Although the #BlackGirlMagic movement was originally meant to celebrate Black women and girls, colleges and universities misused this framework to support a toxic narrative that dismisses the labor it takes for Black women to live out what is perceived as "magic". The misunderstanding around this discourse results in Black women faculty being revered for their academic accomplishments, but isolated and unsupported by their institution in the process of achieving their degree. Embodying two severely marginalized identities, Black and woman, BWGS are often invisible in institutional conversations. In Tinto's Retention Theory Model (1993), Tinto concluded that students who are socially integrated into the college community are more likely to graduate. Facilitating organized mentorship between BWGS and Black women faculty can assist greatly in the socialization of this specific population. In a study by Strayhorn and Terrell (2007) examining mentoring and satisfaction for Black college students, results indicate that Black male and female college students who were engaged in working with faculty mentors were more satisfied with their college experience. Establishing meaningful research-focused mentor relationships with a faculty member was statistically associated with higher levels of satisfaction among Black students (Strayhorn & Terrell, 2007). These positive relationships can also encourage BWGS to consider careers in academia. Institutional leaders who manage student retention rates should take a closer look into the impact that critical and culturally relevant mentorship has on retaining BWGS in their program. In addition to satisfaction and retention, these mentorship relationships can also directly address the intersectional oppressions that Black women and girls face in educational spaces as students. Working-class Black girls experience multilayered oppression informed by the triadic social identity that sits at the intersection of race, gender, and class in their lives and more specifically in their educational experiences (Collins, 1986, 1989; Onyeka-Crawford, Patrick, & Chaudry, 2017). The application of Black feminism, Black girlhood studies, and critical mentoring frameworks found the following major themes to be critical in mentoring Black girls during childhood, adolescence, and university years: (a) individual identity development, (b) development of individual voice, (c) sisterhood and solidarity, and (d) conscientization and resistance. If research connects the benefits of mentorship to retention and student satisfaction, why are there so few opportunities on an institutional level for BWGS to access this opportunity? Another study conducted by faculty at the University of Buffalo (Noel, Miles, & Rida, 2022) examined how minoritized postdoc students, including Black women and students of color, view and engage in mentorship relationships with faculty members. The findings of this study revealed that students valued regular check-ins with their mentors, students found more value in their interactions with junior faculty members who were open to fresh ideas and flexibility, students appreciated informal conversations with their mentors about short- and long-term goals while gaining advice in a safe space. These are all factors that contributed to a successful postdoc experience for graduate students of color and Black women students. Research has shown that those with access to mentoring benefit from their involvement in these relationships, having reported higher salaries, increased promotion rates, greater career satisfaction in the workplace, and lower levels of turnover in their respective field (Blake-Beard et al., 1999). The primary factors that influence the dynamic of a mentorship relationship is race. Results from Cox and Nkomo's (1990) study of 729 Black and White MBA students concluded that Black grad students reported significantly less access to mentors than White grad students.

LOST ONES

The issues and challenges facing Black women in faculty positions are extensive, contributing to high turnover rates. According to Gregory and Jackson (2001), faculty members of color are often excluded from collaborative research projects with their peers and lack sponsorship for research. They also struggle to find resources for their research that could lead to greater prestige, higher future economic gains, and enhanced job mobility (Gregory & Jackson, 2008). Outside of the academy, Black women faculty members also experience the stress of feeling "psychologically divided between home and career" (Trautvetter, 1999, p. 65) or between community and career.

Many feel that they have only two choices: sacrifice family and community commitments for several years or honor non-work commitments as an essential part of their identity at the risk of not earning tenure (Thomas & Hollenshead, 2001). Moreover, Gregory (2001) reported that few successful faculty women were married with children. Recognizing the multiple barriers that Black women in the academy undergo due to racism, sexism, and lack of representation, it is understandable why carving out time for mentorship is not always pertinent on the list of priorities.

In March of 2023, I attended my first ACPA- College Student Educators International Annual Conference. The most memorable session that I attended while at ACPA 2023 was a session entitled, "Shift the narrative, get yo rest sis," presented by Dr. Candace Hall from Southern Illinois University Edwardsville and Dr. Tiffany Steele from the University of Rochester. The session consisted of a panel discussion from Black women graduate students (BWGS) across various institutions detailing how the mentorship they've received from Dr. Hall and Dr. Steele has been paramount to their success in graduate school. These lessons are testaments to the importance of generational mentorship amongst Black women in the academy. Space was also created during this session to discuss how BWGS, faculty, and practitioners exercise rest and wellness in their work. In a breakout session, one of the attendees noted that as the only Black woman in her department, she is not able to fully embrace rest as she would like, resulting in her inability to carve out additional time for mentoring students. Not because she didn't want to, but because the burnout and fatigue that she experienced from being the only one in her department was so extensive that intentional mentorship would require an added level of energy that she could not extend. She is not the only one processing this feeling, so it's important to extend grace to those Black women faculty and administrators who want to mentor students but can't because of the way the system has overburdened them.

As BWGS seek role models and mentors in academic spaces, we often find ourselves looking outside of their cultural group due to the scarcity of Black women faculty in our colleges (Bartman, 2015). In a qualitative study assessing the connection between success and African American mentorship, Black participants noted that self-confidence in their success as students was directly connected to their relationships with their African American mentors (Louis et al., 2014). However, the statistics also support that there are not enough African American women faculty members to mentor these students, which often results in BWGS seeking mentorship outside of their racial group (Bartman, 2015). This is all because of a systematic lack of representation.

WHEN IT HURTS SO BAD

Research into the scarcity of Black women in tenured positions indicates that increasing their representation in faculty roles requires funneling more Black women through doctoral programs. However, Black women, in particular, face significant isolation within academia, hindering the success of this funneling system.

While scrolling through Twitter, I came across a tweet from a fellow scholar, Kaelyn (2024), that deeply resonated with me and many of my peers. Kaelyn noted, "Real talk, it's extremely hard to watch what happens to Black scholars that stay in academia as a Black student and still feel confident about wanting to pursue academia. It's truly a double-edged sword." (Sanders, 2024) Kaelyn, I, and countless other aspiring scholars in academia discern the mistreatment and hurt endured by Black women faculty. For some, this realization encourages them to seek careers outside of academia, while for others, the pain is precisely why we choose to stay.

Throughout my graduate school journey, I grapple with what motivates me to work in a space that inflicts such harm on Black women and why I aspire to contribute to a system that undervalues the work I aim to do. At 24 years old, I am still searching for that motivating factor. Nonetheless, a significant part of my persistence in graduate school is tied to my fellow scholars here at UF and the community we've created. Without the support, love, and motivation of my fellow scholars at UF, my graduate school journey would have been unbearable. As a Black woman graduate student (BWGS), the academy can feel cold, rigid, and isolating without a reliable community to lean on. I am forever thankful that my fellow scholars have always provided a soft and safe place to land when the pain inflicted by my academic environment becomes overwhelming.

As a member of the Black Graduate Student Organization (BGSO) at my institution, I spend the majority of my free time and study time in the company of Black graduate students, specifically BWGS. BGSO quickly became my family and support system at UF. During one of our bi-weekly Tuesday night gatherings at a friend's apartment, we had a conversation about the misconception that people outside of academia have about Black women in doctoral programs. My friend Valarie noted, "We're already trying to navigate a lot as young Black women; mental health, racist classmates, being away from family, dating, financial constraints, searching for jobs, and finding time for self-care, all while trying to get a Ph.D. People just don't understand how much we're going through to reach the finish line." In her book, "Gifted Black Women Navigating the Doctoral Process," Dr. Joy Davis (2024) highlighted how research indicates that the most highly educated population in our nation are Black females (NCES, 2023). However, this statistic fails to capture the challenges faced by this highly educated population in obtaining the resources and support they need to achieve their goals as terminal degree completers (Davis, 2024).

This led me to consider how mentorship from Black women faculty on navigating a doctoral program could be one of the resources that improve this condition for BWGS. During the same Tuesday night gathering, I initiated a conversation and asked my friends, all BWGS, if they had found a Black women mentor while at UF. Despite initial hesitation, they shared their experiences. Out of the eight women present, only one confidently answered yes. This raised concerns and underscored the need for more work focused on culturally responsive mentorship for BWGS. When I asked the other six attendees why they did not have one, they all had similar answers related to the lack of representation and reluctance to burden the only Black woman faculty member in their department, who was already overwhelmed with responsibilities. One friend noted, "If I notice that the only Black woman faculty member in our department is overwhelmed and fatigued, out of respect for her mental health, I'm probably not going to ask her for mentorship, even if I desire it. It's a balancing act between seeking support and understanding that they may not have the capacity to provide it due to lack of support from the department or institution."

The rest of the attendees mentioned that they had mentors who were Black men, White mentors, or no mentor at all. One friend, Sydney, shared her experience of having a Black man as a mentor. However, she expressed discomfort in navigating certain conversations about her experience as a Black woman with him. Sydney noted, "It's challenging when I want to discuss sexism in my program with him. It's uncomfortable because even though he's Black, I know he won't fully understand where I'm coming from." While mentorship from non-Black women can still yield positive outcomes, certain intersectional conversations focusing on the race and gender of BWGS are best addressed by other Black women who share similar experiences.

To gain a deeper understanding of how the lack of representation negatively affects their experience within their programs, I interviewed three friends from UF BGSO, all Black women pursuing Ph.D. degrees at UF. Despite their different disciplines, they all shared similar insights into the impact of the lack of Black women faculty representation on their ability to find mentorship and their overall educational experience as BWGS at UF.

Toni's Story

"To be honest, mentorship for me in my program has been nonexistent. Now that I think about it, I've never had real mentorship from a Black woman while at UF. I've had conversations with a few in passing – but intentional mentorship where someone took the time to show me the ropes... no. Luckily, I've been able to find mentorship at neighboring institutions outside of UF, but it's exhausting always having to go outside of the university that I'm already at to cultivate those relation- ships. I know it's not intentional though; they all have very busy schedules, and I respect that. Plus, The few Black women in my college have either transitioned into administrative roles, such as associate dean, or they are actively grinding toward achieving tenure. I respect what it is, but it also limits how much free time they have. As far as diversity in faculty presence in the classroom, I've never had a Black woman professor. Don't get me wrong though, my non-Black professors are very knowledgeable – some even nationally known, but they aren't as personable as I'd like at times or understanding of why I struggle socially in the program. I can tell that they notice my isolation, but they aren't quite sure how to address it. Sometimes I feel like I'm missing out on the 'secret sauce' and the hidden curriculum on how to navigate the doctoral journey. The advice and lessons you can only learn through real, unfiltered conversations with another Black woman. I have found beneficial mentorship under two of my white faculty members, but they will never truly un- derstand my lived experience, and that creates a barrier in how I show up in spaces and what we discuss. Having a Black woman mentor and seeing more representation here in the college would be great in theory and practice, but once you understand the system, you quickly realize how slim those chances are. I'm not to blame and they're not to blame – it's the system and the way it's intentionally set up that leaves Black girls on the doctoral journey without a lot of guidance or support. I've learned how to figure it out on my own, control the controllable, and lean into my friends."

Sydney's Story

"Luckily, I can say that I've had at least one Black woman faculty member in my department who's accessible for mentorship. She taught a special topics course, and I loved it! It was my favorite class since starting my coursework. I later realized that this faculty member is the 'go-to Black woman' in our department for mentorship which I can imagine becomes tiring on her end. She mentors all of the Black students in our lab, and other Black students outside of our lab including her master's students and even some undergrad students that she helps as well. However, despite her packed schedule, she's great at creating time and space for her Black students specifically. She always reminds me that she didn't go through hell to get this degree for nothing and that she wants us to use her as a resource. Outside of simply seeing another Black woman in the field with her Ph.D., I appreciate the validation I receive when I check in with her. Imposter Syndrome as a Black Ph.D. student is so real! Every time I feel like I'm a 'bad student' or lacking in comparison to my classmates, she reassures me that I'm not either of those things, I'm just entangled in a system that's set up for me to struggle. This kind of validation creates a level of vulnerability that makes my mentorship experience with a Black woman uniquely special. I'm more comfortable being honest and transparent about what I'm going through, good, or bad, knowing that she won't gaslight my experiences. Not having her would make my overall experience a lot harder, and to be honest, I probably would not have continued in my program if I didn't have someone like her cheering me on."

Valarie's Story

"Whew! Girl…. where do I start? Yes, I do have a Black woman mentor here at UF and honestly, she's the only reason I came to UF. I know people say don't select a doc program because of one person, but after doing two years of post-bach research under a racist white man I was desperate! I knew that whatever Ph.D. program I selected, I needed to see at least one Black woman in the department with similar research interests who could also mentor me throughout the process. If a department didn't have that, I didn't apply to that school – that's how important representation and support were to me when selecting the right program. This also narrowed down my options to only four schools. I've been at UF for three years now, and I feel like I've been fighting for my life each year. Thankfully I have my community and an amazing Black woman mentor who has encouraged me along the way.

THE HATE YOU GIVE

By 2010, African American women held 66% of all bachelor's degrees attained by Black Americans. Black women also continue to make up an increasing percentage of all students entering higher educational institutions. While it is true that women exceed their male counterparts in participation and degree completion rates across all demographics, none do so to the degree of African American women (Bartman, n.d.). However, these statistics only tell one side of the story.

In conjunction with this data, research continues to emphasize the importance of representation in higher education because there is still significant scarcity. Aspiring to occupy a space where you rarely see Black women represented can pose additional challenges to the already existing ones that we face in the academy. Whether in higher education or industry, representation remains an ongoing struggle that businesses can't seem to master. Research indicates that increased representation in a space reduces the chances of racial stereotypes and discrimination (Nadal, 2021). Nevertheless, postsecondary institutions still fail to remove obstacles preventing successful recruitment and retention of Black faculty and leadership. According to the Chronicle of Higher Education (2000), only 4% of African Americans represent professors and associate professors compared to their White tenured faculty at 87%. On the instructor and lecturer level, African American representation is at 7% while White colleagues make up 82% of that group. Valarie, whom I interviewed previously, shared her experience of taking a class with a faculty woman of color. It was a required Cultural Competency course for her major. Valarie noted, "I was happy when I saw that my professor was a woman of color, but as the semester went on, I began to empathize with her and resent many of my White classmates. The number of times she was gaslit, disrespected in mid-semester evaluations, and had her expertise questioned by my non-Black classmates was outrageous. Before coming to UF I strongly considered academia as a profession, but after seeing her experience and how she's treated, I'm starting to rethink my career trajectory and consider professions outside of higher education." Even though Valarie's professor wasn't Black, her experience aligns with many of the stories that Black women professors face – contributing to the lack of representation in the academy.

Similar to Sydney, I've had one Black woman professor while in grad school, and her course has been one of my favorites since starting my program. While having a Black woman professor did not alleviate every problem in the classroom, one thing that I knew for sure is that I looked forward to attending her class every week. There would be days when I'd get there early to have 1:1 time with her before the rest of the class came in. We didn't talk about the syllabus or the upcoming assignment. Instead, I took that time to embrace a rare moment with my professor, that I knew I wouldn't get in the rest of my courses. Although these interactions only lasted about 10 minutes before the rest of the class shuffled in, they were still meaningful to me. Within those 10 minutes with her, I felt seen and encouraged. This is a feeling I never fully felt in the rest of my classes with my non-Black professors. I even found myself working a little harder on my assignments in her class because I knew that she truly cared about my success in her class. Many of the required course readings were from scholars of color and she always challenged us to think deeper about the social and cultural implications affecting college students' mental health. I knew she cared about me as a student past the letter grade, and experiencing her class reinforced why, as a BWGS, it's important to see a representation of myself in these spaces.

Historically speaking, there are systematic reasons why my experience is similar to many BWGS while in their programs. Research from the National Center on Education Statistics (NCES) indicates that of the 791,391 faculty in the United States, only 24,283 are Black women, and of that, only 2,647 are tenured professors. The National Center on Education Statistics also notes that of the 4 percent of Black tenured professors, 2 percent are Black women. As of 2021, The National Center for Education Statistics notes that there are 4,811 accredited degree-granting post-secondary institutions in the United States; 4,294 four-year institutions, 517 two-year institutions, and 90 specialized institutions. Given the number of accredited degree-granting institutions in the United States, this scarcity is unacceptable and greatly impacts the grad school experience for BWGS at any level in their program. If historically white institutions understand the power of representation and how it enhances the learning experiences for Black students, why is there not an institutional urgency to rectify this issue? As bell hooks stated, "Sometimes people try to destroy you precisely because they recognize your power. Not because they don't see it, but because they see it and don't want it to exist." One can argue that part of the reason why the academy doesn't prioritize enhancing representation among Black women faculty is because they know how extremely powerful Black women scholars are when we rally together to enact change. Too many Black women in one space would intimidate and disrupt the misogynoir shown towards Black women in higher education. Cynthia Bartman asserts in her work African American Women in Higher Education: Issues and Support Strategies that until academic institutions diversify their faculty, cross-cultural, culturally competent mentoring may be a strategy they'll have to consider. While institutions actively work toward increasing the number of African American female faculty members and students, cross-cultural mentoring is a strategy worth considering to help meet the needs of these students for engagement and support. Not doing anything, however, is no longer an option. As I experience the outcomes of these disparities within the academy as a student, I often ask myself why the scarcity of women who look like me is so prevalent and how I can best prepare myself for what the professoriate will present. I believe that knowing the facts and arming myself with solutions is the first step. In an article by the American Sociological Association, current Black professors share their observations in the academy and implications moving forward to improve the lack of Black representation within women. The first observation that has been validated by research is how Black academics are expected to do antiracist work and "fix" the diversity issues of their department and campus instead of focusing on the expertise that they were hired to work within. This is an outcome of not hiring enough people on campus to do diversity work. Therefore, the expectation is then placed on Black faculty to address diversity, inclusion, and equity issues, even if it is outside of their research expertise. This added pressure and responsibility contributed to the Black academic's decision to leave the academy. My second observation examines the mistreatment of Black faculty. Research by the American Sociological Association (ASA) reports a significant gap in satisfaction between Black and White faculty. Black faculty are 55% less likely than White faculty, who rest at 73%, to feel a sense of satisfaction with diversity and inclusion efforts on their campus. Black women specifically report increased rates of mistreatment and negative experiences in the academy which serves as a byproduct of Black women's lower percentages of achieving tenure (Bartman, n.d.). Workplace discrimination remains at the forefront of the Black woman's academic experience, so, understandably, representation and access to mentorship is limited for Black women grad students at HWI's as a result of Black women, understandably, leaving the field of higher education proper. The hate you give to Black women faculty hurts BWGS who need the support and mentorship of other Black women in this role.

Black women are also forced to deal with the very real reality that we often give our all to institutions that could never fully love or appreciate what we bring into that space. Bridget Love (2021) notes that when operating within the construct of two marginalized identities, Black women experience advancing in the academy in painful ways that impact our sense of self and community, personal and academic well-being, and concepts of a professional trajectory. Amid a growth in social justice-focused academic programs, contemporary politics have undercut the experiences of Black women whose stories are often academicized and co-opted by others and, in turn, told in ways that further marginalize Black women because of our race, gender, or both (Love, 2021). I often ask myself how the academy can truly invest in Black women when they are foundationally rooted in anti-Blackness. In her love letter to Black women in the academy, Dr. Tia Sheree Gaynor (2023) perfectly stated, "Without the presence of Black women, there would be no academy – no hallowed halls of intellectual curiosity and advancement. American institutions of higher learning were built on the backs of Black women" (Gaynor, 2023). It's time that the academy begins treating Black women with the respect that they deserve and provides the support that will garner hope within younger Black women scholars who desire to occupy the profession one day. In the 2022 Netflix documentary, The Black Beauty Effect, Lisa Price, chief executive officer of Carol's Daughter Hair Care said, "When you invest in the mothers, you invest in the daughters." This concept can be tethered to the academy. When you invest in the wellness and needs of Black women in faculty in a way that positions them to prosper in their work, you in return invest in the Black women and girls on your campus.

RECOMMENDATIONS

The recommendations put forth by Ana Branch (2024), Professor of Sociology, emphasize the urgent need for action to support Black women graduate students (BWGS) and Black women faculty within higher education institutions. Professor Branch stresses the importance of establishing an integrated support ecosystem to address the challenges faced by BWGS and Black women faculty. This ecosystem should encompass internal support structures and meaningful resources tailored to their needs, aiming to alleviate the burdens they often bear silently. Collaborative efforts across the institution are essential to create this network, addressing entrenched cultural issues that impact the experiences of Black women.

Furthermore, higher education institutions must prioritize diversity, equity, and inclusion initiatives, translating stated values into concrete actions. Financial equity initiatives are particularly crucial, as they address issues of under-compensation and recognize the additional labor required for tenure by Black women faculty. Allocating sufficient resources to support Black women faculty is imperative to ensure fair treatment and compensation on campus.

In addition to financial equity, peer support networks play a vital role in fostering a sense of community and belonging for BWGS. Normalizing the presence and accessibility of peer support networks, such as sister circles, can provide invaluable mentorship and a safe space for collaboration and discussion. These networks should be promoted across the institution to combat feelings of isolation and provide essential support for Black women graduate students.

Lastly, implementing cluster hiring practices can contribute significantly to building inclusive excellence and faculty diversity. By hiring minoritized faculty members in groups rather than individually, institutions can provide a supportive community and network for new hires, reducing the risk of tokenization and burnout. Effective cluster hiring initiatives should prioritize support and mentorship for minoritized faculty members, ensuring their success within the institution.

These recommendations offer practical strategies for higher education institutions to address the unique challenges faced by Black women graduate students and faculty members. By prioritizing support, equity, and inclusion, institutions can create environments where Black women can thrive academically and professionally, contributing to a more diverse and inclusive academic community.

THE FINAL HOUR

It is Not Me I See is a chapter dedicated to the investment of Black women graduate students. The purpose of this chapter was not to portray a bleak representation of Black women faculty in the academy but rather interrogate a system that has created a lack of representation within Black women faculty and insufficient work environments that haven't allowed them to fully flourish due to systematic and political barriers. The beauty of Black feminist work at its core is the importance of being in a community with other Black women in a world that would rather see Black women disjointed from each other rather than uplifting each other. This narrative is no different within the ivory tower. Creating space in the academy that respects the work of Black women's research, values the scholarly contribution of Black women, and takes the time to listen, understand, and believe the experiences of Black women as essential to the retention and perseverance of BWGS and Black women faculty. We need this to continue doing the work for years to come. To my fellow BWGS reading this chapter, I hope that you continue to do the work your soul must have (Cannon, 1970). I hope that you see your value even when the academy chooses not to. I hope that you take time to rest and disconnect from the heaviness of this work when needed. I hope that you find your garden and water it every chance you get. I hope that you use your lived experience and knowledge gathered from it to create new methodologies that galvanize social change and equity. I hope that you complete the mission you set out to do and discover your unbreak-ability along the way. I'm rooting for you, sis. You got this.

REFERENCES

An Exodus of Black Women in Academia Hurts the Workforce. (2024, January 20). *Bloomberg.com*. https://www.bloomberg.com/ opinion/articles/ 2024-01-20/ an-exodus-of-black-women-in-academiahurts-the-workforce

Anderson, B. N., & Richardson, S. L. (Eds.). (2023). *Gifted Black Women Navigating the Doctoral Process: Sister Insider*. Taylor & Francis. 10.4324/9781003292180

Aya, E. (2023). *Aya: The Enduring Spirit of Black Women in Higher Education* (Order No. 30820060). Available from ProQuest Dissertations & Theses Global. (2917478555).

Bartman, C. C. (n.d.). African American Women in Higher Education: Issues and Support Strategies. *Journal of Women in Higher Education, 2*(2).

Biaggio, M. (2001). Navigating Roles in Mentoring Relationships with Graduate Students. ERIC. https://eric.ed.gov/?id=ED457516

Black Faculty and Radical Retention | American Sociological Association. (n.d.). Retrieved September 30, 2023, from https://www.asanet.org/ footnotes-article/ black-faculty-and-radical-retention/

Blau, F. D., Currie, J. M., Croson, R. T. A., & Ginther, D. K. (2010). Can Mentoring Help Female Assistant Professors? Interim Results from a Randomized Trial. *The American Economic Review*, 100(2), 348–352. 10.1257/aer.100.2.348

Brunsden, V., Davies, M., Shevlin, M., & Bracken, M. (2000). Why do HE Students Drop Out? A test of Tinto's model. *Journal of Further and Higher Education*, 24(3), 301–310. 10.1080/030987700750022244

Cannon, K. G. (2021). *Katie's Canon: Womanism and the Soul of the Black Community, Revised and Expanded 25th Anniversary Edition*. Fortress Press. 10.2307/j. ctv1khdp4b

Colleges Look to Cluster Hires Amid Diversity Hostilities. (2023, September 14). *Diverse: Issues In Higher Education*. https://www.diverseeducation.com/ from-the-magazine/ article/15546498/colleges-look-to-cluster-hir es-amid-diversity-hostilities

Collins, P. H. (2000). *Black feminist thought: Knowledge, consciousness, and the politics of empowerment* (Rev. 10th anniversary ed.). Routledge.

Dillard, C. B. (2000). The substance of things hoped for, the evidence of things not seen: Examining an endarkened feminist epistemology in educational research and leadership. *International Journal of Qualitative Studies in Education : QSE*, 13(6), 661–681. 10.1080/09518390050211565

Gaynor, T. S. (n.d.). A Love Letter to Black Women in the Academy. *Inside Higher Ed*. Retrieved September 30, 2023, from https://www.insidehighered.com/advice/2022/12/16/ letter-support-and-solidarity-black-women-aca deme-opinion

hooks, B. (2014). *Teaching To Transgress*. Routledge. 10.4324/9780203700280

Love, B. H., Templeton, E., Ault, S., & Johnson, O. (2023). Bruised, not broken: Scholarly personal narratives of Black women in the academy. *International Journal of Qualitative Studies in Education : QSE*, 36(10), 2229–2251. 10.1080/09518398.2021.1984607

Price, J. H., & Khubchandani, J. (2019). The Changing Characteristics of African-American Adolescent Suicides, 2001-2017. *Journal of Community Health*, 44(4), 756–763. 10.1007/s10900-019-00678-x31102116

Strayhorn, T. L., & Terrell, M. C. (2007). Mentoring and Satisfaction with College for Black Students. *Negro Educational Review*, 58, 69–83.

Chapter 3
Life, Family, and Academia:
Navigating the Superwoman Schema

Chenell C. Loudermill
Independent Researcher, USA

ABSTRACT

Women began to establish themselves in the workforce during the 1960s and have since entered various professions. Today, Black women make up 65% of all African Americans enrolled in higher education and account for nearly three percent of academic faculty at degree serving institutions. Black women work fervently to find work-life balance but lack the necessary supports to do so. In this chapter, the author details her experiences of battling the Strong Black Woman Phenomenon and her quest for work-life balance. She discusses experiences, lessons learned along the way, and finding the power to resist the demands to exude perfection and wield the double-edge sword of being a superwoman.

INTRODUCTION

Women's role in society, their positions of employment, and the evolution thereof have contributed significantly to the advancement and sustainment of communities and the workforce. Since the mid-1800s, women have expanded their roles outside the home (Webb, 2010). By 1964, with the second wave of the feminist movement, women began to establish themselves in the workplace occupying roles such as teachers, nurses and secretaries (Webb). However, this evolution required women to extend themselves in ways that would eventually lead to stress and burnout as

DOI: 10.4018/979-8-3693-0698-7.ch003

Copyright © 2024, IGI Global. Copying or distributing in print or electronic forms without written permission of IGI Global is prohibited.

they attempted to reach unattainable goals set by society which required them to be everything for everyone in every aspect of life. This was especially true for Black women (Beal, 1975). During the Womanist movement, Black women fought to ensure their story of struggle which included working for low wages in the homes of White women and racism was acknowledged (Beal, 2008; Duran, 2015).

The Black community has historically promoted the strong, Black woman phenomenon, also referred to as the Superwoman Schema (Woods-Giscombé, 2010) which was developed as a means to combat the negative characterizations of Black women. While women have typically embraced their role and natural ability as caregivers and nurturers, they have also embraced and desired the ability to contribute to the workforce. However, functioning in both roles can contribute to external and internal challenges exacerbating the Superwoman Schema (SWS), leaving Black women on a quest to navigate the challenges associated with finding work-life balance.

The term work-life balance, in its simplest form, refers to the equal distribution of time to personal and professional activities (Thomas, 2022). However, when time is the only consideration in this equation, very important aspects of work and life are lost. Furthermore, the distribution of time, effort, and energy is rarely distributed evenly. Kalliath and Brough (2008) provided a more comprehensive definition of work-life balance: "the individual perception that work and non-work activities are compatible and promote growth in accordance with an individual's current life priorities" (p. 326). Women are often encouraged to find work-life balance but rarely given support to do so. For example, working mothers— single or primary caregivers—face challenges when caring for sick children or finding affordable childcare (Arpino & Luppi, 2020). This is especially challenging for Black women working in the academy given the demands of the institution.

There is an added burden placed on women of color—especially in institutions of higher education—that impacts their mental and physical health. Black women in higher education have reported high levels of stress related to bullying (Johnson et al., 2023), racial discrimination and burnout (Jackson et al., 2023), sexual harassment (Dey et al., 1996), and competing demands of home and work. Black women find themselves trying to be the strong, Black woman navigating the five characteristics of the SWS described by Woods-Giscombé (2010): 1) obligation to manifest strength, 2) obligation to suppress emotion, 3) resistance to being vulnerable or dependent, 4) determination to succeed despite limited resources, and 5) obligation to help others.

When I was a child, I remember adults asking, "What do you want to be when you grow up?" Of the responses I gave, none of them was ever, "I want to be an academician." Yet, here I am, a grownup, working for an R1 (research one), predominantly white institution (PWI), and killing it! Or is it killing me? As I reflect on my experiences as a Black woman in higher education, I can, unfortunately, say I have been the strong, Black, woman in many instances, exhibiting the characteristics of the SWS. As I share examples of my experience of trying to navigate life, family and academia, I will discuss lessons learned which I strive to practice daily. However, I am a work in progress and God ain't finished with me yet. Throughout this chapter, I want to discuss how societal views and expectations of women have changed, and how my experiences in academia coupled with finding work-life balance have left me less concerned about how others see me and with a deeper understanding of what is more important, which is how I see myself.

OBLIGATION TO MANIFEST STRENGTH

According to Woods-Giscombé (2010), the obligation to manifest strength can be summarized as being perceived as "the strong one" by friends and family. By the time I started my doctoral program, I had already been established in the profession. I was balancing my roles as a wife, mother, full-time employee, and part-time student. Additionally, I was working a part-time job to pay for school. Being raised to be a strong, Black woman, I believed I could do it all. This came with an extreme amount of stress. I was physically, mentally, and emotionally exhausted as I fell prey to the strong, Black Woman trope.

To be "strong" meant not only did I believe I could carry the weight of the world on my shoulders, but also that it was necessary for survival. I recall juggling responsibilities as the family manager, financial planner, cook, caretaker, team mom, housekeeper, graduate student, and anything else anyone needed me to be. At the time, I had two young sons and while I had a husband, he was typically not available to assist with the day-to-day parenting and homemaker duties. So, I did what my family expected; I carried on. I was, after all, a strong, Black woman. As one of two history-making Black doctoral students to graduate from my program, the obligation to manifest strength was heightened as I matriculated.

I was subjected to discrimination and academic hazing, tasked with supporting my advisor's role as a course instructor as opposed to developing my skills as a scholar. My advisor often shared stories about how difficult her advisor made the process for her. Yet, she treated me in the same manner she complained her advisor treated her. I recall a conversation we had in the early stages of my dissertation research. I had submitted a draft of the first few chapters, and it was taking some time to receive feedback. When I inquired about it, she stated, "Get to the back of the line…. there are other students to get out before you so you should not expect feedback during this semester." To say I was taken aback would be an understatement. I could understand that she had other students. However, I could not understand why she decided I was not worthy of her time, but other students were. It soon became obvious that my place at the end of the line was behind my white peers.

Academic hazing took the form of assigning tedious tasks for me to complete. One summer semester I enrolled in a language seminar. Instead of facilitating the seminar, my advisor tasked me with creating PowerPoint slides for her class. That's it. That's all. I questioned this task to myself; however, I did not question it with her. I kept my head down and did what I was instructed to do. Honestly, I did not have the energy to fight this battle.

In my first academic appointment as an instructor and Director of Clinical Education and Services, I was subjected to racism, sexism, and ageism (damn near any kind of -ism you can think of) by a department administrative assistant and the department chair. Decisions I made that were well within my job responsibilities were consistently challenged by the department administrative assistant. Furthermore, I was treated poorly by the department chair (which I describe in detail in the following section). Nevertheless, I was expected to do my job and "stay strong" in the face of adversity. This was the advice I was given my faculty, family and friends. I know this was with good intent but the impact of trying to do those things weighed heavily on me. The expectation to manifest strength continued and intensified as I was given more responsibility, expectations increased, and family dynamics changed drastically. I was no longer married, and I moved away from home with two sons to a predominately White community. So, there I was trying to find the strength to manage my new job, my new environment and help my sons acclimate to our new lives.

Lesson Learned: I think of strength as the capacity to withstand great force or pressure and exhibiting strength can be a positive attribute. Although strength can be viewed as a renewable resource developed through rest, healthy eating and exercise, manifesting unnecessary strength is an ingredient for self-sabotage. Through my experiences in trying to balance the demands of work and life, I learned there was a need for me to protect my peace by any means necessary. I prioritized what was important to me and gave myself the flexibility to modify which priorities took precedence over others, clearly communicating that in my work and home life without reservation or shame in order to preserve my strength.

OBLIGATION TO SUPPRESS EMOTIONS

Society has conditioned women to believe we are *too* emotional, and that we do not have the right to experience a range of emotions or express how they feel. We have also been conditioned to believe we have to protect the emotions of others. This is especially true for Black women in the workplace serving in leadership roles. In my first academic appointment, part of my role was to serve as the Director of Clinical Education and Services. After serving in this position for a little over a year, I was informed that a new Department Chair, who identified as male and Hispanic, was hired. Three months into his role as department chair, he informed the faculty that he was launching a national search for a Director of Clinical Education and Services. This announcement came as a surprise to the entire faculty, so one can only imagine the range of emotions I felt at that moment. The blatant disrespect and disregard for me was baffling. A man who knew absolutely nothing about me, my role, or my area of expertise had decided he knew more than the faculty who had voted me into the position and the dean who approved my hire. The audacity. I was furious, and I was not alone. When asked about his decision, he gave no legitimate reason. Later, I learned he was not permitted to initiate a search. After senior faculty came to my defense, he quickly reversed course. This individual continued to create a hostile work environment, making each interaction thereafter more and more uncomfortable. There were instances when he raised his voice to me, made disturbing comments about my attire, and dismissed my requests and concerns. I was confused. I had never experienced such disregard and poor treatment in the workplace. I thought to myself, "Am I the problem?" As it turned out, the answer was no. That vote of no confidence found its way to his desk and he found work elsewhere.

Eventually, I transitioned to a different institution but still served in a leadership capacity. Things did not get any easier, however. I experienced a wide range of emotions as I adapted to my new environment. I tend to be very private and this was viewed as impersonal by non-Black, Indigenous, people of color (BIPOC). It has always been my practice to limit the amount of personal information I share with colleagues. Additionally, I operated on the idea that sharing how you feel is unprofessional, and showing emotion was a sign of weakness. So, when my position was threatened, I manifested strength while suppressing my emotions. Through passive-aggressive behavior from individuals who were not BIPOC, constant microaggressions, and feelings of isolation, I manifested strength. Suppressing my emotions became second nature as I reminded myself that I had responsibilities. How would I get my job done? Who would take care of the house, my sons? I had concluded there was no time to deal with emotions, so suppressing them was the only solution.

Lesson Learned: While I tiptoed around my emotions to protect the emotions of others, there was no one protecting me. When emotions are suppressed, one can feel like a ticking time bomb. Ultimately, the repressing of emotions leads to the deterioration of the spirit. I remember feeling reluctant to share how I was feeling with my doctor, partner, family, and close friends. I learned that maintaining privacy does not mean suppressing emotions. The best decision I made was allowing myself to feel, acknowledging those feelings, and taking all the time I needed to heal.

RESISTANCE TO BEING VULNERABLE OR DEPENDENT

The rapid demise of the Black family from systemic oppression and discrimination thrust Black women into the role of breadwinners to survive (Feagin, 2006). Jim Crow laws led to the lynching and killing of many Black men. Once Jim Crow ended, mass incarceration and police brutality became new means of erasing Black male figures from Black families (Feagin). Additionally, domestic violence faced by Black women and the mistrust in the systems that were supposed to protect us threatened our ability to depend on others (Valandra, Murphy-Erby, Higgins, & Brown, 2019). These factors have made it difficult for Black women to seek assistance. As a Black woman, I experienced many challenges as I navigated my personal and professional life. My resistance to vulnerability fed my obligation to manifest strength which led to the suppression of my emotions. The characteristics of the SWS are intricately intertwined and therefore cause a vicious cycle.

When I reflect on my past experiences in higher education and the impact on my physical, emotional, and mental well-being, I cannot help but think about recent tragic events that transpired with Lincoln University alum and Vice President of Student Affairs, Dr. Antoinette Candia-Bailey, who died by suicide due to harassment, bullying, and mistreatment by the university president. Her cries for help went unacknowledged. She was left unsupported with, I imagine, no room to make mistakes. Feelings that are all too familiar to many Black women in academia.

Lesson Learned: How was it that others could depend on me, but I could not depend on them? The strong, Black woman trope had me in a chokehold. It took some time, but I eventually learned that asking for help was not a sign of weakness. Two of the greatest lessons I learned from confronting resistance were that I deserved help, and that people were willing to help without judgment. Some people wanted to see me succeed. I released my fear of seeking help and embraced a life's journey with support from friends, family, community, and allies. Now, when I am in spaces where I don't feel supported, I take the advice of Dr. Nikole Hannah-Jones; I go where I am celebrated, not where I am tolerated.

DETERMINATION TO SUCCEED DESPITE LIMITED RESOURCES

Black women oftentimes attempt to combat negative stereotypes and tropes through strength, resolve, and perseverance even when faced with limited resources. I am no stranger to this concept. One of my mother's favorite sayings was, "Work with what you've got." This idea has been instilled in Black women since childhood: manifest strength, suppress emotions, resist vulnerability, and get the job done no matter what. As I matriculated through my doctoral program, I was determined to succeed no matter what. Help with my children was limited. It didn't matter. I was going to succeed. I went through a divorce. It didn't matter. I was going to succeed. My mother and sister were in the military and deployed. It didn't matter. I was going to succeed. People told me that being geographically constrained would limit my employment opportunities for higher education. It didn't matter. I was going to succeed. All my resources were limited, but my determination was in abundance.

I wanted to work in academia after earning my PhD. So, I left my job in public education, working nine months a year, for a 12-month academic appointment with the same pay. My resources to maintain my current lifestyle were reduced. It didn't matter. I was determined to succeed. The stumbling blocks were numerous and sometimes deliberate. For instance, I began my academic appointment in September but was not provided with a computer until November. My paperwork was processed incorrectly by the administrative assistant (yes, that one), which led to my first paycheck being delayed. I continued to push through, working longer hours, extending my availability to students and colleagues, taking on additional tasks to prove my competency, and code-switching to ensure I was taken seriously. I had been taught that I needed to work twice as hard to be half as good as my white counterparts. It was exhausting.

Lesson Learned: Determination and persistence can be admirable characteristics when harnessed appropriately. Overexertion for the satisfaction or pleasure of others is harmful. Institutions and organizations have unlimited resources to support what they deem to be priorities. I do not have to do more than what I am paid to do. I do not have to masquerade as someone I am not. I do not need to overexert myself to be liked or respected. The truth is, I am enough just as I am.

OBLIGATION TO HELP OTHERS

As I reflect on the question, "What do you want to be when you grow up?" I am reminded that all the professions I considered were helping professions. Growing up, I had numerous examples of women helping others including my mother, grandmother, and community members. As a Black woman, there is a sense of pride that comes with being able to support and meet the needs of others. In some ways, I believe Black women role model how they want to be supported. Often, Black women give of ourselves to the point of exhaustion, depleting their minds, bodies, and souls. In the workplace and at home, the obligation to help others at all costs is unsustainable.

In institutions of higher education, Black faculty often carry the burden of recruiting and supporting students of color. Additionally, Black faculty engage more in service related to engagement and diversity (Joseph & Hirshfield, 2011). Although it can be challenging, it brings me great joy to work with students, stretching them beyond their comfort zone, and expanding their knowledge of cultural humility and cultural responsiveness. In my personal experience, Black faculty tend to be more inclusive of marginalized groups in their research. Although it can be difficult to recruit individuals from marginalized communities to participate in research (with good reason), the reward is great. Despite the massive effort that these activities take, they have been traditionally devalued by senior administration, especially at PWIs.

Lesson Learned: Having a spirit of helpfulness is a great trait to possess. However, pouring into others while neglecting your needs will eventually lead to emptiness. Giving time and talent to institutions that do not actively demonstrate their commitment to fostering inclusive environments where individual differences are embraced and celebrated can lead to resentment. While helping others can be therapeutic, I had to remember to keep my reserves full enough to help myself.

CONCLUSION

With Black women accounting for less than 3% of tenure-track/tenured faculty in degree-granting institutions (Inside Higher Ed, 2021), supportive networks must be developed to uplift and inspire us. Practices that lead to racial and gender discrimination must be disrupted in the academy to release obligations to put work and others before the mental, physical, and emotional health of Black women. One can be as stellar as Dr. Claudine Gay, Harvard University's first Black President, or as committed as Dr. JoAnne Epps, Temple University President, who passed away unexpectedly after 40 years in academia, those that uphold the tenets in which the institution was created will work tireless to keep Black women out. After all, the institution was not created for us. Therefore, Black women cannot expect those individuals to care about our well-being. There must be a critical evaluation of the choices Black women make that bind us to the Superwoman Schema as it is not a badge of honor. Treating it as such puts our peace and livelihood at stake. There is no true benefit to being a superwoman.

REFERENCES

Arpino, B., & Luppi, F. (2020). Childcare arrangements and working mothers' satisfaction with work–family balance. *Demographic Research*, 42, 549–588. 10.4054/DemRes.2020.42.19

Beal, F. M. (1975). Slave of a slave no more: Black women in struggle. *The Black Scholar*, 6(6), 2–10. 10.1080/00064246.1975.11431488

Beal, F. M. (2008). Double jeopardy: To be Black and female. *Meridians (Middletown, Conn.)*, 8(2), 166–176. 10.2979/MER.2008.8.2.166

Dey, E. L., Korn, S. J., & Sax, L. J. (1996). Betrayed by the academy: The sexual harassment of women college faculty. *The Journal of Higher Education*, 67(2), 149–173. 10.1080/00221546.1996.11780254

Duran, J. (2015). Women of the civil rights movement. Black feminism and social progress. *Philosophia Africana*, 17(2), 65–73. 10.5325/philafri.17.2.0065

Feagin, J. (2006). *Systemic Racism: A Theory of Oppression* (1st ed.). Routledge., 10.4324/9781315880938

Jackson Preston, P., Brown, G. C., Garnett, T., Sanchez, D., Fagbamila, E., & Graham, N. (2023). "I am never enough": Factors contributing to secondary traumatic stress and burnout among Black student services professionals in higher education. *Trauma Care, 3*(2), 93–107. 10.3390/traumacare3020010

Johnson, D. S., Johnson, A. D., Crossney, K. B., & Devereux, E. (2023). Women in higher education: A brief report on stress during COVID-19. *Management in Education, 37*(2), 93-100. 10.1177/08920206211019401

Joseph, T. D., & Hirshfield, L. E. (2011). 'Why don't you get somebody new to do it?' Race and cultural taxation in the academy. *Ethnic and Racial Studies*, 34(1), 121–141. 10.1080/01419870.2010.496489

Kalliath, T., & Brough, P. (2008). Work-life balance: A review of the meaning of the balance construct. *Journal of Management & Organization*, 14(3), 323–327. 10.5172/jmo.837.14.3.323

The Systemic Scarcity of Tenured Black Women. (2021, July 15). Inside Higher Education. Retrieved from https://www.insidehighered.com/advice/2021/07/16/black-women-face-many-obstaclestheir-efforts-win-tenure-opinion

Thomas, M. (2022). What does work-life balance even mean? *Forbes*. https://www
.forbes.com/sites/maurathomas/2022/07/26/what-does-work-life-balance-even
-mean/?sh=4450a28a2617

Valandra, M.-E., Murphy-Erby, Y., Higgins, B. M., & Brown, L. M. (2019). African
American Perspectives and Experiences of Domestic Violence in a Rural Community. *Journal of Interpersonal Violence*, 34(16), 3319–3343. 10.1177/0886260516
66954227659684

Webb, J. G. (2010). The evolution of women's roles within the university and workplace. In *Forum on Public Policy Online* (Vol. 2010, No. 5). Oxford Round Table.

Woods-Giscombé, C. L. (2010). Superwoman schema: African American women's
views on stress, strength, and health. *Qualitative Health Research*, 20(5), 668–683.
10.1177/104973231036189220154298

Chapter 4
Navigating Academia the Ultimate Set-Up:
I Knew It Was a Set Up, Because It Was Too Easy!

Andrea "Andi" Toliver-Smith
Howard University, USA

ABSTRACT

This chapter illustrates the academic journey of a Black woman in the field of communication sciences and disorders. Dr. Andi Toliver-Smith started her journey at a Historically Black College or University (HBCU) and transferred to a Predominately White Institution (PWI). She was encouraged by her instructors to continue her education and to obtain her PhD in the field. When seeking out a master's program, she experienced microaggressions for the first time when visiting universities. She completed her master's degree at an HBCU and her PhD at her former PWI university. Her experiences compelled her to develop a support group for BIPOC students. She realized that it was imperative to keep the students in the program in order to expand the field. However, there has been little support for the BIPOC faculty. These experiences led Dr. Toliver-Smith to the forefront of the movement to expand the field of CSD through attraction and retention of BIPOC students and faculty. She has also noted responsibility for faculty of color to maintain a presence in higher education settings.

DOI: 10.4018/979-8-3693-0698-7.ch004

Copyright © 2024, IGI Global. Copying or distributing in print or electronic forms without written permission of IGI Global is prohibited.

INTRODUCTION

Black women in academia face unique forms of oppression that include anti-Blackness, misogyny, misogynoir, which is specific to Black women, and racism. All of these create hostile environments that lead to their departure from their positions and, in some cases, higher education (Gayles, 2022). In this chapter, I share my experiences with racism and oppression from undergraduate and graduate school to my doctoral program and my role as a faculty member while navigating academia.

In 2020, I attended a Speak Up & Speak Out cultural humility seminar by the National Black Association for Speech-Language and Hearing (NBASLH). One workshop presenter posed several questions to attendees that I have adopted and would ask you to ponder as you read this chapter.

1. What is your role in racism?
2. Are you the aggressor, bystander, or victim?
3. As you reflect, consider your position and interaction with racism. What systems do you operate in that have the power to dismantle racism?
4. What is one thing you will do to create a more inclusive, safe, and welcoming environment in your role in education?

BACKGROUND

I must admit that when I entered the Communication Sciences and Disorders field, I was looking for a career that was not contingent upon world events. After the terrorist attacks on September 11, 2001, my job as a professional meeting planner ended after 11 years. It was no longer appropriate to have lavish events as funds were allocated towards the safety of our country. I was a college dropout with experience in the hospitality industry, which was not needed at this time. I left college for financial reasons, which is typical of first-generation Black students (Algers, 2024). Now, I was in a position where I had to make some decisions about my next career move.

I became interested in Communication Sciences and Disorders as an undergraduate student. I initially entered college to become an attorney. However, when I began taking the pre-law curriculum courses, I hated them. I realized I would never be happy constantly searching for loopholes in the law. I also realized that even though I was smart enough to handle being an attorney, I was not swift enough. There was always going to be someone whose mind worked faster than mine and possessed more mentally agility than me. Moreover, my personality did not lend itself to the legal field. I stumbled upon Communication Sciences and Disorders (CSD) while looking for careers that would allow me to use my unique communication skills. Since I was good at "partying and running my lips," I figured, "Why not help others communicate?"

When I decided to re-enroll in college, I was in my mid-thirties. I had already worked in my state's corporate industry and public service. I was married with a child, so I was past the partying stage and the distractions that most undergraduate students experience. I was a mature and sophisticated student with my eye on the prize—my degree. I was also incredibly nervous to return to college with younger women as my peers. I took a deep breath, put my big girl panties on, and jumped into it! I was fortunate in my first semester to meet a Black female professor in the CSD field. She became my mentor and continues to mentor me today.

Mentorship is essential for Black women in academia. Mentors of color pave the way for Black, Indigenous, People of Color (BIPOC) students to grow and become successful in the field. As a Black woman mentored me, I mentor students of color as a university professor. As a mentor, I treat my students like my child, offering them guidance and support. I even tell them that once they are my baby, they are always my baby! When I entered the CSD field, I had no clue how significant my presence would be for BIPOC students or the role I would undertake as a mentor. My hope for my students (and others) was always that they never had to experience the impact of implicit biases and racism in the workplace or the marginalization that comes with being supervised by individuals who neither acknowledge nor understand their culture. I have worked at two PWIs and made astounding discoveries about what underrepresented students in our field must endure to become professionals. While I had great mentors, they did not prepare me for this. I was oblivious to their experiences because I had not had the same experiences in my program.

UNDERGRADUATE EXPERIENCE

I started my post-secondary journey at an HBCU (Historically Black College or University). This was a deliberate decision. I was born in 1970, on the heels of the Civil Rights Movement. My mother instilled a sense of pride in me about my Blackness. How I walked, talked, and dressed, the essence of my being, was all about being Black. You would not have met a little girl prouder to be Black than me! I do not identify as African American because I do not know my African heritage. The institution of slavery stripped away that part of my Blackness. I am as American as apple pie. I will not "go back to Africa" because this country was built on the backs of my ancestors. I have just as much right to it as anyone else. I am Black with a capital "B." My identity as a Black person denotes my culture, not just my race.

Unfortunately, my "culture" let me down financially at the HBCU, so I transferred to a Predominantly White Institution (PWI) to complete the last two years of college, which subsequently became three years. The PWI I attended did not accept some of my history and math courses from the HBCU—no surprise there! Since I had to be there for an additional year, I picked up a minor in Deaf culture. This is when I realized I had an affinity for culture, which is inextricably linked with language. I was in the right place! Deaf culture was my first academic love, and it quickly expanded to multicultural issues and eventually cultural competence, cultural humility, social justice, and culturally responsive practices in CSD.

My undergraduate years at the PWI were wonderful. I was an "A" student, and my professors supported my ideas and goals. I noticed early on that there were only two Black students per class, but I did not question it. I noticed that our classes were mostly comprised of women, but I did not question that either. One of my White female professors encouraged me to consider obtaining my PhD. This was something that I had never considered. I was just thrilled to have the opportunity to complete my bachelor's degree. I should have known then that it was a set-up. Everything about my undergraduate experience was too perfect.

As I matriculated through the program, my mentor explained that I would have to obtain my master's degree to practice. It was not required then, but we all knew it was coming. This is common among many professions to "move the goalpost" or "raise the bar" because more BIPOC individuals gain access to these careers (Hill, 2021). In preparation for the requirement, I applied to several master's programs and was accepted. I decided to visit these programs to make the best selection for my educational goals. This was when the icy fingers of racism reached out to touch me for the first time in my academic career.

MASTER'S PROGRAM SEARCH

During spring break of my last year at the PWI, I visited the CSD masters programs I had been accepted to early in the semester. Since I was a nontraditional student, I was interested in graduate assistantships to help with the cost. I applied to five local graduate programs. One was automatically crossed off the list due to the cost, which left me with four schools to consider.

The first school was a PWI state school. The department staff knew who I was by my name because my grades were "up to here," the young lady said, raising her hand above her head. The white women I met were more interested in how I was going to do it all—work and take classes, and less interested in how they could support me throughout my academic journey. They asked about my marriage and where I worked. They did not ask me about my interest in graduate assistantships. One Black female professor informed me that my clinical interest (accent-dialect modification at that time) did not require a master's degree in CSD. She informed me that I would be better off obtaining a degree in communications. I was shocked she was not as supportive as my undergraduate mentor since so few of us were in the field. When I looked around at the students at this institution, I did not see myself reflected in the student population. I saw much younger women and maybe one BIPOC student of a much lighter skin tone. This was not the place for me.

At the next university, a private PWI, I met a white man who insulted me throughout the entire visit. He insinuated that my American Sign Language level was inadequate for their program. As we discussed the program requirements, he bluntly told me he did not expect me to have any knowledge about the type of projects and research their students were completing. Next, I met with the clinical director, who grilled me about my grade point average and GRE scores, both of which were good. She then explained that graduate assistantships were few and far between. I knew what that meant. They later offered me a full scholarship, which I turned down based on my experience with the faculty. I learned about a situation with a Black woman who had to sue the institution to obtain her master's degree. I had been warned that this may not be the place for me. Although I tried to remain unbiased, they were right. This was not the place for me. I did not want to fight to obtain my master's, and that was not the experience I wanted.

The third university was a state PWI that was very popular in the area. I was excited to visit this institution because it was close to my home. I met with the director, a White woman. I excitedly shared my clinical and research interests with her. She was friendly and listened intently before responding that I should study those areas at another university, out of state, with a group of researchers there. The wind was let out of my sails. I did not apply to the other university because I wanted to attend this particular university. I thanked her and crossed them off my list. This was also not the place for me.

Finally, I returned to the HBCU where I started my undergraduate education. The department chair spoke with me about my areas of interest, introduced me to people in the department that I would benefit from knowing, and put me on the phone with her little boy! I felt accepted and valued. I met trailblazers in the CSD field who were instrumental in establishing cultural and linguistic diversity. It was upon those shoulders I stood. I knew I was home!

GRADUATE SCHOOL EXPERIENCE

In my second year of graduate school, I was awarded a research grant for bilingualism. I also had the opportunity to become a student member of the National Black Association of Speech-Language and Hearing (NBASLH), and in 2008, I won an award for my research. I encouraged more friends to join and attend the conference for fellowship and healing from the traumas we were subjected to at various PWIs and workplaces. Working with such brilliant minds—faculty and students—was a joy.

It took me longer to graduate because I worked during my first year of graduate school. In my last semester, I took a class at the third university I had visited during my graduate school search to graduate on time. In taking that class, a well-respected professor in our field subjected me to numerous indignities. She was a White woman and took great care to scrutinize and grade my papers and assignments stringently. I had a medical emergency toward the end of that semester that led to my absence for the remainder of the semester. When I returned after my surgery, she accused me of attempting to cheat on the makeup exam. She wrote numbers on little bits of paper, then threw them on the floor and asked me to randomly select three so that I could write about those topics during the exam. I had recently had back surgery and could not bend to pick up the pieces of paper. She accused me of attempting to see the numbers written on the bits of paper.

She eventually apologized and admitted to insensitivity once I explained that I still had staples in my back and could not bend to retrieve the pieces of paper. I remember thinking, "Why did she throw paper on the floor at me in the first place?" In the Black community, this is considered rude and implies you are worthless and on the level of a dog. She could have allowed me to select those questions in numerous other ways. This was meant to be demeaning. My experience with this professor was beyond the level of microaggressions - this was blatant racism. It was clear I was not welcome in her class or the profession. She went as far as to request that I repeat her course the following year. Gratefully, my department chair recognized what she was attempting to do and ended her pursuit to be a gatekeeper. That same month, I passed my National Praxis Examination on the first attempt.

PH.D. EXPERIENCE

I had graduated from my beloved HBCU and was working as a speech-language pathologist in a large, predominately Black and Hispanic public school district when my undergraduate mentor called me one day out of the blue. She invited me to return to the university for the Ph.D. program, as they had a grant to cover my tuition. I was delighted with the invitation because I had never imagined doing this. I had been encouraged over the years by faculty from my undergraduate and graduate programs. I was anxious about progressing to this next level because I did not think my marriage could survive the Ph.D., but that is another story!

I applied and was accepted into the program. It was during this time that I met my doctoral mentor and we clicked instantly! We continue to collaborate and conduct research together. The doctoral program went relatively smoothly because of the nature of doctorate programs and my wonderful doctoral mentor. One may take a few basic classes with a cohort, but students are typically alone for most of their classes and while conducting research. So, the feelings of isolation become commonplace during this time – a little advice for students at this level, get used to it! Since my interests had expanded from Deaf culture to many other cultures, which led to my interest in multicultural issues, I had the opportunity to discover my varied interests under the umbrella of cultural and linguistic diversity. I graduated with my Doctor of Philosophy in 2014.

WORKPLACE EXPERIENCES

Armed with my newly minted PhD, I took a position as an assistant professor in the Midwest at a PWI. I thought I would automatically be appreciated for the knowledge and skills I brought to the department. I was wrong. I was subjected to microaggressions daily. Being from the South, I was highly acquainted with racism, but I did not expect it on this level. During meetings, my opinions were often devalued or overlooked. I was saddled with the "heavy emotional lifting" by being assigned the most challenging students under my clinical supervision and students who were struggling academically. These students needed additional assistance and more handholding. I soon got a reputation in the department as the professor caring for students. Many students with learning disabilities and personal problems found themselves in my office for weekly check-ins. This is common with BIPOC professors, who are often seen as caregivers for students of color and other marginalized populations (Mishra et al., 2021). Interestingly, it was my white students that I had to "drag" across the finish line. This was emotionally draining and conveyed that my time was not valued for academic activities. I usually worked late to handle my academic duties because I had been focused on student issues all day.

Since I had an interest in multicultural concerns and I had obtained my Ph.D. in Cultural and Linguistic Diversity, I taught at least two courses per semester in the College of Health Professions related to cultural competence and multicultural issues. My student evaluations were almost always poor because students were offended by the course material or did not appreciate a Black woman professor imparting knowledge to them. Student evaluations are a component of promotion and tenure. Mishra et al. (2021) discussed that professors of color who teach courses related to diversity and multiculturalism often receive low student evaluations and, therefore, shy away from teaching these courses. Promotion and tenure are based on scholarship, teaching, and service. I was often left with little time for scholarships because I was busy supporting struggling students.

Outside of the classroom, I was excluded from activities with peers. My colleagues met for happy hour and other activities, and I was not invited. This was a challenging time for me as a new professor. I needed leadership, guidance, and camaraderie but did not receive it. As a result, I did not advance as I should have during my time there. One of the administrators recognized this and introduced me to other professors of color on campus. This university prided itself on its vibrant and active diversity, equity, and inclusion (DEI) department. Students were able to join groups where they felt acknowledged and heard. They participated in activities across campus and were able to thrive in the PWI environment. However, professionals on campus were not offered opportunities such as these. The administrator who introduced me to other BIPOC professors was an older white woman who had made numerous contributions to education and the community during the Civil Rights Movement. She created a book club that highlighted books with topics told from the perspective of BIPOC individuals. I was asked to join because they needed more "Black" voices at the table. Although she had good intentions, I realized these activities were largely performative.

I have never been afraid to speak out and to voice my opinions. This was problematic for some of the other BIPOC professors who felt as though they had "arrived" and did not want me to rock the boat with what they thought were radical ideas. They had assimilated and believed they had been accepted into the fold, but they had not. They tended to distance themselves from me because I refused to code-switch or change my mannerisms to make others comfortable. My job was not to make others feel comfortable. My only responsibility was to bring my authentic self to all the spaces I had been invited to. I understood I was a diversity hire. I was also there for the students. It was important to me that I was there for representation. Students must see themselves reflected in every aspect of the culture to matriculate and seek similar professions (Gregory, 2020). If they could not see me, they could not be me. I aimed to expand the field, one Black speech pathologist or audiologist at a time.

I began reviewing statistics in my national organization, the American Speech-Language-Hearing Association (ASHA), and I realized our profession comprised 92% white women. However, only 8% of professionals in the field identified as BIPOC. This has not changed over the years and has not changed over the years (ASHA, 2021). According to Whitfield (2022), attempts to improve representation in our professional disciplines have been largely unsuccessful. Of the 8% BIPOC professionals, Hispanics make up 5%, with the African American members bringing up the rear at a mere 3% (ASHA, 2021). There are organizations specifically for BIPOC speech pathologists and audiologists: 8-Percenters, NBASLH, and the Hispanic Caucus. Although they provide a place of solace for its members, they have done little to increase the number of BIPOC professionals in our field.

While researching representation in the field, I noticed that students in our program were also struggling. They were not struggling with the work but with their experience at the university and the treatment they were receiving. Abdelaziz (2021) found that BIPOC students often experienced feelings of isolation and endured adverse treatment from professors, clinical supervisors, and their peers. These experiences led to students changing majors or leaving the institution. To prevent attrition and expand the field, I created a support group for underrepresented students in our program called the BIPOC Check-In. This was a safe space where students could voice their opinions, share their experiences, and meet other BIPOC students in the program. During monthly meetings, I often offered advice on addressing these issues and assisted them in navigating the program and the field. I introduced my graduate students to NBASLH and even took three graduate students to the conference. They were so impressed with the conference that they became interested in starting a local affiliate group, but they graduated before it was established.

I still keep in touch with my students, especially my BIPOC students, because I understand that mentoring never stops. I am forever grateful to my mentor, whom I affectionately call "Speech Mama." I still call her for advice. She has been an amazing resource and a place of refuge for me. Now that I am a "Speech Mama" myself, I must continue to pay it forward.

As I continued my journey toward tenure, I became increasingly aware of how microaggressions played a tremendous role in my day-to-day life at the university. Sue et. al., 2011, discussed microaggressions and how they showed up in the workplace. I always addressed them when they occurred but was challenged or dismissed. I was always assigned to DEI committees and charged to increase support for the BIPOC students in our program. Assistant professors in our program were encouraged to participate in the greater university community. I often gave staff and faculty presentations regarding cultural competence and cultural humility. My presentations were often met with skepticism and resistance from not only my white colleagues but also my BIPOC colleagues because I was seen as radical and because I was unwilling to assimilate.

A few months ahead of the pandemic, I decided to work online to avoid the microaggressions and racism I had endured for the past few years. This was a new opportunity, and I could still pursue tenure. Higher education was blindsided by the pandemic, which changed our world forever. We transitioned to online instruction. I thought I would be safe from racism and microaggressions, but I assure you that I was not. I was paired with a Black woman to design my courses. She often buffered my interactions with middle management. Middle management was primarily white women with master's degrees who took every opportunity to micromanage me. I learned that reports were run that indicated when and how long I had been logged into the system. There was a report that went to my dean every Monday that informed her if I had logged in over the weekend or not. I learned after the fact that we were expected to log in at least one day over the weekend.

As 2020 moved on and the contemporary Red Summer (Ortiz, 2020) ensued with the murders of George Floyd, Ahmad Arbury, and Breonna Taylor, I became more disgusted with the treatment and disregard of Black people as well as the policing of Black and brown bodies in the workplace. The original Red Summer occurred in 1919 and was a period during which White supremacist terrorism and numerous race riots occurred across the country. The term was coined by civil rights activist, James Weldon Johnson. The events of 2020 echoed this awful period in American history.

Later that same year, Nikole Hannah-Jones won the Pulitzer Prize for her work, the 1619 Project, a historical recount of slavery in the United States with African Americans at the center. This award came with a tenured position at the University of North Carolina and the title of Knight Chair in Race and Investigative Journalism. The following year, the academic world watched with revulsion as the university's Board of Trustees did not offer her tenure but a five-year contract with an option for tenure review. This meant none of us were safe from maltreatment based upon criticism, even though we had earned certain privileges with our scholastic work. The two previous Knight Chairs were given tenure but based on the topic of Hannah-Jones's work, she was not awarded tenure. Students and faculty alike protested this decision. After obtaining legal counsel to receive the highly coveted offer of tenure, Hannah-Jones rejected the offer. Instead, she accepted a tenured position at Howard University, explaining her desire to "go where you are celebrated, not tolerated" which is a popular saying in the Black community.

This encouraged me to leave my tenure track position when I was summoned back to campus after a year of working from home. I refused to return and be policed by White women with less education than me. I took a position at the university where I obtained my PhD. When my "Speech Mama" retired, I was offered her position. Although retired, she was still an emeritus faculty member and was always supportive and kind. It was a fantastic opportunity to work with her. Although I had several years of experience as a professor when I was hired, it was a hassle to negotiate my salary and rank. I later found out the administration wanted to hire me at a lower salary than my White female colleague, who had just graduated with her doctorate and had significantly less experience than me. Nevertheless, I was ecstatic to work at this university near my parents' home. My husband had developed some health issues and had become disabled, so he traveled with me when we were not at home with family.

As usual, I was assigned to the multicultural issues course. While I enjoyed teaching this course, it was difficult because of the raw emotions experienced by students, as the course required an examination of personal biases and prejudices. Students complained to my department chair after my first lecture on cultural humility. I was called into a meeting with my chair and program director, two White women. I have noticed that it always takes two of them to talk to one me! No one ever considers how uncomfortable or adversarial these meetings are for BIPOC faculty. The chair and program director wanted to know what I said in my lecture that had upset students so severely. I calmly informed them that they were probably upset when I walked my Black ass into the classroom! They suggested how I could soften the material and relate it to gender instead of race. To be clear, this was my area of expertise, not theirs. Neither one of them had training in this area. I accepted their criticism, but I knew I had no intention of changing a damn thing! The problem was that students were accustomed to hearing this type of information sugarcoated. If I were to enact change in the field, I would have to engage students and faculty in substantial discussion regarding this topic. I knew I could not change their hearts and minds, but I could give them another way of looking at other cultures to develop a healthy level of respect for the clients they would ultimately serve.

As with my previous university, this university needed to support BIPOC students. My program director encouraged me to write a grant to conduct a study on the BIPOC Check-In. After reading my proposal, I was again told to soften my language. I took their advice, and I still was not awarded the grant. The BIPOC Check-In group was well received; however, the students were reluctant to trust me. They considered me to be one of "them" as they stated, referring to the faculty. I had to lessen the professional distance I usually maintained so they would trust me. Every month, I had a BIPOC speaker join us to discuss various topics that impacted us professionally, such as our hair and imposter syndrome. I also implemented an anonymous satisfaction survey. At the end of the academic year, we all went to dinner to celebrate their success and to fellowship with each other. I obtained funding from the student activities office to pay for dinner. Things were good until I had two white women (it always takes two of them for me) come and demand to be a part of the activities. I turned them down because this was not their space. I explained that they were not allowed to participate because students felt unsafe with them. I reminded them that the goal was to retain BIPOC students and avoid attrition. I allowed them to come into our first meeting the next year and introduce themselves because the students needed to know who they were and that they supported them. Affinity groups are important in that students or faculty with shared interests can form to feel included. These groups foster a sense of belonging and combat the feelings of social isolation. These groups may be formal or informal and serve to ensure an environment where all are valued and empowered for success.

In May of 2022, my husband was diagnosed with renal cancer. I informed my "work family" that I would work from home for the summer to care for my husband. This was a reasonable request since I focused on research in the summer and did not teach courses. The administration did not take this kindly. They accused me of "telling" them and not asking. The last time I checked, I was a 52-year-old professional woman. It was perfectly acceptable for me to tell them what was happening, and they should have been supportive. Once again, I was being policed and micromanaged. I had to document and submit everything I did each day. Around this time, I developed high blood pressure for the first time and lost hair around my edges due to the stressful work environment. Of course, my husband's illness and subsequent death contributed to this, but my administration's lack of support did not make it easier to deal with. I managed to work through that academic year. I never stopped working, but I did go to therapy, which was a tremendous help.

After much deliberation, I decided to leave that university as well. I had been dehumanized and treated like a child. I decided they did not deserve me. Once again, I parted ways with an institution before obtaining tenure. The idea that I obtained my PhD and worked hard to create a safe space to attract and retain underrepresented students in our field felt like the ultimate set-up. My entrance into the academy, although easy, was a set-up! It set me up for daily microaggressions which led to additional stress, poor work-life balance, periods of depression, feelings of isolation, and mental health challenges.

When writing this chapter, I took the time to examine the role I played in racism while navigating academia. As both a student and a professor, I have been a bystander and a victim with racist activities around me. However, I realized that as a faculty member, I have the power to dismantle racism within my department by calling out microaggressive behaviors and developing affinity groups for students. I strive to create a safe and welcoming environment in my classes, department, and the field in general. I have provided my service to the university by joining and participating in DEI committees on campus. I hope that my students truly benefited from my efforts and that my clients felt safe and valued in all spaces. I understand that I have a responsibility to the individuals and communities that I serve. However, my personal experiences and maltreatment makes it difficult to continue this work that has become my passion.

In 2023, the Supreme Court struck down affirmative action efforts for colleges and universities. Academia again watched in horror as our hard work to level the playing field for students disappeared along with the dismantling of DEI departments. Again, we were subjected to scrutiny and dismissals on all levels. I decided then only to work where my knowledge and skills were valued. I literally and figuratively went "home" to an HBCU where I am now an associate professor. HBCUs face their own set of problems, but I take solace in the fact that if I am ever mistreated or disliked, it will not be because I am Black.

REFERENCES

Abdelaziz, M., Matthews, J., Campos, I., Fannin, D., Riveria Perez, J., Wilhite, M., & Williams, R. (2021). Student stories: Microaggressions in communication sciences and disorders. *American Journal of Speech-Language Pathology*, 30(5), 1990–2002. 10.1044/2021_AJSLP-21-0003034432987

Alger, R. (2024). Drop Out Rates among First-Generation Undergraduate Students in the United States. Ballard Brief. January 2024. www.ballardbrief.byu.edu

American Speech-Language-Hearing Association. (2020). *Profile of ASHA members and affiliates, year-end 2021.* www.asha.org

Gayles, J. G. (2022). Does anyone see us? Disposability of Black women faculty in the academy. *Diverse.* https://www.diverseeducation.com/opinion/article/15295726/does-anyone-see-us-disposability-of-black-women-faculty-in-the-academy

Gregory, K. (2020). Moving Forward as a Profession in a Time of Uncertainty. *The ASHA Leader Blog.* https://leader.pubs.asha.org/do/10.1044/leader.FMP.25082020.8/full/?fbclid=IwAR3uSS3BGgPGOKGLUMb1O55ozWvPbY-_j30C98PxDN6PcrnmJrHaniv1RwQ

Hill, A. (2021). *Changing the rules changes the game...and not for the better.* https://tnnonprofits.org/blog-posts/2020/7/30/goalpostsmove

Mishra, A., Nunez, G., & Tyson, G. (2021). Faculty of color in communication sciences and disorders: An overdue conversation. Perspectives of ASHA Special Interest Group – SIG 10. *American Speech-Language-Hearing Association*, 6(4), 778–782. 10.1044/2021_PERSP-20-00176

Ortiz, E. (2020). *Racial violence and a pandemic: How the Red Summer of 1919 relates to 2020.* https://www.nbcnews.com/news/us-news/racial-violence-pandemic-how-red-summer-1919-relates-2020-n1231499

Sue, S. W., Rivera, D. P., Watkins, N. L., Kim, R. H., Kim, S., & Williams, C. D. (2011, July). Racial dialogues: Challenges faculty of color face in the classroom. *Cultural Diversity & Ethnic Minority Psychology*, 17(3), 331–340. 10.1037/a002419021787066

Whitfield, J. (2022). Systemic racism in communication sciences and disorders academic programs: A commentary on trends in racial representation. *American Journal of Speech-Language Pathology*, 32(1), 381–390. 10.1044/2022_AJSLP-22-0021036450159

Chapter 5
Leading and Surviving With Aftershocks

Bri'Yana Nicole Merrill
https://orcid.org/0009-0003-8445-9619
George Mason University, USA

ABSTRACT

In this chapter there will be a closer examination into the emotional tax that is experienced by young, Black student leaders within institutions of higher education. The emotional taxes are amplified feelings of isolation and otherness within the workplace due to gender, race, and/or ethnicity. As a result, the person is left with the arduous task of flourishing at work. While this term was originally coined to explain the experiences of marginalized professionals in the workplace, it can also be explained in the context of student leaders in colleges and universities. Throughout this chapter, the author will highlight the impact of racial trauma on Black students and propose strategies for self-care. Through these techniques and self-reflection there is an emphasis on the importance of being bold in one's self-identity and authenticity.

INTRODUCTION

Being a student leader is one of the most rewarding experiences a person can have during their college experience. In leadership positions, one can promote sustainable change while also being a voice for students on campus. Yet, the experience of Black student leaders in white spaces does not necessarily look the same as their non-Black peers. Not only must they show up 100% of the time to lead, but they must also deal with the trauma stemming from the injustices and inequalities that

DOI: 10.4018/979-8-3693-0698-7.ch005

Copyright © 2024, IGI Global. Copying or distributing in print or electronic forms without written permission of IGI Global is prohibited.

plague their identity inside and outside of the bounds of their institution. Moreover, the intersectionality of being Black and a woman takes an even greater toll.

The nature of intersectionality means one cannot extricate a portion of one's identity. Each segment of identity, especially when being a woman and considered a minority can produce unique and specific experiences of discrimination. Experiences of discrimination and prejudice can cause a person to experience aftershocks. In this context, an aftershock is a reaction or feeling after experiencing a racially traumatic event. The aftershock effect often persists well beyond the initial event, which can prolong and even intensify the impact of the event. In this chapter, we will explore this phenomenon from the lens of a student leader, and how the author was able to survive them.

EXPLORING IDENTITY

Words can shape, inspire, and change the world around us. Words are the reason we behave in certain ways, the reason we have certain perspectives, and words often contribute to the reasons we find ourselves in certain circumstances. Identity is a word with the power to disrupt our unique and unfiltered views about ourselves and others, when it seems we are attacked, called out or put down. Self-identity, or the lack thereof, can be altered and/or damaged by a person's speech. Without a clear sense of self-identity, stereotypes can influence a person into believing they are someone they're not. Without a firmly rooted foundation of self-identity, a person can lose themselves and feel the need to impress others by conforming to society's standards, much to their own detriment. When that happens, power, influence, focus, productivity and leadership are sacrificed in favor of being a follower who may not experience confidence nor success. Growing up, I recognized my skin color was different than many of my friends. At the time, however, I didn't understand this difference would impact me, the way I saw myself, and the way I would be treated by those "friends." It wasn't until I heard the phrase, "It was just a joke," that I knew my skin color had more influence than I could imagine. I was eight years old when I experienced this otherness. The feeling of being an outcast made me self-conscious of my appearance. Worried about what others may think of me, I began to change the way I talked to fit in and "sound proper." I even tried to flat iron my hair every day in the hopes that my hair could grow longer like most of the women on TV. As I matured, was exposed to more, and had diverse experiences, my self-identity became rooted in confidence, clarity, and vision. I was finally able to embrace who I am, and who I was created to be. I remember being inspired by a social movement which began when I was about twelve. "#BlackGirlMagic" sparked curiosity in me to learn more about my culture, and to be proud of what I learned about the successes, talents and amazement, Black women in today's society. I stopped identifying with the straight, long hair like some of my old dolls, and non-Black women on TV. I began to wear my hair in its natural state; curly, full and beautiful. I felt unstoppable. Clear self-identity is powerful. It is introspective as it radiates, allowing those in the world to sense our energy, which can also empower those around us. As someone who once had difficulty discovering my true self identity, representing my most authentic self was the best thing that has happened to me.

JOURNEY TO COLLEGE

Three hours and forty-three minutes. This was the time it would take to leave my hometown and arrive at my destination: college. I was excited to embark on this new journey and take on the next four years. Exiting a jammed-pack truck with my family, filled with my belongings, I stepped foot onto campus; the place I would call home feeling proud of myself for what I had done, and excited for what was to come. Becoming a student leader was far from my mind. I was ready to explore what it meant to have freedom. After many welcome speeches and prayers, orientation weekend finally began. This is when it hit me. While I knew I was going from a predominantly black high school to a predominately white institution (PWI), nothing prepared me for this moment. The culture shock was suffocating and paralyzing all at the same time. Culture shock is the feeling of otherness and confusion when entering an environment or culture that is different from your own. In an article on Black acculturation, studies show that the feeling of the outgroup from stressors related to culture can manifest adverse mental health outcomes (Gomez et al., 2011). This was the first time in a school setting when I felt the need to code switch so that I would "fit in" and not "stand out." As if that was possible. Consequently, I found myself dimming my light and personality to appease my white peers. I felt like an imposter; a stranger to the person I once was. And actually, they didn't tell me to behave this way, there was something instinctive inside of me which said, be compliant, choose conformity so you will be safe. Unfortunately, this is not a unique and individualized experience. Many Black students entering the confines of a PWI experience discomfort and disconnect when entering these white spaces. These outcomes can pose a greater difficulty for Black women because we experience greater scrutiny, more stress, less support and less understanding than our white female peers as we navigate college.

BECOMING A STUDENT LEADER

I was grateful for my family and support-system during this time. They encouraged me regularly through conversations, shared experiences, and prayer. Long after orientation and into my second semester of my freshman year, I began to transform and evolve into a more confident version of the person I was before. I was bold, and expressive, recognizing my presence could positively impact my environment, bringing value to those who encountered me. This is when I began my first leadership position as secretary for a social justice student organization. I made a vow that if I was going to be a leader, I would lead with integrity and be my authentic self. I believed my leadership strengths would inspire generations through my innovative thinking, creativity, and strong commitment to building a community around me. This first leadership experience in college was the beginning of a memorable and lesson-filled college journey. Within the next year, I would become a Resident Assistant (RA), and the Public Relations chair of the Black Student Union.

My active participation in Black Student Union (BSU) was pivotal in the connections I was able to make with my Black peers across campus. Not only was BSU a place to learn and immerse yourself into Black culture, but it was also a space for laughter, fun, and connection. The passion and love I have for BSU is truly indescribable. As I continued to get more involved in BSU, I knew that I wanted to take a leap of faith and apply to be the BSU president during my junior year. I wanted to be in the position where I could make sustainable change within the organization and on campus, empower our members, and create a safe environment to have difficult conversations when needed. At the end of my candidate speech, I shared these sentiments: "I do not want you to vote for me because I am your friend. I do not want you to vote for me because I am your RA; and I do not want your vote simply because I am nice. I want you to vote for me because you can feel and see the passion that I have for this organization and in your heart, you believe that I will do everything that I can to propel BSU to new and greater heights and not be intimidated by any hardships along the way."

The speech was well-received, and I was voted in as BSU President, one of my most memorable experiences. This was so impactful to me because I knew what it was like entering college and not knowing anyone around me. The feeling of going into a classroom where no one looked like me made me feel like an outsider. It was so important for me to create and sustain an environment and space where Black students could be one thousand percent themselves. I found peace in learning that being a leader isn't simply about conducting meetings and delegating tasks, but it's also about being the person who will stand through the good times and challenging times. It's about being an emotionally intelligent leader, especially during times of conflict and being open to new ideas and perspectives.

A similar feeling was experienced by Jasmine, a recent college graduate that was interviewed for this chapter. She had many leadership experiences ranging from being a fundraising chair, spirit chair, and concert chair her junior year, all while being an RA. She wanted to be a student leader to give back to her community and make a difference at her university. Another main drive to be a student leader was that she wanted to be a role model for those who were coming behind her. This meant her siblings, cousins, and extended family because she is the first woman in her family who's attending a four-year university. With that came a certain level of expectation. She finished her senior year by becoming the President of our African Student Association. "The most memorable experience I had as a student leader was trying to start a new organization on campus. I had to see it through from creating a constitution, to finding an E-board, and scheduling meetings. These were all the things that go on in the background that many others don't get to see" (Jasmine, personal communication, January 3, 2024). While the creation of the African Student Association was proven to be a success after they became a registered student organization on campus, there were still barriers to its existence that Jasmine had to face: "I had to over explain why an organization like this was needed on campus while most students were white. I also had to explain why Africans and people of color on campus needed a place for themselves to feel free to hang out with people who are similar and have somewhat of the same experiences as them. I had to further illustrate how this organization was going to be different from the Black Student Association. These challenges helped to drive the E-board to keep pushing through and make the mark that is necessary on campus" (Jasmine, personal communication, January 3, 2024). I enjoyed listening to Jasmine's story and how she created more spaces for students on campus. In college, it oftentimes felt like my white peers viewed Black culture as a one-dimensional space. Across the Black diaspora, there's multiple languages, expressive styles, music, and perspectives and it's important to continue to learn and embrace the many facets of Black culture.

I also interviewed Alese, a Black woman who graduated with her bachelor's and master's degree from PWIs. During her time as an undergraduate student, she served as an RA, BSU Vice President, and student body Vice President. To Alese, being a student leader meant leading by example and giving voice to her constituents. In her role as student body vice president, she wanted to make sure there was proper representation of the entire student body and that she was vocal about the things that needed to be changed. The changes included increased opportunities for students, student empowerment, and creating an environment on campus where everyone feels like they belong. She felt a difference in how she was treated in her BSU role versus how she was treated as student body vice president. The Senate leadership did not respect her as much as she wanted them to. From the tone of their voice to the reactions she received after she was done speaking, the people and her environment made her feel ignored. These actions felt as if they did not fully accept that she was in the position to make decisions. She was most comfortable and respected in her leadership role within BSU. She attributed this to having a greater connection because of their shared identity. In addition to this, the people on the leadership team listened to her a lot more than the people on the senate leadership team. One of the drawbacks was that whenever the team would work hard to plan events for the entire campus, the same people attended. After she graduated and the killing of George Floyd occurred, she saw a lot of people on social media from college wishing they did more when they were still in school. However, they gave people on campus many opportunities to have immersive cultural and educational dialogue.

RACIAL EPITHETS AND THE FEELING OF PARALYSIS

A notable time for Black achievement, accomplishment, and remembrance is Black History Month in February. In the year of my presidency within BSU, I was excited and anxious to ensure that all the planning came together for the month of February. We had a month filled with different events and we were excited to kick off our celebration with a virtual Black-owned business panel. This panel incorporated various entrepreneurs from the community. However, the Black excellence that exuded from our panelist was quickly overshadowed by blatant hate speech from Zoom bombers, along with unwanted disrupters in our Zoom meeting. The unknown participants joined the call and screamed racist remarks. The Zoom host was unable to mute or remove the hackers due to them taking over the meeting electronically. The racists screamed, "Black lives don't matter," "White power rules," and repeatedly called everyone on the Zoom call the n-word; over and over again. Not only did this occur, but the hackers began to display child pornography across the screen. Students, faculty, and guests were forcibly exposed to this. The Zoom call finally stopped, and the meeting ended.

At that moment, my body was paralyzed. I began to get a rush of messages and phone calls, but all my body could do was sit there. I felt so dehumanized, triggered, and disgusted by this Zoom call experience. Finally, I forced myself out of paralysis and talked to our advisor and my vice president over the phone. We were all traumatized. There were so many tears that fell on our three-way call. After pouring out the pain, I knew my priority was to first work through the emotions I was feeling so that I could support the other students who were on that Zoom call. Not only was it triggering for myself and many others, but everyone on the executive board agreed that we must first take the time necessary to process.

After a day or so, the executive team began to work on our next steps. We drafted a statement to be sent to the campus, and we created a "Stand for Solidarity" event a week later. We needed to heal. We hoped this event would help us in doing so. At this event, there was a combination of poetry readings, a call-to-action. In this call to action, we created an opportunity for accountability, allyship, and connection. Dressed in all black attire, hundreds of students and faculty attended this event, including a few from the community. The program ended with reflection:

- Take a moment to think about how this disgusting incident made you feel. Did you feel rage, despair, guilt, numbness?
- What were your actions following the event? Did you immediately try to spread the word, educate yourself on the situation, or just take time to process what happened?
- Have you taken time to check in on your brothers and sisters who were affected by the incident?
- Think about what you can do right now to uplift the Black community? What is something you can do that is in your power and control?

After the reflection and remarks, we had a banner which allowed people to pledge and sign. The banner read, "Progress is Continuous" to symbolize justice, intentionality, allyship, and hope. This statement recognizes that the fight for justice is not over and that everyone plays a part in this progress. While there has been improvement in racial justice and equality, there is still work to be done. This is the point we wanted to highlight to all the students, faculty, and staff at our school.

We did not let the incident prevent us from celebrating the rest of our planned events during Black History Month. While this was a terrible experience for any student to have to go through, I was lucky that I was able to lean on my peers within BSU. The connection of the group strengthened, and we were more empowered than ever to advance our organization's mission.

A few months after the Zoom bomb, we found out it was a minor from a different state who had done the damage. Although some students wanted the incident to be reported more broadly, because of the inclusion of pornography, we could not share the recording because we would be breaking the law. It felt like the Federal investigation which ensued, as a result, happened because of that – the porn – rather than the racial violence we faced. The weeks after that event were difficult. The executive board of BSU carried out the rest of the events we had planned for February. While it was a joy celebrating Black history, the racist remarks from the Zoom call rippled through my mind like aftershocks. Life continued for a lot of people around me and yet, I still felt trapped in that paralysis.

SOCIETAL IMPACT ON BLACK STUDENTS

Student organizations across colleges and universities provide an opportunity for students to feel more connected to campus, and the people around them. From multicultural organizations to religious organizations, fraternities, and sororities, these are all ways in which students can get involved on campus. For these organizations' student leaders, there is increased pressure to ensure things run smoothly as they uphold the organizations' mission and values. Outside of these duties, they must also practice self-care and self-awareness to effectively lead the organization and its members, as issues of discrimination, verbal attacks, passive aggressive comments and violence can often open the door to experience undue stress, imposter syndrome, and trouble coping. My personal experience from these events caused a lot of anxiety in addition to the responsibilities which came with being a student in leadership. During the many leadership training sessions in which I participated during my undergraduate years, I was not prepared for the emotional toll of external forces. Local and global issues affected how I would show up in my classes and leadership positions. This had harsh effects on my mental health.

Racial trauma and inequality can have grave effects on a lot of student leaders. In an article by the Washington Post, polls have shown that factors beyond a person's control such as politics, race relations, and inflation can create stress among adults (Johnson, 2023). For those who are constantly battling inequities, stress can multiply within the body. Threats and the anticipations of threats can have life-altering effects on the body. With this, the body will begin to produce an excessive amount of cortisol that makes it difficult for the body to bring itself back to normal (Johnson, 2023). Produced by the adrenal glands, cortisol is released into the bloodstream when a person endures stress (Johnson, 2023). A profusion of cortisol can quickly lead to various health problems (Johnson, 2023). I found it difficult to concentrate at times, especially when I would read so many breaking news articles about Black people being senselessly killed. I vividly remember learning about Breonna Taylor, a beautiful Black woman who was brazenly killed by the police. This prompted a lot of discussions with my friends and family on the matter. We were angry, disappointed, fearful, and most of all, tired. For people to be so senseless and cruel due to prejudice that they use their positions to inflict fatal violence is completely unacceptable. Despite the many social media posts, protests, and public outcries for justice to be served, we mostly felt powerless. A common chant was, "Say her name. Breonna Taylor." Hearing it aloud would send chills up and down my spine, as we share the same name phonetically. Hearing the chants made me more hypersensitive to the world around me. I was unhappy, angry, and fearful all at the same time. This story could have easily been me or any of my friends and family. I was tired. Tired of the same story with the same outcome. I appreciated the professors who would take time to discuss matters happening beyond the university. There was acknowledgement by several that these issues do impact students even if one does not know someone personally. Many of us grieved the pain of the deaths, the multiple, senseless, unaccounted for deaths. The effects of the external issues riddled with violent disparities created a great sense of emotional tax for us, as it does with current Black student leaders. The emotional tax amplified feelings of isolation and otherness within the workplace due to gender, race, and/or ethnicity. These identities within me are inextricable from one another, producing a different level of discrimination. This has posed difficulty for me in the workplace and at school. Jasmine resonated with the experience of emotional tax when she was in college. She constantly felt like she was in a fishbowl and knew her actions were being scrutinized differently than her peers. She also felt the added pressure within the classroom, "When a certain topic regarding people of color would come up in class, all of a sudden, they were expecting me to be the voice of everyone" (Jasmine, personal communication, January 3, 2024). Being the voice of everyone is not possible; however, there were many instances when she forced herself to speak up, using her voice when there was no other voice. "In student organizational leadership meetings, I had to speak up because all of the perspectives that would be given were not considering people who looked like us" (Jasmine, personal communication, January 3, 2024). Overall, that was one of the most challenging things trying to navigate her PWI. While constantly feeling like she was under a microscope, Jasmine also felt like there was no room for failure, "You cannot seem like you do not have it all together. You must be on top of all your responsibilities and the best. I had to be the best at everything because I could not afford to fail in these kinds of situations" (Jasmine, personal communication, January 3, 2024). Alese did not know that there was even a term for the experiences she went through in college until after she graduated. In her sophomore and junior years, she used to welcome educational questions that her white peers had about her experiences as a Black woman. However, she realized that it quickly became emotionally exhausting. She started to feel like a token, as if she had to fit into a specific type of persona; this took a greater toll on her. While her leadership positions made her happy, there were a lot of emotional aspects parts she had to navigate that she had not previously considered. Feeling the need to overcompensate to combat the preconceived notions that plague one's identity is a phenomenon that many Black students experience, especially women.

AFTERSHOCK

Racial trauma can refer to a specific incident of racial discrimination or the ongoing, harmful emotional impact of racial discrimination that builds up over time. In some cases, [these experiences] may lead to PTSD (Va, 2021). This topic is important due to how racial trauma can have neurological effects on individuals. These neurological effects in turn create physical alterations in the brain. Posttraumatic Stress Disorder, commonly known as PTSD, is a psychiatric disorder that can potentially develop in people who have had an experience that was traumatic. This event can threaten the person physically, emotionally, or spiritually (APA, 2023). U.S. Latinos, African Americans, and Native Americans/Alaska Natives are each disproportionately affected and have higher rates of PTSD than non-Latino whites (APA, 2023). Outside of the trauma of the event itself, people oftentimes experience triggers after the event. For instance, a person experiencing racial discrimination may have aftershocks that occur from places, people, or thoughts that reminds them of that traumatic event (Va, 2021). When a person witnesses or experiences an unsettling event, the brain transmits a signal, triggering a reaction. Unfortunately, whether an event occurs once or multiple times, the exposure to racism can have adverse effects on a person's brain which could lead to poor health outcomes (Okeke et al., 2022). There was a study done on Black women who reported having experiences with racial discrimination where scans were done on their brains. After assessing the women's MRI scans, it was found that there were changes in their white matter (Okeke et al., 2022). The white matter tissue of the brain contains axons which form connections between neurons (Okeke et al., 2022). The big picture of this research is to delve into the physical changes that occur when a person develops PTSD, especially within Black individuals. Whether you are going into the medical field, higher education, or even into Corporate America, understanding and acknowledging the way that external factors can impact a person internally is very important.

At the height of racial injustice and violence, I became lethargic, despondent and less productive. While some professors could tell I was not myself at times, others quickly assumed that I was slacking and intentionally ignoring my responsibilities. How could I explain my experience of withdrawal from class to people who do not look like me and just simply would not understand? Sometimes these emotions would come in waves like aftershocks from a rough storm. I did several things to cope and grapple with these feelings. One of which was drafting the following poem to express my attitude and emotions:

> "Aftershocks are earthquakes that follow the largest shock of an earthquake sequence. They are smaller than the mainshock. Aftershocks can last days, weeks, months, or years.

Black people are left with the aftershocks of losing their loved ones.

Actually, let me take a step back and change that.

Black people are left with the aftershocks of their loved ones being taken from them.

Little Black children are being ripped from the grip of their parent's love.

Husbands and Wives are losing their Kings and Queens.

What happens when you give a racist the power to eradicate a human race one by one?

You do not know? Live in America while Black and I am sure you'll find out.

What affects one, will affect all. The Aftershock.

It is crazy how bullets can soar freely through the sky into buildings and homes and not dare harm the structure itself and STILL find a way to gravitate towards the darkest people in the room.

Shattering Black bodies like glass into little pieces; little pieces leaving them to be picked up by families who are left broken themselves.

It pains me how twelve can take so many pieces of me. How 12 can shoot so many bullets into me and play hopscotch over those pieces to their next victim.

What affects one, will affect all. The Aftershock.

That possibility affects me each and every day.

Anxiety becomes a blanket around my brain and the thread weaves into every single brain cell of my mind until I'm held captive of my own self.

So don't you tell me that I shouldn't fear for my life when the red and blue lights of injustice pierce through my rear-view mirror onto my melanated skin.

Don't tell me that my GPA and involvement here on this campus will save me from the racism that is carefully woven into the very fabric of this society and nation.

What affects one, will affect all. The Aftershock

So yes, when I see Black men, Black women, and Black children get brutally attacked and murdered in the racist streets of America, I lose a piece of myself every time.

I lose a piece of my joy.

I lose a piece of my comfort.

I lose a piece of my sanity.

I lose a piece of my patience.

Not because of the simple fact that it could be me, but because every time I walk out my front door the chances are greater that it will be me.

Every time I lay my head down at night in my own home, it could be me.

Every time I walk across the street with my friends, it could be me.

What affects one, will affect all. The Aftershock.

So, when I see that breaking news headline in all caps bold across my television screen,
I cry tears of sadness and anger every single time.
We may not be blood, but Black people will ALWAYS be MY people.
I can still feel the aftershocks of Michael Brown,
I can still feel the aftershocks of Breonna Taylor.
I can still feel the aftershocks of Ahmaud Arbery.
I can still feel the aftershocks of George Floyd.
I can still feel the aftershocks of Daunte Wright.
Because whatever affects one directly,
affects us all indirectly.
And that is what you call the Aftershock."

There would be times when I would sit in class with my heart so heavy, and oftentimes angry. Seeing people who looked like me dehumanized in their homes, at work, at school, and even just out in public. It was exhausting trying to be happy all the time. I found it difficult to give myself emotional grace when societal racial issues arose. Drafting this poem gave me an alternative way to express my emotions rather than internalizing them. This ignited the passion within me to keep going. Every step forward was a way to remember those who were lost along the way, and fight for justice.

STRATEGIES TO COPE WITH AFTERSHOCKS

Being a student leader includes empowering those around you to be the best version of themselves. I think a lot of the time, we identify a student leader as someone with the biggest title while scheduling meetings and telling others what to do. However, I did not want that to be my legacy. I was intrigued by the different ideas of my peers and how we could incorporate everyone's strengths to produce favorable outcomes. Being a student leader means not forgetting who you are. Amid everything going on, it is easy to put others before ourselves. In full transparency, it took me a long time to understand what self-care meant to me. Practicing self-care can be accomplished in different ways like taking naps, manicures, pedicures, cooking a delicious meal, spending time in person or virtually with a favorite friend or family member, taking yourself on a date, or writing and journaling. Alese made sure that she surrounded herself with people who supported her, and those with which she was comfortable. She reflected that she would not have made it through college without her best friends.

In Jasmine's leadership capacity, a way in which she practiced self-care was setting boundaries. Since she was a RA with over thirty residents, she had to be intentional in allocating time for herself. Similarly to Alese, Jasmine also enjoyed spending time with friends. She felt like we sometimes take for granted the time we spend with people we love. Each hour she got to spend with her friends helped and motivated her. She was finally able to not have an entire to-do list in the back of her head. As you can see, different strategies can have a wide array of effects on people. If you are looking for a few ideas, I have some strategies that has helped me in my student leadership roles in college:

1. THERAPY

I later realized that tasks to get my mind off of things did not sustain me over a long time. That is when I began to go to therapy. It has really changed my complete outlook on what it meant to take care of myself, and what it meant to love myself. My therapist gave me the space to work through my emotions rather than working around them. There are still stigmas surrounding mental health and therapy that echo in the back of people's minds. A disconnect can be the lack of diverse representation in the counseling center at PWIs. Black students tend to be more likely to use mental health services on campus if there was a Black counselor, rather than just a white counselor (Nickerson et al., 1994). I found this to be true as I am personally more comfortable with a Black counselor, regardless of their gender. During my time in therapy, I learned that it's okay to be vulnerable to those you trust. Holding my feelings in did so much damage that I convinced myself that nothing was wrong. Another barrier to Black students getting the help that they need is mistrust. As previously mentioned, discrimination and bias have led to great mistrust of American medicine. When examining this, it is important to recognize some of the roots and foundations that have caused it. One of which is the racist experiences that patients have experienced in the healthcare system. An example of this is the Tuskegee Syphilis Study. This study was conducted by the United States Public Health Service and the Centers for Disease Control and Prevention on hundreds of African Americans between 1932 and 1972 (CDC, 2022). This is only one of many ways that diverse populations have been mistreated by the healthcare system. Researchers believed it was permissible to not provide effective care to the African American participants as their disease began to fully progress. This left many of the participants with severe health problems including mental impairment, blindness, or death. Researchers failed these participants greatly and did not collect informed consent. It is important to note that inequities within the healthcare system can happen to any marginalized identity, or vulnerable group of people. Yet, the trust must not fall on the patient themselves to build, but it is the responsibility of the physician (Sullivan, 2020). Although the Tuskegee Syphilis Study occurred in the 1900's, we still see the ripple effects to this day. Not only with continued injustices in the field, but also with the way that Black people respond to health care providers. It is crucial that colleges and universities make a conscious effort to diversify their staff and not let cultural incompetence be the reason a student is not able to receive the help that they need. The first therapists I ever had was a Black woman. Not only was she able to understand some of the different things I was going through, but her approach also made me more comfortable going to therapy regularly. I have noticed a significant shift in my life after taking time for the things that bring me joy while going to therapy. I consistently went to therapy for about 8 months. I journaled more and started to feel more confident in who I was, and the woman I was becoming.

2. REFLECT ON WHAT BRINGS YOU THE MOST JOY

When dealing with compounding issues that happen on and off your campus, it is important to find outlets. This can range from artistic activities, spending time with friends and family, or exploring various places in your city. Having an added activity to look forward to outside of school and work is a fantastic way to decompress and focus your mind on something different. I found myself often writing poetry and enjoying the outdoors. On campus, there was a hammock that few people knew about, and I would lay there and look up at the sky above me with music playing in my ears. In my poetry, I can dissect many of my layers and experiences. From the blessings to the storms in my life, I can write about it and eventually, I can share it with the world. Actions did ease my mind in those tough moments, it oftentimes felt like a quick fix. If I were stressed out for the day and there was a lot going on in the organization that involved conflict management, I would just go home and do those self-care tasks that I knew would help at that moment.

3. JOIN AN AFFINITY ORGANIZATION

Joining clubs like the Black Student Union, African Student Association, and women empowerment organizations are a wonderful way to branch out and meet people who may have similar interests as you. These are great organizations to connect with people with similar experiences. Another advantage to joining these organizations is that you can increase your knowledge about other cultures around you. I remember how I would learn so much from the African Student Association, and I found myself learning something new at every single event I attended. It was also nice to see some of the overlap of our shared experiences while also appreciating our differences. If the organization you are looking for is not on your campus, you can be the one to change that. Jasmine noticed an unmet need on her campus and went through the proper channels to fill the gap. When doing so, it is helpful to find a group of students and faculty who would support and be an ally with you during the process.

REFLECTIONS AND ADVICE

As an African American woman, society expects me to become a certain way due to those attributes about myself; I proved society wrong. Through my efforts to promote racial equality in my community, I reject the notion of conforming to societal standards of who I should be, and continue to embrace who I am. While the college experience was far from easy, I had an amazing village that constantly supported me. I had mentors who instilled so much wisdom and encouragement in me that I could not contain it just for myself. There may be a young Black woman who plans to go to college or are in college right now as you are reading this. There is so much advice that we want to share with you, but here are a few points that stood out. Whether your support system is large or small, we hope these words will empower and uplift, no matter what obstacle college may bring.

I asked Jasmine and Alese if there was any advice they would give to young Black women entering college for the first time:

It is going to be hard but you're going to get through it. I feel like there are a lot of times where I couldn't see the day I would be graduating. I could not see the day when this whole chapter would be behind me. I am like it's a journey and it's a process like everything else in life. Understand that an exam grade was probably not your best but you're going to come up, so just enjoy the process while it's happening because you won't be stuck there forever. Enjoy it while it lasts. Savor every moment of it, the struggles, the experiences, the fun times. Enjoy all of it. You are going to get to the end eventually. (Jasmine, personal communication, January 3, 2024)

Be your most authentic self. There is always going to be someone who doesn't like you, but remember that's their problem, not your problem. If there is something you're passionate about, go for it. Keep saying your opinion, even if you feel like someone is going against your views. At the end of the day, the only person that is going to be with you through life whether you lose friends or gain friends, is you. (Alese, personal communication, November 16, 2024)

I know sometimes you may not be understood, or you may be looked down upon for the way you act, the way you dress, the way you are. However, I feel like being yourself puts you in rooms you were meant to be in. The best way to succeed is to be yourself. You will be able to look back and be proud that you did not have to compromise your character, beliefs, and who you are to fit within a system that was not even built for us anyway. (Jasmine, personal communication, January 3, 2024)

AN OPEN LETTER TO THE BLACK WOMAN

Finally, here is an open letter, specifically for you:

Dear Black girl,

Do you know that your light shines bright?

Do you know that when you walk into a room, your presence commands attention?

Do you know that your words have power, and your feet will walk into places far beyond what you could have imagined?

Black girl, did you know that your voice can impact millions?

Your voice is so powerful that many of those around you will try to silence it. Did you know that you are a queen in every possible way? Your black skin represents beauty, not bondage. Your past represents overcoming, not from the struggles of those who tried to overcome. Your intellect is instilled with exquisite power.

Black girl,

Walk onto your campus with your head held high and show them who you really are.

For this may be a new experience, but you were destined for greatness.

Don't be afraid to be a disrupter.

Push boundaries and shatter glass ceilings.

Black girl, know that we support you, we're rooting for you, and there's nothing you can't accomplish.

Black girl, you got this.

~Your fellow Black girl

REFERENCES

Akilah Johnson, C. G. (2023a, October 17). *Stress is weathering our bodies from the inside out.* The Washington Post._https://www.washingtonpost.com/ health/ interactive/2023/ stress-chronic-illness-aging/?itid=hp-top-table-main_p004_f002

Beatty, C. C., Bush, A. A., Erxleben, E. E., Ferguson, T. L., Harrell, A. T., & Sahachartsiri, W. K. (2010). Black Student Leaders: The Influence of Social Climate in Student Organizations. *Journal of the Student Personnel Association at Indiana University*, 38, 48–63. https://scholarworks.iu.edu/ journals/index.php/ jiuspa/ article/view/5002

Gomez, J., Miranda, R., & Polanco, L. (2011). Acculturative stress, perceived discrimination, and vulnerability to suicide attempts among emerging adults. *Journal of Youth and Adolescence*, 40(11), 1465–1476. 10.1007/s10964-011-9688-921717234

Lewis, J. A., Williams, M. G., Peppers, E. J., & Gadson, C. A. (2017). Applying intersectionality to explore the relations between gendered racism and health among Black women. *Journal of Counseling Psychology*, 64(5), 475–486. 10.1037/ cou000023129048194

Sullivan, L. S. (2020). Trust, risk, and race in American Medicine. *The Hastings Center Report*, 50(1), 18–26. 10.1002/hast.108032068281

Va.gov: Veterans Affairs. Racial Trauma. (2021, August 16). Retrieved October 2, 2023, from https://www.ptsd.va.gov/ understand/types/racial_trauma.asp

What is posttraumatic stress disorder (PTSD)? (n.d.). Psychiatry.org - What is Posttraumatic Stress Disorder (PTSD)? https://www.psychiatry.org/ patients-families/ ptsd/ what-is-ptsd#:~:text= Posttraumatic%20stress% 20disorder%20(PTSD)% 20is,events%20or%20set% 20of%20circumstances

KEY TERMS AND DEFINITIONS

Affinity Organization: An organization that connects people from similar backgrounds. This can be ethnic, cultural, or religious.

Aftershock: A reaction or feeling after experiencing a racially traumatic event.

Black Diaspora: People from African descent scattered to different areas around the world both voluntary and by force.

Culture Shock: The feeling of otherness and confusion when entering an environment or culture that is different from your own.

Dehumanize: To strip someone from their human attributes, such as dignity, in a degrading manner.

Disrupter: A person who is not afraid to break through the barriers of societal norms.

PWI: Known as a Predominantly White Institution, these colleges have more than 50% of white students enrolled.

Student Leader: A student in the position to promote sustainable change while also taking care of their personal needs.:

Section 2
Stories of Us

Chapter 6
That's the Way Love Goes:
On Black Women Leaders, Family Stories, and Higher Education

Eboni L. Sterling
House Esther LLC, USA

ABSTRACT

Black women leaders are daring to reimagine higher education. Infusing love in their leadership practices, they embark on unconventional journeys. Repurposing family stories, these leaders consider love and apply the elusive concept to leadership. The utility of retrospective family storytelling fortifies Black women leaders in this quest. In the challenging realm of academia, Black women battle to survive professionally and personally. Arguably, retrospective family storytelling is a determinant of Black women leaders' survival and sustenance at predominately white institutions of higher education. A complex relationship remains between Black women in academia and the metanarratives manufactured by the dominant group. Even when Black women reach the pinnacle of success, the threat of exclusion and marginalization looms. Often, racial and gender-related stressors are backdrops. Despite these challenges, Black women employ progressive strategies, such as love, as a means of resistance, a tactical force to reconfigure the anatomy of higher education.

INTRODUCTION

In the latter half of the 20th century, the United States workforce experienced significant growth in diversity. Today's workforce is increasingly diverse in age, sex, and ethnicity, necessitating diverse leadership (Holder et al., 2015). Although

DOI: 10.4018/979-8-3693-0698-7.ch006

Copyright © 2024, IGI Global. Copying or distributing in print or electronic forms without written permission of IGI Global is prohibited.

women comprise 47% of the workforce, breaking into leadership roles beyond middle management remains a persistent challenge (U.S. Bureau of Labor Statistics, 2011). Black women's labor force participation rate of 59.4% is projected to decrease to 58.8% by 2026 (Toossi & Joyner, 2018). In the context of these challenges, Bagati (2008) noted a 219% increase in professional and graduate degree attainment among Black women from 1991 to 2001. However, Holder et al. (2015) emphasized that despite being a significant and growing talent pool, Black women, the largest female group with educational degrees, lack representation in leadership.

As Black women ascend beyond the confines of the glass and concrete ceiling to claim leadership positions, they find themselves entangled in racial and social challenges. This turbulent journey involves grappling with the relentless currents of microaggressions, discrimination, stereotyping, invisibility, hypervisibility, surveillance, and racial battle fatigue. While the literature frequently outlines tribulations encountered on their path, a critical void remains in understanding the influence of family storytelling in the lives of Black women leaders. This book chapter attempts to bridge the scholarly gap with a thorough inquiry into the multifaceted layers of their existence.

LITERATURE REVIEW

Black women's resilience and self-development have historically defied oppression's gravity. Well before the proverb "each one, teach one" became ingrained in African American culture, during slavery, Black women risked their lives to acquire proficiency in the English language. Despite the dangers, they became educators, teaching fellow enslaved individuals to read and write (Jones et al., 2012). Before the Civil War, educating a slave was illegal, but some, with allies and bravery, pursued education in secret. Others were granted limited education for labor or religious purposes (Jones et al., 2012; Solomon, 1985). The post-Civil War era marked a turning point, particularly for Black women. Chamberlain (1991) noted that before this conflict, women and African Americans were barred from higher learning experiences. The war's conclusion brought about significant changes with the Morrill Acts of 1862 and 1890; these legislative acts combined to create policies facilitating coeducational attainment for Black women (Chamberlain, 1991).

The momentum towards equity and nondiscrimination gained traction with significant policy changes in the mid-20th century. In 1964, pivotal measures were enacted to prohibit employment discrimination against women and marginalized groups through The Civil Rights Act of 1964 and the introduction of affirmative action (American Association for Access, Equity and Diversity, n.d.). This period also saw the establishment of the Higher Education Act of 1965, which played a crucial role in alleviating the financial burden of higher learning for Black women (Roebuck & Murty, 1993). Building on these policy shifts, the Civil Rights Movement continued to advance. Throughout the 1960s, 1970s, and 1980s, higher education experienced a significant surge in Black student enrollment and an increased presence among administrators and professors (Roebuck & Murty, 1993).

BARRIERS AND CHALLENGES FOR BLACK WOMEN LEADERS

An immediate and persistent need remains to address not only overt acts of racism but also the subtler, pervasive forces that continue to affect the well-being of Black women leaders in the higher education landscape. Within higher education institutions, a system of social control exists, designed to disadvantage Black women leaders (Collins, 2002). Access to advancement and resources available to their counterparts, such as White women and Black males, is systematically denied to Black women leaders. Recruitment and hiring practices at predominantly White institutions (PWIs) align with the needs of the dominant group, impeding the progression of Black women in academia (Hughes & Howard-Hamilton, 2003; Patitu & Hinton, 2003). Compared to other minority groups, Black women face lower salaries and a higher likelihood of unjust reprimands (Gregory, 2001; Jarmon, 2001).

Several reasons surface for Black women's challenges in securing promotion and tenure, including unspoken expectations, insufficient guidance and mentorship, and scrutiny over trivial matters (Patitu & Hinton, 2003, p. 87). Consequently, Black women leaders experience isolation and a sense of not belonging. Lutz et al. (2013) agreed that the limited number of Black women leaders at PWIs contributes to feelings of separation, stress, and loneliness. Stress for Black women leaders is complex and nuanced and manifests in various ways. Vakalahi and Starks (2011) illustrated that the experiences of Black women leaders often lead to an induced state of spiritual, social, and emotional bankruptcy.

RETROSPECTIVE FAMILY STORYTELLING

Storytelling plays a profound role in the Black community, providing evidence of our existence and lived experiences. Through storytelling, moral courage is gleaned, enabling individuals to act in accordance with ethical principles. Amason (2020) emphasized storytelling as a tool for transmitting values, beliefs, and norms across generations. Such practices contribute to the construction of collective identity and legacy. Comparable to the custom of passing down heirlooms, Smith

(2020) suggests that sharing stories within a family reveals the personal history and identity of that family. This process allows family members to make meaning of their ecological context, offering them a subjective family identity. Kellas (2005) explained that members derive meaning by recalling ancestral and current family practices. As families share stories about their identities, members better understand their individual paths.

Retrospective family storytelling has two significant implications for the experiences of Black women leaders. Communication researchers understand retrospective storytelling in and about family as (1) assisting with overcoming challenging experiences and making meaning of one's life and (2) socializing an individual and familial identity and legacy despite societal expectations (Kellas & Horstman, 2014; McAdams, 1993). To successfully navigate higher education politics, Black women leaders must creatively learn to solve or cope with social and racial difficulties. While society characterizes them through the gaze of the dominant culture, within Black families, storytelling has been used to counteract the myths and incorrect characterization of family members by societal constructs. By extension, people use retrospective storytelling to transmit ideas about themselves and the world (Livo & Rietz, 1986). The preservation of self-defined identity is sustained through the engagement of retrospective family storytelling.

In her transformational book *Black Sheep and Kissing Cousins*, Elizabeth Stone (2008) offered a critical commentary on how retrospective family storytelling clarifies its members' personal identities, writing:

Those of little power and status and those of great power and status tend to confirm one another's position. It is the first job of the family, through its stories, to explain to its members where they are positioned socially. (p. 145)

Regarding Black women leaders in higher education, retrospective family storytelling can potentially teach Black women survival strategies. Summarizing the connection between Black women leaders' survival and retrospective family storytelling, Collins (2002) clarified that dialogical relationships between Black women may serve as a resistance tool. As Black families share one-to-another survival stories, Black women leaders carry this acute sense of empowerment into the workplace. Through the power of retrospective family storytelling, Black women maintain their self-defined identities and learn the art of psychological and emotional strategies for resistance in the academy.

EMANCIPATORY KNOWING

Chinn and Kramer (2008) applied the concept of emancipatory functions to storytelling. They defined emancipatory knowing as the human capacity to transform challenging circumstances rather than avoiding them. This process involves recognizing and naming inequitable situations and then redefining and transforming them through creative avenues (Chinn & Kramer, 2008). Emancipatory knowing serves as a lens for Black women leaders to exercise agency to shape their realities through heightened consciousness. The authors emphasized the value of storytelling, stating, "The story has exquisite value as a frame from which to explore avenues of understanding and meaning, to shift experiential ground, and create visions for the future" (Chinn & Kramer, 2008, p. 162). Through various forms of storytelling—whether self, familial, dialogical, or professional—Black women leaders acquire knowledge on enhancing their experiences.

BLACK FEMINIST THOUGHT

The study applies Black feminist thought (BFT) as a theoretical framework as it appropriately frames Black women's lived experiences as a group. Essentially, BFT theorizes and depicts the lives of Black women from the knowledge they produce. Black women's vantage points are unique to their lived experiences, and BFT returns the authorship of these experiences to Black women. Although all Black women are intersectional, this group is not monolithic, so how Black women interpret and respond to daily bouts of discrimination could differ vastly within this group (Collins, 2002). Thus, Black women's challenges may or may not produce contrasting perspectives (Collins, 2002). Collins (2002) likened BFT to the empowerment of Black women. More specifically, she wrote about the matrix of knowledge Black women produce when in dialogue. This dialogical relationship produces a change in thought and, consequently, in actions.

In addition, Collins (2002) proposed the idea of "taken-for-granted knowledge" deriving from everyday experiences, thoughts, and actions (p. 36). Knowledge creation among Black women is interwoven in commonplace occurrences and conversations. Collins claimed that these dialogical relationships can transform Black women's thinking. *Knowing* is conceivable in any space or site where Black women congregate and offer discourse. Collins suggested that even blues clubs or washrooms are sites where *knowing* happens among Black women. Churches, hair salons, their mother's bedrooms, kitchens, and breakrooms all represent sites where *knowing* occurs. In other words, the African American oral storytelling tradition has the potential to liberate and transform the thinking patterns of Black women.

Through the utility of storytelling, Black women can depict their experiences and ultimately shape them. In light of this claim, BFT and storytelling work to aid Black women in survival, coping strategies, resistance, and *knowing*.

METHODOLOGY

This study examines the influence of retrospective family storytelling as a tool for emancipatory knowing in Black women leaders at PWIs. I applied a narratology method to investigate the impact of retrospective family storytelling. This narrative inquiry allowed for the extraction of in-depth stories and was particularly valuable in uncovering insights into sensitive areas often undiscoverable by more traditional methods (Webster & Mertova, 2007). Narrative inquiry proved effective for collecting participants' thoughts, feelings, and knowledge.

Additionally, the study relied on critical art-based research methods such as photo-elicitation and artifact elicitation. Harper (2002) described the value of using photo-elicitation versus words alone, stating, "Images evoke deeper elements of human consciousness than do words; exchanges based on words alone utilize less of the brain's capacity than do exchanges in which the brain is processing images as well as words" (p. 13). He asserted that using elicitation in interviews can draw connections between the participant, society, culture, and history (Harper, 2002, p. 13). To clarify, the use of photographs underscores more than a supportive method; they invite the researcher and audience into the participant's world. Further, photographs and artifacts invite participants into their own worlds beyond a surface-level recollection.

Finley (2008) put forth, "At the heart of arts-based inquiry is a radical, politically grounded statement about social justice and control over the production and dissemination of knowledge" (p. 72). Critical art-based and visual methods defy the dominance of quantitative methods by prioritizing marginalized lives (Finley, 2008). These techniques challenge the notion of quantitative methods as the only factual and trusted data. Hays and Singh (2012) suggested that an advantage of visual methods is the opportunity for participants to express themselves nonverbally (p. 278). Thus, visual and critical arts-based methods are recognized as socially responsible, allowing participants to define their realities as they experience life.

PARTICIPANTS

Participants within this study represented a non-random purposive sample instead of a random sample, ensuring alignment with predefined sample criteria. Table 1 provides an overview of the ten participants' demographics, listing their pseudonyms, ethnicity, age, level of education, marital status, number of children, and religion. The results of a Qualtrics survey revealed that all participants self-identified as African American women holding a graduate or advanced degree. Among the participants, two are Doctors of Philosophy, two are Doctors of Education, and six hold master's degrees. All participants identified as members of the Christian faith to some degree. Participants ranged from 34 to 63 years of age.

Table 1. Participant demographics

Pseudonym	Ethnicity	Age	Level of education	Marital status	Children	Religion
Dr. Naomi	African American	35	PhD	S	0	Christianity
Dr. Miriam	African American	37	EdD	M	2	NC
Priscilla	African American	34	Master's degree	S	0	Christianity
Leah	African American	63	Master's degree	P	3	Catholicism
Dr. Elizabeth	African American	35	EdD	S	0	Christianity
Hannah	African American	36	Master's degree	M	4	NC
Dr. Ruth	African American	59	PhD	S	0	Christianity
Hadassah	African American	36	Master's degree	S	0	Christianity- Baptist
Mary	African American	43	Master's degree	M	6	Christianity
Rachel	African American	37	Master's degree	M	0	Christianity

Note. S=Single, M=Married, P=Partnered, NC=Non-Denominational Christian

DATA COLLECTION

Procedures

The study's data collection consisted of in-depth interviews that included the elicitation of retrospective family stories. These stories are sub-data sources of interviews; thus, the study elicited this sub-source through one-on-one semi-structured interviews (Hays & Singh, 2012). In addition, the family narratives received support through artifact elicitation. I utilized photo-and-artifact elicitation to extract comprehensive material. Graphic imagery played a critical role in eliciting substantial responses regarding participants' lived experiences.

Before the interviews, I emailed each prospective participant detailing the research study's purpose. Once participants confirmed their participation by acknowledging the consent form, I placed an introductory Zoom call to clarify any questions and introduce the study. Importantly, each participant reviewed and approved the IRB consent form before answering any questions related to the study. The study required consent for three major components: Zoom audio and video recordings for data collection and analysis, photographs provided by participants of their artifacts, and disclosure of personal and professional information.

Following the Zoom call, a second email asked participants to spend, at most, two weeks immersed in their family history, stories, and legacies before the scheduled in-depth interview. Participants reviewed family photo albums and collected three to five mementos, heirlooms, and miscellaneous artifacts representing their family stories.

Retrospective Family Story Interviews

I implemented a standardized interview protocol to maintain uniformity across participants. Due to the impact of the COVID-19 pandemic, Zoom audio and video recordings were chosen to capture the family stories. The interviews lasted up to three hours, affording participants the flexibility to respond in a non-sequential manner. Additionally, I encouraged participants to refer to the interview questions, photos, and artifacts to help guide their life reflections and family stories.

During the initial interview segment, participants articulated their perspectives on the definition and purpose of family, their emotional connections to family stories, perceptions of family leadership, and the transmission of family stories. Following this, participants discussed their professional journeys at PWIs, recounting their experiences and observations. They explored the influence of family stories on their leadership approaches and how these narratives served as navigational aids. Finally, participants were prompted to interpret their chosen photograph or artifact.

Participants detailed its significance and relevance to their professional lives and whether it represented a person, place, or object.

Photo-and-Artifact Elicitation

The photographs and artifacts collected by participants were used as a form of archaeological memory (Clandinin & Connelly, 2000). The photos and artifacts provided imagery and representation of their experiences and familial influences. These tools gave insight into their ontology and epistemologies and represented the people, places, and items surrounding their homes and workspaces. Figure 1 and Figure 2 showcase photo and artifact examples. For each image or artifact selected, the participants were asked to generate a caption and respond to a narrative prompt describing and interpreting their feelings, emotions, and observations. Their families' photographic imagery and artifacts guided the discussion around the meaning made throughout their lives.

Figure 1. Artifact examples

Artifact Examples (Not limited to this list)			
Scrapbooks	Books	Photographs	Plants
Collages	Letters	Family Videos	Seeds
Paintings	Poems	Video Diaries	Flowers
Drawings	Scriptures	Heirlooms	Pottery
Sculptures	Sticky Notes	Keepsakes	Tools
Posters	Text Messages	Trophies	
Flyers	Diaries	Obituaries	
Quilts	Quotes	Newspapers	
	Postcards	Awards	
	Maps		
Jewelry	Songs	Recipes	Keychains
Clothing	Playlists	Kitchen utensils	Instruments
Shoes	Movies	Food	Coffee mugs
Comb/Brush	Vinyl Records	Tea	Vehicles
Hair clips	Cassette tapes	Coffee	Games
Handkerchiefs	Voice memos	Candles	Toys
Perfume			
Lapel Pins			

Figure 2. Photograph examples

Photograph Examples (People, Places, and Items)			
Buildings	Family gatherings	Friends	Monuments
Homes	Birthdays	Family	Tombstones
Schools	Births	Co-workers	Gravesites
Restaurants	Weddings	Mentors	Alleys
Parks	Reunions	Siblings	Abandoned buildings
The outdoors	Holidays	Husband	Fields
Churches	Portraits	Wife	Wooded areas
Salons	Family photos	Romantic partner	Bars
Neighborhoods	Engagement photos	Parties	Clubs
Bedrooms	Wedding photo	Anniversaries	Childhood home
Kitchens	Pets	Funerals	A friend's house
Living rooms	Kitchen table		Concert venues
Backyards	Dining room		Sports stadiums
			Museums

DATA ANALYSIS

I implemented a line-by-line coding procedure to identify emerging codes, using verbatim excerpts to develop the initial codes. As codes further developed around the participants' experiences and stories, themes became evident among participant stories. I drafted a matrix via Atlas.ti to further analyze and extract shared and individual themes. Kramp (2003) recommended that "all aspects of a matrix stand in relation to each other. The variations on a theme remain explicit and meaningful at the same time that the common themes are identified and illustrated" (p. 119). I reviewed the interviews once more for patterns within each interview and compared them against other interviews. After the initial coding and theme development phase, I merged and refined the codes.

Collins's (2002) BFT framework provided a filter through which to analyze the interviews further. The analysis revealed the following: (a) the commonality of stories and experiences among Black women leaders from the BFT standpoint, (b) the unique stories, experiences, and responses Black women espoused due to their individuality and positionality, (c) how these common experiences affected their leadership style and attainment of emancipatory knowing, (d) the contribution of intellect from family or other Black women in their village, (e) how the Black women leaders articulated their standpoint in opposition to the dominant narrative, and (f) the coping strategies they used to manage the effects of continual oppression.

FINDINGS

This study deeply explored the utility of retrospective family storytelling as a tool for resistance and emancipatory knowing in Black women leaders at PWIs. The study was designed to elicit "taken-for-granted knowledge" (Collins, 2002) from Black women leaders to provide an in-depth understanding of their experiences interpreted from their standpoint. Utilizing retrospective family storytelling, the research created a platform for Black women to explore the intricacies of their socialization, navigate the challenges of leading as Black women, and define their leadership identity.

NAVIGATING SPACES IN HIGHER EDUCATION

Participants elaborated on the pathology of White supremacy and how it shapes and affects work environments. Their stories were rimmed with the penalties they encountered at the hands of White supremacy. Collectively, the women recounted experiences of professional abuse, exhaustion, microaggressions, workplace terrorism, demeaning perceptions, the duplicity of whiteness, and imposter syndrome. Figure 3 demonstrates the effects of oppressive spaces on Black women leaders.

Reflecting on her grandmother's garden, Dr. Naomi grappled with the current state of her professional life versus the future she imagined for herself. Her reflections clarified the tension of imposter syndrome experienced in oppressive environments. She opened with a penetrating metaphor describing her relationship with higher education institutions:

I think about all the weeds that are currently growing in my professional garden... maybe it's time to burn the garden of my professional life and see new growth because this ain't it. This ain't it. So, I'm starting to see glimpses of what my garden is gonna look like. And it's scary. It's scary because I think I figured out what I want to be when I grow up. Um, and that's scary because you don't really want to tell people that. You know? When I wanted to be a college president, and I still might want to be a college president. I told somebody that, and they said, "You know, that's not something you aspire to." Why the hell not? Why can't the presidency be something I aspire to? So, when I think about that, gardens give you hope... I'm trying to figure out if I'm weeding my garden or if my garden needs to burn entirely and regrow. I didn't think that was gonna make me emotional, but it did.

Dr. Naomi intentionally repeated specific terminology, such as *weeds*. Detailing her use of the word weeds, she expanded on this trope and explained the effects of White supremacy in her workspace:

White supremacy don't grow in my garden. Don't get me wrong, it shades. It shades my garden. So, there are some days I can't get direct sunlight on all my plants. But, White supremacy don't grow in my garden. So, what does grow because of White supremacy? Weeds pop up of self-doubt. Weeds pop up like, am I good enough? Will I be able to publish enough? You know? Those are the weeds that have to go because, ultimately, White supremacy doesn't exist in here. That's mine ... and so, it's my responsibility to cultivate that space because it is mine.

Figure 3. Navigating spaces in higher education

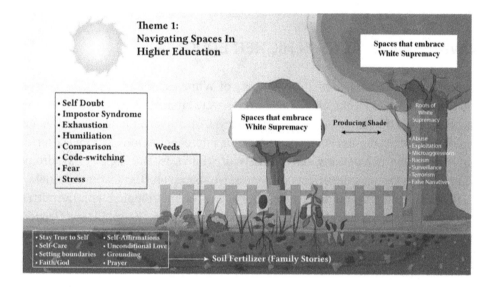

Similar to Dr. Naomi, all the women in the study cited their experience of weeds in their professional gardens. Detailing her early career experiences as a young Black professional, Dr. Miriam expressed the impact of imposter syndrome, highlighting its manifestation under the leadership of a particular department. Dr. Miriam characterized imposter syndrome as follows:

So, what I mean by imposter syndrome is that this person, and I'll include myself, this person and I were very capable of doing the job, right? But, when you are in a toxic environment, um, you question your ability, you question what you're doing and how you're doing it. But you do the work. You do the work well, but the environment that's been created for you in that space goes against what you know you can do and what your resume shows you can do. ... I think with imposter syndrome, you question it, and you feel like you're a fraud. You're not giving yourself the credit.

Participants discussed experiences of isolation and exclusion in PWIs. A common thread throughout their stories involved memories of being shunned and professionally stunted. Leah, for instance, recounted facing negative labels after advocating for students of color on campus. Enduring bullying and slander, she found her reputation tarnished; these acts influenced how other campus departments perceived her and her students. She described how demeaning perceptions can lead to stunted growth professionally: "Any thought or any chance that I had to elevate in any other position was null and void at that point. I wasn't going anywhere else, and I knew that." Following Leah's rebuke of White supremacist tactics, she was Blacklisted. She recognized the cost of speaking up and ultimately paid the price. Leah further shared, "It was truly exhausting. I retired for a few reasons, and one of the reasons was I was exhausted, seriously. … But again, if you, as an African American person, stay in the background, you're okay." Leah continued:

They label you or they labeled me the troublemaker. "Here comes the troublemaker," you know, or, "Here comes the angry Black woman." That's the major title, you know, and I wasn't. I'm not. I don't walk around angry. People that knew me, I'm smiling every day, all day long. That's who I am. But, I'm not gonna put up with deceitfulness. I'm not gonna put up with racism. Period. I'm not. We don't have to, you know?

Continuing the dialogue, participants emphasized the additional challenge of navigating perceptions from White students. They shared instances where White students perceived them as incompetent and questioned their ability to oversee an office, manage a caseload, or lead a classroom. Priscilla, for example, recounted a conversation with a student that swiftly escalated into divisiveness. Humorously, Priscilla shifted the weight of her voice as she discussed the stereotypical perceptions held by a White male student:

It was an academic advising appointment with a student. I was telling the student that he needed to take an additional course, and he did not want to take that additional course. He goes, "Well, what can I offer you to not have to take this additional course?" And I go, "Yeah, this isn't a bribe situation. Like that's not how this works. You're gonna have to take the additional course," and he's like, "Are you sure that I cannot give you some fried chicken or some watermelon to not have to take this course?" My immediate answer was stunned face. Did he really just say this? … The words that came out of my mouth were, "I don't even like fried chicken or watermelon." How stereotypical and just ridiculous was that, right?

For participants, learning to navigate the *duplicity of whiteness* was another common thread. Here, Dr. Naomi explained the notes of disparagement embedded in the duplicity of whiteness:

So, they'll [White colleagues] thank me privately in meetings for stretching them to be more equitable while punishing me publicly for speaking out. So, it's just the duplicity, it's the duplicity of Whiteness. Where, as long as it has some level of interest convergence, some level of symbiosis for them … they're all on board.

For Rachel, the development of demeaning perceptions stemmed from the duplicity of whiteness. Not only did she recognize these perceptions, but she also felt the mental and physical toll of the duplicity of whiteness. Rachel further described the strong Black women phenomenon: "I always have to be this strong person that I can do it all. That I could do 30,000 things, and I don't get tired." Rachel also communicated the stark cultural differences between White and Black women leaders. She explained, "A lot of these director positions and some of the provost positions are these White, middle-aged women who run the show. And they just want to work the hell out of you because this is their world and their whole life." Rachel prioritized her family life over the demands of higher education, a sentiment shared by many women in the study. Furthermore, she expressed that her colleagues perceive her as expendable yet simultaneously subject her decision-making to surveillance. She continued, "I also feel like because I'm not a 50-year-old, middle-aged White woman, that I'm, um, that I'm also not competent and feel like, you know, I have to be watched."

These leaders shared tales of narrowly navigating PWIs and spoke poignantly about exhaustion. It became evident that weathering the higher education landscape took a toll on their physical and mental well-being. Participants perceived these spaces as exhausting, even abusive. For instance, Dr. Naomi disclosed, "Admitting you're in an abusive professional relationship is hard. Because how do you say that? Companies don't like being told they're abusive … I'm sick of negotiating with terrorists. Like that's just what it is."

Hadassah not only detailed the harm caused by oppressive White spaces but also expressed her deliberate efforts to reclaim both her body and soul. It appeared that she sought a form of self-atonement for allowing the harm to persist. Declaring she would no longer allow herself to be haphazardly used in these spaces, Hadassah asserted:

At some point, you have to put the accountability off on them, meaning the White people—men and women. Stop trying to use us to do your shit. And then take the accolades and the praise while we over here burnt out looking dusty and musty. No, we're not doing it. I'm just not doing that. I can't. My body and my soul won't allow me to do that. Because, again, I'm in a different space. Again, I'm not where I fully need to be. I don't know who I am or what it looks like on the other side, but I'm damn sure not where I used to be in terms of that.

In addition to relaying the exhausting burden of navigating oppressive PWIs, a striking concern for participants involved the lack of compensation. Dr. Naomi noted that Black women leaders are not compensated for the cultural strategies they use to survive.

The exhausting work that Black women are not compensated for doesn't go on our CVs and doesn't go on our cover letters. Like, navigate White supremacy all day long. I wish there was a salary attached to navigating White supremacy and, particularly, at the intersection of gender. White women are, oftentimes, in my experience, the gatekeepers of White supremacy.

Dr. Naomi went on to say:

I think I've been used in some pretty harmful ways. That also includes carrying the responsibility of very basic, mediocre White women who don't know their right from left. That's one of the most exhausting parts of my role, is that there is a dotted line to make sure that White women stay afloat. And that's exhausting. I'm tired of it. I just don't understand why White supremacy won't keep White women afloat. I don't understand why White women don't recognize that White supremacy don't keep them afloat."

Navigational tools at PWIs were a preeminent story arc in the participants' narratives. The participants, on the whole, cited the need to be hypervigilant in these spaces. Specifically, they relied on the weight of their voice, boundary setting, faith, and lessons from their families. These navigational tools dually operated as alternative methodologies of survival and resistance. For example, commenting on the power of a Black woman's voice, Dr. Naomi said, "I think there's something really revolutionary about being a Black woman who says no and that's a complete sentence." However, Dr. Naomi understood that exercising these rights could work against her in such spaces. For instance, she described the double-edged sword of setting boundaries in White spaces:

I will tell you that working in this predominantly White space, they are a lot less forgiving, and grace doesn't abound in this space. Right? So, as gracious as I want to be in setting my boundaries, I don't feel like I have the same freedoms to fail. I don't feel like I have the same freedoms to always exercise my boundaries. And that's part of the reason I'm deciding if this is where I want to be, right? So, it's not necessarily a bad thing. But I don't feel like there's the same level of grace, there's not the same shared understanding, there's not the same shared cultural practice. The way I would tell somebody in my personal life, like, "That's enough," is different than how I have to police the imaginations of White people. And that is exhausting. That even in my boundary setting, I still have to figure out a way that White people won't be so threatened that my boundaries equal a death sentence.

THE THERAPEUTIC NATURE OF FAMILY STORYTELLING

Family stories symbolized reservoirs of empowerment and self-affirmation. As participants continued to reflect and share their family stories, two subthemes emerged: (a) know thy self and (b) spiritual compass. By serving as reminders, their family stories aided them in maintaining their identity apart from false meta-narratives. Figure 4 showcases the collective soundtrack of the participants' voices. The following excerpts illuminate the participants' perceptions of the therapeutic nature of family stories.

Figure 4. The therapeutic nature of family storytelling

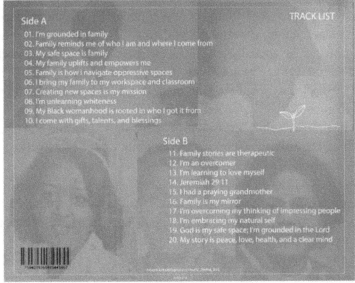

Know Thy Self

This subtheme represents the participants' alternative practices to preserve their identities in cultures of assimilation. These Black women leaders lean on familial strategies to bolster self-love in less-than-loving spaces. They engender a compassionate love for themselves and the people they serve. Their family stories act as mental buffers against the racial challenges Black women face in society and the revictimization they withstand in their workspaces. For example, Dr. Ruth suggested she would only narrowly survive in PWIs if not for the mental fortitude her family instilled. The family narrative of resilience is what cemented self-empowerment in Dr. Ruth. She explained:

I knew once I left our safe space. Oh, I knew not to even think about not being anything but the strong woman that I have been trained to be by both sides of my family. No matter where you are. So, being a part of a university is no different. And as a matter of fact, it made me stronger. Because I never felt I had to belong. I never felt I had to be accepted.

She continued to speak about how her family narratives girded her in preparation for higher education:

Somebody has to say something about it continually, that these spaces [PWIs] are not safe unless you have a strong foundation of support. I don't mean just financially. Someone has to really put some resilience inside of you, something that you can reflect on. Or you're not going to make it because it's designed for you not to make it. There are people staying in these spaces because they're just there; they're not there to help.

In reflecting on her family's narrative of attending church and practicing prayer, full of emotion, Dr. Miriam elaborated on the scripture she provided as an artifact. She reminded herself:

My future is, it's okay. I have hope that I have a future and it's going to be good. That's a promise from God. You know? Like I said earlier, it reminds me, good or bad, that my path is going to be okay. My path is going to be prosperous as long as I am doing right by people, by my job, by my family, so on and so forth.

Referring to her great aunt's affirming words, Dr. Elizabeth reflected, "She's always been the person to say, 'Why would you have to prove anything? You are loved. And I'm going to show you.'" Dr. Ruth's reflections mirrored Dr. Elizabeth's. In revisiting where she learned self-confidence, Dr. Ruth deferred to her family:

So, the sense of security, mainly, the confidence in myself, professionally. I'm secure enough in who I am to be in the world. To be who I am. I'm happy with who I am. I'm confident. I'm committed to what I do, all because that's what was put inside of me, that's what was around me.

Self-affirmations and self-reflection were parallel concepts during the participants' discussion of self and identity. Dr. Elizabeth further pointed out the need to consistently assess herself in PWIs:

I think sometimes we don't self-reflect as Black women in these predominantly White spaces. Because you can't lift and climb if you ain't lifting yourself. Are you spending time with yourself? Or are you evaluating yourself? Who are you in this space? I'm a bold, smart Black woman. I'm bold, I'm plus size. I'm fly. I don't code-switch.

While Dr. Elizabeth discussed self-affirmations as a reflective tool, Hadassah noted how her family's narrative of unconditional support encouraged her to bring the best version of herself to work. She explained how her family has contributed to who she is at work. Hadassah said, "I think about just my family and being supportive of me. Through all these years and loving me the way that they have has allowed me to show up to support the students in the way that I do." She went on, "Really, all I'm doing is bringing who I am. So, I'm bringing my family with me along with my work experiences and my personal experiences into the classroom with me."

In the *telling* of their family stories, Black women are reminded of who they are and to whom they belong. As Dr. Naomi stated, "Right now, I gotta remind myself who I am and whose I am. So that's the space I'm in, professionally." Hannah stated, "I had to remember that I come with gifts and talents that I bring to my role." For all the Black women leaders, affirming their worth was directly tied to the affirmations they received from their family networks.

Spiritual Compass

Throughout the discussion about their self-preservation, the idea of a *spiritual compass* became evident as a subtheme. In unison, the participants spoke about memoirs of faith from the families. The notion of faith in God or a higher power seemed to be regenerative in and among their families. Often, participants communicated the *passing down* of hope and prayer when facing the gauntlet of higher education. For example, with pride, Mary shared, "Whether it be my parents, but mostly my grandparents, like my one grandmother … when I say the prayer warrior, she pleaded the blood on a daily basis." Mary's description of *pleading the blood* refers to calling on the name of Jesus and His host of angels to cover her and her family. For many of these Black women leaders, faith invoked improvisation in their personal and professional lives. Through faith in God, they learned strategies to fight spiritually against perpetual attacks on their personhood. Faith in God implies there is no *hell* that rivals Him [God]. He is more than enough to make it through the day in any space. For these women, God overwhelmed the challenges that would try to overwhelm them. In a profound excerpt, Mary identified God as her source of life. She showcased her grandparents' bible that was passed down to her a year ago:

It's strength. You know, it's tradition, it just, it says everything about who we are. Not only do we have individual purpose but a purpose as a family. I'm grateful for that tradition of Christianity and of loving the Lord.

Mary expressed her gratitude:

Oh, my God. You have smiled on us, God; you continue to smile on us. And that's why my family legacy, our family story, God is the center of it all. He is the one that keeps us when we don't know how to be kept. He is the one who guides and leads and protects us. So, He is always going to be the person that you need to have at the center of your life ... to accept Him, to honor Him, and to reverence Him. So that He can continue to show us how to walk this journey because it's not going to be easy every day, but it's gonna be worth it.

Many of these leaders practiced a form of contemplation. This practice strengthens their inner person, allowing them to project hope and courage in the face of defeat. Dr. Miriam explained, "I know my faith in God has set me up for more. I can lean into that during those tough times, knowing that this is a phase ... you're going to come out of it and keep pushing forward." In light of their perpetual challenges, many participants' family narratives form the foundation of their personal and professional lives, supporting their mental and spiritual wellness.

Many participants coupled their family narratives of faith and authenticity as resistance factors in PWIs; their most critical endeavor was to remain true to themselves. They made conscious efforts to root themselves in God's promises. Their family stories were emancipators. The modes of oppression used against Black women leaders stood in contrast to the pedagogies of love imprinted by their families—a love seared into their identities.

Here, Leah put into context and summarized the importance of *walking in God's light* despite her professional hurdles:

So, always walk in God's light; I have to do that ... Like I said, I could be bitter about some things, I can be angry about some things, but I choose not to be. I choose to walk in God's light. I feel like when God gives you grace and blessings, then that is a heck of an honor. To be able to know that, I think it's huge. It's amazing.

REDEFINING LEADERSHIP

Leading in Love

The stories shared by each Black woman leader served as crucial building blocks for shaping a culturally relevant leadership profile. Figure 5 illustrates the blueprint for *leading in love*. Notably, while higher education functions as a system, systems, by nature, may not prioritize virtues such as *compassionate love*. Nevertheless, every system relies on people, and people inherently need care.

Figure 5. Leading in love

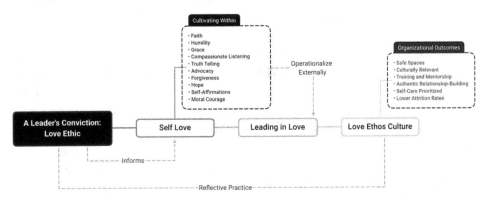

Unlike common perceptions of compassion and love, compassionate love surpasses conventional notions of kindness, sympathy, and romantic affection (Fehr & Sprecher, 2009). The experience of compassionate love goes beyond an expression practiced only between "loved ones" and extends toward *others*. This phenomenon—expressing compassionate love toward non-family—warrants further investigation. Fehr and Sprecher (2009) put it this way: "Compassionate love merits scientific study because people can experience this kind of love for close others as well as for strangers (or perhaps even for all of humanity), and it may well be the kind of love that contributes to the greatest social good" (p. 343).

The term "compassionate love" originated at a convening of the World Health Organization (WHO) organized by Lynn Underwood. Among the thought leaders present were researchers, health professionals, and religious and non-religious (Buddhist, Hindu, Muslim, Christian, Jewish, indigenous, Agnostic, atheist) groups. This meeting of the minds and hearts aimed to develop a measurement tool for "quality of life" (World Health Organization Quality of Life Spirituality, Religion, and Personal Beliefs Group, 2006). The word "love" alone raised concerns for the

Buddhist participants, who preferred the term "compassion." In stark contrast, the Muslim participants favored the word "love" because it offered an aspect of *feeling* (Underwood, 2009). Perhaps the most relevant depiction of compassionate love derived from various members of the WHO assembly. They put forward the construct of compassionate love as the holistic experience of responding to human suffering and spurring human flourishing. Their conceptualization suggests that compassion addresses suffering and love fosters empowerment, but both are required to enhance an individual's *quality of life*.

For Black women leaders, transforming higher education spaces involves placing compassionate love at the core of their strategic plan. This commitment leads to the development of a love ethic—a set of principles propelled by the force of love. Their love ethic serves as a root system for self-love—an internal love planted by their families that germinates into qualities such as hope and faith, forgiveness and grace, humility and advocacy, compassionate listening and truth-telling, and self-affirmations and moral courage. Through the cultivation of self-love, these leaders not only internalize the essence of love but project it outward. Meticulously fostering a culture immersed in a love ethos. Crucially, while these leaders may not embody every facet of this framework, they remain in continuous pursuit. They prioritize and engage in reflective practices while striving for a leadership approach that is both meaningful and relevant.

Here, Dr. Elizabeth visited a memory of her great aunt. In this recollection, Dr. Elizabeth recalled her great aunt's demonstration of leading in love on her neighborhood block. Confronted by a group of young men littering in her yard, she navigated the situation with a profound love for people and community. Dr. Elizabeth remembered:

Watching her navigate the fact that she didn't know this car. She didn't know these people, but she still led in love. So, not to accuse them. Not to yell at them. Not to shame them. Not to belittle them. But to make it a teachable moment. She treated them as if they were her kids, as if they were family.

Further describing her aunt's leadership profile, Dr. Elizabeth went on to say:

She did it with love and good intentions. I think that's sometimes what's being missed in leadership. Sometimes it's like, I'm just trying to show that I know more than you; I'm better than you. I'm superior. She wasn't demanding respect, she was respected. … The way she navigated those men really showed me that you can love anybody. You can love anybody. You don't necessarily know who needs that example of love at that moment.

Bearing witness to her aunt's leadership practices helped Dr. Elizabeth refine her own leadership profile. Dr. Elizabeth established herself and her space as safe places for both her colleagues and her students. She explained:

I think I navigate every space as—assume good intentions. Leading with love ... and when I say leading with love, even in the workplace. You never know who's navigating trauma or not having a good home life themselves, not just the students but also the faculty and staff. I might be just a small glimpse of what they could be missing at home. Maybe at home, you're not feeling respected. But here, I'll respect you. You know, maybe at home, you're feeling not motivated or heard. But I'm going to motivate you and hear you.

Similar to Dr. Elizabeth, Rachel's leadership style involves creating safe spaces for her followers. Her comments revealed her desire to reimagine a work–life balance. She outlined:

I enjoy working with teams. I do. I enjoy motivating people, I enjoy pouring into people, developing them, allowing them to get a feel of what they like and don't like about the job and best practices and stuff like that. I always have side conversations with people, and whenever you're ready to move on, just let me know how I can prepare you for the next thing. The next level, phase, whatever it may be of your life. I think that upsets a lot of people because they just want to keep people at the same level that they're at and work the hell out of them. I don't believe in that. I believe in giving people autonomy. I believe in providing flexible schedules because work–life balance is real. It should be encouraged at work. People don't believe it.

Rachel further elaborated:

Work is hard, and life is hard, too. So how can we make the best of both worlds so that we can have great workers but also healthy people whose families need them to be there for them? So, how can we do that? How can we create those spaces? I don't think higher ed is ready for that.

Dr. Miriam expanded on a culturally shared view of leadership. Reflecting on a past encounter with a divisive and manipulative supervisor, she recounted how this experience inspired her to lead with honesty at her helm:

I also think that experience showed how truthful I want to be in this work. I think that's where it's always hard for me because I want to be truthful. I want to be honest, transparent, and accountable. But I don't think a lot of PWIs, especially when it comes to the DEI work, they're not willing to be honest and transparent. I think that's where it gets hard for me with doing this type of work. You want to have the right intentions, you want to work hard, but you don't have the resources and the transparency behind you to do it. That makes it hard.

For Leah, leadership is synonymous with unconditional love. She described the resistance she encountered from her peers regarding her leadership philosophy. Here, Leah clarified that she led with unconditional love, a love that starts with self:

That's exactly how I led. ... Some people embraced it very well. Some people, in my opinion, were just like me; they loved unconditionally. Those were your for real people. The people that had their own agenda, they, you know, they made it an issue, you know, "Oh, she's just too involved," or "She's just fake," "That's not how she feels." How you gon' tell me how I feel? ... So again, they're being judgmental because they're not that way. They don't understand because it's not in their heart. Sometimes, they don't love themselves. So, you can't love someone else. Once I realized that and realized who those people were, then I knew how to handle myself around those people.

The analysis of the data has addressed three critical inquiries regarding the participants' leadership pedagogies: (a) how Black women leaders conceptualize leadership, (b) where they acquire their leadership skills, and (c) the approaches they employ in leadership. These Black women leaders view leadership as both an honor and a means to disrupt generational challenges on personal and professional fronts. Their leadership styles merge insights from family narratives and life experiences. For these Black women, leading in love is their framework.

DISCUSSION

Practitioners of Love

Black women leaders are poised to unveil unorthodox, nuanced leadership definitions and approaches. They contribute novel perspectives on leading in love based on their unique vantage points. Acutely aware of the traditional leadership styles used in higher education, they recognize a spiritual and cultural gap. Consequently, their focus centers on showcasing leadership practices that bridge these gaps. Acknowledging the inseparability of personhood from leadership, Black women leaders argue against excluding personal identity in professional spaces, considering it inauthentic. Lord and Hall (2005) argued that a leader's identity is shaped by the construction of their self-concept, while McCain and Matkin (2019) understand the development of a leader's identity as connected to meaning made from family stories.

Within this study, participants envisioned their leadership identity through the prism of Sankofa practices, griot culture, self-love, compassionate and unconditional love, humility, and grace. They painted the canvas of their identity as a leader against the backdrop of family stories, a compelling influence on their sense of self (Kellas, 2005). The concept of love had the highest impact on the participants' leadership identity. Love as a practice remains a highly sought-after ability, however elusive. hooks (2001) described the necessity of cultivating a love ethic that informs a leader's daily life:

Domination cannot exist in any social situation where a love ethic prevails. ... When love is present the desire to dominate and exercise power cannot rule the day. All the great social movements for freedom and justice in our society have promoted a love ethic. Concern for the collective good of our nation, city, or neighbor rooted in the values of love makes us all seek to nurture and protect that good. (p. 98)

In this same vein, Sir John Templeton (2000) wrote about the effects of a loveless person on others, warning:

When we can love enough, we find a fulfillment and a true closeness to others that satisfies our desire to reach another person's heart. When we do not love enough to enter into this wholesome, freeing union with others, we tend to seek to solve our basic problem of separation by gaining power over others. We may tend to live by comparison. We may try to analyze how much better or more important we are than others. We may tend to be competitive rather than cooperative and creative and helpful. (p. 24)

In one of His many parables, Jesus taught His followers to love others as they loved themselves. That is, love should extend beyond homogenous groups. He commanded: You shall love your neighbor as yourself [that is, unselfishly seek the best or higher good for others] (The Amplified Study Bible, 2016, Matthew 22:39).

What also became evident in the study is that one must first see *love in leadership* as a possibility. These Black women leaders bore witness to *love in leadership* from their multi-layered family systems. According to their family stories, the possibility of *love in leadership* was always apparent. Their praying grandmothers and grandfathers, mothers and fathers, and aunts and uncles demonstrated *love in leadership* within their families and in a world that refused to reciprocate love. Family inspired their confidence and comfortability to embrace a love ethos. As Dr. Miriam and Dr. Naomi described, what makes it challenging to *lead in love* are environments built on the foundations of selfishness and domination. For these leaders, this humane love spreads beyond theory and manifests in how they care for themselves first and then others. Their family narratives of love aided in counteracting internalized oppression. Furthermore, it began decolonizing their perceptions about self-image and ability in professional spaces.

As the participants continue to explore the practice of embracing both inner and outer self-love, the fruits of this endeavor radiate wherever they dawn. For a Black woman leader, cultivating self-love becomes a revolutionary act. This act gradually drowns out the steady hum of oppression. As hooks (2015) aptly articulated, "The choice to love has always been a gesture of resistance for African-Americans" (p. 98). Given the historical context of Black women in America, self-love holds particular significance for this critical demographic. Returning to hooks's (2015) insights, she further underscores love as a necessity for Black women:

It is the absence of love that has made it so difficult for us to stay alive or, if alive, to live fully. When we love ourselves we want to live fully. Whenever people talk about Black women's lives, the emphasis is rarely on transforming society so that we can live fully, it is almost always about applauding how well we have "survived" despite harsh circumstances or how we can survive in the future. ... To live fully, Black women can no longer deny our need to know love. (p. 103)

In the corridors of academia, a shift seems to have occurred so that Black women leaders no longer find it necessary to suppress their need for and practice of love. Love emerges as a budding best practice for leadership—a cornerstone.

THE IMPLICATIONS OF SERVANT LEADERSHIP

The landscape of contemporary leadership literature reveals a striking alignment between the leadership profile articulated by the study's participants and the principles of servant leadership. This offers Black women leaders a platform to affirm their distinctive leadership style, though such validation is unnecessary. It is crucial to clarify that while justification is not a requisite, an exploration is warranted to evaluate the viability of servant leadership as a sustained practice among Black women leaders. Within this dialogue, certain elements prove particularly valuable while others do not. Greenleaf's (1970) philosophy of servant leadership introduces a perspective suggesting various positive outcomes:

It begins with the natural feeling that one wants to serve, to serve first. Then conscious choice brings one to aspire to lead. The difference manifests itself in the care taken by the servant—first to make sure that other people's highest priority needs are being served. The best test is: Do those served grow as persons; do they, while being served, become healthier, wiser, freer, more autonomous, more likely themselves to become servants? (p. 4)

Servant leaders work to empower their followers and facilitate their holistic growth. Leaders who practice servant leadership enable their followers to become more self-confident and proactive. Their followers can meet personal and professional goals with their leaders' support. Ultimately, the potential long-term outcomes of servant leadership enable the leader to lead in a culture of trust. The Black women leaders within this study required trust and honest relationship building. Their sole request as leaders was for their colleagues and followers to genuinely work toward a synergy and culture without gender and racial microaggressions, surveillance, and conditions of visibility. Black women leaders thrive in cultures of care where forgiveness is actively valued, gratitude is freely expressed, humility is viewed as self-awareness, noble purpose provides meaning, moral courage incites risk-taking, empowerment inspires creativity, future-mindedness encourages forward-thinking, and stewardship is the new leadership. A culture built on servant leadership principles can potentially build community and strong personal relationships. Perhaps servant leadership cultures value others' differences and support the practice of compassion (Goffee & Jones, 2011).

The Black women leaders in this study led from a sense of calling. In Jones's (2003) research on Black women instructional administrators, spirituality emerged as a prominent concept from her discussions with participants. Her participants identified spirituality as a source of inspiration, leading with a noble purpose, and connecting with students, colleagues, and families within the institution as components of their leadership style. Servant leadership, along with spirituality, has the potential to support the resilience, well-being, and survival of Black women leaders.

While acknowledging the positive characteristics of servant leadership, it is vital to examine this practice critically with Black women leaders in mind. Conservation of resources (COR) theory can be used to comprehend the negative and positive consequences of practicing servant leadership. The COR theory explains that leaders are motivated to gain resources and protect against resource loss. Hobfoll (1989) defined resources as "those objects, personal characteristics, conditions, or energies that are valued by the individual or that serve as a means for attainment of these objects, personal characteristics, conditions, or energies" (p. 516). The premise of servant leadership is to cultivate high-quality relationships between leaders and followers. The challenge for a servant leader, however, is how to support all their followers' needs without nearly depleting their resources. The well-being of such leaders is potentially at risk, especially for Black woman leaders.

The paradox between the COR model and servant leadership suggests a relationship between servant leadership and leader fatigue. Black women leaders face many stress offenders, and one could argue that the tax of servant leadership emphasizes unique challenges. In contrast, the COR theory suggests a possibility of resource gain. In their systematic review, Eva et al. (2019) demonstrated how servant leaders gain resources—such as well-being, self-actualization, and satisfaction—from developing others. The theory suggests that resources obtained through servant leadership practices protect against negative consequences, defined as resource losses, such as leader fatigue or emotional exhaustion. This uncertainty underscores the importance of careful consideration, emphasizing the need for Black women leaders to avoid specific leadership styles that they do not define.

The leadership competencies of Black women leaders transcend conventional Western notions, expanding to encompass cultural and spiritual practices. Their leadership emerges from a multidimensional profile shaped by their intersectional identity. In articulating her definition of leadership, Dr. Naomi stressed the necessity for leadership practices free of Western ideology. She recommended the following:

Most of the literature on leadership is centered around whiteness. I don't know that I will use any of those definitions because I don't know if they fully can encompass who Black women show up as leaders. Leadership writ large has been Whitewashed, and we don't know what that means for other folks. If I had to describe my leadership, I don't know. It's like a combination of connectedness … I've figured out how to make stories and tell stories that make people want to act. I think that I'm a griot culture leader; I'm a leader in griot culture. I'm a leader in impact. So those are probably better ways to describe how I would think about leadership because I've never seen a White person define something around leadership that I was like, "That's the one. Count me in like." No, White people don't understand the premise of Sankofa, you know? Sankofa isn't built into Western ideology and Western culture. You don't have to go pick up what's at risk of being left behind. Sankofa is a part of the leader that I am. All of these things baked in and I don't know what to call it. But I'm grateful for the little okra stew that is the leadership that I am and how I show up.

RECOMMENDATIONS

Seeing Love as a Possibility

Recognizing that some PWIs may deem the following recommendations irrelevant, the persistence of such a perspective reinforces the relevance of this research agenda. Failing to acknowledge these implications will further jeopardize the relationship between Black women leaders and higher education. The following recommendations are compiled for both parties respectively in Table 2.

Table 2. Seeing love as a possibility

Black women leaders	Predominately White institutions of higher education
Cultivate an internal love and recognize your inherent worthiness of self-care. Extend the same compassion to yourself that you generously offer to others.	*Realize* love in leadership as a possibility and embrace a love ethos. Attention to this significant detail is critical to mitigating attrition rates among Black women leaders.
Fearlessly practice love in your leadership journey. Allow grace to permeate within and around you.	Move from theory to practitioners and intentionally curate spaces void of oppression. Evaluate and eradicate spaces that embrace and induce intersectional harm.
Allow this love to serve as a guiding force, propelling you towards virtuous actions and nurturing meaningful change.	Engage in compassionate inquiry, actively listening to and prioritizing the visions of Black women leaders.
Elevate the importance of your well-being and self-care, ensuring it becomes an ingrained and consistent practice in your routine.	Improve policies to support work–life balance.
Evaluate your actions and motivations. Reflect on the intentions behind your decisions and the spirit guiding your responses.	Revisit the strategic plan. Create a diverse task force to ensure the plan is effective in word and deed.

continued on following page

Table 2. Continued

Black women leaders	Predominately White institutions of higher education
Share your leadership wisdom to uplift yourself and the organizational culture you influence.	Require robust, continuous, culturally relevant leadership training for all staff, administration, and faculty.
Contribute to your community by offering mentorship and coaching to those who are following in your footsteps and walking alongside you on their own journeys.	Institute long-term mentorship and coaching programs specifically tailored for Black women staff, administration, and faculty.

CONCLUSION

Across generations, the Black family has embraced storytelling, playing a crucial role in shaping collective and individual identities. Beyond bridging the past and present, storytelling serves as a vessel for passing down family histories and identities to the next generation. Culturally, storytellers intricately weave together the threads of the past, present, and future. This study cements the profound significance of family storytelling, particularly for the leadership pedagogies of Black female leaders in higher education. The findings highlight family storytelling as a positive force contributing to the resilience of Black women leaders at PWIs. Seeking mentoring and support from their families, the participants demonstrated their resourcefulness. The narratives shared in this study meaningfully contribute to the development of a culturally relevant leadership profile for Black women. While the notion of love in leadership may challenge traditional paradigms in higher education institutions, Black women leaders have boldly redefined leadership, positioning leading in love as a central and effective practice. Perhaps hooks's (2015) conclusion is the most fitting:

When we as Black women experience fully the transformative power of love in our lives, we will bear witness publicly in a way that will fundamentally challenge existing social structures. ... When we know what love is, when we love, we are able to search our memories and see the past with new eyes; we are able to transform the present and dream the future. Such is love's power. Love heals. (p. 111)

REFERENCES

Amason, P. (2020). Family stories: Collections of narratives revealing family identity. *The Journal of American Culture*, 43(1), 49–62. 10.1111/jacc.13117

American Association For Access. Equity and Diversity. (n.d.) Affirmative action policies throughout history. https://www.aaaed.org/aaaed/history_of_affirmative_action.asp

The Amplified Study Bible. (2016). Zondervan.

Bagati, D. (2008). Women of color in US securities firms. *Catalyst : Feminism, Theory, Technoscience*.

Chamberlain, M. (1991). *Women in academe: Progress and prospects*. Russell Sage Foundation.

Chinn, P. L., & Kramer, M. K. (2008). *Integrated theory and knowledge development in nursing* (7th ed.). Mosby Elsevier.

Clandinin, D. J., & Connelly, F. M. (2000). *Narrative inquiry: Experience and story in qualitative research* (1st ed.). Jossey-Bass Publishers.

Collins, P. H. (2002). *Black feminist thought: Knowledge, consciousness, and the politics of empowerment*. Routledge. 10.4324/9780203900055

Eva, N., Robin, M., Sendjaya, S., van Dierendonck, D., & Liden, R. C. (2019). Servant leadership: A systematic review and call for future research. *The Leadership Quarterly*, 30(1), 111–132. 10.1016/j.leaqua.2018.07.004

Fehr, B., & Sprecher, S. (2009). Prototype analysis of the concept of compassionate love. *Personal Relationships*, 16(3), 33–364. 10.1111/j.1475-6811.2009.01227.x

Finley, S. (2008). Arts-based research. In Knowles, J. G., & Cole, A. L. (Eds.), *Handbook of the arts in qualitative research: Perspectives, methodologies, examples, and issues* (pp. 72–82). SAGE Publications, Inc. 10.4135/9781452226545.n6

Goffee, R., & Jones, G. (2001). Followership. *Harvard Business Review*, 79(11), 148.

Grassley, J. S., & Nelms, T. P. (2009). Tales of resistance and other emancipatory functions of storytelling. *Journal of Advanced Nursing*, 65(11), 2447–2453. 10.1111/j.1365-2648.2009.05105.x19737319

Greenleaf, R. K. (1970). *The servant as leader*. Greenleaf Center for Servant Leadership.

Gregory, S. T. (2001). Black faculty women in the academy: History, status, and future. *The Journal of Negro Education*, 70(3), 124–138. 10.2307/3211205

Harper, D. (2002). Talking about pictures: A case for photo elicitation. *Visual Studies*, 17(1), 13–26. 10.1080/14725860220137345

Hays, D. G., & Singh, A. A. (2012). *Qualitative inquiry in clinical and educational settings*. The Guilford Press.

Hobfoll, S. E. (1989). Conservation of resources: A new attempt at conceptualizing stress. *The American Psychologist*, 44(3), 513–524. 10.1037/0003-066X.44.3.5132648906

Holder, A. M. B., Jackson, M. A., & Ponterotto, J. G. (2015). Racial microaggression experiences and coping strategies of Black women in corporate leadership. *Qualitative Psychology*, 2(2), 164–180. 10.1037/qup0000024

hooks, b. (2001). *All about love: New visions*. Harper Perennial.

hooks, b. (2015). *Sisters of the yam: Black women and self-recovery*. Routledge.

Hughes, R. L., & Howard-Hamilton, M. F. (2003). Insights: Emphasizing issues that affect African American women. *New Directions for Student Services*, 2003(104), 95–104. 10.1002/ss.110

Jarmon, B. (2001). Unwritten rules of the game. In Mabokela, R. O., & Green, A. L. (Eds.), *Sisters of the academy: Emergent Black women scholars in higher education* (pp. 175–182). Stylus Publishing, LLC.

Jones, S. N. (2003). The praxis of Black female educational leadership from a systems thinking perspective [Unpublished doctoral dissertation]. Bowling Green State University.

Jones, T. B., Dawkins, L. S., McClinton, M. M., & Glover, M. H. (Eds.). (2012). *Pathways to higher education administration for African American women*. Routledge.

Kellas, J. K., & Horstman, H. K. (2014). Communicated narrative sense-making: Understanding family narratives, storytelling, and the construction of meaning through a communicative lens. In Turner, L. H., & West, R. (Eds.), *The SAGE Handbook of Family Communication* (pp. 76–90)., 10.4135/9781483375366.n5

Kellas, J. K. (2005). Family ties: Communicating identity through jointly told family stories. *Communication Monographs*, 72(4), 365–389. 10.1080/03637750500322453

Kramp, M. K. (2003). Exploring life and experience through narrative inquiry. In deMarrais, K. B., & Lapan, S. D. (Eds.), *Foundations for research: Methods of inquiry in education and the social sciences* (pp. 119–138). Routledge.

Livo, N. J., & Rietz, S. A. (1986). *Storytelling: Process and practice*. Libraries Unltd Inc.

Lord, R. G., & Hall, R. J. (2005). Identity, deep structure and the development of leadership skill. *The Leadership Quarterly*, 16(4), 591–615. 10.1016/j.leaqua.2005.06.003

Lutz, K. F., Hassouneh, D., Akeroyd, J., & Beckett, A. K. (2013). Balancing survival and resistance: Experiences of faculty of color in predominantly Euro American schools of nursing. *Journal of Diversity in Higher Education*, 6(2), 127–146. 10.1037/a0032364

McAdams, D. P. (1993). *The stories we live by: Personal myths and the making of the self*. Guilford Press.

McCain, K. D., & Matkin, G. S. (2019). Emerging adults leadership identity development through family storytelling: A narrative approach. *Journal of Leadership Education*, 18(2), 159–170. 10.12806/V18/I2/T3

Patitu, C. L., & Hinton, K. G. (2003). The experiences of African American women faculty and administrators in higher education: Has anything changed? *New Directions for Student Services*, 2003(104), 79–93. 10.1002/ss.109

Roebuck, J. B., & Murty, K. S. (1993). *Historically Black colleges and universities: Their place in American higher education*. Praeger.

Smith, K. (2020). Hidden Heirlooms: Black Families and Their Stories of Continuity. *Journal of Narrative Politics*, 6(2).

Solomon, B. M. (1985). *In the company of educated women: A history of women and higher education in America*. Yale University Press.

Stanley, C. A. (2009). Giving voice from the perspectives of African American women leaders. *Advances in Developing Human Resources*, 11(5), 551–561. 10.1177/1523422309351520

Stone, E. (2008). *Black sheep and kissing cousins: How our family stories shape us*. Transaction Publisher.

Templeton, J. (2000). *Pure unlimited love*. Templeton Foundation Press.

Toossi, M., & Joyner, L. (2018, February). *Blacks in the labor force*. U.S. Bureau of Labor Statistics. https://www.bls.gov/spotlight/2018/Blacks-in-the-labor-force/pdf/Blacks-in-the-labor-force.pdf

Underwood, L. (2009). Compassionate love: A framework for research. In Fehr, B., Sprecher, S., & Underwood, L. (Eds.), *The science of compassionate love: Theory, research, and applications* (pp. 1–25). Blackwell Publishing Ltd.

U.S. Census Bureau. (2011). *The Black population: 2010*. U.S. Department of Commerce. Economics and Statistics Administration. https://www.census.gov/prod/cen2010/briefs/c2010br-06.pdf

Vakalahi, H. F., & Starks, S. H. (2011). Health, well-being and women of color academics. *International Journal of Humanities and Social Science*, 1(2), 185–190.

Webster, L., & Mertova, P. (2007). *Using narrative inquiry as a research method: An introduction to using critical event narrative analysis in research on learning and teaching*. Routledge., 10.4324/9780203946268

WHOQOL SRPB Group. (2006). A cross-cultural study of spirituality, religion, and personal beliefs as components of quality of life. *Social Science & Medicine*, 62(6), 1486–1497. 10.1016/j.socscimed.2005.08.00116168541

Chapter 7
Reclaiming the Mainstream Depiction of Black Women:
The Modern–Day Representation of Black Women in Academia

Lovis M. Nelson-Williams
Baylor University, USA

ABSTRACT

Black women faculty in academia face unique challenges in the workplace, some of which stem from the historical marginalization of Black women in mainstream media. These challenges manifest as tokenism and lack of equal pay. Even in the face of these complexities, Black women have been able to permeate the bounds of the professional workspace by acquiring professional degrees at high rates at the turn of the 21st century. Black women faculty in academia are, unfortunately, negatively impacted by the unwelcoming environments of their academic institutions. The depiction of Black women in mainstream outlets acts as a barrier to workplace achievement for Black women professionals. For example, representations include the mammy, the asexual house servant, or Jezebel, the hypersexual Black woman. This chapter examines the history of controlling images of Black women in mainstream portrayals, the challenges faced by Black women faculty in academia, and the modern-day media representations of Black women faculty that aid in normalizing their presence in higher education institutions.

DOI: 10.4018/979-8-3693-0698-7.ch007

Copyright © 2024, IGI Global. Copying or distributing in print or electronic forms without written permission of IGI Global is prohibited.

INTRODUCTION

Black women have had to overcome a myriad of negative portrayals in popular culture from television advertisements to cinema in the United States. Black women have been able to permeate the bounds of so many facets of society, even though they were consigned to the fringes of society because of their once-enslaved status. Black women were relegated to roles such as low-wage workers (i.e., nannies and housemaids). Their portrayals in popular culture would reflect as such even after they began to enter different domains in society at the turn of the 20th century. Common portrayals solely highlighted their hypersexuality, asexuality, or sassy and uncompromising attitudes.

In the 21st century, Black women occupy some of the most competitive leadership roles in society; and while many strides still need to be made to increase their presence in these roles, popular culture has started to highlight Black women in roles where they were virtually absent on screen. One such role is Black women collegiate faculty members. Black women faculty in higher education have struggled in higher education environments, as Collins (1986) labeled the experience as The Outsider Within. Many Black women faculty struggle to be accepted in these spaces and are often isolated by the institutions they work for. They may face, for example, a lack of support for their research endeavors or lower pay. Amid these challenges, more and more representations of Black women faculty have begun to emerge. It is important to understand the historic controlling images of Black women in mainstream media in the United States; the challenges faced by Black women faculty in higher education environments and, how mainstream media depictions of Black women faculty in modern-day shows such as *The Chair* (2021), *Harlem* (2021) *and How to Get Away with Murder* (2014) help to reclaim the narrative that Black women do not belong as faculty in the academy.

THE LITERATURE

The history of Black women representations in popular culture. The marginalization of Black women in mainstream representation continues to be a challenge that undermines Black women professionals (Collins, 2009; Marshall-Wong, 2000; Woyshner & Schocker, 2015). The controlling images of Black women have historically been a challenge as Black women make efforts to reclaim the distasteful narratives that include portrayals such as mammies and Jezebels (Collins, 2009). Mainstream representations such as the docile Aunt Jemima in pancake advertisements undermine authentic depictions of Black women (Morgan, 1995). Research on the visual representation of Black women in history textbooks, which included mainstream and African American history books, also revealed that Black women are the most underrepresented compared to White men, White women, and Black men (Woyshner & Schocker, 2015). Marshall-Wong (2000) conducted a research study on portraying Black professional women in fiction and found a lack of exemplary representations of powerful Black professional women. Empowerment and agency were absent in portraying Black women and did not provide a guiding narrative for Black professional women today.

The historical portrayals of Black women in US popular culture (i.e., the media) are explicated in what Collins (1990) describes as oppressive controlling images, such as the mammy, the Jezebel, and the matriarch. The image of the mammy is the obedient, passive, asexual housemaid who works to serve the White family. She is embraced with love by the family she serves, however, her "place" in the household is that of a servant. She is paid a low wage, which keeps her in a state of poverty. She is a symbol of oppression because of her economic reality. Her status as a mother is also key because the image perpetuates the notion that Black women are defined by their motherhood and subservient status in society (Collins, 1990; Henderson, 2019). Mainstream depictions of the Mammy include television shows such as *Maude* (1972) and *Beulah* (1950). The Jezebel is a hypersexual, immoral, aggressive Black woman who is defined by her sexuality. This image of the Black woman was an opportunity to justify the sexual assaults of White men during the time of slavery as she was also economically exploited. The children produced during these sexual assaults were another source of labor and a commodity (Collins, 1990; Henderson, 2019). Mainstream depictions of the Jezebel were characterized in films such as *Foxy Brown* (1974) and *Birth of a Nation* (1915). The matriarch is overly dominant, emasculating, and assertive. Much like the Jezebel and the mammy, the matriarch is relegated to a life of poverty because of her unwillingness to conform to stereotypical ideals of "womanly behavior" (being docile and gentile). Therefore, she is abandoned by her male partner and forced to become the breadwinner in her household. Matriarchs are also coined as mothers but as mothers who are neglectful of their children as they struggle to provide for their single-parent households (Collins, 1990; Henderson, 2019). Popular culture depictions of the matriarch are found in shows such as *Good Times* (1974) and *Thea* (1993).

A recent study by Tyree and Powell (2022) examined whether or not the common stereotypes of African American women still prevail on television in the 50 years between 1970 and 2020. Tyree and Powell (2020) reviewed shows such as *The Cosby Show, Living Single, Road Rules, Insecure,* and *The Bachelor.* While Black women's representation increased in number, the common tropes such as the Jezebel and the mammy could be found throughout the decades. The findings in the shows reviewed during the 2010s provide insight into how reality television has contributed to disparaging images of Black women. According to Tyree and Powell (2022):

Reality television became the genre for the ghettoization of African American women's representations. This type of programming set up roles where Black women had extreme aggression and hostility compared to every other race and allowed for the sexual subjectification of their bodies. (pp. 286-287)

Reality television has highlighted the most unsavory elements of Black women and has been replicated because these shows are so popular. They magnify stereotypes such as the Jezebel.

There were common themes that emerged in the researchers' examination of studies conducted on representations of Black women in mainstream media. Tyree and Powell (2022) offer insight into the perpetuation of problematic stereotypes. For example, a key observation was that there was a smaller pool of family shows to utilize for research, there are not enough television shows that explore Black family life. For shows that are in existence, many of them highlight portrayals of single-parent homes or Black women dominating their husbands in two-family households (Baptiste, 1986; Tyree & Powell, 2022). Another notable observation was that in the 1970s, there was an oversaturation of Black women professionals depicted in television that was not representative of their reality during that time in history. There was an emphasis on conveying Black women as having a place in professions such as lawyers and doctors (Seggar & Wheeler, 1973; Tyree & Powell, 2022). And lastly, there was an absence of representing Black women in affectionate relationships. Many representations show Black women at two extremes, either they are hypersexualized or asexual. While this is a reflection of Collin's (1990) research on controlling images, this research is an overall assessment of the many studies conducted on the representation of Black women in television over the last 50 years.

A study conducted by Mctaggart et. al (2019) explored how Black women and Black girls are represented in television shows and films in the United States. Mctaggart et. al (2019) conducted a content analysis by reviewing highly watched films and television shows between 2009 and 2010. They explore facets of representation such as sexuality, stereotypes, skin color, and hairstyle. The findings are segmented by positive findings in film and television representations and negative findings in television and film representations of Black women and girls. Regarding cinematic works, a key finding was that while Black women and girls make up about 6.7% of the population, approximately less than half play leading or co-leading roles in the most popular films of the decade (Mctaggart et. al, 2019). Similar to what Collins (1990) coins as the Jezebel, the prevalence of sexualizing Black women at a higher rate than White women was a finding. According to Mctaggart et. al (2019), "When it comes to sexualization, Black women (13.5%) and other women of color (14.8%) are more likely to be depicted as partially/fully nude than white women (9.0%)." In addition, seeds of Collins' (1990) controlling image, the matriarch (depictions that highlight Black women as aggressive) are present as Black females are approximately 5% more likely to be shown as violent than White female characters (Mctaggart et. al, 2019).

In addition to some of these negative findings regarding Black females in films, there were some positive findings. Black women were more likely to be depicted as leaders, working in the STEM field, and less likely to be shown working in a service job in comparison to White females (Mctaggart et. al, 2019). The change in Black women being portrayed in service jobs directly counters, The Mammy, one of the most common historical portrayals of Black women in a domestic role.

There were also a considerable number of findings, both negative and positive regarding representations in television. In stark contrast to the big screen, according to Mctaggart et. al (2019), "Black female characters are twice as likely as white female characters and other female characters of color to be shown in a service industry job (56.3% compared to 26.4% and 20.6%, respectively)." In addition, Black women in television were also more sexualized than their White counterparts as they were more likely to be depicted without having a romantic partner, but they were still linked to another individual with whom they had sexual encounters. Black women were also more likely to be objectified and without a job in comparison to White women. Some positive results of the study were that Black females were more likely to be conveyed as "smart" and attractive than White women and more likely to be leading characters in a television series.

BLACK WOMEN FACULTY IN HIGHER EDUCATION

Extensive literature has explored Black women faculty's workplace challenges. Black women faculty have limited growth opportunities and lack support from higher education institutions that employ them. Black women have existed in these institutional spaces without a sense of belonging. Many higher education institutions are grounded in ideologies of White supremacy (Collins, 1986, 2002; Harley, 2007; Love & Jiggetts, 2019) that often undermine the professional development of Black women faculty.

Collins (1986) establishes and defines the phenomenon, the outsider within—feelings of isolation as a higher education faculty member. Black women in academia have acquired the accolades and education to teach within the walls of higher education institutions. However, their identities and experiences counter the White dominant culture—this divergence creates a feeling of alienation. Although different iterations of the outsider within now exist, the original intent was to begin a conversation about the unique collective position of Black women in the United States (Collins, 1986). Black women are marginalized and face discrimination due to their intersecting identities, such as race, gender, and class (Collins, 2002; Crenshaw, 1991). Collins (1986) specifically charges Black women intellectuals with challenging and revamping the systems that have made the outsider within phenomenon possible.

THEORETICAL FRAMEWORK

According to Collins (1990), Black Feminist Thought (BFT) is a theoretical framework that aims to explain the unique position and experiences of Black women in society. Black women face discrimination based on intersecting identities, such as race, sex, and class. BFT is a theoretical framework grounded in empowering Black women, as the theory unearths insight into what has contributed to forming a Black woman's identity (Howard-Hamilton, 2003). BFT acknowledges that Black women's experiences can be multifaceted and unique—however, there are undeniable generalities. The crafting of these generalities that shape the Black woman's identity is by individuals who are not Black women (Collins, 2002; Howard-Hamilton, 2003). According to Howard-Hamilton (2003), disparaging imagery and stereotypes about Black women have become normalized in society, "therefore, self-valuation, self-definition, and knowledge validation must replace the negative images of self in the minds of these women" (p. 22). Therefore, BFT provides an essential justification for the need to understand how Black women faculty are portrayed in popular culture. Collins (2002) is essentially positing a call to action; Black women must work to redefine what society has deemed as normative when it comes to how Black women are perceived and revamp the imagery.

METHODOLOGY

To explore the portrayals of Black women faculty in popular culture I examined two television shows with central characters that are Black women faculty. This research analyzed the characters, Yaz McKay from *The Chair* (2021), Camille Parks from *Harlem* (2021) and Annalise Keating from *How to Get Away with Murder* (2014). In watching season one of each show, notations of their portrayal as Black women were made. Each character was examined by exploring their commitment to teaching and their students, their relationship with the administration, and the complexities of their lives outside of their roles as faculty members.

FINDINGS

The Chair. The character Yaz McKay is an English Professor at Pembroke University. Her role is intertwined with the premise of the show, which is centered on the character Ji-Yoon, who is the first woman (who is also a woman of color) to become the Chair of the English Department. Ji-Yoon takes an interest in Yaz because of her progressive teaching methods and because she is a woman of color. Ji-Yoon's goal is to revamp the English department's traditional make-up, stoked in White privilege and male dominance by attempting to highlight Yaz's accomplishments and help elevate her career in the department. Ji-Yoon wants to offer Yaz the opportunity to become tenured.

Yaz is depicted as a faculty member who is fiercely committed to teaching and invested in the education of her students. Her approach in the classroom is known as progressive because of her ability to make the classical material she teaches relatable to the lives of her students. She utilizes the designated material, such as Melville's *Moby Dick* but allows students to explore these works with modern-day outlets such as social media and rap music. She encourages their literary exploration through the forms of expression she knows will allow students to express their creativity while learning about important literary works. Her methods are so beloved by the student population that her English course has the highest enrollment in the English Department. The student interest in her course becomes the basis for another English section at the same time as her course to be combined with her class because of its low enrollment. She is forced to work with Elliot Rentz, a professor who had for decades dominated the English department and was well accomplished, but his methods had become outdated, especially in comparison to Yaz. According to Peet and Wyman (2021), during a joint class, a student asks Elliot about Herman Melville's abusive behavior toward women and he is dismissed. Yaz interjects by saying they will discuss the topic during the discussion she leads as well as the women who contributed to Melville's work. Her students are visibly excited by her comment, and it depicts her willingness to explore the ideas and interests of her students to encourage their investment in the material.

Yaz's relationship with the administration is complex but authentic in its depiction. While the new Chair of the department genuinely wants to secure Yaz's place at Pembroke, there is staunch opposition by the administration. While Yaz works closely with Elliot because of their combined class, he criticizes her use of social media to connect with students. She assigns her students the task of tweeting their favorite line from the assigned reading and Elliot comments that it is a superficial way of getting the students to engage. Eliot explains to Yaz that his goal is to have the students immerse themselves in the story in its entirety. He describes her tweeting activity as "low-hanging fruit". In another tense interaction with Elliot,

Yaz confronts him because she gets a glimpse of the report he crafts for her tenure committee meeting. His report is critical of her work, and she wants an explanation. In this interaction, Elliot conveys that a critique of her work is the norm and that he is one of her supporters. Yaz lashes out at him revealing that she was forced to combine their classes because of Elliot's low enrollment and Elliot once again criticizes her teaching methods, labeling them as pandering to her students which is something he refuses to do.

Early in the season, the Chair of the department announced at a faculty party that Yaz would be the first Black woman to receive the Distinguished Lectureship. Unfortunately, the administration undermines the Chair's decision and offers it to an outsider, a celebrity who is a White man. Yaz again, confronts the administration after this change in plans by meeting with the Chair of the English Department. The Chair tries to assuage Yaz's concerns by making excuses for the individuals behind the decision such as Elliot, who is resentful because of his low enrollment. According to Robbins (2021), Yaz replies to the Chair, "I see why you feel sorry for him. He only got to rule Pembroke for the last 40 years". Faced with this disappointment, Yaz decides to give her lecture at Yale University. In communicating this opportunity to the Chair, she also reveals that Yale is also looking to recruit her to be a faculty member. According to Kim (2021), the Chair is visibly worried about this potential loss and says "You are going to be the first tenured Black woman in the department", to which Yaz replies, "That's why I'm leaving". Yaz refuses to be the token Black professor in a setting that is outdated in its thinking about who should be tenured professors in the English department.

The character of Yaz is virtually relegated to being seen within the walls of the institution she works for; her role as a faculty member is the sum of what viewers get to see. Yaz does attend a social function for Pembroke professors. Viewers get a small glimpse into Yaz outside the halls of the institution or the classroom (Peet & Robbins, 2021). Her style of dress is in direct opposition to the sea of faculty and administrators in suits and ties. She wears a half-floral, half-polka-dotted dress with a natural hairstyle. She considers not drinking alcohol at the party in a room filled with Pembroke elites and tries to connect with Elliot, her complete opposite. After opening a book Elliot wrote in years past, with a dedication to his students, she makes an effort to connect with him. They find common ground by discovering that they both like to take refuge in the archives entitled the North Star.

HARLEM

Camille Park is an adjunct professor at Columbia University who teaches Anthropology courses. As the main character, Camille lives in Harlem and has formed strong bonds of friendship with three other Black women whom she met in college. She finds strength and support in these relationships as they all navigate the nuances of career goals, romance, and surviving their 30s in the quickly transforming neighborhood of Harlem.

The character of Camille is portrayed as a professor whose courses are incredibly popular with the students because of her commitment to exploring interesting and captivating concepts in anthropology. In every scene depicting her course, she is lecturing to a packed lecture hall of engaged students. Her classes have waiting lists and her character is portrayed as someone willing to work through the night because she is dedicated to her profession. The pilot episode opens with Camille giving a lecture on Cultural and Social Anthropology: Sex and Modern Love. She discusses a tribe in the Himalayan Mountains that has completely transformed the concept of gender norms in society. It is a society in which women have dominion over men and choose their spouses. The concept is fascinating to the students as she charges them to do mini self-case studies by asking them to take on the gender norms of those who live in this tribe. She pushes her students to actualize these concepts in their lives for a deeper understanding of the ideas. Most of the episodes open up with Camille in the classroom utilizing a concept in Anthropology to explain the nuances of modern-day relationships (Oliver et al., 2021). According to Dungey (2021), Camille flashes across her projector, images of different mating customs in Latin, European, Asian, and African nations to depict the wide range of customs that exist. Camille says, "Across all cultures, mating is very often a dance of deception. In the name of sex, love, and everything in between, perceptions are played with in order to enhance or hide certain realities". She uses the topic of mating rituals as a window into how students interact in their dating relationships and what they may or may not allow others to see.

The administration in *Harlem* is explicated through the relationship Camille has with the Chair of her department; Camille struggles to further her career in the world of academia. The Chair of Camille's department is a White woman who is quickly replaced at the very beginning of season one for making insensitive comments at a rally for women. However, in Camille's first interactions with her, she is trying to prove her value by showing her an offer letter she received from Kansas State University. Kansa State is offering her a full-time professorship and tenure. According to Oliver (2021), Camille complains to the Chair and says "Columbia is what I want, Columbia is my soulmate, but the bitch won't commit. Sorry, I just need to know that I'm not going to wind up being Columbia's oldest adjunct professor." Camille's advisor reveals that she will be making room in the department, so that she can become full-time, but that good news is short-lived when the Chair is let go from Columbia University. The new Chair is a Black woman but Camile's relationship with her develops into a very tense and uncomfortable one after she misses an appointment with her to work on a research project. The climax of their tense relationship occurs when the Chair refuses to endorse Camille for the full-time professorship she had been promised by her predecessor. She is told that she is not ready to take on the position, due to her lack of academic journal publications and field work. Her use of social media to engage in anthropological discourse is seen as in direct opposition to the norms of the traditional academic discourse. In addition, she is charged with carrying "the weight" of all Black women academics, and that her failure would reflect poorly on the entire group. The new Chair is unwilling to take a risk on Camille. She is left feeling dejected and unsure of what her next steps should be.

Outside of the academic environment, Camille is a woman struggling to find love yet finds a way to ground herself in the comfort of her friends and therapist. Her character is portrayed as driven and strong. Her wardrobe is stylish and unapologetically sexy. However, her vulnerability is conveyed when she encounters her ex-lover. She is unsure of what to say when she sees him. She allows herself to be honest with him about still having feelings for him. When he rejects her because he is engaged, she finds a new love interest. She tries to enjoy her newfound love but battles the emotions she still feels for her ex-lover. She juggles life, friends, and work but her wellbeing comes last because she has put off meeting with her therapist for weeks. Camille admits that it is difficult to balance everything. In finally meeting with her therapist, Camille lays bare her life plan. She had imagined she would have already been tenured, married, and two years away from family planning at her age. Instead, she is single, and her career is in a tenuous place. According to Matt (2021), Camille says "This is not how I pictured my life. I thought that by now I'd be a renowned tenured anthropologist that little Black girls would want to dress like for Halloween". Her therapist proposes the possibility of letting go of a life plan she made in her teens and allowing herself to explore the possibility of taking life as it comes. In doing so she could chart a new path for herself and stop mourning the loss of what she thought her life would be.

HOW TO GET AWAY WITH MURDER

Annalise Keating is an adjunct professor at Middleton University who teaches Criminal Law 100. Her introductory course is entitled How to Get Away with Murder. She is a criminal defense lawyer who also has a law clinic that enables her students to ascertain real-world criminal law experience. The show is built on the premise of the murder of her husband by her students. As the show unravels, viewers are provided with insight into Annalise's traumatic past and her ultimate commitment to keeping her students safe. Her reputation precedes her as she is known for her no-nonsense approach in the classroom and the courtroom.

Criminal Law 100 with Annalise is considered to be "the class" to take, as students are eager to take her course because of her real-world experience in the courtroom. The pilot episode displays a packed lecture hall with students discussing the rigor of the class, comparing their level of preparedness and even fear of being called upon because of what they have heard about the intensity of the material. On day one of her course, Annalise makes a clear distinction between her course and other law courses at Middleton University. I According to Nowalk (2014), Annalise says "Unlike my colleagues, I will not be teaching you about how to study the law or theorize about it, but rather how to practice it in a courtroom." Her classroom is a Socratic-style environment as students dissect criminal cases by way of rapid-fire questing from Annalise. Students are challenged to "think on their toes" and provided with honest feedback when needed. When Annalise shoots a question to a student who is unable to answer, another student quickly stands up, providing the class with the answer. Instead of thanking her, according to Nowalk (2014), Annalise says "Never take a learning opportunity from another student, no matter how smart you want everyone to think you are."

Students are presented with active cases that Annalise's firm is working on to merge theory and practice. On day two of classes Annalise has already tasked her students with providing a reasonable defense for her client. Those who come up with the most compelling reasons are drafted into her law clinic to work on her active cases. She consistently imparts the knowledge she has come to be confronted with as a defense attorney. According to Nowalk (2014), Annalise says, "That was one case that opened my eyes to the fact that the justice system doesn't always reward those who tell the truth, but those that have the power to create their own." She wants her students to truly understand the realities of what it means to be a defense lawyer.

Annalise is virtually autonomous in her role as an adjunct professor as is depicted by her classroom methods. Her interactions with the administration are almost non-existent in season one. She has the power to dismiss students who underperform and has complete disregard for the other courses that her students are enrolled in. In challenging her students to collect evidence for one of her cases which required them to show up to court the next morning, she dismisses her student's pushback about missing classes if she attends court. Everyone has Torts at 10 am and then Property at 11 am. Annalise's reply challenges her student. According to Nowalk (2014), Annaliese replies, "The way you're whining right now makes me think I'm your mother Ms. Pratt. Show up tomorrow or drop out of the competition, it's that simple". Her student does indeed show up to court and does not miss out on the opportunity to engage in an active criminal case. After the death of her husband, Annalise's dean places a substitute in her class so that she can have some time to grieve. Instead, she shows up to class ready to work. In the short interaction with her colleague, she tells him to leave, and he does so without any objection, outside of telling her the dean instructed him to fill in. She begins class and within five minutes she is brought information about one of her criminal cases. She dismissed her class right away and proceeded to work on her case.

Annalise's worlds of academia and criminal defense work are merged but outside of them, she has so many facets to her personality and personal life. She is married but infidelity exists within her relationship. Both her husband (who is also a professor) and herself are unfaithful in their marriage. When she finds out that her husband has slept with a student, she confronts him. According to Bellomo (2014), she retorts, "Don't you dare say you were just sending pictures because I know you were screwing her. How long did it go on? How many times? Where?" Her disappointment and anger resound as she scolds her husband. Annalise's character is "laid bare". After a grueling day, she sits in front of a mirror and removes her wig, her eyelashes, and her makeup. Her hair underneath is a short natural style. She is completely stripped of all of the layers of preparation she applies to be "ready" to face the world she operates within (Swafford, 2014). She is vulnerable in this moment and viewers get a glimpse of the real Annalise.

Another key layer to Annalise is revealed when her mother visits her. Her relationship with her mother is tense at best but she comes to visit Annalise when she takes some time away from work because her lover is accused of killing her husband. First viewers are made aware that Annalise's name is Anna Mae. Second, during the visit, viewers get a glimpse into the trauma that Annalise has endured in her life which is the reason she has an estranged relationship with her mother. She is angry with her mother because she was sexually assaulted as a child. According to Stockstill and Swafford (2015), Annalise lashes out and says to her mother, "Did you know? Did you know what he did to me? So, you knew." She is extremely hurt by finding out that her mother knew that her uncle sexually abused her. According to Stockstill and Swafford (2015), Annalise expresses "My sorry ass husband may have been a lowlife, but he saw me. Why I am this way? Sam knew exactly what happened to me the moment I stepped into his office. Everything." The impact of this abuse has contributed to how she operates in the world.

CONCLUSION

Each character is an example of versatile Black women portrayals in popular culture. The empowerment component of BFT is embodied in these characters because they are depicted as amazingly creative in connecting with their students and sharp in their application of the material that they present in the classroom. Their ability to engage in the classroom reshapes the identity of Black women on screen by positing characterizations such as capable, educated, and brilliant (Collins, 2002; Howard-Hamilton, 2003). Each character by virtue of their roles is self-defining and validates their undeniable place in the world of academia (Collins, 2002; Howard-Hamilton, 2003). The characters Yaz and Camille are told that their non-traditional approaches, such as the use of social media in the world of academia have no place. It is clear that the world academia needs to "catch up" with them if it wants to continue to retain students given the strong student interest in their approaches to the material. Annalise is also unconventional in her approach as students get the opportunity to work on active criminal court cases rather than studying cases that have already been decided upon. Each character's commitment to their students' ability to understand the content of the coursework is undeniable. These portrayals are vehicles of empowerment for other Black women who see their triumphs as Black women.

Each character challenges the one-dimensional historical portrayals (Collins, 1991) of Black women that zero in on their sexuality or domesticity. Not only are these women faculty member, but they have nuisances that make them complex individuals. While Yaz's portrayal outside of the academic setting is limited, her style of dress and natural hair directly counters the norm of what it means to be a professor. Camille's character does the same with her stylish outfits and long Nubian twists. The traditional portrayal of older White males in suits standing in front of students as the norm is challenged. Camille's character is not relegated to any one aspect of her being as she is a professor, but she is also unsure about love, in therapy, and needs the support of her friends. Annalise is a whip in class and in the courtroom, but she is also a woman who has endured immense suffering. Her strength in some settings may even dehumanize her very essence. However, when viewers get to see her without makeup, the sadness she feels when confronting her husband's infidelity and then confronting her mother about her history of sexual abuse—Annalise is multidimensional. In these moments these characters are self-defining the complex nature of the identity of Black women.

Another key aspect of these portrayals was the insight that Yaz and Camille provide in depicting the struggle that Black women faculty face in career advancement (Collins, 2002; Gregory, 2001). While Annalise's focus is not solely her academic advancement, it a major focal point for Yaz and Camille. Both, provide a realistic depiction of how Black women find it difficult to secure tenure. Yaz is continuously being undermined by the administration, first by having her Distinguished Lectureship taken away and then by realizing a colleague who has a say in her advancement had a negative assessment of her work. She is made to feel like an outsider, as she is the only Black woman in her department. The Chair of her department wants to advance her, but the establishment wants to preserve the "traditional" makeup of the department—White and male-dominated. Camille is also met with disappointment, but in her case, she is told by another Black woman that she is not accomplished enough to secure a full-time tenure track position at Columbia University. Her academic contributions, much like many Black women who may concentrate efforts in the classroom rather than on publications are undercut when it is time to seek opportunities for growth (Collins, 2002; Gregory, 2001; Love & Jiggetts, 2019).

Overall, these characters are the gateway to re-envisioning representations of Black women. Popular culture depictions of Black women faculty highlight the undeniable place they have in the world of academia. Not only do these characters convey their capability but provide much-needed attention to the career advancement struggles Black women face in the academy.

REFERENCES

Baptiste, D. A.Jr. (1986). The image of the black family portrayed by television: A critical comment. *Marriage & Family Review*, 10(1), 50. 10.1300/J002v10n01_03

Bellomo, A. T. (Writer), & Listo, M. (Director). (2014, October 23). We're Not Friends. (Season 1, Episode 5) [TV Series]. In Rhimes, S., Beers, B., D'Elia, B., Nowalk, P. (Executive Producers), How to Get Away with Murder. Shondaland. NoWalk Entertainment. ABC Studios.

Collins, P. H. (1986). Learning from the outsider within: The sociological significance of Black feminist thought. *Social Problems*, 33(6), S14–S32. 10.1525/sp.1986.33.6.03a00020

Collins, P. H. (1990). *Black feminist thought in the matrix of domination*. Unwin Hyman.

Collins, P. H. (2002). Learning from the outsider within: The sociological significance of Black feminist thought. In C. S. Turner, A. L. Antonio, M. Garcia, B. V. Laden, A. Nora, and C. Presley (Ed.), *Racial and ethnic diversity in higher education* (1–9). Pearson Custom.

Collins, P. H. (2009). *Black feminist thought*. Routledge.

Crenshaw, K. (1991). Mapping the margins: Intersectionality, identity politics, and violence against women of color. *Stanford Law Review*, 43(6), 1241–1298. 10.2307/1229039

D'Elia, B. (Writer), & Foley, M. (Director). (2014, October 30). Freakin' Whack-a-Mole. (Season 1, Episode 6) [TV Series]. In Rhimes, S., Beers, B., D'Elia, B., Nowalk, P. (Executive Producers), How to Get Away with Murder. Shondaland. NoWalk Entertainment. ABC Studios.

Dungey, A. (Writer), & Mendoza, L. (Director). (2021, December 3). Rainbow Sprinkles. (Season 1, Episode 3) [TV Series]. In Oliver, T., King, S., Poehler, A., Becky, Lessing, K., Williams, P., Valdez, M., Bausch, D., Mendoza, L., Dungey, A., Brown, N., Free, T., Matt, B., Breece, J., Saxton, s., Varga, S. (Producers), *Harlem*. Amazon Studios.

Gregory, S. T. (2001). Black faculty women in the academy: History, status, and future. *The Journal of Negro Education*, 70(3), 124–138. 10.2307/3211205

Harley, D. A. (2007). Maids of academe: African American women faculty at predominately White institutions. *Springer Science and Business Media, 12*(1), 19–36. 10.1007/s12111-007-9030-5

Henderson, M. (2019). Portrayals of Black women in TV shows that aired in 1997 versus 2017: A qualitative content analysis. *Elon Journal of Undergraduate Research in Communications*, 10(1), 64–69.

Kim, J. (Writer) & Longino, G. D. (Director). (2021, August 20). The Last Bus in Town. (Season 1, Episode 5) [TV Series]. In Peet, A., Benioff, D., Weiss, B. D., Caufield, B., Longino, G. D., Oh, S., (Executive Producers), *The Chair*. Netflix.

Love, B. J., & Jiggetts, V. D. (2019). Black women rising: Jumping double-dutch with a liberatory consciousness. In Evans, S. (Ed.), *Black women and social justice education: legacies and lessons* (pp. 1–20). State University of New York Press. 10.1515/9781438472966-002

Marshall-Wong, C. R. (2000). Challenges to agency in the workplace: An analysis of Black professional women in fiction and in their lives. [Doctoral dissertation, University of Chicago]. ProQuest Dissertations and Theses Global.

Matt, B. (Writer), & Muhammad, S. (Director). (2021, December 3). The Strong Black Woman. (Season 1, Episode 7) [TV Series]. In Oliver, T., King, S., Poehler, A., Becky, Lessing, K., Williams, P., Valdez, M., Bausch, D., Mendoza, L., Dungey, A., Brown, N., Free, T., Matt, B., Breece, J., Saxton, s., Varga, S. (Producers), *Harlem*. Amazon Studios.

Mctaggart, N., Cox, V., Heldman, C. (2019). Representations of Black women in Hollywood. *Geena Davis Institute on Gender in Media*, 1–15.

Morgan, J. (1995). Mammy the huckster: Selling the old south for the new century. *American Art*, 9(1), 87–109. 10.1086/424235

Nowalk, P. (Writer), & Offer, M. (Director). (2014, September 25). Pilot. (Season 1, Episode 1) [TV Series]. In Rhimes, S., Beers, B., D'Elia, B., Nowalk, P. (Executive Producers), *How to Get Away with Murder*. Shondaland. NoWalk Entertainment. ABC Studios.

Oliver, T. (Writer), & Lee, D.L. (Director). (2021, December 3). Pilot. (Season 1, Episode 1) [TV Series]. In Oliver, T., King, S., Poehler, A., Becky, Lessing, K., Williams, P., Valdez, M., Bausch, D., Mendoza, L., Dungey, A., Brown, N., Free, T., Matt, B., Breece, J., Saxton, s., Varga, S. (Producers), *Harlem*. Amazon Studios.

Oliver, T., King, S., Poehler, A., Becky, Lessing, K., Williams, P., Valdez, M., Bausch, D., Mendoza, L., Dungey, A., Brown, N., Free, T., Matt, B., Breece, J., Saxton, s., Varga, S. (Producers). (2021). *Harlem* [TV. Series]. Amazon Studios.

Peet, A., Benioff, D., Weiss, B. D., Caufield, B., Longino, G. D., Oh, S., (Executive Producers). (2021). *The Chair* [TV Series]. Netflix.

Peet, A., & Robbins, E. R. (Writer) & Longino, G. D. (Director). (2021, August 20). The Faculty Party. (Season 1, Episode 2) [TV Series]. In Peet, A., Benioff, D., Weiss, B. D., Caufield, B., Longino, G. D., Oh, S., (Executive Producers), *The Chair.* Netflix.

Peet, A., & Wyman, J. A. (Writer) & Longino, G. D. (Director). (2021, August 20). The Town Hall. (Season 1, Episode 3) [TV Series]. In Peet, A., Benioff, D., Weiss, B. D., Caufield, B., Longino, G. D., Oh, S., (Executive Producers), *The Chair.* Netflix.

Rhimes, S., Beers, B., D'Elia, B., Nowalk, P. (Executive Producers). (2014). *How to Get Away with Murder* [TV. Series]. Shondaland. NoWalk Entertainment. ABC Studios.

Robbins, E. R. (Writer) & Longino, G. D. (Director). (2021, August 20). Don't Kill Bill. (Season 1, Episode 4) [TV Series]. In Peet, A., Benioff, D., Weiss, B. D., Caufield, B., Longino, G. D., Oh, S., (Executive Producers), *The Chair.* Netflix.

Seggar, J. F., & Wheeler, P. (1973). World of work on tv: Ethnic and sex representation in tv drama. *Journal of Broadcasting,* 17(2), 201–214. 10.1080/08838157309363684

Stockstill, D., & Swafford, G. E. (Writer), & Foley, M. (Director). (2015, February 19). Mama's Here Now. (Season 1, Episode 13) [TV Series]. In Rhimes, S., Beers, B., D'Elia, B., Nowalk, P. (Executive Producers), How to Get Away with Murder. Shondaland. NoWalk Entertainment. ABC Studios.

Swafford, G. E. (Writer), & Innes, L. (Director). (2014, October 16). Let's Get to Scooping. (Season 1, Episode 4) [TV Series]. In Rhimes, S., Beers, B., D'Elia, B., Nowalk, P. (Executive Producers), *How to Get Away with Murder.* Shondaland. NoWalk Entertainment. ABC Studios.

Tyree, C. M. T., & Powell, A. (2022). African American women's representations on television. *Journal of African American Studies,* 26(3), 277–296. 10.1007/s12111-022-09587-1

Woyshner, C., & Schocker, J. B. (2015). Cultural parallax and content analysis: Images of Black women in high school history textbooks. *Theory and Research in Social Education,* 43(4), 441–468. 10.1080/00933104.2015.1099487

Chapter 8
From Mammy
to Matriarch

DeNiece Kemp
Confluence Academies-South City, USA

ABSTRACT

This chapter provides an insightful perspective on two stereotypes unique to Black women, the mammy and the sapphire, and how they contribute to the formation of the matriarchal model in Black women educators. It offers an understanding of how these experiences can be shaped to positively impact all students, especially African American students and their families. Interwoven throughout the chapter are personal narratives from five African American women who work in education in varying roles to further illustrate how these stereotypes manifest in their work. This chapter also includes the author's personal narrative of her experiences with two students and their mothers, providing a powerful testament to the multifaceted impact of Black women embracing the matriarchal model. The narratives provide a framework for understanding the importance of the matriarchal model and the mentorship and community that are associated with it. In this chapter, stereotypes about Black women are challenged, and Black women are encouraged to take ownership for their identity.

INTRODUCTION

When an underrepresented social identity group appears to be a threat to the majority, the majority forms fabricated narratives to describe the perceived threat (Seo & Hinton, 2009). Several negative stereotypes have been associated with black women throughout history: loud, aggressive, welfare queen. Black women's personal and professional experiences have been profoundly impacted by these stereotypes,

DOI: 10.4018/979-8-3693-0698-7.ch008

Copyright © 2024, IGI Global. Copying or distributing in print or electronic forms without written permission of IGI Global is prohibited.

historically and presently. These stereotypes frequently portray Black women inaccurately and are harmful. In Zora Neale Hurston's 1937 novel, *Their Eyes Were Watching God*, the heroine Janie Crawford said that Black women were the mules of the earth (p. 14). Typically, gentle and docile animals, mules are known as loyal and hardworking. Furthermore, mules are regarded as stubborn, resulting in the commonly used expression "as stubborn as a mule."

Apart from the fact that this comparison diminishes Black women to the status of animals, mules are generally not the type of animal the average person would desire for any reason other than their capability to perform hard, backbreaking work. Thomas and Hill (2022) assert the idea that Black women are somehow less than human persists in some aspects of contemporary American life. McDole (2017) contended that Black stereotypes act as powerful tools that reinforce social inequalities. These stereotypes are created to portray racism, sexism, and classism as natural and unavoidable aspects of Black people's lives, rather than as systemic issues. Among many stereotypical terms used to dehumanize African American women, mammy, and sapphire are but two examples. These caricatures present images of Black women as mules: docile, hardworking, and stubborn. Warren-Gordon and McMillan (2022) assert that the influence these images have on Black women and how they are regarded impacts every aspect of their lives.

The mammy and sapphire stereotypes may appear to be opposed, but they work in concert to preserve white supremacy and power. These stereotypes restrict Black women to pre-defined roles that don't challenge the status quo. The Mammy is overly devoted to white families, diminishing her own agency and reinforcing the idea that Black women are subservient. The Sapphire is seen as angry and aggressive, making her a target for control and silencing legitimate grievances. This chapter argues that Black women navigate a unique space where they must reconcile two seemingly contradictory stereotypes: the nurturing "mammy" and the assertive "sapphire." By drawing on both of these stereotypes, Black women can establish a matriarchal model that allows them to be both caring and powerful figures. This influence can positively impact Black women educators, their students, and their educational community. In this chapter, I will discuss the impact of these stereotypes on the experiences of Black women educators. Additionally, I will provide an alternative perspective of these stereotypes opportunities to be reshaped to positively impact all students, particularly African American students. Interwoven throughout the chapter are personal narratives from several African American women who work in education in varying roles to further illustrate how these stereotypes manifest in their work. My personal narrative as an educator will complement the stories of the educators highlighted in this chapter to serve as testament to the multifaceted impact of Black women that favors embracing those traits we inherently possess, denying those traits that have been imposed on us, and taking ownership of defining ourselves.

In his preschool year, Malik's mom spent all of her time at the hospital with his older brother. His brother had suddenly become terminally ill and would eventually succumb to his illness. She was a single mom, raising her boys with the support of her sister and mother. I'd see his mom during dismissal at parent pick-up and we eventually began bonding over sneakers. Having experienced the same thing as she, losing a son suddenly to an illness, my heart went out to her and I always made a point to connect with her in a positive way because I understood how important it was for a grieving mother to feel connected and grounded through relationship, even if it was only a casual relationship built on a love for sneakers. A small reprieve from the grief and others reminding you of the grief by expressing their condolences which often felt like pity. Kindergarten year, Malik spent the majority of his school days in the hallway with the resource officer if he was not sent to in-school suspension or home. Unable to be successful in his classroom, he had become disruptive and explosive. His first-grade year is when I began building a relationship with him. I had sons at home who had lost a brother also. I was hypersensitive to the fact that children are not immune to the trauma of grief that we adults experience. Teaching second grade, my classroom was just a couple doors away from his first-grade classroom, which he spent sitting outside of a great deal of the time. He would come to school late just about every day and would refuse to go into his classroom. Throughout the day, you'd see him either in the hall again, or hanging out of the classroom door while his teacher was delivering instruction. Whenever I would see him in the hall, I would go and briefly talk to him, trying to coax him into his room. His teacher was kind and recognized his struggles and did what she could to be supportive while still holding him accountable. Eventually, he would begin taking breaks with me in my classroom, or I'd take extra time to talk to him when I saw him in the hall. We developed a pretty good relationship. I was able to see how smart and witty he was. Now, Malik is in second grade, in my second-grade class. The transition was seamless because he and I had already built a relationship during his first-grade year. He was excited to be with me and I was happy to have him. I knew the road ahead for us was not going to be an easy one, but most certainly necessary for both his growth and my own. **Personal Narrative, 2nd Grade Teacher**

JUST KEEP THEM CALM

I feel like being a caregiver and providing emotional support to students is an unspoken expectation for me as a Black woman educator. Administration has assumed that I have the ability to deal with students with repeated and aggressive behavior problems with no support from them. I have been told to "just keep them calm," but nothing has been said regarding my teaching skills or a plan to get certain students support for their mental health issues. **Nylette Farmer, First Grade Teacher**

The image most have of Harriet Tubman is that of an escaped enslaved woman who became an abolitionist and social activist. However, Tubman was born Araminta 'Minty' Ross, loaned out by her owner to be a house or nursemaid in neighboring homes at a young age. (McGowan & Kashatus, 2011). She was expected to be obedient and respectful to her owners, docile and subservient. McDole (2017) explained that mammy is usually associated with grandmotherly or elderly women; however, "mammies" who nursed white children were typically teenagers or young girls assigned to sleep in the master's house. While the dominant figure of Tubman is far from "mammy", her role as nursemaid as a child provides context about the origins of the stereotype.

The earliest use of the term, mammy, was in 1810 and appeared in a travel guide about the American South in reference to enslaved Black women who cared for white children (McDole, 2017). Mammy, a hybrid of the words ma'am and mamma, was the first caricature assigned to Black women in the United States to denote a controlling, yet obediently subservient, nurturing, and caring Black woman (Collins, 2000; McDole, 2017). Hattie McDaniels, Ethel Waters, Louise Beavers, and Butterfly McQueen were actresses from the 1930s cast as mammies in Hollywood cinema. Their roles in film and movies represented a pivotal moment in the development of the stereotype (Wallace-Sanders, 2010). Pilgrim (2008) affirmed that the mammy image was designed to influence and control images of Black women's maternal behavior.

While the image of the mammy is not as overt today, there still exists a subtle, yet insidious image in film and theater. Whoopi Goldberg's portrayal as Corrina Washington in the 1994 film, Corrina, Corrina, and Viola Davis's role as Aibileen Clark in the 2011 film, The Help, illustrate this point.

Film and other forms of media are not the only sources of the mammy image. This image also exists in education. Seo and Hinton (2009) discussed the emergence of the "modern mammy, Black, middle-class Black women in academia. In the same way that various film representations dehumanize and demean Black women, academia also implicitly denigrates them. The mammy image effectively marginalizes black women and places them in a position of inferiority to all other binary groups (McDole, 2017). Black women in academic settings are not typically in positions of authority, resulting in subordinate roles to white and/or male authority (Seo & Hinton, 2009). Furthermore, Seo and Hinton (2009) stated that the duties of Black women in education illustrate the expectation that they are to fulfill the role of a devoted, nurturing, and caring team player.

Mrs. Farmer, a first-grade educator, described the expectation of administration that she "just keep them calm" rather than offer psychological and social-emotional support for students.

If we were to take a look at Malik's attendance records, it would show that he arrived to school late just about every day of his first-grade year. The school day begins at 7:30 a.m. Malik would arrive well into the morning somewhere between 8 and 10 a.m. depending on the day. Many students arrive late. My colleagues and I are used to it, but once Malik got to second grade, he began arriving at school on time. In fact, he is always one of the first students to enter the room just about every morning. Usually with a smile on his face. One day I decided to ask him about it. I asked what had changed that made him begin coming to school on time. In my mind, I had expected him to say that his mom was now working a different schedule, or something to that effect. He told me he enjoyed coming to school to be in my class. What I later found out from the school social worker is that Malik was not late because his mother was lazy, negligent, or had a work schedule that made them late, but because he did not want to come to school and his mother had a hard time getting him to get dressed and out of the door at a decent time. But now, he readily came to school because he enjoyed being in my class. An honor I do not take lightly, and a heavy responsibility I am well aware of. The care and concern that I showed him had caused him to want to be at school. This desire to be present would be one of the first steps in our journey together. **Personal Narrative**

Mrs. Farmer, like many in her position, was tasked with a role that should be the responsibility of school counselors and social workers who are specifically trained and employed for this purpose. Her experience further illustrates the expectation of unpaid emotional labor placed on many Black women educators. It is this expectation of many Black, women educators that perpetuate the stereotype of the mammy in academic settings. Mammy, while portrayed as the manager of the household, had perceived authority, but was aware of her position in the household. Seo and Hinton (2009) termed this "appropriately subordinate". Collins (2009) contended, "even though she may be well loved, and may wield considerable authority in her "white" family, the mammy still knows her "place" as obedient servant"(p. 80). The perception of authority within the domestic sphere is comparative with Black women in education and the mammy image especially as it relates to authority and discipline. In many cases, Black women are regarded as the experts on behavior management and consulted by their white counterparts on the matter.

Five of us, three classroom teachers and two English Language Learner teachers, were gathered for an impromptu meeting during one of our plan times. One of the ELL teachers had a student with him who was refusing to follow directions in his classroom. While we were talking, the student stood silently across the room from us. As the other three continued to talk, I and one of my teammates drifted off into a side conversation. At some point, their conversation had shifted to the student. Unaware of this, I heard one of them say, "Have Kemp do it." I was drawn back to the group by the sound of my name, turning my attention to them to see what they were discussing. "Have Kemp do what?" I asked. According to my colleague, the three of them had asked the student to take a seat, but he had been silently refusing. As a result, they requested that I ask him to take a seat. I immediately turned to the child. Without even thinking, calm and firm in tone, I told him to "Have a seat... now." He did as he was told, without hesitation or response. **Personal Narrative**

The maternal instincts and willingness of Black women educators to go the extra mile for students is praised, while their professional skills and knowledge are downplayed. McDole (2017) referred to the mammy as an icon created to convey the message that suggests Black women are relegated to the role of supporter/protector and the backbone for white women and children. Often their expertise is seen to begin and end with keeping Black and brown children 'in their place'. The role of black women in academic settings is often to manage the psychological, social-emotional, and behavioral needs of students, while remaining humble.

When working at a school with 97% White co-workers, I was often seen as the authority on the experiences of our Black students. I was once asked how we could "better reach them" in a 7th-grade team meeting. In retrospect, I should have refused to provide any input at all. **Dina Moore, Author and Former Teacher**

When I was at a charter school, I felt like being one of the few black women at the school, I was pushed harder than my white counterparts. It was almost like I was being hazed while the white women that started with me were coddled, put on a pedestal, and given room to make mistakes. I have expressed my disagreement regarding a math district assessment that was given to my students not being an adequate predictor of what my students know. I feel like my comment was ignored, but when a white educator said the same thing, their comment was taken into consideration. **Nylette Farmer, First Grade Teacher**

Perceived authority is a double-edged sword for Black women in academic settings. Often looked to for assistance in managing Black and brown children, Black women are seldom recognized outside of this context.

I was asked to participate in a district-wide public panel instead of my more experienced colleagues. A white colleague expressed that I was invited because I was a black woman. This comment attempted to completely negate my education, clinical experience, and confidence. **Andrea Eagan, School Social Worker**

On one hand, they are encouraged to be authentic while on the other hand, they are expected to assimilate to white norms and standards. Authenticity can be met with criticism and devaluation. Most times Black women's value is centered around serving and caring for others; they are the mammy, jolly, docile, hardworking, and motherly. Despite being overburdened and undervalued, Black women carry pride in themselves and their work, which can be misconstrued as contentment. The balancing act of authenticity and acceptance can stifle Black women's potential by mistaking cautious self-regulation for contentment. Their boldness, confidence, education, and talent cannot exceed what is expected in order to prevent our colleagues from feeling intimidated.

HE MAY HAVE BEEN INTIMIDATED BY ME

I worked for eight years in a district where I eventually found myself being the only Black woman teacher in the building. It was not the most comfortable situation as the district was beginning to change. When I decided to leave, having 14 years of experience, I applied for an instructional coach position in a different district. Even though that principal was ready and willing to hire me for the position, it was denied because I did not score high enough from my previous principal. It took former colleagues of the school I was in for eight years to make me realize he may have been intimidated by me. The things he said in his portion of the interview were not all true. He did not see me as a leader, and he did not think I would be good for the job. Five years later, I have been the instructional coach for four years, seeing as I could be hired after working a year in the district as their math interventionist. And I am really great at what I do. **Mary Bryant, Instructional Coach**

The sapphire characterized as aggressive, domineering, unfeminine, emasculating, and emotionally unstable, has also been associated with Black women (Pilgrim, 2008). Amos n' Andy, a radio and television program from the 1940s and 1950s, introduced the character Sapphire Stevens, who shaped the sapphire image. Contrary to the docile, subservient, contented mammy image, the sapphire was portrayed as loud, argumentative, stubborn, rude, and overbearing (Pilgrim, 2008). As punishment for violating social norms, Black women were often depicted as this caricature to encourage them to become more 'mammified' (Pilgrim, 2008). As opposed to the mammy image, which was more accepted and palatable, the sapphire image portrayed Black women as intimidating.

Today, Black women are more likely to be portrayed in this way. According to Stevenson (2023), modern reality TV has become a major source for seeing how Black women are stereotyped. In these shows, Black women are frequently depicted as "Sapphires," a stereotype that portrays them as angry and aggressive. Despite protests against the mammy image resulting in the rebranding of well-known products, television shows, and marketing campaigns, the sapphire image persists. She exists on the big screen, reality television, and popular sitcoms. Actresses like Techina Arnold, Taraji P. Henson, and Wendy Raquel Robinson have been associated with this image of the sassy Black woman in film and real life. A wonderfully satirical portrayal of this caricature is provided by Oprah Winfrey's character Sophia in the film adaptation of Alice Walker's *The Color Purple*. Sophia illustrated other's discomfort with Black women's strength and autonomy. While this character advocated for herself, there were multiple times she was encouraged to be and ultimately was physically beaten into submission. Although Oprah's depiction of Sophia has become one of the most beloved portrayals of a protagonist, it is still a reflection of how Black women are perceived and thus a denial their full humanity.

In the position where the district was changing and becoming less diverse, I came across parents who often did not understand me. They thought I was mean because I held their children accountable for their actions. I remember one thought I must not like children because I had standards and high expectations for all children in the class and was not willing to allow children to be the boss. One year, I had a para in the room the majority of the day and I had to ask her, an older white woman who I knew to be honest, if she saw the traits I was hearing from my principal (that he was hearing from the parents). She did not. That year because I didn't feel I could trust the parents and the students were too young to accurately express what was going on - they just didn't like being told to do what was expected - I began recording my classes. I set up my laptop to record my lessons just waiting for the day someone would say I was yelling or being mean to their children. I never had to use the recordings, but I was ready to defend myself. I'm firm and unmoved by misbehaving children. They learn that I only want the best for them collectively and I will not allow one or two to spoil our bunch. **Dina Moore, Author and Former Teacher**

The experiences of Black women in education are impacted by the Sapphire caricature, the sassy, loud-mouthed, opinionated, aggressive Black woman. Often, Black women are considered aggressive, intimidating, or even threatening when they advocate for themselves. Aggression is considered appropriately acceptable when it is expressed to benefit others while expressing aggression on behalf of themselves can be seen as problematic (Seo & Hinton, 2009). When Black women present assertiveness and confidence, they are misjudged, their authority and knowledge questioned, and they met with disrespect. Black women are held to higher standards than their non-Black counterparts while being constantly scrutinized.

A co-worker once referred to me as loud because I advocate for myself in situations. She even mentioned that it was an undesired quality of her biracial daughters. **Andrea Eagan, School Social Worker**

Despite the appearance of contradiction, sapphire and mammy are two sides of the same harmful coin. A critical examination of both caricatures can lead to the development of positive narratives about Black women in general, but specifically those in academic settings.

MATRIARCHS AND MENTORSHIP

While working as a long-term substitute at a low-income school, I became a role model and confidant for a lot of the students. Several students shared that the love I showed them is what they were missing at home. To help improve overall literacy and test scores, the students had an additional hour of reading at the end of every day. There were four fifth-grade classes, and the reading classes were separated by reading levels. I was assigned students in the second-highest group. Some of the children shared that they had never seen "someone like me" read with so much inflection and feeling. They all looked forward to our reading hour because they wanted to be around me. After two weeks with the readers, a group of Black girls gave me a gift bag full of handwritten notes and trinkets they had made or gathered from home. They asked me if I could be their mother and expressed their appreciation for my kindness, beauty, and intelligence as a Black woman. **C.B. Rodgers, Substitute Teacher**

I feel like I am able to relate to our black students more than my white counterparts. I am looked at as a role model or inspiration to the black students. They can see themselves in me. **Nylette Farmer, First-Grade Teacher**

Despite its controversy, the N-word serves as a clear example of how Black people are masters of redefining words and situations to serve a different purpose. In the same way, the mammy and sapphire caricatures must be critically examined, not in terms of their intended purposes, but to determine the specific characteristics worth reclaiming. Although the two images have been used as opposing representations, there are specific qualities to isolate to create narratives that reflect the unique role that Black women sometimes fulfill as the matriarch.

Generally, matriarch refers to the female head of a community; although, the term can be used in a variety of contexts. According to the Cambridge Academic Content Dictionary (n.d.) a matriarch is a woman holding leadership within a family or a female-led society. Matriarchs have historically been powerful forces in many cultures, and their role celebrated and honored. According to Stanford (2018), several problems in the Black community, including criminal activity, drug abuse, poverty, and unemployment, are often attributed to the failure of Black matriarchs. However, systemic oppressive factors such as racism, sexism, and classism tend to lead to these pathologies (Stanford, 2018). How can we reconcile the historical reverence for Black matriarchs as symbols of strength, wisdom, and mentorship with the internal narratives that often portray them as failing mothers within their own families?

Brandon struggled in kindergarten and first grade with aggression. The weight of raising him alone left his mom feeling hopeless. Knowing her struggle, I focused on a fresh start with Brandon, ignoring his past behavior. During parent-teacher conferences, his mom's tense body language spoke volumes. When I assured her Brandon was doing well, her relief was clear. She, like many single Black mothers, felt the burden of raising a son alone. My role became crucial, supporting Brandon and offering the guidance she might not have had the resources for. **Personal Narrative**

Black women commonly suppress traits that are characteristic of their nature for fear of affirming harmful tropes imposed on them. However, Black women have autonomy in defining who and what they are irrespective of what others think, especially as their opinions are based on their prejudices, biases, and views They have the power to embrace what is and deny what is not as it pertains to their identities. Considering this, perhaps they might move beyond the docile and subservient traits of the mammy image, defying the limitations of the mammy trope. The matriarch embraces those nurturing traits that allow her to be a source of stability, wisdom, and support for her family and community. Providing care, building community, and mentoring are the responsibilities of the matriarch.

Malik's mom showed up to parent teacher conferences ready to discuss her son. Which, we did. However, the majority of our conversation ended up being about mothering, grief, and raising Black sons through the grief. I had not intended for our conversation to go there, as I'm sure she did not either, but it was a necessary deviation. She was not aware of me losing my son, so as it came up she was a bit shocked at the news. It was in that moment that we were able to really build a connection that allowed us an opportunity to really partner with one another to do what was best for Malik. I wasn't just another teacher, I was a single Black mother of Black sons who lost a son just like her. We text almost daily now, especially and particularly during the work week, and our working relationship allows me to support her in ways Malik's previous teachers could not. Not because they were unwilling or because they were not good teachers, but because they could not provide her with the sense of community and mentorship that I could. **Personal Narrative**

In the same way that Black women can break free from those undesiring traits of the mammy image, they may also deny the notion that their passion, assertion, and advocacy perpetuate the sapphire image. By reclaiming the traits of these images that are valid and empowering, they can begin to define for themselves a more accurate and affirmative representation of Black women. This helps to recognize the unique power of Black women and the importance of their matriarchal role. Additionally, it serves as a reminder that Black women are not confined to the perceptions of others, but that as individuals they have the freedom to define themselves by their own unique stories and experiences. This work allows them to recognize their strength and resilience as well as the importance of honoring their cultural legacy.

Considering the long history of racism and sexism behind these images, any appropriation of them should be done carefully and responsibly. The mammy is presented as nurturing, hardworking, and motherly, while the sapphire is presented as passionate, confident, and assertive. By reclaiming these qualities, Black women can be seen as powerful, independent, and multifaceted. Unlike the polarity of the mammy and sapphire images, these self-affirming qualities can be juxtoposed to create maternal dynamism. This allows Black women to create a more balanced and nuanced representation of themselves and their matriarchal importance in the academic setting.

MAMAS, TE-TE'S, AND GRANNIES

One of the best compliments I've received as a Black woman educator came not from my colleagues or administration, but from my students. The compliment was not about my teaching, stylish clothes and sneakers, or my hair, although I receive those compliments frequently. Among the most rewarding compliments I have received were the times when students accidentally called me Mama, Te-Te, or Granny. **Personal Narrative**

Auntie is a term widely used throughout the diaspora, often reserved for older women, regardless of blood relationship, as a sign of respect and endearment. Spruill et al. (2014) state that West Africans used terms like "Aunt" and "Uncle" to address older people, even strangers, demonstrating how kinship defined their social interactions. An aunt in the African American community may be a sibling of a parent, a close family friend, a cousin who belongs to an older generation, or even a non-related Black woman who is being referenced in passing or casual conversation. There is an implied kinship in the use of the term regardless of whether it is fictive or an actual blood relationship. The significance of kinship to Black women extends beyond family ties. Among black communities and families, kinship is a crucial survival strategy (Stanford, 2018). It is intricately crafted from strands of history, resilience, cultural richness, and steadfastness. Mamas, Te-Tes, and Grannies are typically regarded as maternal figures who provide a nurturing presence, protection, wisdom, and discipline rooted in love and concern. They are the matriarchs, historically known for assuming the responsibility of caring for the community's children, whether that responsibility is imposed or voluntary. Jimenez (2002) shared that this collective responsibility for the community's children, combined with a broad kinship and caretaking culture, was brought from Africa, and became an inevitable way of life for us. Stanford (2018) contended that Black women had to assume the role of matriarch for the advancement of the Black family and community. When students refer to a teacher as any of these terms, it reflects the nature of the relationship between teacher and student, as well as qualities indicative of a felt kinship between teacher and student. This relationship creates the feeling of safety, care, and love.

In one of our conversations, Malik's mom said to me, "Ms. Kemp, the way he calls me you at home, I KNOW you gotta be tired of how much he says your name here. Every five minutes he's calling me you!" I laughed, because she wasn't wrong. But I also was well aware that I make such an impact on him that he accidentally refers to his mother as me, which I found ironic because he constantly mistakenly calls me momma at school. It was an indication that the lines of safety, care, and love for him were blurred because I in some way mirrored what he was receiving from his mother. **Personal Narrative**

FROM ONE SEGREGATION TO ANOTHER

I think every student needs to experience non-white educators. So often students go through a decade or more of schooling and are only faced with Caucasian, often women, teachers. And that is not to say they lack the ability to be stellar educators. But there are cultures and experiences that students miss out on by not having a person of color educate them. The school I currently work in is overwhelmingly African American, and those students benefit by seeing me from day to day. In my position, I am able to be an extra person they can come to and work out issues or get assistance with class work. They know they can trust me and that I have their best interest at heart. **Mary Bryant, Instructional Coach**

Desegregation of public schools remains a controversial topic in the United States following Brown v. Board of Education of Topeka (1954). Due to the ruling in Brown v. Board of Education, schools could no longer be segregated. In the process of desegregating schools across the country, a different form of segregation emerged. There was a lack of integration of Black teachers into the schools, which resulted in a large number of African American teachers becoming displaced. Will (2022) argued that the decision:

Afforded Black children access to the same educational opportunities as white children, while causing the dismissal, demotion, or forced resignation of many experienced, highly credentialed Black educators who staffed Black-only schools. In the 17 states with segregated school systems prior to Brown, black principals and teachers constituted 35 percent to 50 percent of the educator workforce. (p. 2)

Black students were now subject to harm caused by being in class with and taught by white Americans who despised them. The loss of Black educators had a profound impact on the quality of education African American students received in public schools (Milner & Howard, 2004). Those percentages are much lower today, with only 7% of teachers and 11% of principals being Black (Will, 2022). This implies that Black students are taught by predominantly white and other non-Black educators which particularly affects school districts in urban areas. To provide "better" education and more resources to African American students, both teachers and students alike no longer benefited from the sense of community and kinship experienced before the ruling. Studies have shown that students benefit from having a teacher who shares their same racial identity. Milner and Howard (2004) affirmed that "for many Black students, Black teachers represented surrogate parent figures, acted as disciplinarians, counselors, role models, and overall advocates for their academic, social, cultural, emotional, and moral development" (p. 286). Blazar (2021) also found that "teachers of color have large and lasting effects on the social-emotional, academic, and behavioral outcomes of their students" (p. 3). These findings applied to all students, regardless of students' race, when compared to students assigned to white teachers. Blazar (2021) attributed this to teachers of color being more likely than their white colleagues to view student intelligence as flexible, lead highly organized classrooms, cultivate good relationships with students and families, and plan instruction more carefully with attention to individual students' needs.

I was assigned a large caseload of black female students who had never had a black therapist. They would always mention how easy it was to speak with me without feeling judged. **Andrea Eagan, School Social Worker**

I once worked in a school system that was approximately 93% Black. The high school had one White student and one White teacher out of more than 1,000 students and dozens of faculty. As a result, many of the students were wary of the existence of racism and didn't want to learn about "Black stuff." I countered by sharing my own experiences growing up in a town that was nearly 93% White. I pointed out the bigotry and sexism I faced as the only Black person in many of my high school classes. **Dina Moore, Author and Former Teacher**

I was a substitute teacher in one of the largest school districts in the United States. The school district ranged from schools in upper class to rich communities to schools in impoverished neighborhoods. The schools with low-income students paid more because most of the schools required an extra hour per school day for reading and literacy. The second time I visited one of the low-income schools, I was pulled from the class I was supposed to work for. I was asked to assist a white male substitute teacher in one of four fifth-grade classrooms. I ended up taking on most of the responsibilities—especially student interaction—because the original substitute seemed overwhelmed and out of touch. We had a moderately successful day. The next morning, the school called and offered me a position as a long-term substitute for the class. I expressed my gratitude but told them that I didn't want to take the other substitute's job. The sub-coordinator told me that they had already let him go. She said that the staff and students felt that I identified better with the children. They thought my approach and communication with the students was appropriately motherly. The school was predominantly Black, similar to the schools I attended as a child. **C.B. Rodgers, Substitute Teacher**

Considering these findings, the importance of the Black matriarch must be acknowledged, seen as the center of their families and communities, for providing support, guidance, and nurturing environments for children to thrive. Black matriarchs often must navigate complicated systems and overcome challenges to ensure children's success. Similarly, Blazar's findings implied that teachers of color may be more adept at working with students of all backgrounds, supporting their academic success despite obstacles. This shared focus on resilience and overcoming adversity can be linked to the legacy of Black matriarchs.

BREAKING FREE AND BUILDING BRIDGES

Black women must present authentically since it is this version that benefits them most. They must be committed to the work of breaking free from all of the stereotypes and labels that confine them and be about the business of defining who they are and being present as that which they have defined. When viewed through the problematic lens of the sapphire image, assertiveness is often discouraged; however, when viewed through the lens of an assertive matriarchal figure, it is a powerful asset. It supports advocacy, loving discipline, structure, and agency. Likewise, when the nurturing traits of the mammy is viewed through the same matriarchal lens, there is safety, love, mentorship, kinship, and community.

For seven years I worked as a special education paraprofessional, then several more years as a preschool teaching assistant before becoming a classroom teacher. At the school where I currently teach,, approximately half of the students are African American and the other half Hispanic. Yet, the staff are predominantly white women. There have been many instances where students respond more positively to me than to my colleagues who are not Black. Parents and family members greet me with smiles, hugs, and sometimes kisses as if I were family. **Personal Narrative**

Black women educators are strong, resilient, and resourceful. They have a unique ability to connect with and empower students and families of all backgrounds. The matriarchal model is a coin, with two sides that are inextricably linked and complementary. One side of the coin represents the power of nurturing, which can create a supportive environment for Black women educators, their students, and their families. The other side of the coin represents the power of assertiveness, which can create a motivating and challenging environment for students of all backgrounds.

Both Malik and Brandon continue on their second-grade journey with me as they learn to be loved, affirmed, and held accountable to being better than what they believed they could ever be. My ability to show up for them and their mothers with such empathy and unwavering support is the result of self-work. Focusing on shedding the limitations of a self-image that no longer served me, I found the courage to forge a new identity, a truer reflection of who I am. The moment I decided to be my authentic self is the moment I became everything they needed…everything I needed. A bridge of community and kinship has been built and no longer do we exist on our islands alone. Having mutual understanding of the support necessary as Black mothers and those who want nothing but the best for their sons. Our sons. Shared resiliency and overcoming adversity, intergenerational connection and mentorship, and fostering positive relationships that benefit all of our emotional well-being.

CONCLUSION

In conclusion, by strategically combining nurturing support and assertive strength, Black women educators defy the limitations imposed by stereotypical portrayals. This matriarchal model fosters a safe and empowering environment, particularly for Black students. It challenges the societal belief that nurturing and assertive qualities are mutually exclusive. This unique approach not only provides Black women with the necessary support to thrive but also offers a sense of cultural affirmation that extends to others in their community. Furthermore, it empowers them to see themselves beyond the confines of stereotypes and embrace their full potential. Black women educators, through their strength and resilience, pave the way for a more inclusive and equitable educational landscape where all students can flourish. This chapter explored the concept of Black women reclaiming their power through a reframing of the mammy and sapphire stereotypes. The stereotypes were compared with Black women educators' personal experiences, highlighting the complexities they face in the educational system. By embracing the nurturing and supportive qualities inherent in the mammy image, while rejecting its limitations, Black women can embody the nurturing aspects of the matriarch. Similarly, by reclaiming the confidence and assertiveness associated with the sapphire stereotype, they can redefine it as strength and advocacy. This matriarchal model empowers Black women to define themselves on their own terms, fostering a sense of safety, care, and love for others, while remaining true to their unique cultural heritage. This reframing not only benefits Black women but specifically Black women educators and their students, particularly Black students who can see themselves reflected in their teachers and leadership figures. While the world has attempted to define who they believe Black women are and should be, they are admonished to embrace what is, deny what is not, decolonize their views of self, and break free from harmful ideologies that have previously defined them. Black women possess the power to define who they are and show up their authentic selves. It is through this process that a bridge for those around them to join in doing the same can be built. They are not confined to the mammy and sapphire tropes. Black women are multidimensional. They can be nurturing, assertive, and so much more. There is no need to limit themselves to what Chimimanda Ngozi names the "single story" (Adichie, TED Talks, 2009). Black women have full agency over their identities.

They assert their power and authority in defining themselves to better serve others, and more importantly to serve themselves.

REFERENCES

Adichie, C. N. (2009, July). The danger of a single story [Video]. TED Talks. https://www.ted.com/talks

Blazar, D. (2021). *Teachers of color, culturally responsive teaching, and student outcomes: Experimental evidence from the random assignment of teachers to classes.* (EdWorkingPaper: 21-501). Annenberg Institute at Brown University. 10.26300/jym0-wz02

Cambridge English Dictionary. (n.d.). Matriarch. In website dictionary. Retrieved December 19, 2023, https://dictionary.cambridge.org/us/dictionary/english/matriarch

Collins, P. H. (2009). *Black feminist thought: Knowledge, consciousness, and the politics of empowerment* (1st ed.). Routledge.

Hurston, Z. N. (1998). *Their eyes were watching God.* HarperPerrenial.

Jimenez, J., Hinton, K., Branyon, A., Greenfield, E. A., Baker, L. A., Mutchler, J. E., & Schwartz, A. (2002). The history of grandmothers in the African-American community. *The Social Service Review*, 76(4), 523–551. 10.1086/342994

McDole, A. (2017). Mammy representations in the 21st century [Master's thesis, Syracuse University]. https://surface.syr.edu/thesis/194

McGowan, J. A., & Kashatus, W. C. (2011). Harriet Tubman: a biography (illustrated ed.). Greenwood Biographies. Bloomsbury Academic.

Milner, H. R., & Howard, T. C. (2004). Black teachers, black students, black communities, and Brown: Perspectives and insights from experts. *The Journal of Negro Education*, 73(3), 285. 10.2307/4129612

Pilgrim, D. (2008, August). *The sapphire caricature.* Jim Crow Museum. https://jimcrowmuseum.ferris.edu/ antiblack/sapphire.htm

Seo, B.-I., & Hinton, D. (2009). How they see us, how we see them: Two women of color in higher education. *Race, Gender & Class (Towson, Md.)*, 16(3), 203–2017.

Spruill, I. J., Coleman, B. L., Powell-Young, Y. M., Williams, T. H., & Agwood, G. (2014). Non-biological (fictive kin and othermothers): Ebracing the need for a culturally appropriate pedigree nomenclature in African-American families. *Journal of the National Black Nurses' Association. Journal of National Black Nurses' Association*, 25(2), 23–30. https://www.ncbi.nlm.nih.gov/ pmc/articles/PMC4847537/27134343

Stanford, T. N. (2018). African American grandmothers as the black matriarch : You don't live for yourself. (ThinkIR). The University of Louisville's Institutional Repository. https://ir.library.louisville.edu/etd/2944/

Stevenson, E. J. (2023). Impacts of the Sapphire stereotype seen on reality television in college-aged Black women [Senior Honors Thesis, Eastern Michigan University]. https://commons.emich.eduhonors/766

Thomas, T. D., & Hill, M. (2022). Reversing the dehumanization of black women. In *Black women and public health: strategies to name, locate, and change systems of power* (pp. 36-40). State University of New York Press, Albany 10.1515/9781438487335-003

Wallace-Sanders, K. (2010). *Mammy: A century of race, gender and Southern memory*. University of Michigan Press.

Warren-Gordon, K., & Mencias McMillan, D. (2022). Analysis of Black Female Belizean Stereotypes in Visual Media: Jezebel, Mammy, Sapphire, and their Contributions to Violence against Women. *Journal of International Women's Studies*, 23(1), 248–262. https://doi.org/https://vc.bridgew.edu/jiws/vol23/iss1/23/

Will, M. (2022, May 17). "Brown v. Board" decimated the black educator pipeline. A scholar explains how. *Education Week.* https://www.edweek.org/ teaching-learning/ brown-v-board-decimated-the-black-educator-pipeline-a-scholar-explains-how/2022/05

Chapter 9
Too Much of My Rhythm Causing Them So Much Blues

Asueleni E. Deloney
Hand 'N Hand Coaching, USA

ABSTRACT

In this chapter, the author examines the manifestations of workplace discrimination in educational settings and other industries where Black women hold leadership positions. This analysis includes an exploration of equity vs. equality, psychological safety, and the concept of diversity dishonesty, among other relevant topics. The discussion is supported by various research methodologies, including focus groups and auto-ethnography. The chapter aims to raise awareness of these discriminatory practices and their persistent impact on Black women's professional advancement which ties directly with this book, Sharing the Legacy and Narrative Leadership Experiences of Black Women in Education. It highlights the psychological burden Black women often bear as they navigate the complexities of workplace presentation and behavior to avoid conflict, jeopardizing career progression or facing wrongful termination. The author contends that confronting these discriminatory environments directly is essential for mitigating their detrimental effects on Black women's professional experiences.

THE JOURNEY: MY RHYTHM

How many of us can relate to the mental and emotional acrobats of "what card to play at work?" I have created a workplace "rule." I allow myself to be considered "the angry Black woman" three times a year, when necessary, to either defend my

DOI: 10.4018/979-8-3693-0698-7.ch009

Copyright © 2024, IGI Global. Copying or distributing in print or electronic forms without written permission of IGI Global is prohibited.

teaching practices or advocate for one of my students. As we all know, whenever we stand our ground, we are angry and disgruntled and unable to control our emotions.

As a Black Woman Educator with a Bachelor's in Broadcast Journalism and Master's in Education, with over 21 years of educational experience, thinking back on my career as an early professional reminded me of how I had feelings of anger, inferiority, belittlement, disrespect, and more of that lived in my nervous system. I had allowed racism, unprofessionalism, and the need to become likable and not be "combative" to have a seat at the table. However, it catalyzed becoming the un-apologetic advocate that I am today, never wanting the next person to have the same lived experience that I did. What became necessary as I matured was learning to empower myself to stand in my truth, stand for what was right, and, when necessary, in a perfect world, "knock their heads off." Metaphorically speaking, of course.

At the onset of my professional career 20 years ago, I began at a television station as a programming production assistant, an older white male coworker—arguably the leader of the "good 'ol white boys' club"—and I were having a conversation as to why it was okay for Black people to use the "N" word, but unacceptable for him and his white community to do so. In a burst of frustration, he yelled: "Oh, so you can say nigger and it is okay, but I say it and it is wrong?" My instant thoughts were: "Hell yeah, it is wrong, and saying it in front of the wrong crowd will get your head knocked off." However, I said nothing. My 24-year-old self was scared that speaking up would cost me my dream career and the residue of blind obedience and submission from my childhood was still present and I had yet to question why I functioned that way. My voice was still finding its way to the surface.

Due to industry layoffs, I transitioned into education, where I was initially hired as a classroom teacher. My coworker was excited and all too willing to collaborate with me. As I grew professionally and the larger organization learned of my skill set and what I was able to bring to the table and sought my professional advice and opinion, that collaboration quickly turned into questions such as "why does every-one think she is so great?" Even though this situation is isolating and confusing and causes self-doubt, there is danger in shrinking, defined as drawing back, as in retreat or avoidance (dictionary.com, 2024) will cause one to unknowingly set the tone for how one will be handled in the workplace.

Yes, Black women indeed have to navigate differently; we have to work a little bit harder and grow thicker skin for the dismissiveness and outright disrespect that we receive. What one cannot allow is sending the message that one is going to lie down and take it. It has to be known that we are not opposed to defending our processes and pushing back when our ideas are overlooked. We have to fight for ownership of our hard work and accept on occasion the nauseating title of "angry Black woman." True enough, showing up in the workplace and bringing our "rhythm" with one is a balancing act; nevertheless, putting it into proper perspective should show how it can be a superpower. Look at what it can cause us to become; working harder causes us to become more knowledgeable and intellectual in our prospective field, having to constantly defend why we do what we do develops our oration and presentation skills. Also, being thorough in what we believe, and being forced to grow a thicker skin, gives us the ability to show up without concern for how we will be received, garnering all these skills for our personal use. It is important to clarify that I am not asserting that the appropriate approach is to settle into an "it is what it is mindset" and just deal with it. I am stating this to say perspective is *everything* in the workplace, and the faster this mindset is adopted as a positive perspective, the easier it becomes to navigate.

Black women are among the most educated groups in the U.S., 20% of Black women are being told they are not qualified and 55% of Black women have their professional judgment questioned regularly (Brownlee, 2022; Castrillon, 2022 Davis, 2020 Forbes). The irony is that, although we are educated, our competence and place in our respective fields are consistently questioned. For me, this begs a deeper question: Why?

My study focuses on the experiences of Black women in various industries, comparing them to those of Black women in education. As a Black woman educator, I have encountered numerous challenges and forms of disrespect, particularly regarding my intellectual leadership and abilities. This prompted me to explore whether Black women in other industries face similar experiences. Specifically, I wanted to investigate if they, too, encounter the same dismissiveness and disrespect that I have faced in education. I also chose to explore this angle because, oftentimes, while working in education, at some point we begin to explore the possibilities of transitioning into other fields and I wanted to present an open awareness of what Black women are up against in other industries as a comparison.

In this chapter, I will analyze the experiences of Black women leaders in various industries in relation to those of Black women educators. The central question guiding this study is: Are the experiences of Black women educators and Black women leaders in other industries similar or different? Drawing from my own experiences, as well as those of my colleagues, mentors, and mentees, I have a deep understanding of the challenges faced by Black women in education. This investigation is crucial, as it provides valuable insights for educators who are new to the field or considering a transition, helping them to navigate their career paths more effectively.

METHODOLOGY

In this study, I explored the lived experiences of four Black women in various industries through a qualitative research design, aiming to dive deeply into their professional lives. An in-person focus group approach would be employed, consisting of five carefully crafted questions to facilitate in-depth conversations. These discussions centered on their narrative experiences and the strategies they employed to navigate their professional environments.

PARTICIPANTS

The population of the participants of this study consisted of Black women who currently serve in leadership positions in their prospective industries. These women were recruited through my professional network using electronic communication invites. After the acceptance of the invite, the women completed a demographic questionnaire that assisted with the development of focus group questions. Table 1 provides a breakdown of the participants' backgrounds.

Table 1. Participant demographics

Name	Level of degree	Years of experience	Industry
Summer	Numerous certifications and certificates as it relate to her field.	20	Health care
Melissa	Bachelor of Science Biology	15	Pharmaceuticals
Mia	Bachelor of Science in Business Administration and MBA	30	Human resources and technology
Morgan	Bachelor of Arts in Communication and Master of Arts in Management	20	Insurance

FINDINGS

I conducted a focus group using four professional women in various career fields and at different stages in their careers. I chose this approach because I was curious to see if these inequalities show up in other industries. I asked very poignant questions as well as allowed room for them to express their experiences. I discovered that every woman found community and comfort in each other's experiences as well, and they found solace in knowing that they were not alone in their experiences.

A comprehensive collection of workplace incidents underscores a variety of inequitable experiences and practices, highlighting the shortcomings of diversity programs. One notable case involves an employee who was promoted to manager at a major corporation, only to face immediate resistance and disapproval from her white subordinates. This opposition culminated in the removal and destruction of essential files and materials required for her new role over the weekend. The employee's transition was facilitated by a supportive group of Black women who were aware of the incident and rallied around her.

Another case involves a Black woman who grappled with the decision to straighten her natural hair or to assert her right to wear it naturally. Shortly after beginning her job, she was summoned to a meeting and advised to alter her hairstyle, as it was deemed incongruent with the company's conservative image and clientele. This incident illustrated the absurdity of such discriminatory practices, when the objective is to discredit, dismiss, and disregard Black employees, any form of discrimination is utilized.

The first three narratives are representative of the majority of experiences faced by Black women, whereas the final narrative is an aspirational one. Each story is critical and provides valuable insights into the necessity of remaining vigilant regarding the nuances of professional environments. These narratives serve as instructive examples of the pervasive experiences that Black women are challenged with concerning workplace diversity efforts.

SUMMER: EQUITY VS. EQUALITY

Equity speaks to the quality of being fair or impartial (Dictionary.com, 2024). It is about the understanding that we are not all equal in front of a similar situation and making adjustments to give everyone the same chances (Sombret, 2023). If done right, a company can create a healthy environment conducive to inclusive diversity of thought and safe spaces to address bias that may arise in the future.

Summer's experience allows us to dig into the difference between equity and equality as well as fair treatment under the law. Summer has been working in her chosen industry of the healthcare field for more than 10 years. While doing a job for which she is very skilled and after performing for years in multiple departments, she was being questioned about her ability to do her job due to her recent hair change of going natural. Her immediate supervisor approached her needing to know if she was "okay." Furthermore, those that she served no longer wanted her assistance and services, to the degree of requesting someone else, and requesting the items she touched to be cleaned and disinfected.

While grappling with her new workplace environment, Summer encountered a situation involving an elderly patient from a prominent white family. Explicit instructions were given that only the family's chosen staff members were to attend to the patient. As the patient's condition deteriorated and she nearly fell from her bed, Summer, adhering to her professional duty and ethical obligation to assist anyone in need, intervened to help. Despite her commitment to her role, the family pursued legal action against the company for failing to comply with their specific request to have only Caucasian staff attend to the patient.

In response to this incident, the company attempted to terminate Summer's employment and had her publicly escorted from the premises. This case exemplifies the persistent struggle that Black women face in their efforts to secure workplace equality. These challenges highlight the frequent necessity for Black women to advocate for their rightful place and treatment within professional settings, often against significant opposition.

Summer refused to settle for the treatment that she was receiving, having worked for this company for years and realizing her reputation and her time invested in the company were on the line. She decided to engage the National Association for the Advancement of Colored People (NAACP) to help fight on her behalf to retrieve her back pay and preserve her position (Equal Employment Opportunity Commission, 2022). Founded on February 12, 1909, the NAACP was established in part to guarantee the rights of all people given to them under the 1st, 14th, and 15th amendments written in the U.S. Constitution (NAACP, 2013).

The Equal Employment Opportunity Commission (2022) has enforced Title VII's prohibition of race and color discrimination in numerous cases since 1964. Title VII falls under the Civil Rights Act and protects employees based on discrimination against race, color, religion, sex, and national origin. Their data state that, in 2022, 19,805 individual charges were filed in the area of race discrimination. This is a 1,043 increase from the year before, which speaks to this increasing issue.

MELISSA: PSYCHOLOGICAL SAFETY

Melissa's experience is an example of how large companies love to tout being inclusive and welcoming to all creeds and intellects but are not practicing what they preach from the inside. Melissa works in pharmaceuticals and was highly sought after and promised a career doing what she earned a degree in and growth opportunities. Unbeknownst to her, she started working for a company that currently has language written in their bylaws that instruct upper management "never to hire

Black people." Little did she know she would soon find herself in an environment where her psychological safety would be jeopardized, a growing concern for Black women in the workplace (Gallo, 2023).

Psychological safety is the absence of interpersonal fear. It embodies the ability to take interpersonal risks, be able to have hard conversations without fear of repercussions or feel encouraged and rallied around when sharing one's ideas (Gallo 2023). It also includes accepting fault and being supported in taking accountability and not being ridiculed, reprimanded, or demoted, Melissa was still able to ascend and become an employee who was top in her department, earning several accolades due to her work performances, which were all well-deserved given she was the only one who was trained over the years and educated on multiple procedures and practices throughout the department. With her professional raise, the promises made to her of a fair and progressive work environment were short-lived. Below is her story.

Working in production for 13 years, she encountered many prolonged incidents that went on for three years with two white female supervisors who were friends, one being in an intimate relationship with the chief operating officer. As she was pulled away from her regular job duties of processing pharmaceutical medications, she was told that she needed to mop floors and attend to the sanitation of her department. In addition, being faced with cycles of upper management profiling her with accusations of not performing up to par started to wear thin on Melissa. As educated as she was regarding not only her job duties, but also the job duties of her coworkers, she was seen and treated as less than at work, falsely accused, to dismantle her character and causing her to have to choose her "battles" very wisely to not put her employment in jeopardy. Being tired of having to constantly defend her work practices set the tone for a contentious work environment and prompted Melissa to take her grievances to human resources (HR).

The final straw came in the form of being the only Black female in her department. She was accused of having one of her false eyelashes fall in the product and was escorted to HR. She was questioned in an attempt to stereotype her and built a paper trail regarding her work habits. After calling out the workplace practices handbook that they required her to read every year, she exposed their zero-tolerance harassment policy as this was the latest in a long line of baseless and asinine write-ups.

Melissa finally chose to take back her power, protect her psychological safety, and defend herself using their by-laws against them. Psychological safety is when one feels safe to take interpersonal risks, to speak up, to disagree openly, and to surface concerns without fear of negative repercussions or pressure to sugarcoat bad news (Gallo, 2023).

MIA: DIVERSITY DISHONESTY

Diversity dishonesty occurs when organizations position themselves as diverse and inclusive; however, their inner workings tell a very different story (Wilton et al., 2020). Mia agreed to work for a company that outwardly prided itself as inclusive, regularly holding diversity and inclusion development; she was met, however, with interworking circumstances that spoke directly against that. The most commonly used strategies to increase organizational diversity are often not effective, and prodiversity organizational portrayals can be inaccurate or disconnected from the reality of the organization (Wilton et al., 2020). For example, although 87% of all Fortune 500 companies have a dedicated Web page expressing their commitment to diversity, only 3% of those companies report their employee demographics and 72% of the senior executives at those 16 companies that report this information are white men (Jones & Donnelley, 2017).

Mia had to endure microaggressions after receiving a promotion while working in the banking industry, which is a white male-dominated industry. Like many of us moving into adulthood, we cling to the advice and guidance of our mothers, and Mia was no different. She shared how her mother advised her to handle unwanted attention: "My mom would say ignore it, work harder, do not let that bother you, because that was her lived experience." While stating this, she retrospectively realized some important realizations about her growth and strength:

When I look backward and think about it with everything that is happening now with Diversity and Inclusion, Me Too, all of those things, I think back to my experiences and I know I have experienced racism, been sexually harassed—all of these things were not detrimental, but, at that time, there was a certain point where you just let them know "I do not play those games" and I'm not that person; and you just move on and work harder, until you finally get to a place where you feel it is okay to use your voice for corrective action.

After being at her company for some time, she was placed on a Diversity, Equity, and Inclusion (DEI) "heat map" and began getting much positive exposure for her work and potential in the company. With this, her superiors began to groom her for larger roles in the company. However, the ones who worked in her immediate department did not agree with her possible ascension in the company, as she was beginning to outshine them. After returning from maternity leave, she found that her immediate manager, who was loved and had a loyal following, had been fired and she replaced her. This promotion gave her leadership over the unit, and she would now gain leadership and become a supervisor over the entire department, including the loyalist of the previous manager. Her district manager praised the promotion stating, "I have been waiting for you to get back from maternity leave so that I could do this, you should have been leading these units all along." All of the loyalists who were once her coworkers had now become her subordinates and had to report to Mia. Needless to say, Mia encountered immediate issues. Her subordinates, as well as the fired supervisors, spent the weekend before Mia's start date emptying the office of every file that she needed to perform her job duties successfully. They also scrutinized her unit before her promotion, attempting to undermine her leadership skills. They struggled to understand her ability to lead, frequently questioning, "how do you get these people to walk the line for you?" This clearly revealed the longstanding threat they felt from her. Mia's previous unit, predominantly Black, not only supported her, but also stood firmly by her side during the transition, ensuring she had their unwavering backing.

Mia, being of a "keep-your-head-down-and-work" generation, has had to endure these unjust conditions, making it easier for her to be professionally suppressed once her skill set became more of a threat, rather than an asset. In Mia's growth, she realized the value of her voice and the value of no longer allowing a "go-along to get along" disposition at work as she professionally pushed back, stood on what was right, and solidified her position at work as a valuable member of the team.

MORGAN: THE OUTLIER

An outlier is something that lies outside of the main body or group of which it is part. Morgan serves as our outlier for this study because she represents the minority of Black women in the workspace. What she encountered was discrimination, but she also experienced having management support her and come to her aide. As an excited young adult fresh out of college, going into one's chosen career can bring on a myriad of emotions from nervousness to excitement. Wanting to make a good impression, and navigating a new environment tends to be the number one priority. The idea of having to file a grievance on an established employee is not on anyone's bingo card early in their career. Morgan, who had worked for the same insurance company the entirety of her professional career, was met with serious discriminatory practices early on. While working closely with her manager, Morgan decided to make a major change to her hair and landed on a big chop, which sent her from relaxed hair to essentially no hair. When she arrived at work after a holiday, she encountered her manager who said directly: "Oh I did not know you were one of *those* Black girls." Feelings of confusion, sadness, insignificance, and being scared to respond robbed her of feeling empowered, having fully embraced her big chop. After working all day under these traumatic circumstances, she went home to have a conversation with her mom. Her mom advised her that it was unacceptable and supported her in going to HR to report what happened.

Solidarity is defined as a union or fellowship arising from common responsibilities and interests, between members of a group, between classes, and between people (Solidary,Dictionary.com, 2024). Morgan was able to experience solidarity in reporting her concerns as her grievances were taken seriously and addressed. After extensive interviews with all parties involved the manager was subsequently fired. This is one of the many ways we can minimize the Work Pet to Work Threat—by not only creating safe spaces among our sisters at work but also speaking up against inequality and prejudices.

Morgan is our outliner in this study because of the unwavering support she received not only when dealing with HR, but afterward, having another manager to step up and support her. Jackson (2022) stated that less than 25% of Black women feel included and supported at work. This would then conclude that more than 75% of Black women do not feel supported or included in the workspace. Thus, as a culture, we are groomed to expect isolation, unfair treatment, assessment, and more because, more often than not, we will not have the same experience that Morgan had.

DISCUSSION

I conducted this study because I felt that it is prudent to gather Black women across various industries and create a safe space where their stories could be shared. Ironically, I found that, regardless of the industry, there were similarities in how each woman was treated. Upon revisiting and analyzing each experience, it becomes evident that, despite the presence of DEI initiatives in most companies, these efforts frequently fail to generate consistent and sustainable change across various contexts.

DIVERSITY DISHONESTY

Imagine interviewing for a highly coveted career position, seated before your prospective employers as they assure you of an inclusive environment where your potential can be fully realized. They emphasize that your diversity of thought and leadership is both welcomed and encouraged. However, once you are hired and incorporated into the company's diversity statistics, the reality starkly contrasts with these promises.

Highlighting this discrepancy is crucial because many companies project a facade of commitment to diversity and inclusion. Behind these public affirmations, there may lie hidden agendas and outdated beliefs that implicitly favor certain races or genders. Essentially, these issues reflect structural racism embedded within the company's foundation, which has not been adequately addressed.

These companies manipulate diversity figures and data to protect their interests, presenting a misleading image of compliance with affirmative action requirements. This practice occurs even as affirmative action policies are being systematically dismantled, as Gretzinger (2024) noted in the context of higher education. Black women are often led to believe that they are joining an organization that genuinely values their perspectives, intellect, and creativity. However, they frequently discover that this supposed inclusivity comes with significant personal and professional costs that many are unwilling or unable to bear. Dobbin and Kalev (2016) discussed the heightened focus on diversity within businesses following several high-profile lawsuits in the financial industry. They highlighted the substantial multimillion-dollar settlements paid over the years and noted that, as a consequence, Wall Street firms now require new hires to sign arbitration agreements precluding them from participating in class action lawsuits. This approach is particularly noteworthy, given that many companies publicly commit to diversity, fairness, and racial equality by establishing dedicated departments for DEI. This raises a critical question: If a company genuinely fosters an environment of fairness and equality, why is there a perceived necessity for employees to waive their rights to collective legal action?

THE REALITY OF DIVERSITY PROGRAMS

The onboarding process for many employees often includes diversity training, with promises of an ideal, inclusive work environment. However, there is a widespread perception that these trainings yield minimal tangible benefits. It can be argued that diversity training often fails to tackle the hard questions or to address the specific needs related to the racial climate within the company. Consequently, these sessions fall short of addressing critical issues. This deficiency may explain the persistence of discriminatory practices in the workplace, where racial and gender disparities remain unchallenged, fostering environments where Black women can be easily marginalized for simply fulfilling their job roles.

Those tasked with facilitating diversity training might concur that it is counterproductive to invest in programs that are, at best, limited in effectiveness and, at worst, divisive among employees. Nonetheless, such trainings are routinely implemented across various corporations and institutions (Redstone, 2020). Despite efforts to demonstrate the necessity of diversity programs, research often reveals shortcomings because these programs lack genuine buy-in and proper execution from leadership. Additionally, diversity programs frequently fail to consistently and effectively address the unique needs and issues of each company.

Some companies aim to bridge racial disparities and create inclusive environments that welcome and embrace diversity (Pedulla, 2020). When it works, diversity training allows employees to feel like a common goal and team. It fosters collaborative environments and safe spaces to disagree and have hard conversations without fear of repercussions. In creating effective diversity training, it has to include a common goal, the ability to confront unconscious bias, and an intent focus on inclusion. This requires a certain type of leadership and open-mindedness from staff. Having the resources to address the undertones that threaten the health of a company and restructuring the system or replacing individuals if needed. This is not an issue that can be dismantled by simply speaking up for oneself; just like with racism, this is an issue that has to start with the ones perpetuating it and those who call themselves allies. They have to be willing to start these conversations in their circle, not be afraid to stand for what is right, and call out what is systematic racism and inequality.

PROTECTING YOUR PSYCHOLOGICAL SAFETY

Dr. Antoinette "Bonnie" Candia-Bailey was the Vice President for Student Affairs at Lincoln University of Jefferson City Mo. who tragically took her life after enduring months of mistreatment by the president of the university by Dr. John Moseley.

Dr. Candia-Bailey's experiences provide a compelling illustration of the absence of psychological safety in her workplace. Despite her profound love and passion for her university, Dr. Candia-Bailey prioritized her commitment to the institution over her well-being, even as she faced daily trauma inflicted by Dr. Moseley. This conflict between her dedication to the university and her personal health needs was explicitly articulated in her correspondence with the university leadership, stating: "I have had dark days, but I have never been this dark in my 25 years in the field. Student affairs was my love, and my love killed me." Further down in the letter she stated, "You were made aware of my mental health by email before I sent the email to the Board of Curators (agenda items for discussion). You scheduled a meeting on 10/26. Your demeanor was that of rushing; you stood the entire meeting, and you appeared heartless" (Martin, 2024).

In her end-of-summary letter, Dr. Candia-Bailey detailed multiple incidences of bullying and attempts to voice the need for help regarding her mental health; she was met with ridicule from Dr. Moseley, who chose to ignore the request while engaging with other employees to tease and openly discuss this private and personal condition (Lawrence, 2024).

Dr. Candia-Bailey went on to outline how Dr. Moseley was not pleased with her work performance; however, he would never provide a plan to help her be successful, noting that he did this to ensure her failure. She stated:

When I respectfully challenged you, you agreed to "strike a concern." I could not even finish the meeting because you did not hear me. I left in tears. You intentionally harassed and bullied me and got satisfaction from sitting back to determine how you would ensure I failed as an employee and proud alumna. (Martin, 2024, pg.2.)

Given the experience of Dr. Candia-Bailey, we understand that we do not have complete control over how colleagues or coworkers may choose to treat us in the workplace, this should not render us powerless. Implementing certain practices can provide mental peace and clarity while at work (Castrillon, 2022). Start your day with a peaceful mindset by setting clear intentions and understanding what aspects of your workday you can and cannot control. Deciding on your goals for the day allows for planning and execution. Throughout the day, avoid dwelling on comparisons regarding who can perform a task or project better. Recognize and value your unique strengths. Establishing and pursuing your goals with determination and fostering positive work relationships and supportive environments are crucial for maintaining a constructive and fulfilling work experience.

EQUITY VS. EQUALITY

According to Pendell (2022), equity is the allocation of resources based on individual needs, acknowledging that different circumstances require different levels of support. In contrast, equality involves treating every person the same, regardless of their unique situations.

Summer's struggle for these fundamental rights, which should be guaranteed to all employees, exemplifies the injustice she faced from her employers. This led to a prolonged and unnecessary battle to restore her reputation and secure appropriate compensation. Ultimately, Summer achieved justice and had her name cleared, but continuing to work in that environment became increasingly challenging. A physician who recognized her hard work and ethics offered her a promoted position in his office, where she continued to excel.

Summer's experience suggests either a lack of appropriate diversity training or the presence of what can be termed "diversity dishonesty." In theory, equality in the workplace entails providing the same opportunities and resources to everyone. However, this approach can be problematic, as different racial groups have varying needs. Failure to manage this properly can perpetuate inequalities.

THE OUTLIER: REPRESENTATION AND SUPPORT

Although HR supported Morgan, the consequences included being blackballed and perceived as problematic, which impeded her ability to advance within her department. However, solidarity emerged in Morgan's story through a leader who chose to ally with and support her. Morgan recounted, "Having a Black manager changed everything for me. I love her for that and always will. She saw something others ignored." She further emphasized the importance of representation, stating, "Having people who look like you in rooms that you cannot be in, speaking up for you, is what Black women need in the workplace. Additionally, being in leadership and not being afraid to challenge our colleagues is crucial." (Personal Communication, focus group September 2023)

This supportive manager recognized Morgan's potential and work ethic, facilitating her promotion to a different state, where she thrived for eight years. Upon her return, Morgan was appointed as the manager of the department where she had previously been blackballed. This narrative underscores that the challenges Black women face in the workplace are not of their own making but rather a result of systemic issues.

Intentional support and advocacy are critical. When one Black woman is promoted, it is imperative to lift up the next by mentioning her in influential spaces and standing up for her when she faces injustice. Solidarity and collective advancement in leadership are vital, ensuring we remember our struggles while helping others rise. As Black women, it is essential to recognize our collective strength and stand united.

CONCLUSION

In conclusion, the findings of this study reveal that, across various industries, Black women consistently encounter similar oppressive experiences and psychological burdens. These challenges arise from the pervasive dishonesty in diversity initiatives and the ineffectiveness of diversity programs that fail to significantly improve their work experiences. Despite their extensive experience, advanced education, and substantial expertise—attributes that make Black women one of the most educated demographics—they continue to face undue scrutiny regarding their attire, leadership abilities, and overall competence. This scrutiny is exacerbated by a glaring lack of support and representation within professional environments.

To address the questions guiding this study—whether the work experiences of Black women educators and Black women leaders in other industries are similar or different—it is clear that they are, unfortunately, alike in their adversity.

The imperative for organizations and educational institutions is evident: there must be a deliberate and sustained effort to create work environments that not only welcome and accept Black women, but also support and retain them. This necessitates the implementation of meaningful DEI initiatives that specifically address the unique challenges Black women face, ensuring they receive the respect, recognition, and opportunities they deserve. Only through intentional and genuine commitment can we hope to foster workplaces that are truly inclusive and equitable for Black women.

REFLECTION QUESTIONS

1. Is it possible for the experience that Morgan had to become more of the norm? If so, what steps would need to be taken to ensure that this happens?
2. Considering that diversity training exists and is provided at every company, what real changes can and should be made to make it more effective and sustainable?
3. How can we cultivate the next generation of Black women to recognize and address Work Pet to Threat when they encounter it or witness it?
4. What steps can you take personally if you find yourself in a situation where you are experiencing Work Pet to Threat?

REFERENCES

Bradford, J. H. (2022). *Session 254: Black women in the workplace.* https://therapyforblackgirls.com/2022/04/06/session-254-black-women-in-the-workplace/

Brownlee, D. (2022). Black women leaders are more ambitious but less supported at work, McKinsey and Lean in study finds. https://www.forbes.com/sites/danabrownlee/2022/10/21/black-women-leaders-are-more-ambitious-but-less-supported-at-work-mckinsey-and-lean-in-study-finds/

Castrillon, C. (2022). 10 ways to improve your mental health at work. *Forbes.* https://www.forbes.com/sites/carolinecastrillon/2022/05/08/10-ways-to-improve-your-mental-health-at-work/ https://www.dictionary.com/browse/solidary

Dobbin, F., & Kalev, A. (2016, July-August). *Why diversity programs fail.* https://hbr.org/2016/07/why-diversity-programs-fail

Equal Employment Opportunity Commission. (2022). *Title VII of the Civil Rights Acts of 1964.* U.S. Equal Employment Opportunity Commission.

Gallo, A. (2023). *What is psychological safety?* https://hbr.org/2023/02/what-is-psychological-safety

Jackson, A. (2022). *Less 25% of Black employees feel included at work-what companies can be doing better.*CNBC.https://www.cnbc.com/2022/04/01/less-than-25percent-of-black-employees-feel-included-at-work-what-companies-can-be-doing-better.html

Lawrence, A. (2024, February 28). "She endured cruelty:" What led to a leader's death at a historically Black university? *The Guardian.* https://www.theguardian.com/us-news/2024/feb/28/antoinette-candia-bailey-lincoln-university-death

Martin, R. (2024). *State of hopelessness: Lincoln Univ. VP of student affairs died by suicide after workplace bullying.* Roland Martin Unfiltered. https://www.youtube.com/watch?v=rx3FQusVBsU

Miles, M. (2022). *9 ways to promote equity in the workplace (and how to lead by example).* Betterup.https://www.betterup.com/blog/equity-in-the-workplace

National Association for the Advancement of Colored People. (2023). *NAACP support worker's rights as civil rights opposed to so-called "right to work" legislation and initiatives.* National Association for the Advancement of Colored people. https://naacp.org/resources/naacp-supports-workers-rights-civil-rights-opposed-so-called-right-work-legislation-and

Paulise, L. (2023). How can women overcome the pet to threat phenomenon in 7 tips. *Forbes*. https://www.forbes.com/ sites/lucianapaulise/ 2023/02/23/ how-black-women-can-overcome-the-pet-to-threat-phenomenon-in-7-steps/

Pendell, R. (2022, September 22). Workplace equity: The "E" in DEI and why it matters. https://www.gallup.com/ workplace/401573/ workplace-equity-dei-why-matters.aspx

Sombret, P. (2023, March 21). Workplace equity vs. equality: What's the difference? RSS. https://www.deskbird.com/blog/ workplace-equity-vs-equality

orkplace equity vs. equality: Two small letters, one big difference. Deskbird.

Turman, L. (2024). *Emails surface from LU's VP of Student Affairs sent the day she died by suicide.* KRCG13.https://krcgtv.com/ news/local/ emails-surface-from-lus-vp-of-student-affairs-sent-the-day-she-died-by-suicide

Wilton, L. (2020). *Show don't tell: Diversity dishonesty harms racial/ethnic minorities at work.* Sage Journals. Show don't tell: Diversity dishonesty harms racial/ ethnic minorities at work. Sage Journals.

Pedulla. (2020). Diversity and Inclusion efforts that Really work. https://hbr.org/ 2020/05/ diversity-and-inclusion-efforts-that-really-work

Redstone, I. (2020, November 18). *This is why diversity programming doesn't work.* Forbes.

KEY TERMS AND DEFINITIONS

Disproportionate: Something being too large or small in comparison with something else.

Diversity Dishonesty: When organizations position themselves as diverse and inclusive, but the inner workings of the company tell a very different story.

Diversity Programs: Measures taken to enhance the well-being of members of underrepresented groups.

Equality: Unlocking opportunities for every employee by treating them equitably and without bias at every stage of employment.

Equity: The quality of being fair and impartial.

Heat Map: A tool to identify candidates that have potential to be developed to move into upper/executive management roles.

Microaggressions: Subtle but offensive comments or actions directed at a member of a marginalized group, especially a racial minority, that are often unintentionally offensive or unconsciously reinforce stereotypes.

Outlier: Something that lies outside the main body or group.

Pet to Threat: The phenomenon of Black women being embraced and groomed by an organization until they start demonstrating high levels of confidence and excel in their roles.

Psychological Safety: Feeling safe to take interpersonal risks, speak up, disagree openly, and surface concerns without fear of negative repercussions or pressure to sugarcoat bad news.

Solidarity: A union or fellowship arising from common responsibilities and interests, as between members of a group, between classes or between people.

Unconscious Bias: Social stereotypes about certain groups of people that individuals form outside of their own awareness.

White Fear: A deep-seated fear that white people will become the intellectual minority and lose their political, social, and economic power.

Section 3
Stories of Now

Chapter 10
The Price of a Token:
The Effects of Tokenism on Black Women in Higher Education

Chinyere Turner
Partners in Justice LLC, USA

ABSTRACT

Tokenism is the practice of making only a perfunctory or symbolic effort to do a particular thing, especially by recruiting a small number of people from underrepresented groups to give the appearance of equality within a workforce. Tokenism has always been a point of contention in diversity and inclusion conversations, mainly because tokenism can affect those of any marginalized community. However, tokenism through the lenses of professional Black women has not been explored as thoroughly. "The Price of a Token" will analyze the various factors of tokenism that Black women experience in professional settings and the price they unwillingly must pay in being assigned a token.

FROM ONE TOKEN ROLE TO ANOTHER

Tokenism involves making only perfunctory or symbolic efforts to include individuals from underrepresented groups to give the appearance of diversity and equality within an organization (Jackson, Thoits, & Taylor, 1995). Furthermore, it requires the elevation of those individuals above others within the same identity group, causing hostility among them because of limited opportunities (Childress et. al, 2023). In higher education, tokenism is often presented as black women widely appearing in marketing materials or honored in magazines but one or few black women in senior leadership positions. It can also look like a staff member of color having to speak on behalf of their race or ethnic group after social issues

DOI: 10.4018/979-8-3693-0698-7.ch010

Copyright © 2024, IGI Global. Copying or distributing in print or electronic forms without written permission of IGI Global is prohibited.

arise. Tokenism is generally ascribed to groups with marginalized identities with the added burden of group representation. For example, a cyber security specialist may be referred to as a female cyber security specialist. A professor of chemistry may be referred to as the disabled chemistry professor. Kanter (1977) argued that the term "token" refers to one's status as a symbol of their kind. Tokenism not only contributes to the mental health issues of the Black women who are tokenized in higher education it also negatively affects individuals of the same identity group and creates dishonestly in the institution. In this chapter, I will analyze the various levels of tokenism Black women experience in professional settings as well as the impact of tokenism on their personal and professional development.

My first experience with tokenism in higher education was while I was an undergraduate student. My experience as an undergraduate student at a small, private, predominantly white institution (PWI) in the Mid-western United States is not uncommon for Black women in similar situations. The undergraduate institution I attended had a small population of traditional undergraduate students which led to an average classroom size of less than 20 students. This meant I was the only Black person, and sometimes the only person of color, in most of my classes. As a student, I wanted to make the most of my college experience. I was a student-athlete, a member and leader within several organizations, and a student employee. My role as an executive board member of cultural student organizations and with the Office of Diversity and Inclusion shaped my undergraduate experience. As my involvement with the Office of Diversity and Inclusion increased, so did my recognizability among students, faculty, and staff. In many ways, I felt I had become the "Black student leadership girl" or the "Black diversity girl." This further complicated my undergraduate experience. There were times I felt like a contradiction. On one hand, while most people knew my name or recognized me, I felt invisible because I experienced bias like other students of color on campus. On the other hand, I had become the poster child for diversity which made me hyper-visible and contributed to my being tokenized.

An example of this is when I was asked to be interviewed for an article in support of a university department. As part of the interview, I was photographed for the publication. Eventually, the picture I took for the interview became the university's favorite photo for marketing campaigns and recruitment. I was never compensated for the interview, or the mass printing of my face on the university's marketing publications. Even after I had graduated, my image and likeness were used for years. It is hard to describe the feeling of having your face used for banners, magazine advertisements, websites, and in the international airport while being encumbered due to finances and experiencing bias and discrimination. No amount of publicity could stop the microaggressions or stereotypes I experienced. Not only did I feel invisible, but also, I felt silenced. I noticed that I was being invited into spaces off limits to other students to be seen but not heard. This was evidenced by the fact that the suggestions I made were never implemented. Experiences with tokenism are not limited to college students. This was confirmed when I became a professional employee at my alma mater and the race-based issues I faced as a student plagued students who followed me.

Having experienced hyper-visibility and tokenism as a student and eventually as a professional staff member, I became self-conscious. As I bared the weight of being the token, I grappled with my identity as a Black woman as I became careful not to behave in ways considered stereotypical. I was overly aware that my behavior would be the measuring stick with which Black women who came after me would be judged. Eventually, I began code-switching to avoid being labeled. Code-switching is when people from marginalized groups find themselves as the numerical minority in a setting and alter their language, dialect, slang, mannerisms, behaviors, and/ or appearance due to the environment, setting, or people present (Conner, 2020). While code-switching can manifest in various ways, I altered my verbal communication. The African American Vernacular English/Ebonics, Black cultural phrases, and slang I once used during conversations and presentations slowly decreased. My attire was impacted as well. The bright colors and patterns I once proudly donned were replaced with neutral tones. Code-switching became a defense mechanism and a form of protection in an environment where stereotypes and biases became unbearable.

This took an emotional toll on me and led to me policing my mannerisms as not to be viewed as aggressive and silencing my voice. I soon realized that doing this led to feelings of depression and turmoil. I eventually decided to make my emotional well-being a priority. I chose to assert my voice even when it fell on ears that refused to listen. However, I was never able to shake the pressure to be perfect or combat stereotypes.

Tokenism leads to exploitation. It requires the token to be the representative for those in their identity group. The lure of tokenism is the "privileges" afforded to the individual. Initially, it was an honor to be invited to speak at events, sit on committees, and attend meetings because it felt exclusive. But as time progresses, the tokenized individual is expected to take on more responsibility. At one point early in my professional career, I was transitioning from position to another at the same university. During the transition, I was asked and expected to learn my new duties as a program coordinator while also performing my previous responsibilities as an admission counselor. My contributions were praised in words but overlooked during salary negotiations or promotions. Invisible labor in academia is not just limited to Black faculty. Connor (2022) described invisible labor as the extended university and student services that Black faculty provide that goes unnoticed by university leadership and is not considered for tenure and promotion. The labor I provided to the institution was considered voluntary and therefore not considered as professional development when being considered for salary increases. I often felt conflicted with the encouragement from senior professionals to "be thankful" for the chance to be in the room. The tokenism and exploitation I experienced were always masked as an opportunity, a special privilege not offered to others in my identity group.

Soon, my presence felt like a hollow fixture; I was ushered into rooms to display the university's efforts toward inclusion. For some institutions, performative actions and valued more than meaningful strides toward equity. Initially, I believed the loneliness and isolation I felt was unique. However, the more I shared my experiences with Black women, I realized I was, unfortunately, one of many Black women who felt exploited, silenced, and unappreciated. Black women continue to be subjected to racial and gender-based discrimination like wage inequity.

If Black women across professions in and outside of higher education share this feeling, then Black women are not the problem. The system is the problem. The institutions that employ us are the problem. It is the structures that uphold capitalism, white supremacy, and patriarchy. It is the society that continuously devalues Black women. Tokenism gravely affects the black women who are subjected to it but it also the professional environment and the interactions between employees. The experiences of those who are tokenized can be categorized by the ratio of uniform groups.

A QUOTA OF TOKENS

Tokenism supports the use of quotas in institutions and encourages unhealthy competition among individuals in marginalized identity groups. When organizations feel they "have enough Black women" or have met their "quota" for people of color and those from marginalized communities, the organization and its employees are placed at a disadvantage. Limiting the number of people of color in an organization or a professional space added pressure and challenges on those individuals and creates tokenism. There are several research studies that explore the experiences of tokenized individuals and the quota system used by some organizations.

Kanter (1977) was one of the first researchers to study tokenism. Kanter's research focused on professional women in marketing and sales who were the only or one of few women in a male-dominated environment. Kanter sought to understand the male-female interactions in professional settings and how those interactions shaped women's experiences. From her research, Kanter developed a framework for conceptualizing the interactions between tokens and dominates or marginalized and advantaged individual. The framework included four group types based on proportional representations of a specific identity: uniform, skewed, tilted, and balanced.

Uniform groups have one identity that is shared by all and are homogeneous with respect to identities such as sex, race, or ethnicity. The ratio of uniform groups is 100:0. Skewed groups have a ratio of 85:15 and below. These groups have a large numerical dominance of one identity over another with the dominant identity controlling the work culture. It is in skewed groups where dominate and token roles are formed. Tokens are the numerical minority and are seen as representatives of their identity group rather than as individuals. The third group type, tilted, has less extreme distributions with a ratio of 65:35. In this group, minority identity members can build relationships as allies and form coalitions that shape work culture. Minority identity members are also able to maintain individual identities without fear of being expected to represent an entire identity group. Balanced groups have ratios of 60:40 to 50:50. These groups are called "balanced" based on the numerical balance as well as the culture and interaction that reflect it. Kanter's research focused on the experiences of tokens from skewed, tilted, and balanced groups and found that group structures shaped the interaction context and influence patterns between men and women in professional settings. Kanter's (1977) ground-breaking work on tokenism further revealed three typical types of interactions that dominant groups and tokenized have in groups that have skewed numbers. Token responses were comprised of three themes: visibility, polarization, and assimilation. Visibility describes the heightened awareness the dominant group has of the token including similarities between those who share the same identity and the differences of the token. Polarization, then, describes the exaggeration of differences. The dominant group often applied generalizations and stereotypes to the token to highlight their differences. Assimilation involves the use of stereotypes to distort individual characteristics to fit into negative beliefs. Each type of interaction affected the treatment of tokenized individuals and their personal experiences. Kanter (1977) stated, "Visibility creates performance pressures on the token. Polarization leads to group boundary heightening and isolation of the token. And assimilation results in the token's role entrapment" (p. 972). Through her research, Kanter was able to articulate the experiences of tokenized women and in many ways explain the phenomenon that other social identities face when they are victims of tokenism.

This research, while focused on women in predominantly male spaces, can be applied to any social identity category such as race, religion, sexual orientation, ability status, etc. Furthermore, other identity groups that have stereotypes or assumptions based on their culture or behavior fit into this framework.

Kanter's research also suggested that having a handful of women (or any marginalized group) in a male-dominated work environment does not change the negative experiences of the marginalized group because numerically, they are still in the minority. In essence, quotas do not make significant differences to work culture.

Kanter argued that balanced ratios between majority and minority groups is the first step in ensuring an inclusive work culture.

While Kanter's research on tokenism in the workplace was groundbreaking, it has come under scrutiny by some scholars since its publication. Specifically, Kanter's assumption that tokenism can be eliminated by drastically increasing the number of women in male-dominated spaces. Opponents of Kanter's research contend that increasing the number of already marginalized individuals in an already toxic work environment only subjects a larger number of people to the toxicity.

One critic of Kanter's research, Zimmer (1988) argued that issues facing women in the workplace cannot be solved without first working to eradicate racism. Moreover, the societal issues faced by women is also present in their professional places of employment and is a result of sexist and discriminatory practices. Zimmer further noted that focusing on tokenism alone diverted attention away from the root problem of sexism. Zimmer wrote, "Tokenism alone, without attention to sexism, offers little insight into the organizational behavior of women or the relationships that develop between men and women in newly integrated occupations" (p. 72).

To fully understand tokenism, one must understand the societal issues that create the environment for tokenism to exist. As Zimmer (1988) argued, tokenism, in this context, exists because of sexism. For Black women specifically, tokenism exists because of racism and sexism which leads to misogynoir. Misogynoir is a term coined by Moya Bailey (2021) that describes the specific hatred, dislike, distrust, and prejudice directed towards Black women. How society views Black women has a direct impact on how we are viewed professionally. (Bailey, 2021) The societal norms that exist, specifically in Western countries, of discrimination against all marginalized groups including those with disabilities, LGBTIQ+ individuals, and people of color are rampant. The prejudice and discrimination that marginalized communities face in society extend to their workplaces. In their professional roles, tokenized individuals contend not only with the stressors of everyday life, but also navigate t experiences of bias. Many of the experiences that tokenized individuals face as under-represented communities in their workplaces are similar to the ones that Black women experience. Unfortunately, being a token comes at a price – a price of mental and emotional frustration, challenges toward professional advancement, invisibility, and exhaustion. Bizzell (2023) research study captured the experiences of black women in higher education who expressed these same concerns regarding the effects of tokenism.

A participant from Bizzell's (2023) study noted how tokenism affects other black women in the workplace stating

"Look at our shiny or fill-in-the-blank marginalized identity. Because I feel like that was one of my friends. The Dean of Students took a liking to her and mentored her. But then I think she was also like the black pet and kept getting promotions, which I don't take away from her. But then I think about my particular self, of course. You know, the Black people at the institution, we found each other, and we became the caucus. But, like the other two, we can't get promoted here. Like they don't even see us." (page 11).

Tokenism can professionally advance one person and showcase their intellect or experience while also dismissing and disregarding others of that same identity. Bizzell (2023) also notes token fatigue is caused by job stressors and performing in a manner that is unnatural and not just by the overexposure of black bodies for marketing and rebranding of the institutions' imagery." Code-switching for many is very unnatural and is a continuous effort and for some can be a conscious effort to defy stereotypes, which is another contributing factor to fatigue.

THE PRICE OF TOKENISM

While Kanter's research has received criticism, there were critical points that arose from the research that should be further explored. Tokenized individuals in an organization can feel isolated, trapped, and pressured. The women Kanter (1977) interviewed indicated several job stressors from their token status including performance stressors, boundary heightening, and role entrapment. Managers, specifically, reported that they were often the subject of scrutiny and gossip, and their skills and abilities were questioned. Tokenized individuals experienced performance stressors related to stricter standards and work conditions than their peers. They also reported feeling additional pressure to perform above expectations and have their achievements noticed by others. Boundary heightening involves repeated reminders of the differences between tokenized individuals and the majority through jokes, interruptions, exclusion from activities, and various "loyalty tests". Boundary heightening led to code-switching behaviors to fit in with the majority. When tokenized individuals are typecasted and stereotyped, this results in adaptive responses that create additional stressors like working harder or "laying low", accepting isolation, hostility towards other tokenized individuals, and perpetuating or combatting stereotypes. Stereotyping of black women also enables role entrapment because it limits them to the responsibilities or positions that others believe they should fulfill instead of advancing in their careers.

What the women experienced in Kanter's experiment can also be applied to the tokenism experienced by black women in higher education. Black women's experience of isolation in their professional spaces is something that persists. Isolation in this context refers to the feeling of loneliness, being aware one doesn't fit in, and being forced to be your own support system. (Bizzell, 2023)

Carroll (1982) described the experiences of isolation by Black women stating,

Black women in higher education are isolated, underutilized, and often demoralized. They note the efforts made to provide equal opportunities for Black men and white women in higher education, while they somehow are left behind in the work of both the Black and feminist movements. (Carroll, 1982)

Similar sentiments from Carroll's study in 1982 were shared in Bizzell's recent 2023 study describing the "ideal black" employee who is often isolated from other black colleagues due to their tokenization causing a divide and inability to share knowledge or skills they might have learned. (Bizzell, 2023) Isolation often leads to psychological stressors. Those who experience race-based tokenism have higher experiences with depression and those who experience gender-based tokenism experience greater anxiety levels. Tokenism is seen as a significant predictor of depression. Black professionals are outnumbered by white professionals who report token stress and higher rates of depression. Those who are elite and our outnumbered by the opposite gender report work overload that increases in both depression and anxiety. "Blacks who are outnumbered by whites report more token stress and increased depression. (Jackson et. al.,1995).

An additional cost of tokenism is invisible labor. As discussed earlier, invisible labor involves completing tasks that are unpaid, unacknowledged, and unregulated (Connor, 2022). Women and professionals of color take on a disproportionate amount of invisible work in education A study conducted by the Social Sciences Feminist Network Research Interest Group (2017) revealed that invisible labor included, for study participants, department-level committee meetings to evaluate curricula, university-level goal development, or discipline-related article reviews. Another aspect of invisible labor "care work". Care work focuses on the care and attention of others and can include teaching, mentoring, and advising students through organization, one-on-one student leader meetings, writing letters of recommendation, providing professional recommendations on job opportunities, or general advice (Social Sciences Feminist Network Research Interest Group, 2017).

An unfortunate price Black women pay is the effects of the phenomenon "leaky pipeline". The "leaky pipeline" describes the gradual disappearance of women and people of color at each stage of academia. (Social Sciences Feminist Network Research Interest Group, 2017). Women and people of color become less represented in senior-level positions and as tenured faculty. For example, women represent 51 percent of non-tenured instructors compared to 46 percent of assistant professors, 36 percent of associate professors, and 21 percent of full professors. The same can be said for tenured faculty of color. As faculty of color move up the academic ranks their proportion diminishes. This is the complete opposite for white faculty members who make up 90 percent of associate and full professors (Social Sciences Feminist Network Research Interest Group, 2017). Black women in higher education must navigate numerous landmines to get through the leaky pipeline.

In addition to the hardships that Black women face in trying to advance in higher education, we also have to counter the bias of professional peers. A huge burden Black women shoulder in society and the workplace are that carries on from society into their professional careers in higher education is microaggressions. Microaggressions are brief and commonplace daily verbal, behavioral, or environmental indignities, whether intentional or unintentional, that communicate hostile, derogatory, or negative prejudicial slights and insults toward marginalized groups (National Conference for Community and Justice, 2024). Black women experience microaggressions at the intersection of race and gender. While some of the day-to-day microaggressions are not problematic enough to meet standards for harassment complaints, they still create a negative experience. Microaggressions can look like not being invited to social interactions to build a network, sexist jokes, and being referred to as "Miss" or "Ms." instead of professional titles (Social Sciences Feminist Network Research Interest Group, 2017)

Black women regularly experience microaggressions, specifically microinvalidations, from white colleagues and microinsults from white or male students. Microinvalidations are verbal comments or behaviors that exclude or negate the thoughts, feelings, or experiences of a marginalized group (Bormann, 2020). On the other hand, microinsults convey rudeness or insensitivity that demean a person's social identity (Bormann, 2020). Microaggressions based on race can present as Black women having colleagues question their merit or professional experience, lack of comradery in predominately white spaces, or being subjected to racial stereotypes. The Social Sciences Feminist Network Research Interest Group (2017) mentioned that the persistence of microaggressions and slights creates "double doubt" where employees of color "feel both an internalization of not being good enough and external pressures to do more and be twice as good as white colleagues." (SSFNRI, p. 6) This burden also has an emotional impact on employees of color because they experience more stress and anxiety as a result.

For employees of color, there is often the expectation that they will and should address diversity-related issues, regardless of their role at the institution. They are asked to serve on committees, draft statements, or edit goals that demonstrate the department's commitment to inclusion. These are examples of service burdens and invisible work. Black women are affected twice-fold, having to speak to issues facing women and people of color. Often tokenized individuals take on emotional labor as a result of a greater service burden than their colleagues. Invisible labor can present as an emotional burden as well. An example of this is the emotional, invisible labor many tokenized individuals experienced in higher education after the murder of George Floyd. The tragic murder of George Floyd impacted the world and had a unique impact on the lives of Black people. Many Black professionals in higher education, whether faculty or staff, found themselves caring for Black students on an emotional level while also caring for themselves. Police brutality, civil rights violations, and social justice issues are, unfortunately, embedded in the fabric of the United States. When any civil rights incident or event with racial undertones happens in the U.S., commonly, professional staff of color are called upon to speak on the incident. In my experience, Black women are always the first to be called on to vocalize the injustices.

The expected role of Black women to support the campus community in times of social injustice is an example of cultural taxation. Amado Padilla coined the term 'cultural taxation' in 1994 to describe the burden on education professionals of color to address diversity-related department and university issues. In addition to the specified responsibilities in their job description, employees from underrepresented groups are expected to engage in diversity work including diversity committees, advising students of color, or public lectures on equity. Oftentimes, marginalized professionals are asked to speak on behalf of their race or identity group. Asking faculty and staff of color to speak publicly and be at the forefront of the university's efforts to address a current event around racism results in tokenism. The expectation of black women addressing race-related issues or serving on committees and panels related to diversity issues also stems from hypervisibility. Black women are hyper-visible in professional spaces where few look like us. Hypervisibility allows those of the majority to scrutinize and create assumptions or continue stereotypes of us. (Bizzell, 2023)

Another unfortunate effect of tokenism is the unhealthy and unnecessary competition between Black employees. When a company has a history of employing one or a handful of Black women it creates the belief that only one can be successful at a time. The same can be said when a professional environment only promotes one of a few people of color into senior leadership roles. Tokenism perpetuates the idea that only one person from a racially diverse or minoritized group is needed to show diversity and inclusion. Therefore, when another person of color is added to the team, it can make the tokenized employee believe they no longer have job security. This relates to Zimmer's critique of Kanter's assertion that recruiting more diverse employees alone does not positively affect the experience of marginalized employees. It must be a combination of work culture shifts and the recruitment of diverse individuals.

To create an equitable work environment for Black women, institutions must go beyond the performative Black History Month celebration. This will involve cultivating community among Black women. There are several ways to cultivate community among employees who share a similar background to combat competition. One of which would be creating and maintaining affinity groups. Affinity groups are employee-led and facilitated gatherings for employees from a particular marginalized group to build community through professional development, discussing issues specific to their identity, and personal growth (Indeed, 2024). Allowing Black female employees, the opportunity to network and build relationships can prevent toxic competition and foster a healthy work environment. Furthermore, it can help retention efforts because it allows new Black women employees to enter an established community of support. Affinity groups are one way in which institutions of higher education can practice honest representation.

HONEST REPRESENTATION

One way to eradicate tokenism is to move towards honest representation. Representation is often discussed in terms of the media through film, TV shows, and other forms of entertainment. However, this form of representation is just as important in higher education. Students from marginalized populations must see themselves reflected in the positions in which they aspire to achieve. Research suggests there are long-term sustained impacts on Black students who have instructors who are the same race (Gershenson, Hart, Lindsay, & Papageorge, 2017). In a 2017 research study entitled, *The Long-Run Impacts of Same-Race Teachers* experts found that exposure to one Black teacher had a meaningful effect on students' long-term outcomes. Additionally, students who had three Black teachers had a stronger desire for educational attainment. There was a substantially larger impact on Black students who were also socioeconomically disadvantaged (Gershenson et al., 2017). While this study focused on elementary and secondary education students, the results can be applied to post-secondary education as well. Representation in faculty, staff, and administrative leadership is not only meaningful for those who share similar backgrounds but also for those who are of other backgrounds because it promotes intellectual authority and success as characteristics not associated with race and gender. Having Black women at all levels of leadership and in various positions dismantles tokenism.

The benefits of diversity and inclusion have been researched and are well-known. Racial and ethnic diversity on a college campus improves the social experience and learning environment (Nam, 2023) Graduates from diverse colleges and universities can expect to earn a little over five percent more than those who attended institutions with homogeneous populations. This was especially true for Hispanic and Latino students (Wolfe & Fletcher, 2013)

According to the United States Census Bureau (2012), the United States people of color will represent the majority by 2043. The ecosystem of higher education, from entry-level to senior level, should reflect racial diversity. While six in ten higher education professionals are women, only one in five positions are held by racial and ethnic minorities (Whitford, Who Holds Professional Positions in Higher

Ed, and Who Gets Paid?, 2020) Currently, in leadership positions, including administration and tenured faculty, women and people of color are few and far between (Whitford, 2020). Overwhelmingly, leadership in higher education are white (80 percent) with less than eight percent of administrators being Black. Black people and people of color are disproportionately underrepresented across the higher education workforce (Whitford, 2020). Representation at all levels within the institution is necessary to cultivate an environment where employees can grow, develop, and advance professionally.

Many universities support diversity, equity, and inclusion in theory, but not in practice. In the name of tokenism, institutions have created marketing campaigns with racially ambiguous models; ensured their websites and other recruitment materials feature minoritized groups; and spotlighted their lone person of color in senior-level administration. When institutions engage in performative diversity, equity, and inclusion efforts when their actual demographics tell another story, institutions can be perceived as deceptive. Deception manifests when there is a lack of policies that ensure equity in recruitment, pay, professional opportunities, or workplace treatment. To ensure diversity and inclusion efforts do not result in tokenism, institutions of higher education must actively and intentionally create an inclusive campus culture. The first step in creating an inclusive campus culture is to understand that equity is not a checklist. There must be policies that ensure equity of pay, closing the gender-race wage gap. Next, institutions must document requirements for professional advancement, promotions, and pay increases. Then, educational opportunities must be provided that include continued support toward cultural competency and dismantling systems of oppression. I would encourage institutions to empower those in roles centering on diversity and inclusion to lead and facilitate workshops and training around equity. Institutions can also seek assistance from social justice advocates and consultants outside the institution to facilitate workshops with deliverables for the campus community. Having an equity-based culture also means holding accountable those employees whose behavior violates the campus equity-based community standards.

Inclusive policies should also be demonstrated in hiring practices. Developing an inclusive recruitment strategy is another way to shift campus culture. Diversifying the institutions' recruitment strategies would mean targeted advertising of open positions. While "Higher Ed Jobs" is a great resource, it is not a strategic approach. A strategic approach would be to develop relationships with community organizations, professional networks, and associations that directly support Black women. Some examples include the Black Career Women Network and the National Coalition of 100 Black Women. Institutions should partner with organizations like the National Association of Black Accountants, National Black Nurses Association, or National Association of Black Engineers, especially for faculty positions. There are professional organizations geared toward Black professionals for almost every profession and sector. Creating an intentional pipeline for recruitment can help to eradicate tokenism.

Institutions must also acknowledge the invisible labor done by Black women by providing recommendations for advancement and promotions, salary raises, bonuses, and professional development opportunities. The impact of invisible labor on student retention and campus culture cannot be underestimated. The reward for the good works of Black women in higher education should not be additional work.

There is much work to be done to shift this trend. Compensation, including bonuses and non-monetary compensation like additional paid time off, flex time, company technology, and professional development are all ways in which the invisible labor of Black women can be acknowledged.

Changes such as these take time to implement. In the meantime, institutions can begin addressing tokenism by increasing opportunities for staff to develop cultural competence to reduce workplace microaggressions and isolation experienced by Black women. Intentional cross-cultural mentoring that expands employees' professional network is essential to reducing isolation.

These recommendations are the minimum institutions should do to create working environments that are inclusive of marginalized communities. Moreover, these steps are more effective when senior leadership leads the charge to implement these strategies. Equity efforts are most successful when they are embedded within the culture of the organization. That commitment starts at the top. Senior leadership must be devoted to progress and take intentional, strategic, and measurable steps towards equity or these initiatives will fail (Harvard Business Review Analytic Services, 2021). One study found that diversity, equity, and inclusion initiatives were hindered by a lack of commitment among leadership. 72 percent of respondents stating they were held back by a lack of diversity at senior levels of the organization (Harvard Business Review Analytic Services, 2021) . Overall, organizations and institutions that truly desire to move the needle toward equity must resist having a sole Black woman as a token.

CONCLUSION

The research on tokenism had several similarities to my own experiences as a student and professional. From heightened visibility, mental health challenges, and invisible labor, Black women, like myself, desire to be authentically themselves without scrutiny, code-switching, and the pressure of confronting stereotypes. To eradicate the tokenism of Black women, higher education must first address issues of sexism, racism, and misogynoir. While systemic changes would take tremendous effort and time, institutions can begin making significant changes to address current issues of tokenism. Additional research is necessary as remains a scarcity surrounding research about Black women in higher education. Moving away from tokenism towards honest representation has benefits for Black women as well as the educational institutions they inhabit. Providing honest representation is beneficial for the overall campus community of an institution.

REFERENCES

Bailey, M. (2021). *Misogynoir Transformed: Black Women's Digital Resistance.* NYU Press.

Bartman, C. C. (2015). African American Women in Higher Education: Issues and. *College Student Affairs Leadership.*

Belland, J. (2021, June 23). *Higher Education Trends for Colleges and Universities.* Retrieved from Salesforce.org: https://www.salesforce.org/blog/higher-education-connected-student-report-second-edition/

Bizzell, C. V. (2023). How does it feel to be a problem: Tokenization of black women student affair professionals in white academic spaces. *International Journal of Qualitative Studies in Education : QSE.*

Bormann, O. (2020). *Microaggression.* Retrieved from University of Portland: https://www.up.edu/inclusion/files/101---microagressions-accessible.pdf#:~:text=A%20microinsult%20is%20a%20comments%20or%20action%20that,or%20disregard%20for%20a%20person%E2%80%99s%20identity%20or%20heritage

Bouchrika, I. (2020, August 4). *11 Top Trends in Higher Education:2021/2022Data, Insights & Predictions.* Retrieved from Research.com: https://research.com/education/trends-in-higher-education#ment

Carrasco, M. (2021, October 26). Addressing the Mental Health of LGBTQ+ Students. *Inside Higher Ed*, 1. Retrieved from Inside Higher Ed: https://www.insidehighered.com/news/2021/10/26/lgbtq-students-face-sizable-mental-health-disparities

Carroll, C. (1982). Three's A Crowd: The Dilemma of the Black Women in Higher Education. *But Some of Us Are Brave*, 115-128.

Childress, C., Nayyar, J., & Gibson, I. (2023). Tokenism and its long-term consequences: Evidence from the literary field. *American Sociological Review*, 89(1), 31–59. 10.1177/00031224231214288838313415

Conner, K. O. (2020, December 3). *What is Code-Switching.* Retrieved from Psychology Today: https://www.psychologytoday.com/us/blog/achieving-health-equity/202012/what-is-code-switching

Conner, T. (2022). Black faculty and radical retention. *Footnotes: A Magazine of the American Sociological Association, 50*(2), 1-7.

Gershenson, S., Hart, C. M., Lindsay, C., & Papageorge, N. (2017). *The Long-Run Impacts of Same Race Teachers.* Institute of Labor Economics. 10.2139/ssrn.2940620

Harvard Business Review Analytic Services. (2021). *Creating a Culture of Diversity, Equity, and Inclusion: Real Progress Requires Sustained Commitment*. Harvard Business School Publishing.

Holgersson, C., & Romani, L. (2020). Tokenism Revisited: . *When OrganizationalCulture Challenges Masculine Norms, theExperience of Token Is Transformed*, 649-661.

Howard-Vital, M. R. (1989). African-American Women in Higher Education: Struggling to Gain Identity. *Journal of Black Studies*, 20(2), 180–191. 10.1177/002193478902000205

Indeed. (2024, April 1). *What is an Affinity Group in the Workplace*. Retrieved from Indeed for Employers: https://www.indeed.com/hire/c/info/what-is-an-affinity-group

Jackson, P., Thoits, P., & Taylor, H. (1995). Composition of the Workplace and Psychological Well-Being: The Effects of Tokenism on America's Black Elite. *Oxford Journals*, 543-557.

Kanter, R. M. (1977). Some Effects of Proportions on Group Life: Skewed Sex Ratios and Responses to Token Women. *American Journal of Sociology*, 82(5), 965–990. Retrieved June 11, 2023, from https://www.jstor.org/stable/2777808. 10.1086/226425

Magley, J. (2023, February 14). *How Toxic Work Culture Breeds Unnecessary Competition Between Black Employees*. Retrieved from Forbes: https://www.forbes.com/sites/jennifermagley/2023/02/14/how-toxic-work-culture-breeds-unnecessary-competition-between-black-employees/?sh=24492a703690

Nam, J. (2023, March 31). *Diversity in Higher Education: Facts and Statistics*. Retrieved from Best Colleges: https://www.bestcolleges.com/research/diversity-in-higher-education-facts-statistics/

National Conference for Community and Justice. (2024). *Resources*. Retrieved from National Conference for Community and Justice: https://nccj.org/resources/age/

National Student Clearinghouse. (2023, July 27). *Persistence and Retention*. Retrieved from National Student Clearinghouse Research Center: https://nscresearchcenter.org/persistence-retention/

Social Sciences Feminist Network Research Interest Group. (2017). The Burden of Invisible Work in Academia: Social Inequalities and Time Use in Five. *Humboldt Journal of Social Relations*, 2828–245.

United States Census Bureau. (2012, December 12). *U.S. Census Bureau.* Retrieved March 19, 2024, from Newsroom Archive: https://www.census.gov/newsroom/releases/archives/population/cb12-243.html#:~:text=The%20U.S.%20is%20projected%20to%20become%20a%20majority-minority,comprise%2057%20percent%20of%20the%20population%20in%202060

Whitford, E. (2020, October 27). *There are so few that have made their way.* Retrieved from Inside Higher Ed: https://www.insidehighered.com/news/2020/10/28/black-administrators-are-too-rare-top-ranks-higher-education-it%E2%80%99s-not-just-pipeline

Whitford, E. (2020, May 5). *Who Holds Professional Positions in Higher Ed, and Who Gets Paid?* Retrieved from Inside Higher Ed: https://www.insidehighered.com/news/2020/05/06/report-details-gaps-women-and-minority-professionals-higher-ed

Wolfe, B., & Fletcher, J. (2013). *Estimating Benefits from University-Level Diversity.* National Bureau of Economic Research. 10.3386/w18812

Zimmer, L. (1988). Tokenism and Women in the Workplace: The Limits of Gender-Neutral Theory. *Social Problems*, 64-77. Retrieved 6 11, 2023, from https://www.jstor.org/stable/800667

KEY TERMS AND DEFINITIONS

Code-Switching: Altering one's language, dialect, slang, mannerisms, behaviors, and/ or appearance due to the environment, setting, or people present that puts one in the minority (Conner, 2020).

Marginalized: Groups of people or social identities that are treated inferior or insignificant and have historically experienced discrimination. Communities that are marginalized refer to communities of color, those with disabilities, women, the LGBTQ+ community, religious minorities, and have a low socioeconomic status (National Conference for Community and Justice, 2024).

Microaggressions: Brief and commonplace indignities that communicate hostile or negative assumptions towards a marginalized group of people through behaviors, actions, environment, or verbally (National Conference for Community and Justice, 2024).

Micro-Insults: Subtly conveying rudeness or demeaning a person's social identity (Bormann, 2020).

Micro-Invalidations: Invalidating the experience of someone from a marginalized social identity group as false or inaccurate (Bormann, 2020).

Misogynoir: The combination of racism and sexism that is displayed as dislike, contempt, or prejudice against Black women (Bailey, 2021).

Racism: A pervasive system of advantage and disadvantage based on race that is enacted intuitionally, culturally, interpersonally, and individually. Racism happens when one has racial prejudice against a community of color and social and institutional power to carry it out (National Conference for Community and Justice, 2024).

Retention: Students who re-enroll at the same higher education institution from one year to the next towards degree progression (National Student Clearinghouse, 2023).

Sexism: A system of oppression where privilege is afforded to cisgender men (National Conference for Community and Justice, 2024).

Social Identity: A socially constructed characteristic such as age, race, gender, class, sexual orientation, religion, etc. shared by a group of people that sets them apart from others (National Conference for Community and Justice, 2024).

Chapter 11
Who Said I Can't Lead:
The Journey to Leadership in Higher Education as a Black Female

Ty Jiles
https://orcid.org/0009-0001-4949-5353
Prairie State College, USA

Megan N. Lyons
North Carolina Central University, USA

ABSTRACT

This chapter provides a personal account of the author's journey toward achieving a leadership role in higher education as a young black female. By sharing these experiences and insights, the authors hope to shed light on the importance of representation and why it is crucial for minorities and females in higher education. Throughout the chapter, the authors address four major concerns that make the path to leadership particularly challenging for women. These concerns encompass various aspects, such as societal biases, gender stereotypes, limited opportunities for advancement, and lack of support systems. By examining these challenges in detail, readers can better understand women's unique obstacles on their journey toward leadership positions. Furthermore, the chapter will provide strategies for retaining and supporting women in leadership roles within higher education settings. These strategies will focus on creating inclusive environments, providing mentorship opportunities, advocating for equal opportunities, and fostering a supportive network.

DOI: 10.4018/979-8-3693-0698-7.ch011

Copyright © 2024, IGI Global. Copying or distributing in print or electronic forms without written permission of IGI Global is prohibited.

INTRODUCTION

In recent years, there has been an increasing focus on diversity and inclusion across various sectors. Despite the progress made, there remains a significant underrepresentation of African American women in leadership roles, specifically within higher education. A 2019 study by the American Council on Education (ACE) revealed that Black women make up only 3.5% of college and university presidents in the United States despite their accounting for a more significant portion of the student population. In terms of numbers, this translates to approximately 148 Black women out of a total of 4,398 leaders surveyed by ACE. Similarly, the representation of Black women in other high-level administrative positions within higher education institutions is also limited. According to the same ACE study, Black women hold only 2.6% of chief academic officer positions and 2.7% of chief financial officer positions. These statistics underscore the systemic barriers and biases that hinder their progress and limit their access to leadership opportunities. Further, this issue has broader implications for diversity and representation within the higher education landscape. To address this disparity and create a more equitable and inclusive environment, it is essential to examine the contributing factors and identify potential strategies for change.

UTILIZING INTERSECTIONALITY TO UNDERSTAND MINORITY FEMALES IN HIGHER EDUCATION

African American women face numerous challenges when pursuing leadership positions in higher education. These obstacles can be understood and analyzed through the theoretical framework of intersectionality. Coined by Kimberlé Crenshaw in 1989, intersectionality has become a vital tool for examining the complex intersection and interaction of different social identities (2005). In the context of African American women in higher education, intersectionality helps us understand the unique challenges they face due to the intersection of their race and gender, influencing their experiences and opportunities. The storytelling elements of intersectionality allow for a personalized perspective, spotlighting the need for representation through real-life viewpoints and experiences.

THE JOURNEY BEGINS

My career in higher education started in 2005, yet the challenges and adversities that awaited were unforeseen. As a young Black female, I embarked on this journey with determination and a passion for teaching. Initially beginning as an adjunct faculty member, I worked hard, moving up to the position of assistant professor in early childhood education. Throughout my tenure, I taught with tenacity, wrote grants, and demonstrated dedication to service and scholarship for the university.

Throughout my academic journey, I faced numerous obstacles unique to my identity as a Black woman in higher education. Although many individuals face challenges and obstacles along their path to academic success, minorities like me often confront a particularly treacherous road to tenure, marred by discrimination, bullying, and a hostile work environment. Despite my dedication and hard work, I was subjected to bullying and discrimination for nearly six years, particularly due to my age. The mistreatment was not an isolated incident but rather a sustained campaign that left me feeling marginalized and undervalued. Colleagues belittled my ideas and dismissed my contributions, undermining my confidence and sense of belonging in academia. Constantly plagued by doubt and self-questioning, I developed imposter syndrome, grappling with feelings of inadequacy and fear of being exposed as a fraud. The lack of support from my administration only reinforced these feelings, perpetuating the cycle of mistreatment and causing undue emotional duress and physical tolls on my overall health. It also sent a message that such behavior was acceptable within the institution, further deepening my sense of disillusionment within the academic environment.

One example of mistreatment I faced was being consistently excluded from important departmental meetings and decision-making processes. Despite my status as a tenure-track professor, I was left out of crucial discussions directly pertinent to my work and career. This exclusion not only undermined my authority within the department but also deprived me of opportunities to contribute to its growth and development.

Additionally, I faced age-based discrimination, with some colleagues dismissing my ideas and expertise solely due to my young age. They insinuated that my lack of experience and knowledge invalidated my contributions, adhering to narrow-minded preconceived notions of what a professor should look like or how they should behave. This not only undermined my credibility but also made it more challenging for me to assert myself and be taken seriously within an already hostile work environment.

I also experienced direct bullying from specific individuals within the department. They would mock my ideas, publicly criticize my work, and even spread unfounded rumors about my professional conduct. These acts of bullying were not only hurtful but also created a toxic atmosphere that hindered my ability to thrive and succeed in my academic pursuits.

This unsupportive work environment had a significant impact on my hopes and ambitions, especially regarding leadership roles in higher education. Without role models or mentors who shared similar backgrounds and experiences, it was difficult to envision myself in leadership positions or believe in my potential to succeed. Unfortunately, the negligible presence of Black females in leadership positions rendered me hopeless. Despite these challenges, I persevered and continued to push myself academically and professionally. I knew that breaking through these barriers was essential not only for my advancement but also to pave the way for others like me. I dedicated myself to writing grants, conducting research, and engaging in service activities that would enhance my career and uplift the voices of marginalized communities.

Finally, after years of hard work and perseverance, I achieved tenure in 2014. This achievement was not only a personal victory but also a testament to the resilience of Black women in academia. As one of the first Black females to receive tenure in that department, it was a significant moment. However, the mistreatment I endured took its toll, diminishing my vision to pursue leadership roles. I began to accept that being a great professor was the extent of my ambitions, and that I had reached the pinnacle of my career.

While I thought teaching was fulfilling enough, each semester, several students would approach me, expressing their aspirations to become professors like me. It was then that I realized that I would not want my students to experience the challenges I faced. I recognized the urgent need to advocate for change and make things better for future generations. I knew that I needed to step into a leadership role within academia to make meaningful change.

It is important to note that the underrepresentation of African American women in higher education leadership roles is due to the persistent existence of systemic barriers and biases within the industry. Research has consistently shown that African American women face unique challenges in their career advancement, including racial and gender discrimination, lack of access to networking opportunities, and unconscious biases that perpetuate stereotypes and limit their professional growth (Moss, 2014). These barriers not only hinder the advancement of individual African American women but also create a climate of exclusion that discourages aspiring African American women from pursuing leadership roles in higher education.

IMPORTANCE OF REPRESENTATION

Minority females face unique challenges and barriers that can hinder their academic and professional advancement. The lack of representation of minority females in higher education and leadership positions exacerbates these challenges by limiting their access to role models, mentors, and opportunities for advancement. A study by Gurin et al. (2002) highlighted that when minority females see individuals who look like them in positions of power and authority, it helps to dismantle the notion that certain roles are reserved for a specific gender or racial group. This representation instills confidence in minority females and motivates them to strive for leadership positions.

Moreover, representation is essential for minority females in higher education because it gives them a sense of belonging and validation. Minority females often feel isolated and marginalized in predominantly white institutions where they may be the only person of color, especially women, in their field of study. This lack of representation can exacerbate imposter syndrome and feelings of inadequacy. However, seeing minority females who share their experiences and backgrounds succeed in higher education and leadership roles reinforces their belief that they belong in these spaces too. According to Sáenz et al. (2007), representation fosters a supportive environment where minority students feel valued and included, which is essential for their academic success and retention in higher education.

Representation serves as a crucial tool in breaking down stereotypes and challenging societal norms (Hooks, 1981). Minority females are often depicted as submissive, exotic, or intellectually inferior, which can have detrimental effects on their academic and career aspirations. However, when minority females are represented in higher education and leadership roles, it challenges these stereotypes by providing alternative narratives that showcase their intelligence, resilience, and leadership capabilities. As Turner et al. (2018) noted, representation helps disrupt the dominant narratives that perpetuate bias and discrimination amongst minority females.

Gurin et al. (2002) found that the presence of individuals who resemble minority females in positions of authority significantly dismantles the notion that certain roles are exclusively designated for specific genders or racial groups. Thus, representation is a powerful catalyst, instilling confidence in minority females and inspiring them to strive for leadership positions. For instance, representation provides role models who can guide and mentor Black women through their educational journey, helping them navigate the complexities of academia and develop the skills necessary for success. Additionally, having Black women in leadership positions can promote a more inclusive and equitable campus culture.

Historically, African American women have faced numerous challenges and barriers in their pursuit of leadership roles. Despite these obstacles, they have made significant contributions to various industries, shaping the history and progress of African American communities. From the civil rights movement to politics, education, and entrepreneurship, African American women have emerged as powerful leaders, defying societal expectations and shattering glass ceilings. In the field of education, Mary McLeod Bethune stands as a trailblazer and visionary. In 1904, she founded a school for African American girls in Daytona Beach, Florida, which grew into Bethune-Cookman University. Bethune believed that education was essential for empowerment and poverty alleviation within the African American community. Throughout her career, she fought tirelessly for equal educational opportunities for all children, regardless of race or gender. Bethune's leadership and commitment to education serve as an inspiration for African American women leaders in the education sector today.

CHALLENGES FACED BY MINORITY FEMALES IN HIGHER EDUCATION

Underrepresented groups, particularly Black women, still encounter significant challenges in attaining leadership roles within higher education. Systemic barriers, including biased hiring practices and limited networking opportunities, often prevent their access to such positions. Additionally, a lack of mentorship and sponsorship further hinders the professional growth and development of Black women in academia.

Stereotypes and Biases

Implicit bias and stereotypes can affect how Black women are perceived and evaluated, leading to unfair treatment and limited opportunities for advancement. Moreover, stereotypes about Black women's leadership capabilities can create additional hurdles, subjecting them to higher expectations and scrutiny compared to their counterparts. Overcoming these barriers requires a concerted effort from institutions to address systemic inequities and create a more inclusive and supportive environment for underrepresented groups.

Women from minority backgrounds often encounter several key challenges as they strive to attain leadership roles in higher education. One particularly significant obstacle is the prevalence of societal biases. Many people hold preconceived notions about traditional gender roles and expectations, which can hinder the progress of women in leadership roles. As Eagly and Carli (2007) noted, these biases can portray women as less competent or suitable for leadership positions than their male counterparts. These deeply ingrained societal biases create significant barriers for women working to break through the glass ceiling and attain leadership roles.

Societal biases can manifest in various ways, hindering women from minority backgrounds in their pursuit of leadership positions in higher education. One example is the assumption that women are less competent or skilled than men or are too emotional to lead effectively. Discrimination based on race, ethnicity, or religion compounds these biases, making it even more challenging for these women to succeed. For example, a woman who wears a headscarf may be perceived as less competent or qualified simply because of her religious affiliation, as societal norms and stereotypes may influence others' perceptions.

Societal biases can also be seen in the workplace, where women are often expected to take on more domestic responsibilities, such as childcare and housework, limiting their ability to pursue career opportunities. This expectation stems from traditional gender roles that view women as primary caregivers and men as primary breadwinners. As a result, women may be unfairly penalized for taking time off to attend to family needs or for not being as readily available for work-related commitments as their male counterparts.

Women are often subjected to stereotypes that portray them as more nurturing, emotional, and less assertive than men, which can hinder their advancement into leadership roles. For example, women may be overlooked for promotions or leadership positions because they do not conform to the traditional masculine image of a leader (Eagly & Carli, 2007). Overcoming these stereotypes requires confronting societal norms and advocating for gender equality in the workplace.

Lack of Mentorship and Sponsorship

Recent studies underscore a significant concern for limited advancement opportunities for women in the workplace. Despite having similar qualifications and experience as their male counterparts, women often need help accessing the same career growth and development opportunities. This challenge is particularly evident in the underrepresentation of women in higher-level and executive positions, as highlighted by Eagly and Carli (2007). Their research highlights the issue of inadequate support systems for women aspiring to leadership positions. Women often face unique challenges that make it difficult to effectively balance their professional and personal responsibilities. However, with adequate support systems like flexible work arrangements, mentorship programs, and childcare support, women can find it easier to achieve their leadership aspirations. These support systems not only benefit individual women but also contribute to creating an inclusive and diverse organizational culture. Organizations can foster an inclusive workplace culture that values diversity and promotes equality by providing an environment conducive to supporting women's professional growth.

The reasons for this lack of support are numerous and complex. Biased hiring practices, limited access to networks, and a lack of mentors are just a few factors contributing to this issue. Networking is equally important, as it allows individuals to build connections and gain exposure to leadership roles. Attending conferences, workshops, and other professional development events lets individuals meet leaders in their field, learn from their experiences, and explore potential career opportunities. Networking also provides a platform for individuals to showcase their skills and expertise, increasing their visibility and potential for advancement.

Institutions can play a crucial role in facilitating mentorship and networking opportunities. By establishing formal mentorship programs, institutions can connect aspiring leaders with experienced mentors who can provide guidance and support. Additionally, institutions can organize networking events and create spaces for individuals to connect and collaborate. By investing in mentorship and networking initiatives, institutions can empower underrepresented individuals and create pathways to leadership opportunities.

Glass Ceiling Effect

The glass ceiling effect continues to be a significant concern in our society, particularly in academia. This term refers to the invisible barrier hindering women's career advancement and their reaching the highest levels of leadership. Despite their qualifications and skills, women find themselves facing limited opportunities for advancement, leading to a lack of diversity and representation at the top level.

Numerous studies, such as Eagly and Carli (2007), have highlighted the existence and impact of the glass ceiling effect. Even when women are equally qualified and competent, there are issues that hinder their progress to leadership roles. The consequences of the glass ceiling effect in academia are far-reaching, with limited opportunities for advancement. Many talented and qualified women fail to break through to leadership positions, resulting in a lack of female representation at the highest levels of academia, including university presidents, deans, and department chairs. This underrepresentation has significant implications for the overall diversity and inclusivity of academic institutions.

The glass ceiling effect extends beyond its impact on individual women, affecting society as a whole. When women are excluded from top leadership positions, diverse perspectives and voices are not adequately represented in decision-making processes. This lack of diversity limits innovation and hinders progress within organizations and institutions.

Addressing the glass ceiling effect requires a multifaceted approach. Organizations must implement policies and practices that promote gender equality and nurture the advancement of women. Initiatives like mentorship programs, leadership development, and flexible work arrangements benefit both men and women. Additionally, increasing awareness about the glass ceiling effect and challenging gender biases are essential for lasting change.

Work-Life Balance

Achieving work-life balance is a constant challenge for women in leadership positions. Balancing professional responsibilities with personal commitments can be particularly overwhelming, compounding societal expectations and traditional gender roles. Women in leadership positions often face additional pressures to excel in their roles and exceed expectations, leading to a sense of guilt and inadequacy (Bureau of Labor Statistics, 2018). Furthermore, traditional gender roles and societal expectations dictate that women should prioritize their families over their careers, creating added conflict when juggling both aspects of life (Blair-Loy, 2004).

The struggle for work-life balance is not limited to women in leadership positions but it is often exacerbated by the expectations placed on them. Women leaders often face higher expectations and scrutiny as compared to their male counterparts (Eagly & Carli, 2007). They may feel the need to work longer hours or take on more responsibilities to prove themselves. This can result in a constant cycle of overwork and neglect of personal commitments. Additionally, women in leadership may face challenges related to the lack of support systems and resources, highlighting the value of organizations that provide flexible work arrangements, mentoring programs, and access to childcare facilities (Blair-Loy, 2004).

Work-life balance is crucial for overall well-being and job satisfaction. When individuals can effectively balance their professional and personal responsibilities, they are more likely to experience lower levels of stress and burnout, leading to increased productivity and job satisfaction (Greenhaus & Beutell, 1985). Women in leadership positions who achieve work-life balance serve as role models for other women in their organizations, encouraging them to pursue leadership roles while demonstrating that success is possible without sacrificing personal commitments (Blair-Loy, 2004).

STRATEGIES TO INCREASE REPRESENTATION OF BLACK FEMALES IN HIGHER EDUCATION LEADERSHIP

To increase representation in higher education leadership, institutions must implement strategies that address the barriers faced by underrepresented groups. One effective approach is to establish targeted recruitment and retention programs. These initiatives should actively seek out and support individuals from underrepresented backgrounds, equipping them with the resources and opportunities to advance their careers. Institutions should also prioritize diversity and inclusion in their hiring practices, ensuring that search committees are diverse and trained in recognizing and mitigating bias.

By implementing targeted recruitment and retention programs, supporting mentorship and networking initiatives, and investing in diversity training and education, institutions can create pathways to leadership for individuals from underrepresented backgrounds. By valuing and celebrating diverse leadership styles and perspectives, institutions can foster a culture of inclusion that empowers individuals to realize their full potential.

Another crucial strategy is to provide mentorship and networking opportunities for aspiring leaders. Mentorship programs can pair underrepresented individuals with experienced leaders who can provide guidance, support, and advocacy (Black et. al, 2018). Networking events and professional development opportunities can also help individuals build connections and gain exposure to leadership roles. By investing in mentorship and networking, institutions can help underrepresented groups overcome barriers and develop the skills and relationships needed for success.

Several successful initiatives have been implemented to promote representation in higher education leadership. One notable example is the University of California's Presidential Postdoctoral Fellowship Program. This program aims to increase faculty diversity by providing funding and mentorship opportunities to postdoctoral scholars from underrepresented backgrounds. The program has been effective in increasing the number of diverse faculty members and has had a positive impact on student success and campus climate.

Another successful initiative is the American Council on Education's Moving the Needle initiative (2014). This program aims to increase the number of women in higher education leadership positions through targeted training, mentoring, and networking opportunities. Participating institutions have seen an increase in the number of women in leadership roles, leading to a more diverse and inclusive campus environment.

These case studies demonstrate that with the right strategies and commitment, institutions can make significant progress in promoting representation in higher education leadership. By learning from these successful initiatives, other institutions can develop their own programs and initiatives to increase diversity and ensure equal opportunities for all.

Overcoming implicit bias and stereotypes is essential for promoting representation in higher education leadership. Institutions must take proactive steps to address and mitigate bias in their hiring and evaluation processes. Training and education are key in addressing implicit bias. Institutions should provide training for search committee members, administrators, and faculty to raise awareness about bias and its impact on decision-making. This training should include strategies for recognizing and mitigating bias, as well as creating inclusive evaluation criteria. Institutions should also regularly review and assess their policies and practices to ensure they are fair and unbiased.

Addressing stereotypes is equally important. Institutions should challenge stereotypes about leadership and create a culture that values and celebrates diverse leadership styles and perspectives. This can be achieved through targeted professional development programs and initiatives that provide individuals with the skills and confidence to challenge stereotypes and advocate for themselves.

THE JOURNEY CONTINUES

Promoting representation in higher education leadership requires a collective effort from institutions, individuals, and organizations. Together, we can break down barriers, challenge stereotypes, and create a more inclusive and equitable landscape within academia. Through robust representation, we possess the power to inspire future generations of leaders and drive positive transformation within our institutions and communities.

Through perseverance and dedication, I gradually earned the respect and recognition of both my colleagues and superiors. My leadership skills became evident as I adeptly managed complex projects, navigated through challenging situations, and demonstrated a commitment to nurturing excellence in higher education. As a result, I was promoted to increasingly higher positions of authority.

Today, as a dean in higher education, I pause to reflect on the obstacles I have overcome and the strides I have made. My journey has been far from easy, but it has been immensely rewarding. I take pride in knowing that I have shattered stereotypes and carved a path for upcoming generations of young Black females aspiring to leadership roles within academia.

To address the need for representation, I prioritized supporting and uplifting other faculty members who shared my background. I recognized the importance of building a community rich in diverse voices and perspectives within academia. By mentoring and advocating for other minority female professors, I hoped to cultivate an environment where individuals from underrepresented backgrounds could thrive and succeed. This commitment meant actively seeking out opportunities for collaboration, resource sharing, and offering guidance to my colleagues.

Moreover, my supporting other faculty members who looked like me extended to bolstering their research and scholarship endeavors. I understood the challenges and barriers that minority scholars often face in obtaining funding and recognition for their work. Therefore, I made it a point to engage with their research, attend their presentations, and amplify their voices whenever possible. By championing the contributions of my peers, I aimed to challenge prevailing narratives and dismantle stereotypes that limit opportunities for minority scholars.

Alongside my own journey, there are numerous success stories about Black women professors in higher education. These narratives not only celebrate the achievements of these remarkable individuals but also challenge stereotypes while promoting diversity and inclusivity within academia. One such tale is that of Dr. Mae Jemison, the first African American woman to travel into space. After her groundbreaking career as an astronaut, Dr. Jemison went on to become a professor of environmental studies at Dartmouth College. Her success as both a scientist and educator stand as a testament to the immense talent and perseverance of Black women in academia.

Equally inspiring is the story of Dr. Kimberlé Crenshaw, a renowned scholar and professor of law at Columbia University and University of California, Los Angeles. Crenshaw's groundbreaking work on intersectionality, which examines how different forms of oppression intersect and impact individuals, has had a significant impact on the fields of law, feminist theory, and critical race studies. Through her research and teaching, Dr. Crenshaw not only advances academic knowledge but also serves as a driving force in the fight for social justice and equality.

Dr. Anita Hill is another Black woman professor who has made a significant impact in higher education. She gained national attention in 1991 when she accused Supreme Court nominee Clarence Thomas of sexual harassment during his confirmation hearings. Despite facing backlash and attacks, Dr. Hill remained resilient and pursued her career as a professor of social policy, law, and women's studies. Her courage and determination have inspired countless individuals, urging them to confront injustice and fight for gender equality.

Beyond these individual success stories, there exists a tapestry of collective achievements by Black women professors in higher education. For example, the National Black Women's Health Project and the Coalition of 100 Black Women are testaments to this effort. These organizations provide a platform for Black women scholars to collaborate, advocate for their rights, and support one another in their academic endeavors. Their existence is vital in promoting the representation and success of Black women professors in higher education.

The success stories of Black women professors in higher education not only highlight their individual achievements but also underscore the importance of diversity and inclusivity in academia. These women have shattered stereotypes and overcome systemic barriers to excel in their respective fields. Through their invaluable contributions to knowledge production, teaching, and mentorship, they have enriched higher education institutions and paved the way for future generations of Black women scholars.

CONCLUSION

Representation in higher education leadership is crucial for fostering an inclusive and equitable environment. It is essential to ensure that the needs and perspectives of all students are taken into account and to drive innovation and excellence in higher education institutions. To promote representation, institutions must address the barriers faced by underrepresented groups, provide mentorship and networking opportunities, and challenge implicit bias and stereotypes.

Having diverse leadership in higher education institutions brings numerous benefits. First, diverse leadership ensures that the needs and perspectives of all students are represented and taken into account when making decisions. This leads to policies and practices that are more inclusive and responsive to the challenges faced by underrepresented groups. Diverse leadership also fosters a more inclusive and equitable campus culture, where individuals from all backgrounds feel valued and supported.

Representation in leadership brings a wealth of perspectives and experiences to the table. This diversity of thought leads to more innovative and creative solutions to complex problems. By bringing together individuals with diverse backgrounds, institutions can tap into a wider range of skills, knowledge, and experiences, leading to better decision-making and outcomes.

Finally, diverse leadership serves as a powerful symbol of what is possible. When students see leaders who look like them and share their backgrounds, they are inspired to aspire to leadership roles and reach their full potential. Diverse leadership provides role models who can guide and mentor students through their educational journey, helping them overcome challenges and achieve their goals.

REFERENCES

American Association of University Women. (2016). *Barriers and bias: The status of women in leadership.* https://www.aauw.org/app/uploads/2020/03/Barriers-andBias-nsa.pdf

American Council of Education. (2012) American Council on Education. United States. Moving the Needle Initiative, Retrieved from the Library of Congress. https://www.acenet.edu/Programs-Services/Pages/Communities/Moving-the-Needle.aspx

Black, V. G., & Taylor, Z. W. (2018). Nobody's talking to the mentees. *Mentoring & Tutoring*, 26(5), 606–626. 10.1080/13611267.2018.1561027

Blair-Loy, M. (2004). Work devotion and work time. In Epstein, C. F., & Kalleberg, A. L. (Eds.), *Fighting for time: Shifting boundaries of work and social life* (pp. 282–316). Russell Sage Foundation.

U.S. Bureau of Labor Statistics. (2018). U.S. Department of Labor. *Occupational Outlook Handbook.*

Crenshaw, K. (2005). Mapping the margins: *Intersectionality, identity politics, and violence against women of color (1994).* In Bergen, R. K., Edleson, J. L., & Renzetti, C. M. (Eds.), *Violence against women: Classic papers* (pp. 282–313). Pearson Education New Zealand.

Eagly, A. H., & Carli, L. L. (2007). *Through the labyrinth: The truth about how women become leaders.* Harvard Business School Press.

Espinosa, L. L., Turk, J. M., Taylor, M., & Chessman, H. M. (2019). *Race and ethnicity in higher education: A status report.* American Council on Education. https://1xfsu31b52d33idlp13twtos-wpengine.netdna-ssl.com/wpcontent/uploads/2019/02/Race-and-Ethnicity-in-Higher-Education.pdf

Greenhaus, J. H., & Beutell, N. J. (1985). Sources of conflict between work and family roles. *Academy of Management Review*, 10(1), 76–88. 10.2307/258214

Gurin, P., Dey, E. L., Hurtado, S., & Gurin, G. (2002). Diversity and higher education: Theory and impact on educational outcomes. *Harvard Educational Review*, 72(3), 330–366. 10.17763/haer.72.3.01151786u134n051

Hooks, B. (1981). *Ain't I a woman: Black women and feminism.* South End Press.

Moss, Y. (2014). *The role of mentoring and career advancement: A phenomenological study examining Black female mid-level community college administrators* (Order No. 3662311). Available from Education Database; ProQuest Dissertations & Theses Global. (1650557450)

Sáenz, V. B., Hurtado, S., Barrera, D., Wolf, D., & Yeung, F. (2007). First in my family: A profile of first-generation college students at four-year institutions since 1971. *Higher Education: Handbook of Theory and Research, 22*(1), 141–183.

Turner, K., Myers, S., Creswell, J., Sherraden, M. S., Loke, V., & Smith, A. W. (2018). Women's career advancement: An examination of the influence of representation on women's pursuit of leadership roles. *Journal of Women & Aging*, 30(1), 3–18.29558298

Chapter 12
Crowned in Authenticity:
Black Women Redefining Leadership by Leading With Value and Purpose

Ashley N. Storman
The Storman Group LLC, USA

ABSTRACT

Authentic leadership is the cornerstone of the leadership style adopted by Black women educators. Grounded in Patricia Hill Collins's Black feminist thought theory, this research explores the lived experiences of Black women leaders in education. Through a qualitative focus group of K-12 and higher education leaders, participants share their narratives. The researcher addresses key inquiries: What is the current leadership experience, how is it evolving, and what is the future of leadership for Black women? From the findings, the author developed a framework titled "Managing the Consciousness of Oppression" to help Black women proactively equip themselves with strategies to resist and challenge discriminatory practices in their professional journeys. It is crucial that stakeholders, including administrators, supervisors, and mentors, recognize and incorporate the indispensable leadership style of Black women leaders. Failing to do so may result in these women forging their own path toward equity, fairness, and inclusivity.

INTRODUCTION

Without hesitation, the words flowed effortlessly from my lips, "I know my worth, and I am worth more than what you are trying to offer me." In that pivotal moment, carrying an air of self-assurance and an unwavering belief in my abilities.

DOI: 10.4018/979-8-3693-0698-7.ch012

Copyright © 2024, IGI Global. Copying or distributing in print or electronic forms without written permission of IGI Global is prohibited.

With utmost respect, I conveyed to the President that I deserved more than what was being offered. As the words left my mouth in a bit of surprise, I felt a surge of empowerment running through my veins, and an indescribable sense of pride filling my being. It was in that very instant that I walked away, secure in the knowledge of my own worth, a testament to my unwavering determination and unyielding self-confidence. Immediately I realized my value exceeded what was being presented before me.

This was my experience, after being in higher education for 13 years serving underrepresented populations and advancing diversity, equity, and inclusion, this is when I finally decided it was time to step away from higher education. Although I just worked tirelessly for my Doctorate of Education, in Higher Education Leadership with an emphasis in Teaching about three years before, I decided to step away. Because I checked all the boxes: I had the highest level of education, I was a thriving Director, myself and my team received various university awards, and we elevated everything that we touched. It was never a decrease, it was ALWAYS an increase whether it be an increase in recruitment, retention, or new implementations based on data, we showed up, ALWAYS!

As a higher education educator during my trials and hard times I often questioned my experiences and thought "Well, the textbook didn't teach me this, or no one told me about that". That's when I started to realize the need for the narrative experiences of Black Women who served in Leadership roles in education. We needed to hear their stories, I needed to hear their stories, to be empowered, to know my worth, and not to take anything less than what I deserved.

The knowledge and wisdom shared in this chapter will empower the next generation of Black women leaders and educators, providing them with invaluable insights into the lived experiences of Black women educators. It's imperative that they are aware of and familiar with what they will more than likely experience, and witness in education. Patricia Hill Collins Black Feminist Thought specifically her concept on African American Women's Culture focuses on the oppression that women experience and the importance of sharing narratives to assist women with gaining consciousness and awareness of these unique experiences. My hope is to provide Black women educators with an awareness and understanding of what oppression is and looks like, in order to develop strategies to protect themselves and still flourish (Hill Collins, 1986).

As the researcher and author, I aim to answer the following questions:

- What is the leadership experience for Black women educators?
- How is leadership evolving for Black women educators?
- What is the future of leadership for Black women educators?

The candid sharing of participants' lived experiences coupled with relevant theoretical framework will assist Black women and their supporters in creating a sense of camaraderie, awareness, and knowledge among Black women educators through narratives, reflections, and findings.

It is crucial to acknowledge that there is no comprehensive class or textbook that adequately prepares Black women for the unique challenges they will face as educators. The researchers, leaders, and educators in this study are deeply committed to making a difference by equipping women with tools to strategize, establish boundaries, recognize their worth, prioritize mental health, and ultimately thrive as Black women leaders in education.

BACKGROUND

In the Face of Oppression, Still I Rise

Historically speaking the intersecting identities of Black women has always been and still to this day is one that faces oppression. Despite ongoing challenges and barriers Black women are continually emerging as leaders across all industries, organizations, nonprofits, government agencies, and academia. Leadership ambitions of this group are high, such that Black women are nearly three times more likely to aspire to senior leadership with prestigious titles than their counterparts (Leiba, 2022).

Furthermore, there is much literature and data that speaks to the persistence of Black women in education, as being the most educated group in the United States. According to the American Association of University Women. Black women obtained the following: bachelor's degrees, 71.5% of master's degrees and 65.9%of doctoral, medical, and dental degrees. (American Association of University Women, 2020).

According to Miles (2012), even after obtaining their doctoral degrees Black women were least likely of racial identities to serve in roles of authority. Although Black Women are excelling and receiving their education to the highest and fullest potential, unfortunately Black women are still falling short, after checking all of the educational requirements and earning their doctoral degrees, Black women are still not enough for the academy.

Despite facing persistent structural racism and oppression within the educational system, Black women have demonstrated remarkable resilience, excelling both in the classroom and as leaders in education. Despite being the most educated demographic, the full benefits of their doctoral degrees elude them, with Black women still contending with inequitable pay. Shockingly, they earn approximately 38% less than their white male counterparts annually. With the lack of pay and recognition we find that Black women either leave, underperform, or leave the academy altogether. (Center for American Progress, 2023; Nzinga, 2020).

MENTAL HEALTH

In the harsh reality of academia for Black women, the toll on mental health has become an alarming consequence of injustice and oppression. When Black women make even the slightest mistake, there's an immediate attack targeting our credentials, scholarly efforts, and anything that could devalue us.

Take Dr. Claudine Gay, the first Black President of Harvard University, for instance. In addressing antisemitism on campus, her unpopular stance on students' freedom of speech led to massive backlash. People misconstrued her intentions, questioning her scholarly work and accusing her of plagiarism. Despite being a Stanford and Harvard University alumna and serving as faculty for Government and African American Studies, this distressing experience, marked by personal attacks fueled by racial animus, ultimately forced her resignation after a short six month tenure. The question that echoes through this tragedy is whether a white man or woman would face such obnoxious backlash and questioning of academic integrity. This real-life example vividly illustrates how systemic, racism, misogyny, and oppression systematically push Black women out of leadership roles and the education system (Brown, 2024; Haidar & Kettles, 2024; Schuessler et al., 2024).

Tragically, the narrative takes an even darker turn with the story of Dr. Antoinette "Bonnie" Candia-Bailey, Vice President of Student Affairs at Lincoln University. Her termination on January 3, 2024, led to her taking her own life just a few days later. In a letter to President Mosely and the Board of Curators, she detailed her mental health struggles and accusations of harassment. Despite reaching out for help and making repeated complaints to the Board, she faced dismissal and a stunning lack of support (Turman, 2024).

Candia-Baily, who had received a shockingly low performance evaluation, stated that she received no guidance and felt abandoned after seeking direction which drove her to severe depression and anxiety. In her words, "If it was so bad, you should have provided me with an improvement action plan to work with me on my poor performance. You had no intention of retaining me as the VPSA." The aftermath of her tragic death sparked protests from students, faculty, and alumni, prompting the Board to commit to making mental health a priority at Lincoln University (Wong, 2024).

This narrative surrounding mental health is unfortunately not new for Black women educators. It's disheartening that universities are only now prioritizing a commitment to mental health after the loss of a beloved Black woman educator.

The question remains: how many more tragic stories will it take for institutions to truly commit to the well-being of their Black women leaders?

AUTHENTIC LEADERSHIP

Many of the values and characteristics of Black women in this survey illustrate Authentic Leadership. Authentic leadership derives from the Greek philosophy "To thine own self be true". The more modern idea focuses on self-direction, trustworthiness, and consistency. Furthermore, authentic leadership can be seen as owning your own personal experiences which entail ones: thoughts, emotions, and beliefs, coupled with simply being your true self which means behaving and expressing what you really think and believe. (F. Luthans & B. Avolio, 2003). With an ever-changing world that is evolving and seeking belonging and inclusivity the traits and characteristics of authentic leadership are needed today and thereafter. If we consider the role that politics plays which then influences policy, then trickles down to practice, employees are looking for more transparent leaders.

According to Luthans & Avolio 2003:

The authentic leader is confident, hopeful, optimistic, resilient, transparent, moral/ ethical, future-oriented, and gives priority to developing others to be leaders. The Authentic leader is true to themselves and exhibits behavior that positively transforms or develops associates to be leaders too. The authentic leader does not try to coerce or even rationally persuade associates, but rather the leaders' authentic values, beliefs and behaviors serve to model the development of associates.

The dimensions and traits of Authentic Leadership assist with guiding this study as they align with the characteristics of the participants of this study and those they mention through mentorship and role modeling.

BLACK FEMINIST THOUGHT

The theory most appropriate for this study is Patricia Hill Collins, Black Feminist Thought. Hill Collins developed this theory to assist with empowering Black Women who are often oppressed to create a sense of awareness by using stories, experiences, and knowledge allowing Black women to be the producers of their own stories and experiences (Hill Collin, 2000).

Moreover, the utilization of Black Feminist Thought serves to center the experiences of Black women in the analytical process. This approach not only empowers Black Women by offering them new insights into their own experiences but also plays a crucial role in shedding light on and redefining those experiences. By taking control and actively sharing their narratives, individuals contribute to the creation of awareness and elevate the consciousness of Black women regarding the diverse range of experiences they may encounter.

METHODOLOGY

The goal of this qualitative study is to grapple with the idea of Black women and leadership in education and to get an in-depth understanding of their experiences to shed light on their narrative to inform and prepare readers in hopes to develop the changes needed in order for Black women leaders to thrive in the educational system.

Participants

The target population for this semi-structured virtual focus group is Black Women who currently serve or previously served in leadership roles in education ranging from K-12 to higher education. Purposive sampling was utilized to recruit participants via email inviting Black Women leaders in education to participate in a 1 hour 30-minute focus group (ATS Scholar, 2021).

Participants completed a demographic questionnaire and interview release form. The researcher interviewed four Women who currently or most recently served in roles of leadership in education. The experience of the participants is very diverse. Of the participants 1 was currently working on their Master's degree. Two participants obtained their Doctoral Degree in Education. One participant was currently working on their Doctoral degree. The years of experience ranged from 2 -15 years working in education. The age range of participants was 22-37 years old. All participants identify as Black women.

DATA COLLECTION

Focus Group

As the researcher I developed questions before conducting the formal focus group that would highlight the experiences of the participants and would allow participants the opportunity to provide advice and suggestions. Pseudonyms were assigned to each participant. Interview release forms and demographic forms were collected prior to the focus group.

The virtual focus group was 1 hour 30 minutes using Zoom to allow participants to engage and participate regardless of where they were located. Participants were provided the opportunity to answer each question if they wanted, and had the option to skip or not answer any questions as well. Participants shared their personal narratives, and the narratives of their mentors and supervisors, and the ones they witnessed or learned about from. These narratives focused on what it's like to lead, the qualities that Black women bring to leadership, necessary changes in the education system, and the opportunity to share advice and lessons learned with the next upcoming leaders in education.

DATA ANALYSIS

The data analysis process was initiated to assist with understanding the experiences of Black women who serve in leadership roles in education. The hope is to shed light on the unique experiences of Black women in education, but to also to create more awareness around the uniqueness of these experiences. Furthermore, providing insight to assist with the evolution of education as it pertains to this specific population. The focus group was recorded via Zoom and then transcribed by Rev.com, a professional transcription service. Data coding included free reading of focus transcripts and interview notes several times. The coding software used was Dedoose (Dedoose, 2023; Rev.com, 2023).

FINDINGS

This study examined the experiences of Black Women educators and leadership. Participants engaged in reflective discussions, responding to a series of questions that prompted exploration of their ideas, experiences, and insights within the context of being Black Women educators and leaders. The research aimed to unravel the future and evolution of Black Women in leadership roles within education, offering valuable insights for Black Women themselves and those in positions of hiring, supervision, and mentorship. The objective was to shed light on the significance of representation and, ensuring they have a rightful place at the table. The following findings will highlight the lived experiences of four participants as they provide their narrative of their journey.

The Burden of Leadership

As these four Women started to reflect on their experiences contemplating the essence of leadership for Black women in education, a common theme emerged for all of them: leadership roles were perceived as burdensome. Whether in K-12 or higher education, the leadership positions held by these women, ranging from were characterized by demanding expectations. Many of the women expressed the sentiment that when Black Women assume leadership roles, they often find themselves shouldering a heavier workload than their counterparts, without receiving recognition. Tosha shares her experiences as educator with an emphasis on K-12 education:

From my perspective and from my experiences in K-12, I believe that leadership in education requires us to put on additional hats, just because of how Black Women are often required to show up in spaces and sometimes have to mother, care, and nurture other people very differently than what is expected of men, white men and very different than what is expected or received from white women.

Simone has the same sentiments but shares her experiences as a higher education professional using the ideology of heroism and how Black women are still not recognized appropriately for their impact:

Oftentimes it's almost like we have to put on our cape to save them, whether that be a department or individual. It's like they want our labor, but they don't want us to succeed too much, but want us to put in the work. They are completely fine with us almost breaking our backs, putting in all this effort, and behind closed doors, give you a pat on the back or say "oh my gosh, we appreciate you", but when it comes to actual advancement, whether it be through pay, title, whether that be through actual elevation...that's not really done.

Tosha has similar instances but provides insights to how such burdens can become unhealthy for women:

I believe it looks like we are the ones who can do a lot, and so when it's seen that we can do what needs to be done and accomplished were seen as an asset, then we are more likely to be propelled into those leadership positions. I also feel like once were in those leadership positions depending on the demographic that you're leading, I feel like it can be unhealthy for us as Black women because of the burden and lack of boundaries. They don't give room for our boundaries in the same way they do for other people. I do feel like there's a burden to get there, because you have to be able to do a lot, show a lot, prove a lot, and then the burden grows once you are there.

Maya shares some insight when asked what leadership looks and feels like for her and all participants agreed, she was not at all alone in her sentiments:

Leadership is becoming more of a burden. I guess that is where I'm at in my workspace right now, and the spaces I've been in. Leadership is burdensome, and I think it's

because of the type of leadership that I bring to the table. It's not always welcome. It's not a westernized leadership style, so leadership has become a burden because people are unfamiliar with authentic leadership. I think they are not used to it and then when you bring it to a space and they're not used to it, they don't respond well to it, even though it may be good for them. They're used to these westernized leadership styles, and so it's been a burden.

As these women discussed the experiences that proved to make it burdensome and hard for them. They also shared how mentorship played a pivotal role in their existence and success in leadership.

MENTORSHIP: WHISPERS OF WISDOM

Whether it was from very transparent open and honest conversations with mentors and supervisors or being able to first hand witness the experiences of Black Women leaders, these Women spoke about and highlighted the many instances of mentorship and role modeling that assisted them with shaping their own leadership styles.

Simone talks about how all her supervisors have been Black women and offer a certain level of transparency through mentorship:

All my supervisors have actually been Black Women, and the vast majority of my experiences have been positive. One thing that has been common is the level of transparency that was provided to me on how things operate behind closed doors or what things look like, how meetings go when you're not in the room. I think that has been more beneficial to me, and this is something I've learned from the most, is them being transparent about their own experiences, them being transparent about when they have to tell me no on something, when they don't agree with something leadership has instructed them to do. Also, the way the transparency looked was different, but they were very transparent in their feelings and also what it means to be a Black Woman in leadership at predominately white institutions, and how they felt like they had to show up in that space.

Bella the youngest participant shares how through her mentorships she has had the opportunity to witness various leadership styles and take what traits and practices fit her personality to assist her with developing her own leadership style:

I've been mentored by a lot of Black Women and then supervised by Black Women as well. I think more in my mentorship, I've been able to see Black Women lead and use that as the foundation of how I lead. I think applying their leadership style to fit my own leadership style has helped me to evolve personally. I think Black Women who undergo mentorship or have supervisors that look like them will evolve in that where they can cultivate their own leadership style. So I'm just pulling from each of their leadership styles to figure out what is my own, since I am fresh in higher education and student affairs.

The participants also discuss how the sharing of their mentors' narrative and experiences assisted them with developing boundaries and exit plans. Maya shares her experience:

I can count on three hands Black Women that I've either seen supervising others or been supervised or mentored me in their leadership style was to take on so much, they kept taking roles, taking on hats to the point where they were no longer prioritizing their health....I can also count on two hands of Black Women who have either died or got sick because of their jobs. And if you have a candid conversation with them they will tell you that. Some of them are still in those roles, but they have relinquished some of the stress and of the added responsibilities or tasks. I remember asking a Professor in administration Why she didn't take vacation, and her response: "What vacation? If I take a vacation when I come back, I might not have a job or when I come back things may not be running." However, when I talk to them now that has completely changed. It took them getting sick or witnessing others dying literally.

After hearing of Maya's experience Simone shares similar sentiments and reflections:

I feel like as you were talking, I could pinpoint the specific Black Woman in my mind that this specifically happened to, but also, multiple people that used to supervise me left higher education as well. I feel like Black Women now are very much okay with saying no and no being a full sentence and there being a period behind it and that being it. I also ... think Black women are okay with leaving.... with just walking away. And I've seen a good amount of Black Women decide that I'm going to walk away and not even have anything lined up and be like, "I'm going to just trust God on this and that's what it is. I'm out. I know that I can get another job. I know who I am, I know my purpose, and if you're not going to welcome me, I'll find somebody else who will."

Mentorship for these women also consisted of strategizing ways to develop exit plans to get out of bad roles or situations. Maya shares some insight from one her mentors:

My mentors told me upon entertaining a job to already have an exit plan in mind. Get what you need and go. A Black Man told me to get what you need from this institution, they're using you so use them and then bounce. Now I struggle with this because I am a loyal person but at the same time I need to understand what is actually good for me. So I'm leaning into the whole mentality and once you understand that, act accordingly.

The wisdom that the participants have received throughout their professional and personal experiences and the opportunities to build community are so good and full of wisdom they are referred to as gold. Maya goes into detail:

It's like the whispers. And what I mean by that is Black Women sharing wisdom with other Black Women is like gold. When I was deciding between two jobs offers, I did a lot of research and reached out to a lot of people....And what I was getting from that is people telling me, "Set your boundaries now before you even say yes to this job in the interview or in the negotiation phase or whatever, set your boundaries now." And so for me, it was just hearing them say that and share their experiences with me and then really taking note and acting on that. Oftentimes, we're always looking for mentors or we're looking for people who can pour into us. That's such a huge theme in Black Women in leadership or in education, is mentorship.

As the idea of leadership being burdensome evolves, so does the idea and concept of why leadership may be burdensome, due to the way in which Black women educators lead and care. It became evident that these Women all exemplify the characteristics and traits and thrive to have an Authentic Leadership approach.

AUTHENTICITY: BLACK WOMEN'S LEADERSHIP STYLE

Authentic leadership is a concept and idea that evolved heavily when the questions regarding the qualities that Black Women exemplify in their leadership style. Traits of authentic leadership include genuine, transparent, reliable, trustworthy, and real. Such one finds ownership in their personal experiences- thoughts, emotions, or beliefs and is able to show up as their real selves and behave as such (F. Luthans and B. Abolio).

Maya talks about her leadership style and how it's rooted in her values which was developed and cultivated through family values:

I do consider myself a leader, if you look at all my credentials, and if you look at all the history of the work that I've done on paper, society would say, "Yes, she's a leader," but I've been grappling with this topic and really deconstructing what it means to be a leader. It was part of my dissertation, and all of my credentials and all of the stuff that I've done is not what defines me as a leader. Toni Morrison ... One quote from her that always sticks out to me is that "we teach values by having them", and to me, that's what makes up the anatomy of a leader". And so for me, I am a leader because of my value system, and that value system, that standard, comes from where I come from, so it comes from my family. And that's why I consider myself a leader, but oftentimes, as I stated earlier, in society, value system isn't what is defining leadership. It's, "Can you meet this quota?" or, "Can you lead this team?" But do we take considerable care of people? Are we doing that? Are we taking considerable care of them? That, to me, is what defines leadership. And so yeah, I do consider myself a leader, but always, always on this continuum of reflecting and bettering myself. I don't think I've arrived, and I think the term "leadership" is so absolute. I am a leader, but I am still re-arriving, always, at leadership. I haven't arrived. It's not the pinnacle. I haven't got there yet.

Simone is in alignment with Maya and describes how her values and humanity for people speaks to authenticity in leadership and relationships:

I think I'm a leader because, regardless of my title or my credentials.....and I think that that goes back to my values and how I treat people, and the relationships that I've built with people, and also being authentically myself, and knowing that I am always going to come from a good place. I'm always going to come from a place of humanity and see the humanity in others, regardless of what an institution or a university may want to do. I think now, being at a public institution, policies and other things may shift, and what you may be allowed to say or do may be completely different one year to another, but one thing that's not going to change is my values and what I hold sacred and what I believe. And I think that's what makes me a leader, is that I still have respect outside of my title.

Beyond values there was a trait of caring that women exemplified in their work and the people they lead that came from their leadership styles. Tosha speaks to the idea of caring:

For me, it's that word "care." I haven't come across many Black Women who don't only care as far as they're thinking of things and the places in which they are, but also care in the act of doing and being for others. And I just don't think it's something that can be removed from the way that we do leadership, but it's something that I have seen not be present in the way that other people lead ... men and then white women ... and then they're still able to be successful. But I believe that us caring, while it's a part of who we are and how we show up, I also believe that in some ways it is how we, I would say subconsciously or consciously, have to compensate for the narratives and tropes that exist about us being Angry Black Women, especially going into leadership. Because you can't get here without being assertive, you can't get here without being direct about different things, and I think the care gives us that space to navigate that without offending or creating conflict or dissatisfaction in how we show up.

With Tosha's sharing of care within Black Women's leadership style, Maya speaks to how some Black Women do not care, and through her family's love and upbringing that taught her how to lead authentically and care.

I've been under the leadership of Black Women who might as well have been a white man. They did not care...and I have experienced Black Women who did care, and that's where I learned a lot about how to lead people, but I was loved well. Where I come from, I was loved very well in my home, and there was a safe space that was created for me, and so because I was loved well and I know what it feels like to be safe, I can then cultivate that as a leader in space. So those are the qualities that I bring to the table, cultivating safe spaces and leading in love, because I've bore witness to that. I am a product of that....so my leadership style is different because of how I know what I know. It goes back to that....

Maya expounds more on how her leadership style is who she is, both and at home and at work and how this speaks even more to the authenticity of leadership:

Leadership is synonymous to the person that I am. And I feel like oftentimes when people hear that phrase or that term, that concept, leadership, it's like apart from who they are genuinely as a person, and I don't separate the two, and I don't do that because it's authenticity to me. And please understand me when I'm saying this, I don't mean that I don't have a work life and a home life, but what I'm saying is at the core of who I am, does not change, doesn't change from office to home or from home in the office.....The qualities that I bring and the leadership style that I have is because of who I've grown to be and the people who instilled that in me. It's who we are that we bring to the table and what we've learned from the environments that we come from, the homes that we come from, the people who have poured into us, we bring that to the table. And so our leadership style is different in that way.

Tosha discusses in the traditional sense she is a leader because of her vision and ability to make change happen with a sense of urgency:

I would say that I'm a leader, and I would say that some of it is the traditional answer around, "I have people that I lead, I create change," and whatnot. But for me, I really would say outside of my title and my role, I'm a leader because of the vision that I have and the ability ... an almost inability to do nothing about making necessary changes happen, even when I'm like, "I don't want to be the one that does that work," because I go back to the fact that we have to do so much labor. But I feel like in many ways we have such a conviction around what needs to get done, because there's a different level of urgency in this work, especially because we recognize that us being here is on the backs of our ancestors, and there was blood, sweat, tears, a lot of sacrifice for us to do here, so much done. I am someone's answered prayer. And so I feel like I don't look at this as, "My uncle worked in this job, and so he got me a position there." I worked to get here. My reputation precedes me before you even invite me to sit down in an interview. And everything on my resume, everything in my background, says that I believe work needs to be done for us to have space in these settings where we can be successful.

THE FUTURE OF LEADERSHIP FOR BLACK WOMEN

As the concept of Black women and leadership evolved, questions regarding the future of leadership for Black Women were asked, and participants were asked to share advice for upcoming Black Women leaders who pursue education as their career.

A theme of boldness and faith arose when speaking of the need to walk away from a toxic role or experiences. Many participants shared this sentiment and saw this as an evolution for Black Women in leadership. Simone spoke to the importance of knowing when to walk away and having boundaries:

I think it's really about being okay with getting up out of there when you need to. Know what your boundaries are, know what your values are as well. Know the things that you are not going to compromise on. Know how to say no, essentially, and get the hell on when you need to. When you see that they're not going, things are not changing, they're not interested in really listening to you, be okay with getting up out of there and get up out of there quickly. It's going to get worse if you stay.

Tosha immediately shares very own similar experience:

I've done that. I quit my principalship, a good paying job with nothing lined up. It was like, "You know what? High blood pressure. I don't want to be on medication, all that kind of stuff." And quit, nothing lined up, and I'm not afraid to do it again.

The evolution of Black Women and leadership and the changes that needed to be made became a very big idea that included systemic structures, government, policy, and practice. With that in mind we focused on the things that could happen quicker to make Black Women experience more equitable and the topic of fairness and pay arose. Simone shares some ideas:

I think that in terms of what are things that can be done, the simplest thing would be to pay people equitably. And I mean that from entry level positions like program coordinators all the way on up. I'm going to be very honest, $40,000 is not a livable wage nowadays and let alone below $40,000. And there are a lot of positions that are trying to say that they want people who have Masters and they want them making $35,000. That's absolutely ridiculous. I think the main thing that can be changed that I think is not going to take years, a bunch of things structurally, is to pay people equitably and to pay people for the level of education that they hold.

As the conversation revolved around the evolution of leadership for Black Women the question came up as to what is next for Black Women education leaders and these women shared their authentic thoughts and adventures that focus on using their own intellect and passion to fulfill them personally and professionally. Tosha shares how she ready to make her knowledge work for herself:

I'm about to write books because I feel like so much of what we have experienced and what we have learned and what we have to offer needs to be heard throughout academia and not just by people within our networks, but also because I feel like many of us, have a brilliant minds and I believe that why I've been successful as a leader. And so I feel like I can make my brilliance work for myself and I can make a living and make an impact without laboring like that. And then in doing so and leaning into that, then I can do the work that I want to do, not that I need to do.

Simone shared similar ideas and how more Women are creating and working for themselves:

I think it's working for yourself. I think that it's creating opportunities for ourselves and entrepreneurship. I also think about the people, the Black Woman who left higher education and creating avenues for ourselves to where we don't have to answer to anyone, where it's being able to work with who we want to work with, us being able to take our expertise, take our knowledge and our intelligence in doing what we feel like needs to be done.

Maya added another level of how she tired of decolonizing work environments, and many agreed as this is another part of the burdensome in education and fighting the system:

I'm in a space right now where I'm over it, trying to save and decolonize and all that I am. And I know it's part responsibility, our ancestors, things of that nature. I get it. But I want to put my energy in places and spaces where I don't need to decolonize. It just is what it is. It is good because I created it that way.

Tosha speaks to the evolution of leadership but need for more work that speaks to the unique experiences of Black Women:

I will say leadership has changed and evolved for me, but this speaks to the necessity of this book, I don't believe that I've yet to read anything that addresses some of the unique and nuanced experiences that I have as a Black Woman in leadership, in education spaces and institutions because I feel like in some ways it's like you should just be happy that you're in that role. So the things that I want guidance on or I want to grow in, and I may ask about this unique thing that might be happening or I'm noticing it with other Black Women or whatnot, it's like, "Oh, well that's just a thing." There's such a level of dismissiveness around some of our experiences, our questions and our needs.

And so that said, where my level or my understanding of leadership has evolved is that I know that, I've read what's in the books, I've learned a lot of what's in the books, but moving forward, I need to learn from other Black Women. I don't need another book, I don't need another conference. They'll be nice, I'll go to them, shit, I'll present at them, but I don't need them.

DISCUSSION

The goal of this study is to understand the lived experiences of Black Women leaders in education. The researcher used Black Feminist Thought and Authentic Leadership to guide this study to develop a framework titled: Managing the Consciousness of Oppression, which will assist Black women with utilizing Black Feminist Thought as Framework and the dimensions of Authentic Leadership as lens to the leadership style that these Black exemplify.

The Managing the Consciousness of Oppression Framework incorporates key principles from Black Feminist Thought to create a foundation for understanding and addressing the unique challenges faced by Black women. Embracing intersectionality, the framework acknowledges the interconnected nature of race and gender in shaping Black women's identities. Furthermore, it advocates for the development of a critical consciousness that actively challenges conventional power structures. By doing so, the framework aims to empower Black Women with the awareness and understanding necessary to navigate and confront the systemic oppression they are likely to encounter in various aspects of their lives

Authentic Leadership dimensions consist of self-awareness which promotes Black Women leaders to understand their own values, strengths, authentic selves, and aligning personal values with their leadership style. In addition to learning your own values it's important to utilize transparency in relationship building to promote honest communication, trust, and authentic connections when in leadership. Lastly, is advocacy for processes,and valuing diverse perspectives and experiences (Inside Higher Ed, 2022).

The integration of Black Feminist Thought and Authentic Leadership allows one to embrace diversity by utilizing Black Feminist Thought to emphasize the importance of diverse perspectives in leadership and acknowledging and valuing the unique contributions of Black Women. Moreover, this integrated approach actively resists stereotypes by empowering Black Women leaders to embrace their authentic selves. It urges them to defy traditional expectations, fostering an environment where self-expression is promoted without the constraints of conforming to preconceived notions. Advocating for equity combines Black Feminist thought's emphasis on social justice with authentic leadership's focus on fairness to advocate for equity and inclusivity in leadership practices.

Recognizing that Black women will inevitably face barriers and challenges, it becomes crucial for them to proactively equip themselves with strategies rooted in Black Feminist Thought. These strategies serve as a powerful means to resist and challenge discriminatory practices and biases that may arise in their professional journeys. By drawing on the principles of Black Feminist Thought, will assist Black women with navigating these hurdles with resilience and assertiveness, fostering a more equitable and inclusive environment.

Furthermore, the incorporation of self-care practices, guided by authentic leadership principles, takes center stage. The importance of acknowledging that self-care is not just a personal benefit but an essential aspect of effective leadership. By embracing self-care within the framework of authentic leadership, Black Women leaders emphasize the necessity of prioritizing their well-being, recognizing that their ability to lead effectively is inherently tied to their own physical, emotional, and mental health. This holistic approach contributes to sustainable leadership and resilience in the face of challenges.

Lastly, when it comes to leadership impact and legacy it's important to encourage Black Women leaders to empower others through mentorship and support by fostering a legacy of leadership that uplifts and encourages future generations. Doing so will shape Black Women's narrative using both Black Feminist and Authentic Leadership to reclaim and reshape the conversation around Black Women's leadership. In doing so, these leaders leave a lasting legacy that transcends their individual journeys, positively impacting the trajectory of Black women's leadership in the long run.

This integrated framework seeks to leverage the strengths of Black Feminist thought and Authentic leadership, providing a comprehensive understanding of Black women's leadership styles while addressing challenges and promoting empowerment which will assist Black Women with Managing the Consciousness of Oppression.

Figure 1. Managing the consciousness of oppression framework

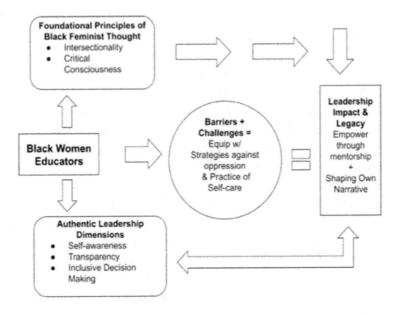

LET'S ANSWER THE QUESTIONS

A vital part of this study was to answer the following the questions regarding Black Women and leadership in the education system:

- What is the leadership experience for Black women educators?
- How is leadership evolving for Black women educators?
- What is the future of leadership for Black women educators?

WHAT IS THE LEADERSHIP EXPERIENCE FOR BLACK WOMEN EDUCATORS?

The leadership experience for Black Women educators encompasses unique challenges and expectations, often requiring them to go above and beyond with minimal recognition, in addition to showing up differently from their counterparts. These women are expected to take on nurturing roles, caring for both students and white colleagues. In this study there was mention of how Black women's labor is desired and wanted but the promotions and pay are slow to come with little to no actual elevation for Black women, even after they have achieved their advanced degrees. This disparity contributes to the perception that leadership for Black Women is burdensome, as their authentic leadership style, rooted in care, transparency, accountability, and mentoring, may not align with the prevailing desire for westernized leadership in institutions (Chance, 2022; Tynan, 2023).

Mentorship, particularly through transparent relationships, plays a crucial role in raising awareness and consciousness among Black Women educators. Mentorship provides a platform for candid discussions about the challenges faced by Black leaders, offering insights into behind-the-scenes dynamics and fostering open dialogue on disagreements with new practices or policies. The mentorship model allows younger Black leaders to observe and learn from seasoned leaders, incorporating admired aspects into their own leadership styles. This exchange of wisdom contributes significantly to the growth and development of women in leadership roles.

Mental health emerges as a critical aspect of the leadership journey for Black Women educators. The relentless expectations placed on them can lead to a lack of boundaries, causing the burdens of leadership to intensify as they climb the professional ladder. Mentorship becomes a source of support in addressing mental health concerns, offering valuable lessons on setting boundaries, asserting the importance of saying no, and prioritizing mental well-being. Through observation and candid conversations, these women gain insights into the significance of maintaining a healthy work-life balance and protecting their mental health in the demanding field of education leadership.

How is leadership evolving for Black women educators?

The evolution of leadership for Black Women educators is marked by a transformative shift towards prioritizing mental health and self-worth. An observed trend is the growing number of Black Women choosing to depart from higher education, fueled by a newfound empowerment to say 'no' without the need for detailed explanations. Faith and religion have become influential factors, guiding these women to be bold and to trust in divine guidance for their next professional endeavors because they know their worth and what they offer.

A significant transformation in leadership style is the abandonment of the separation between personal and professional values. Black women educators now integrate their familial background and value system into their leadership, making it distinct, indispensable, and authentic. The women in this shared that the westernized leadership style, which often revolves around quotas and numbers no longer serves them as they prioritize caring for and putting the well-being of the people they supervise at the forefront. Their leadership is rooted in a value system that surpasses titles and credentials, focusing on humanity regardless of one's position (Inside Higher Ed, 2022).

Care emerges as a prominent characteristic in the evolving leadership style of Black Women, extending to both individuals and broader initiatives. This care is deeply rooted in the love provided by participants' families, shaping their ability to create safe spaces, cultivate authentic relationships, foster mentorship, and promote transparency within their leadership roles. The evolution is not just a professional adaptation but a holistic integration of personal values, faith, care, and resilience in the pursuit of authentic and impactful leadership (Inside Higher Ed, 2022).

WHAT IS THE FUTURE OF LEADERSHIP FOR WOMEN IN EDUCATION?

The future of leadership for Black Women in education is undergoing a profound shift due to the systemic racial injustices misogynoir that Black Women have to navigate. The challenges faced by these Black Women in education have led to many Black Women exiting and choosing entrepreneurship as a means of creating a work environment that is aligned with their values and needs.

According to (Laszloffy, 2022 as cited in Leiba, 2022)

It's a double bind. No matter what you do, you're damned. You stay silent. That's a problem. You speak out," says Tracy Laszloffy, PhD, from the Center for Relationship Healing. "There's no way that is acceptable and that you will be validated and rewarded for. That is the nature of oppression. There is no option you can choose that is considered acceptable. That is the dilemma," she adds—a dilemma Dr. Laszloffy says is forcing Black women to choose between unbearable psychological and emotional stress and leaving corporate cultures to create their own work environment (p.121).

This is why entrepreneurship emerges as a notable theme, with participants expressing a desire to leverage their expertise independently, bypassing an educational system perceived as unwelcoming and unfair. The notion of making one's brilliance work for oneself rather than laboring for others represents a transformative evolution in leadership for Black Women. Furthermore, studies reveal from 2014-2019 that the number of businesses owned by Black women grew by 50% (American Express, 2019; Leiba, 2022;).

Boundaries and values emerge as crucial considerations for future leadership. This study emphasizes the importance of knowing when to walk away, what compromises are acceptable, and the power of saying no. The participants of this study advise upcoming Black educators not to compromise their health for any role, highlighting instances where individuals, including themselves, have prioritized mental health over their jobs(Inside Higher Ed, 2022).

Pay equity for the participants became a very important topic. Many shared the inequities of having to obtain a Master's degree for an entry level position that pays $40,00 as unacceptable and not livable wage in the current state of America. The demand for better pay is identified as a vital aspect that must change to retain brilliant and dedicated Black Women in the educational system (Leiba, 2022).

Many of the leaders in this study who engaged in diversity, equity, and inclusion work in their current roles, are no longer working to decolonize workplaces. These women are now looking for primary roles and workplaces without the added challenge of constantly fighting for equity.

The leadership style exemplified by these Black Women educators and leaders, is assured to play a pivotal role in shaping the next generations of employees and educators. Studies suggest that the alpha generation values authenticity, transparency, and empathy in their leaders. This generational shift indicates an increased expectation for leaders to be inclusive and aware of the unique challenges faced by underrepresented groups, further reinforcing the relevance of Authentic Leadership in the evolving landscape of education leadership, which is already represented in Black Women's leadership style (Communication Generation 2023).

CONCLUSION

Black Women educators epitomize the very essence of Authentic Leadership, a quality that is not just relevant but absolutely pivotal for the future workforce. The demand for this distinctive leadership style necessitates an urgent transformation within the education system. Should the system fail to adopt policies and practices that embrace the unique contributions of Black Women, we risk witnessing a surge of these brilliant individuals forging their own paths, independently or collaboratively, to establish a system where authenticity reigns supreme. The question is not whether the education system can afford to make room for them; it's whether it can afford not to."

REFERENCES

America Express. (2019). Woman-Owned Businesses Are Growing 2X Faster On Average Than All Businesses Nationwide. Retrieved from: https://about.americanexpress.com/ newsroom/ press-releases/news-details/2019/ Woman-Owned-Businesses-Are-Growing-2X-Faster-On-Average-Than-All-Businesses-Nationwide-09-23-2019/ default.aspx

Brown, K. (2024, January 8). *A second look at the resignation of Harvard's first Black president.* Black Girl Nerds. https://Blackgirlnerds.com/ a-second-look-at-the-resignation-of-harvards-first-Black-president/

Career strategies for Black women staff members in higher ed. (2022). Inside Higher Ed. Retrieved from: https://www.insidehighered.com/ advice/2022/04/29/ career-strategies-Black-women-staff-members-higher-ed-opinion

Chance, N. (2022). Resilient Leadership: A phenomenological exploration into how Black women in higher education leadership navigate adversity. *Journal of Humanistic Psychology*, 62(1), 44–78. 10.1177/00221678211003000

Communication Generation. (2023). Meet the Inclusive Leaders of Generation Alpha. Retrieved from: https://www.communication-generation.com/ meet-the-inclusive-leaders-of-generation-alpha/ #:~:text=They %20are%20also%20more %20 likely,unique%20challenges %20facing%20 underrepresented%20groups

Dedoose. (2023). Home. Retrieved from: https://www.dedoose.com/

Fast facts: Women of color in Higher ed. AAUW. (2020, August 12). Retrieved from: https://www.aauw.org/ resources/article/fast-facts-woc-higher-ed/

Haidar, E. H., & Kettles, C. E. (n.d.). *Harvard president Claudine Gay resigns, shortest tenure in University History: News: The Harvard Crimson.* News | The Harvard Crimson. https://www.thecrimson.com/ article/2024/1/3/claudine-gay-resign-harvard/

Hill Collins, P. (1986). Learning from the outsider within: The sociological significance of Black feminist. *Social Problems*, 33(6), S14–S32. 10.2307/800672

Hill Collins, P. (2000). *Black feminist thought: Knowledge, consciousness, and the politics of empowerment.* Routledge.

Laine Cibulskis, E. M. (2024, January 17). *Lincoln University protesters fight freezing temperatures to demand justice.* Columbia Missourian. https://www .columbiamissourian.com/ news/higher_education/ lincoln-university-protesters-fight-freezing-temperatures-to-demand-justice/ article_3a9b2114-b4b9-11ee-83cb-cbd6367ee0c4.html #:~:text=Antoinette%20%E2 %80%9CBonnie%E2%80%9D %20Candia%2DBailey,Moseley %20of%20harassment %20and%20bullying

Leiba, E. (2022). *I'm not yelling: A Black woman's guide to navigating the workplace.* Mango Publishing.

Luthans, F., & Avolio, B. J. (2003). Authentic Leadership: A Positive Developmental Approach. In Cameron, K. S., Dutton, J. E., & Quinn, R. E. (Eds.), *Positive Organizational Scholarship* (pp. 241–261). Barrett-Koehler.

Miles, S. (2012). Left behind: The status of Black women in higher administration (Doctoral Dissertation).

Schuessler, J., Hartocollis, A., Levenson, M., & Blinder, A. (2024, January 2). *Harvard president resigns after mounting plagiarism accusations.* The New York Times. https://www.nytimes.com/2024/01/02/us/harvard-claudine-gay-resigns.html

National Library of Medicine. (2023). Zooming into Focus Groups: Strategies for Qualitative Research in the Era of Social Distancing. Retrieved from: https://www .ncbi.nlm.nih.gov/pmc/articles/PMC8357072/

Nzinga, S. M. (2020). *Lean semesters: How higher education reproduces inequity.* Johns Hopkins University Press. 10.1353/book.77153

Rev.com. (n.d.). *Ai speech to text transcription service.* Retrieved from: https:// www.rev.com/

Turman, L. (n.d.). (2024). *Emails surface from Lu's VP of Student Affairs sent the day she died by suicide.* KRCG. https://krcgtv.com/ news/local/ emails-surface-from-lus-vp-of-student-affairs-sent-the-day-she-died-by-suicide

Tynan, J. (2023). *Inclusive sponsorship a bold vision to advance women of color in the workplace.* Rowman & Littlefield.

Woman of Color and the Wage Gap. (2023). Center for American Progress. Retrieved from: https://www.americanprogress.org/ article/women-of-color-and-the-wage-gap/

Wong, A. (2024, January 16). *An HBCU administrator died by suicide. the school's president is now on leave.* USA Today. https://www.usatoday.com/ story/news/education/2024/01/12/lincoln-university-president-leave-sudden-death/72205406007/

Compilation of References

Abdelaziz, M., Matthews, J., Campos, I., Fannin, D., Riveria Perez, J., Wilhite, M., & Williams, R. (2021). Student stories: Microaggressions in communication sciences and disorders. *American Journal of Speech-Language Pathology*, 30(5), 1990–2002. 10.1044/2021_AJSLP-21-0003034432987

Abrams, J. A., Maxwell, M., Pope, M., & Belgrave, F. Z. (2014). Carrying the World With the Grace of a Lady and the Grit of a Warrior: Deepening Our Understanding of the "Strong Black Woman" Schema. *Psychology of Women Quarterly*, 38(4), 503–518. 10.1177/0361684314541418

Adichie, C. N. (2009, July). The danger of a single story [Video]. TED Talks. https://www.ted.com/talks

Akilah Johnson, C. G. (2023a, October 17). *Stress is weathering our bodies from the inside out.* The Washington Post._https://www.washingtonpost.com/health/interactive/2023/stress-chronic-illness-aging/?itid=hp-top-table-main_p004_f002

Alger, R. (2024). Drop Out Rates among First-Generation Undergraduate Students in the United States. Ballard Brief. January 2024. www.ballardbrief.byu.edu

Amason, P. (2020). Family stories: Collections of narratives revealing family identity. *The Journal of American Culture*, 43(1), 49–62. 10.1111/jacc.13117

America Express. (2019). Woman-Owned Businesses Are Growing 2X Faster On Average Than All Businesses Nationwide. Retrieved from: https://about.americanexpress.com/newsroom/press-releases/news-details/2019/Woman-Owned-Businesses-Are-Growing-2X-Faster-On-Average-Than-All-Businesses-Nationwide-09-23-2019/default.aspx

American Association For Access. Equity and Diversity. (n.d.) Affirmative action policies throughout history. https://www.aaaed.org/aaaed/history_of_affirmative_action.asp

American Association of University Women. (2016). *Barriers and bias: The status of women in leadership.* https://www.aauw.org/app/uploads/2020/03/Barriers-andBias-nsa.pdf

American Council of Education. (2012) American Council on Education. United States. Moving the Needle Initiative, Retrieved from the Library of Congress. https://www.acenet.edu/Programs-Services/Pages/Communities/Moving-the-Needle.aspx

American Speech-Language-Hearing Association. (2020). *Profile of ASHA members and affiliates, year-end 2021.* www.asha.org

An Exodus of Black Women in Academia Hurts the Workforce. (2024, January 20). *Bloomberg.com.* https://www.bloomberg.com/opinion/articles/2024-01-20/an-exodus-of-black-women-in-academiahurts-the-workforce

Anderson, B. N., & Richardson, S. L. (Eds.). (2023). *Gifted Black Women Navigating the Doctoral Process: Sister Insider.* Taylor & Francis. 10.4324/9781003292180

Arpino, B., & Luppi, F. (2020). Childcare arrangements and working mothers' satisfaction with work–family balance. *Demographic Research*, 42, 549–588. 10.4054/DemRes.2020.42.19

Aya, E. (2023). *Aya: The Enduring Spirit of Black Women in Higher Education* (Order No. 30820060). Available from ProQuest Dissertations & Theses Global. (2917478555).

Bagati, D. (2008). Women of color in US securities firms. *Catalyst : Feminism, Theory, Technoscience.*

Bailey, M. (2021). *Misogynoir Transformed: Black Women's Digital Resistance.* NYU Press.

Baptiste, D. A.Jr. (1986). The image of the black family portrayed by television: A critical comment. *Marriage & Family Review*, 10(1), 50. 10.1300/J002v10n01_03

Bartman, C. C. (2015). African American Women in Higher Education: Issues and. *College Student Affairs Leadership.*

Bartman, C. C. (n.d.). African American Women in Higher Education: Issues and Support Strategies. *Journal of Women in Higher Education, 2(2).*

Beal, F. M. (1975). Slave of a slave no more: Black women in struggle. *The Black Scholar*, 6(6), 2–10. 10.1080/00064246.1975.11431488

Beal, F. M. (2008). Double jeopardy: To be Black and female. *Meridians (Middletown, Conn.)*, 8(2), 166–176. 10.2979/MER.2008.8.2.166

Beatty, C. C., Bush, A. A., Erxleben, E. E., Ferguson, T. L., Harrell, A. T., & Sahachartsiri, W. K. (2010). Black Student Leaders: The Influence of Social Climate in Student Organizations. *Journal of the Student Personnel Association at Indiana University*, 38, 48–63. https://scholarworks.iu.edu/journals/index.php/jiuspa/article/view/5002

Belland, J. (2021, June 23). *Higher Education Trends for Colleges and Universities*. Retrieved from Salesforce.org: https://www.salesforce.org/blog/higher-education-connected-student-report-second-edition/

Bell, E. L. J. E. (1990). The Bicultural Life Experience of Career-Oriented Black Women. *Journal of Organizational Behavior*, 11(6), 459–477. 10.1002/job.4030110607

Bellomo, A. T. (Writer), & Listo, M. (Director). (2014, October 23). We're Not Friends. (Season 1, Episode 5) [TV Series]. In Rhimes, S., Beers, B., D'Elia, B., Nowalk, P. (Executive Producers), How to Get Away with Murder. Shondaland. NoWalk Entertainment. ABC Studios.

Biaggio, M. (2001). Navigating Roles in Mentoring Relationships with Graduate Students. ERIC. https://eric.ed.gov/?id=ED457516

Bizzell, C. V. (2023). How does it feel to be a problem: Tokenization of black women student affair professionals in white academic spaces. *International Journal of Qualitative Studies in Education : QSE*.

Black Faculty and Radical Retention | American Sociological Association. (n.d.). Retrieved September 30, 2023, from https://www.asanet.org/footnotes-article/black-faculty-and-radical-retention/

Black Feminisms. (2019, July 16). The Matrix of Domination and the Four Domains of Power. Black Feminisms. Retrieved from https://blackfeminisms.com/matrix/

Black, V. G., & Taylor, Z. W. (2018). Nobody's talking to the mentees. *Mentoring & Tutoring*, 26(5), 606–626. 10.1080/13611267.2018.1561027

Blair-Loy, M. (2004). Work devotion and work time. In Epstein, C. F., & Kalleberg, A. L. (Eds.), *Fighting for time: Shifting boundaries of work and social life* (pp. 282–316). Russell Sage Foundation.

Blau, F. D., Currie, J. M., Croson, R. T. A., & Ginther, D. K. (2010). Can Mentoring Help Female Assistant Professors? Interim Results from a Randomized Trial. *The American Economic Review*, 100(2), 348–352. 10.1257/aer.100.2.348

Blazar, D. (2021). *Teachers of color, culturally responsive teaching, and student outcomes: Experimental evidence from the random assignment of teachers to classes.* (EdWorkingPaper: 21-501). Annenberg Institute at Brown University. 10.26300/jym0-wz02

Bormann, O. (2020). *Microaggression.* Retrieved from University of Portland: https://www.up.edu/inclusion/files/101---microagressions-accessible.pdf#:~:text=A%20microinsult%20is%20a%20comments%20or%20action%20that,or%20disregard%20for%20a%20person%E2%80%99s%20identity%20or%20heritage

Bouchrika, I. (2020, August 4). *11 Top Trends in Higher Education:2021/2022Data, Insights & Predictions.* Retrieved from Research.com: https://research.com/education/trends-in-higher-education#ment

Bradford, J. H. (2022). *Session 254: Black women in the workplace.* https://therapyforblackgirls.com/2022/04/06/session-254-black-women-in-the-workplace/

Brown, K. (2024, January 8). *A second look at the resignation of Harvard's first black president.* Black Girl Nerds. https://blackgirlnerds.com/a-second-look-at-the-resignation-of-harvards-first-black-president/

Brownlee, D. (2022). Black women leaders are more ambitious but less supported at work, McKinsey and Lean in study finds. https://www.forbes.com/sites/danabrownlee/2022/10/21/black-women-leaders-are-more-ambitious-but-less-supported-at-work-mckinsey-and-lean-in-study-finds/

Brunsden, V., Davies, M., Shevlin, M., & Bracken, M. (2000). Why do HE Students Drop Out? A test of Tinto's model. *Journal of Further and Higher Education*, 24(3), 301–310. 10.1080/030987700750022244

Cambridge English Dictionary. (n.d.). Matriarch. In website dictionary. Retrieved December 19, 2023, https://dictionary.cambridge.org/us/dictionary/english/matriarch

Cannon, K. G. (2021). *Katie's Canon: Womanism and the Soul of the Black Community, Revised and Expanded 25th Anniversary Edition.* Fortress Press. 10.2307/j.ctv1khdp4b

Career strategies for Black women staff members in higher ed. (2022). Inside Higher Ed. Retrieved from: https://www.insidehighered.com/advice/2022/04/29/career-strategies-black-women-staff-members-higher-ed-opinion

Carrasco, M. (2021, October 26). Addressing the Mental Health of LGBTQ+ Students. *Inside Higher Ed*, 1. Retrieved from Inside Higher Ed: https://www.insidehighered.com/news/2021/10/26/lgbtq-students-face-sizable-mental-health-disparities

Carroll, C. (1982). Three's A Crowd: The Dilemma of the Black Women in Higher Education. *But Some of Us Are Brave*, 115-128.

Castrillon, C. (2022). 10 ways to improve your mental health at work. *Forbes*. https://www.forbes.com/sites/carolinecastrillon/2022/05/08/10-ways-to-improve -your-mental-health-at-work/ https://www.dictionary.com/browse/solidary

Chamberlain, M. (1991). *Women in academe: Progress and prospects*. Russell Sage Foundation.

Chance, N. (2022). Resilient Leadership: A phenomenological exploration into how black women in higher education leadership navigate adversity. *Journal of Humanistic Psychology*, 62(1), 44–78. 10.1177/00221678211003000

Childress, C., Nayyar, J., & Gibson, I. (2023). Tokenism and its long-term consequences: Evidence from the literary field. *American Sociological Review*, 89(1), 31–59. 10.1177/00031224231121428838313415

Chinn, P. L., & Kramer, M. K. (2008). *Integrated theory and knowledge development in nursing* (7th ed.). Mosby Elsevier.

Clandinin, D. J., & Connelly, F. M. (2000). *Narrative inquiry: Experience and story in qualitative research* (1st ed.). Jossey-Bass Publishers.

Cockley, K. (2024, March 14). It's time to reconceptualize what imposter syndrome means for people of color. *Harvard Business Review*. https://hbr.org/2024/03/its-time -to-reconceptualize-what-imposter-syndrome-means-for-people-of-color

Colleges Look to Cluster Hires Amid Diversity Hostilities. (2023, September 14). *Diverse: Issues In Higher Education*. https://www.diverseeducation.com/from-the -magazine/article/15546498/colleges-look-to-cluster-hir es-amid-diversity-hostilities

Collins, P. H. (2000). *Black feminist thought: Knowledge, consciousness, and the politics of empowerment* (Rev. 10th anniversary ed.). Routledge.

Collins, P. H. (2002). Learning from the outsider within: The sociological significance of Black feminist thought. In C. S. Turner, A. L. Antonio, M. Garcia, B. V. Laden, A. Nora, and C. Presley (Ed.), *Racial and ethnic diversity in higher education* (1–9). Pearson Custom.

Collins, P. H. (1986). Learning from the outsider within: The sociological significance of Black feminist thought. *Social Problems*, 33(6), S14–S32. 10.1525/ sp.1986.33.6.03a00020

Collins, P. H. (1990). *Black feminist thought in the matrix of domination*. Unwin Hyman.

Collins, P. H. (1990). *Black feminist thought: Knowledge, consciousness, and the politics of empowerment*. Routledge.

Collins, P. H. (2009). *Black feminist thought*. Routledge.

Collins, P. H., & Bilge, S. (2016). *Intersectionality*. Polity Press.

Communication Generation. (2023). Meet the Inclusive Leaders of Generation Alpha. Retrieved from: https://www.communication-generation.com/meet-the-inclusive-leaders-of-generation-alpha/#:~:text=They%20are%20also%20more%20likely,unique%20challenges%20facing%20underrepresented%20groups

Conner, K. O. (2020, December 3). *What is Code-Switching*. Retrieved from Psychology Today: https://www.psychologytoday.com/us/blog/achieving-health-equity/202012/what-is-code-switching

Conner, T. (2022). Black faculty and radical retention. *Footnotes: A Magazine of the American Sociological Association, 50*(2), 1-7.

Crenshaw, K. (2016, October). The urgency of intersectionality [Video]. TED Conferences. https://www.ted.com/talks/kimberle_crenshaw_the_urgency_of_intersectionality

Crenshaw, K. (1991). Mapping the margins: Intersectionality, identity politics, and violence against women of color. *Stanford Law Review*, 43(6), 1241–1298. 10.2307/1229039

Crenshaw, K. (2005). Mapping the margins: *Intersectionality, identity politics, and violence against women of color (1994)*. In Bergen, R. K., Edleson, J. L., & Renzetti, C. M. (Eds.), *Violence against women: Classic papers* (pp. 282–313). Pearson Education New Zealand.

D'Elia, B. (Writer), & Foley, M. (Director). (2014, October 30). Freakin' Whack-a-Mole. (Season 1, Episode 6) [TV Series]. In Rhimes, S., Beers, B., D'Elia, B., Nowalk, P. (Executive Producers), How to Get Away with Murder. Shondaland. NoWalk Entertainment. ABC Studios.

Davis, A. Y. (1983). *Women, Race & Class*. Random House.

Dedoose. (2023). Home. Retrieved from: https://www.dedoose.com/

Dey, E. L., Korn, S. J., & Sax, L. J. (1996). Betrayed by the academy: The sexual harassment of women college faculty. *The Journal of Higher Education*, 67(2), 149–173. 10.1080/00221546.1996.11780254

Dickens, D. D., & Chavez, E. L. (2018). Navigating the Workplace: The Costs and Benefits of Shifting Identities at Work among Early Career U.S. Black Women. *Sex Roles*, 78(11-12), 760–774. 10.1007/s11199-017-0844-x

Dillard, C. B. (2000). The substance of things hoped for, the evidence of things not seen: Examining an endarkened feminist epistemology in educational research and leadership. *International Journal of Qualitative Studies in Education : QSE*, 13(6), 661–681. 10.1080/09518390050211565

Dobbin, F., & Kalev, A. (2016, July-August). *Why diversity programs fail.* https://hbr.org/2016/07/why-diversity-programs-fail

Dungey, A. (Writer), & Mendoza, L. (Director). (2021, December 3). Rainbow Sprinkles. (Season 1, Episode 3) [TV Series]. In Oliver, T., King, S., Poehler, A., Becky, Lessing, K., Williams, P., Valdez, M., Bausch, D., Mendoza, L., Dungey, A., Brown, N., Free, T., Matt, B., Breece, J., Saxton, s., Varga, S. (Producers), *Harlem.* Amazon Studios.

Duran, J. (2015). Women of the civil rights movement. Black feminism and social progress. *Philosophia Africana*, 17(2), 65–73. 10.5325/philafri.17.2.0065

Eagly, A. H., & Carli, L. L. (2007). *Through the labyrinth: The truth about how women become leaders.* Harvard Business School Press.

Equal Employment Opportunity Commission. (2022). *Title VII of the Civil Rights Acts of 1964.* U.S. Equal Employment Opportunity Commission.

Espinosa, L. L., Turk, J. M., Taylor, M., & Chessman, H. M. (2019). *Race and ethnicity in higher education: A status report.* American Council on Education. https://1xfsu31b52d33idlp13twtos-wpengine.netdna-ssl.com/wpcontent/uploads/2019/02/Race-and-Ethnicity-in-Higher-Education.pdf

Eva, N., Robin, M., Sendjaya, S., van Dierendonck, D., & Liden, R. C. (2019). Servant leadership: A systematic review and call for future research. *The Leadership Quarterly*, 30(1), 111–132. 10.1016/j.leaqua.2018.07.004

Fast facts: Women of color in Higher ed. AAUW. (2020, August 12). Retrieved from: https://www.aauw.org/resources/article/fast-facts-woc-higher-ed/

Feagin, J. (2006). *Systemic Racism: A Theory of Oppression* (1st ed.). Routledge., 10.4324/9781315880938

Fehr, B., & Sprecher, S. (2009). Prototype analysis of the concept of compassionate love. *Personal Relationships*, 16(3), 33–364. 10.1111/j.1475-6811.2009.01227.x

Finley, S. (2008). Arts-based research. In Knowles, J. G., & Cole, A. L. (Eds.), *Handbook of the arts in qualitative research: Perspectives, methodologies, examples, and issues* (pp. 72–82). SAGE Publications, Inc. 10.4135/9781452226545.n6

Frank, T. J. (2022). *The waymakers: Clearing the path to workplace equity with competence and confidence.* Berrett-Koehler Publishers.

Gallo, A. (2023). *What is psychological safety?*https://hbr.org/2023/02/what-is-psychological-safety

Gayles, J. G. (2022). Does anyone see us? Disposability of Black women faculty in the academy. *Diverse.* https://www.diverseeducation.com/opinion/article/15295726/does-anyone-see-us-disposability-of-black-women-faculty-in-the-academy

Gaynor, T. S. (n.d.). A Love Letter to Black Women in the Academy. *Inside Higher Ed.* Retrieved September 30, 2023, from https://www.insidehighered.com/advice/2022/12/16/letter-support-and-solidarity-black-women-aca deme-opinion

Gershenson, S., Hart, C. M., Lindsay, C., & Papageorge, N. (2017). *The Long-Run Impacts of Same Race Teachers.* Institute of Labor Economics. 10.2139/ssrn.2940620

Givens, S. M. (2021). Black Women and Stereotypes: Implications for the Education and Socialization of African American Children. *The Journal of Black Psychology*, 47(6), 399–417.

Goffee, R., & Jones, G. (2001). Followership. *Harvard Business Review*, 79(11), 148.

Gomez, J., Miranda, R., & Polanco, L. (2011). Acculturative stress, perceived discrimination, and vulnerability to suicide attempts among emerging adults. *Journal of Youth and Adolescence*, 40(11), 1465–1476. 10.1007/s10964-011-9688-921717234

Grassley, J. S., & Nelms, T. P. (2009). Tales of resistance and other emancipatory functions of storytelling. *Journal of Advanced Nursing*, 65(11), 2447–2453. 10.1111/j.1365-2648.2009.05105.x19737319

Greenhaus, J. H., & Beutell, N. J. (1985). Sources of conflict between work and family roles. *Academy of Management Review*, 10(1), 76–88. 10.2307/258214

Greenleaf, R. K. (1970). *The servant as leader.* Greenleaf Center for Servant Leadership.

Gregory, K. (2020). Moving Forward as a Profession in a Time of Uncertainty. *The ASHA Leader Blog.* https://leader.pubs.asha.org/do/10.1044/leader.FMP.25082020.8/full/?fbclid=IwAR3uSS3BGgPGOKGLUMb1O55ozWvPbY-_j30C98PxDN6PcrnmJrHaniv1RwQ

Gregory, S. T. (2001). Black faculty women in the academy: History, status, and future. *The Journal of Negro Education*, 70(3), 124–138. 10.2307/3211205

Gurin, P., Dey, E. L., Hurtado, S., & Gurin, G. (2002). Diversity and higher education: Theory and impact on educational outcomes. *Harvard Educational Review*, 72(3), 330–366. 10.17763/haer.72.3.01151786u134n051

Haidar, E. H., & Kettles, C. E. (n.d.). *Harvard president Claudine Gay resigns, shortest tenure in University History: News: The Harvard Crimson*. News | The Harvard Crimson. https://www.thecrimson.com/article/2024/1/3/claudine-gay -resign-harvard/

Hajela, D. (2022, February 24). Trayvon Martin's death 10 years later: A family's pain, a community's push for change. *AP News*. https://apnews.com/article/trayvon -martin-death-10-years-later-c68f12130b2992d9c1ba31ec1a398cdd

Hall, E. J., Everett, J. E., & Hamilton-Mason, J. (2012). Black Women Talk About Workplace Stress and How They Cope. *Journal of Black Studies*, 43(2), 207–226. 10.1177/0021934711413327222457894

Hampton, R. (2021, November 8). Being a Black woman in the workplace can be like starring in a thriller. *SLATE News & Politics*. https://slate.com/culture/2021/ 11/other-black-girl-all-her-little-secrets-review-work-horror.html

Harley, D. A. (2007). Maids of academe: African American women faculty at predominately White institutions. *Springer Science and Business Media, 12*(1), 19–36. 10.1007/s12111-007-9030-5

Harper, D. (2002). Talking about pictures: A case for photo elicitation. *Visual Studies*, 17(1), 13–26. 10.1080/14725860220137345

Harris-Perry, M. V. (2011). *Sister Citizen: Shame, Stereotypes, and Black Women in America*. Yale University Press.

Harvard Business Review Analytic Services. (2021). *Creating a Culture of Diversity, Equity, and Inclusion: Real Progress Requires Sustained Commitment*. Harvard Business School Publishing.

Hays, D. G., & Singh, A. A. (2012). *Qualitative inquiry in clinical and educational settings*. The Guilford Press.

Henderson, M. (2019). Portrayals of Black women in TV shows that aired in 1997 versus 2017: A qualitative content analysis. *Elon Journal of Undergraduate Research in Communications*, 10(1), 64–69.

Hill Collins, P. (1986). Learning from the outsider within: The sociological significance of black feminist. *Social Problems*, 33(6), S14–S32. 10.2307/800672

Hill, A. (2021). *Changing the rules changes the game…and not for the better.*https://tnnonprofits.org/blog-posts/2020/7/30/goalpostsmove

Hirsch, W. (1942). Assimilation as concept and as process. *Social Forces*, 21(1), 35–39. 10.2307/2570428

Hobfoll, S. E. (1989). Conservation of resources: A new attempt at conceptualizing stress. *The American Psychologist*, 44(3), 513–524. 10.1037/0003-066X.44.3.5132648906

Holder, A. M. B., Jackson, M. A., & Ponterotto, J. G. (2015). Racial microaggression experiences and coping strategies of Black women in corporate leadership. *Qualitative Psychology*, 2(2), 164–180. 10.1037/qup0000024

Holgersson, C., & Romani, L. (2020). Tokenism Revisited: . *When OrganizationalCulture Challenges Masculine Norms, theExperience of Token Is Transformed*, 649-661.

Holmes, T. E. (2020, October 27). Black women at work: How we shape our identities on the job. *Essence*. https://www.essence.com/news/money-career/black-women-work-how-we-shape-our-identities-job/

hooks, b. (2001). *All about love: New visions*. Harper Perennial.

hooks, b. (2015). *Sisters of the yam: Black women and self-recovery*. Routledge.

Hooks, B. (1981). *Ain't I a woman: Black women and feminism*. South End Press.

Hooks, B. (2014). *Teaching To Transgress*. Routledge. 10.4324/9780203700280

Howard-Vital, M. R. (1989). African-American Women in Higher Education: Struggling to Gain Identity. *Journal of Black Studies*, 20(2), 180–191. 10.1177/002193478902000205

Hughes, R. L., & Howard-Hamilton, M. F. (2003). Insights: Emphasizing issues that affect African American women. *New Directions for Student Services*, 2003(104), 95–104. 10.1002/ss.110

Hurston, Z. N. (1998). *Their eyes were watching God*. HarperPerrenial.

Indeed. (2024, April 1). *What is an Affinity Group in the Workplace*. Retrieved from Indeed for Employers: https://www.indeed.com/hire/c/info/what-is-an-affinity-group

Jackson Preston, P., Brown, G. C., Garnett, T., Sanchez, D., Fagbamila, E., & Graham, N. (2023). "I am never enough": Factors contributing to secondary traumatic stress and burnout among Black student services professionals in higher education. *Trauma Care, 3*(2), 93–107. 10.3390/traumacare3020010

Jackson, A. (2022). *Less 25% of Black employees feel included at work-what companies can be doing better*. CNBC. https://www.cnbc.com/2022/04/01/less-than-25percent-of-black-employees-feel-included-at-work-what-companies-can-be-doing-better.html

Jackson, P., Thoits, P., & Taylor, H. (1995). Composition of the Workplace and Psychological Well-Being: The Effects of Tokenism on America's Black Elite. *Oxford Journals*, 543-557.

Jarmon, B. (2001). Unwritten rules of the game. In Mabokela, R. O., & Green, A. L. (Eds.), *Sisters of the academy: Emergent Black women scholars in higher education* (pp. 175–182). Stylus Publishing, LLC.

Jean-Marie, G., & Brooks, J. S. (2019). *Black women scholars in educational leadership: Critical perspectives on race, gender, and social justice*. Peter Lang Publishing.

Jimenez, J., Hinton, K., Branyon, A., Greenfield, E. A., Baker, L. A., Mutchler, J. E., & Schwartz, A. (2002). The history of grandmothers in the African-American community. *The Social Service Review*, 76(4), 523–551. 10.1086/342994

Johnson, D. S., Johnson, A. D., Crossney, K. B., & Devereux, E. (2023). Women in higher education: A brief report on stress during COVID-19. *Management in Education, 37*(2), 93-100. 10.1177/08920206211019401

Jones, S. N. (2003). The praxis of Black female educational leadership from a systems thinking perspective [Unpublished doctoral dissertation]. Bowling Green State University.

Jones, C., & Shorter-Gooden, K. (2003). *Shifting: The double lives of Black women in America*. HarperCollins.

Jones, M. K., Lee, L. H., Gaskin-Wasson, A. L., & McKee, A. D. (2021). The psychological impact of racism: Emotional stress among African American women. *The Journal of Black Psychology*, 47(3), 170–193. 10.1177/00957984211007339

Jones, T. B., Dawkins, L. S., McClinton, M. M., & Glover, M. H. (Eds.). (2012). *Pathways to higher education administration for African American women*. Routledge.

Joseph, T. D., & Hirshfield, L. E. (2011). 'Why don't you get somebody new to do it?' Race and cultural taxation in the academy. *Ethnic and Racial Studies*, 34(1), 121–141. 10.1080/01419870.2010.496489

Kalliath, T., & Brough, P. (2008). Work-life balance: A review of the meaning of the balance construct. *Journal of Management & Organization*, 14(3), 323–327. 10.5172/jmo.837.14.3.323

Kanter, R. M. (1977). Some Effects of Proportions on Group Life: Skewed Sex Ratios and Responses to Token Women. *American Journal of Sociology*, 82(5), 965–990. Retrieved June 11, 2023, from https://www.jstor.org/stable/2777808. 10.1086/226425

Kellas, J. K. (2005). Family ties: Communicating identity through jointly told family stories. *Communication Monographs*, 72(4), 365–389. 10.1080/03637750500322453

Kellas, J. K., & Horstman, H. K. (2014). Communicated narrative sense-making: Understanding family narratives, storytelling, and the construction of meaning through a communicative lens. In Turner, L. H., & West, R. (Eds.), *The SAGE Handbook of Family Communication* (pp. 76–90)., 10.4135/9781483375366.n5

Kim, J. (Writer) & Longino, G. D. (Director). (2021, August 20). The Last Bus in Town. (Season 1, Episode 5) [TV Series]. In Peet, A., Benioff, D., Weiss, B. D., Caufield, B., Longino, G. D., Oh, S., (Executive Producers), *The Chair*. Netflix.

Kramp, M. K. (2003). Exploring life and experience through narrative inquiry. In deMarrais, K. B., & Lapan, S. D. (Eds.), *Foundations for research: Methods of inquiry in education and the social sciences* (pp. 119–138). Routledge.

Laine Cibulskis, E. M. (2024, January 17). *Lincoln University protesters fight freezing temperatures to demand justice*. Columbia Missourian. https://www .columbiamissourian.com/news/higher_education/lincoln-university-protesters-fight-freezing-temperatures-to-demand-justice/article_3a9b2114-b4b9-11ee-83cb -cbd6367ee0c4.html#:~:text=Antoinette%20%E2%80%9CBonnie%E2%80%9D %20Candia%2DBailey,Moseley%20of%20harassment%20and%20bullying

Lawrence, A. (2024, February 28). "She endured cruelty:" What led to a leader's death at a historically Black university? *The Guardian*. https://www.theguardian .com/us-news/2024/feb/28/antoinette-candia-bailey-lincoln-university-death

Leiba, E. (2022). *I'm not yelling: A black woman's guide to navigating the work-place*. Mango Publishing.

Lewis, T. (2020, October 27). New ESSENCE study: Hiding your authentic self at work can damage your career. *Essence*. Retrieved from https://www.essence.com/ news/money-career/essence-study-hiding-authentic-personality-work-damaging/

Lewis, J. A., Mendenhall, R., Harwood, S. A., & Browne Huntt, M. (2017). Coping with gendered racial microaggressions among Black women college students. *Journal of African American Studies*, 21(1), 32–48. 10.1007/s12111-017-9342-0

Lewis, J. A., Williams, M. G., Peppers, E. J., & Gadson, C. A. (2017). Applying intersectionality to explore the relations between gendered racism and health among Black women. *Journal of Counseling Psychology*, 64(5), 475–486. 10.1037/cou000023129048194

Livo, N. J., & Rietz, S. A. (1986). *Storytelling: Process and practice*. Libraries Unltd Inc.

Lord, R. G., & Hall, R. J. (2005). Identity, deep structure and the development of leadership skill. *The Leadership Quarterly*, 16(4), 591–615. 10.1016/j.leaqua.2005.06.003

Love, B. H., Templeton, E., Ault, S., & Johnson, O. (2023). Bruised, not broken: Scholarly personal narratives of Black women in the academy. *International Journal of Qualitative Studies in Education : QSE*, 36(10), 2229–2251. 10.1080/09518398.2021.1984607

Love, B. J., & Jiggetts, V. D. (2019). Black women rising: Jumping double-dutch with a liberatory consciousness. In Evans, S. (Ed.), *Black women and social justice education: legacies and lessons* (pp. 1–20). State University of New York Press. 10.1515/9781438472966-002

Luthans, F., & Avolio, B. J. (2003). Authentic Leadership: A Positive Developmental Approach. In Cameron, K. S., Dutton, J. E., & Quinn, R. E. (Eds.), *Positive Organizational Scholarship* (pp. 241–261). Barrett-Koehler.

Lutz, K. F., Hassouneh, D., Akeroyd, J., & Beckett, A. K. (2013). Balancing survival and resistance: Experiences of faculty of color in predominantly Euro American schools of nursing. *Journal of Diversity in Higher Education*, 6(2), 127–146. 10.1037/a0032364

Magley, J. (2023, February 14). *How Toxic Work Culture Breeds Unnecessary Competition Between Black Employees*. Retrieved from Forbes: https://www.forbes.com/sites/jennifermagley/2023/02/14/how-toxic-work-culture-breeds-unnecessary-competition-between-black-employees/?sh=24492a703690

Marshall-Wong, C. R. (2000). Challenges to agency in the workplace: An analysis of Black professional women in fiction and in their lives. [Doctoral dissertation, University of Chicago]. ProQuest Dissertations and Theses Global.

Martin, R. (2024). *State of hopelessness: Lincoln Univ. VP of student affairs died by suicide after workplace bullying*. Roland Martin Unfiltered. https://www.youtube.com/watch?v=rx3FQusVBsU

Matt, B. (Writer), & Muhammad, S. (Director). (2021, December 3). The Strong Black Woman. (Season 1, Episode 7) [TV Series]. In Oliver, T., King, S., Poehler, A., Becky, Lessing, K., Williams, P., Valdez, M., Bausch, D., Mendoza, L., Dungey, A., Brown, N., Free, T., Matt, B., Breece, J., Saxton, s., Varga, S. (Producers), *Harlem*. Amazon Studios.

McAdams, D. P. (1993). *The stories we live by: Personal myths and the making of the self*. Guilford Press.

McCain, K. D., & Matkin, G. S. (2019). Emerging adults leadership identity development through family storytelling: A narrative approach. *Journal of Leadership Education*, 18(2), 159–170. 10.12806/V18/I2/T3

McCall, L. (2005). The complexity of intersectionality. *Signs (Chicago, Ill.)*, 30(3), 1771–1800. 10.1086/426800

McCluney, C. L., & Rabelo, V. C. (2020). Conditions of visibility: An intersectional examination of Black women's belongingness and distinctiveness at work. *Journal of Vocational Behavior*, 118, 103373. 10.1016/j.jvb.2020.103373

McDole, A. (2017). Mammy representations in the 21st century [Master's thesis, Syracuse University]. https://surface.syr.edu/thesis/194

McGowan, J. A., & Kashatus, W. C. (2011). Harriet Tubman: a biography (illustrated ed.). Greenwood Biographies. Bloomsbury Academic.

Mctaggart, N., Cox, V., Heldman, C. (2019). Representations of Black women in Hollywood. *Geena Davis Institute on Gender in Media*, 1–15.

Miles, M. (2022). *9 ways to promote equity in the workplace (and how to lead by example)*. Betterup.https://www.betterup.com/blog/equity-in-the-workplace

Miles, S. (2012). Left behind: The status of black women in higher administration (Doctoral Dissertation).

Milner, H. R., & Howard, T. C. (2004). Black teachers, black students, black communities, and Brown: Perspectives and insights from experts. *The Journal of Negro Education*, 73(3), 285. 10.2307/4129612

Mishra, A., Nunez, G., & Tyson, G. (2021). Faculty of color in communication sciences and disorders: An overdue conversation. Perspectives of ASHA Special Interest Group – SIG 10. *American Speech-Language-Hearing Association*, 6(4), 778–782. 10.1044/2021_PERSP-20-00176

Morgan, J. (1995). Mammy the huckster: Selling the old south for the new century. *American Art*, 9(1), 87–109. 10.1086/424235

Moss, Y. (2014). *The role of mentoring and career advancement: A phenomeno-logical study examining Black female mid-level community college administrators* (Order No. 3662311). Available from Education Database; ProQuest Dissertations & Theses Global. (1650557450)

Naeem, M., Ozuem, W., Howell, K., & Ranfagni, S. (2023). A step-by-step process of thematic analysis to develop a conceptual model in qualitative research. *International Journal of Qualitative Methods*, 22(11), 16094069231205789. Advance online publication. 10.1177/16094069231205789

Nam, J. (2023, March 31). *Diversity in Higher Education: Facts and Statistics.* Retrieved from Best Colleges: https://www.bestcolleges.com/research/diversity-in-higher-education-facts-statistics/

National Association for the Advancement of Colored People. (2023). *NAACP support worker's rights as civil rights opposed to so-called "right to work" legislation and initiatives.* National Association for the Advancement of Colored people. https://naacp.org/resources/naacp-supports-workers-rights-civil-rights-opposed-so-called-right-work-legislation-and

National Conference for Community and Justice. (2024). *Resources.* Retrieved from National Conference for Community and Justice: https://nccj.org/resources/age/

National Library of Medicine. (2023). Zooming into Focus Groups: Strategies for Qualitative Research in the Era of Social Distancing. Retrieved from: https://www.ncbi.nlm.nih.gov/pmc/articles/PMC8357072/

National Student Clearinghouse. (2023, July 27). *Persistence and Retention.* Retrieved from National Student Clearinghouse Research Center: https://nscresearchcenter.org/persistence-retention/

Nowalk, P. (Writer), & Offer, M. (Director). (2014, September 25). Pilot. (Season 1, Episode 1) [TV Series]. In Rhimes, S., Beers, B., D'Elia, B., Nowalk, P. (Executive Producers), *How to Get Away with Murder.* Shondaland. NoWalk Entertainment. ABC Studios.

Nzinga, S. M. (2020). *Lean semesters: How higher education reproduces inequity.* Johns Hopkins University Press. 10.1353/book.77153

Oliver, T. (Writer), & Lee, D.L. (Director). (2021, December 3). Pilot. (Season 1, Episode 1) [TV Series]. In Oliver, T., King, S., Poehler, A., Becky, Lessing, K., Williams, P., Valdez, M., Bausch, D., Mendoza, L., Dungey, A., Brown, N., Free, T., Matt, B., Breece, J., Saxton, s., Varga, S. (Producers), *Harlem.* Amazon Studios.

Oliver, T., King, S., Poehler, A., Becky, Lessing, K., Williams, P., Valdez, M., Bausch, D., Mendoza, L., Dungey, A., Brown, N., Free, T., Matt, B., Breece, J., Saxton, s., Varga, S. (Producers). (2021). *Harlem* [TV. Series]. Amazon Studios.

orkplace equity vs. equality: Two small letters, one big difference. Deskbird.

Ortiz, E. (2020). *Racial violence and a pandemic: How the Red Summer of 1919 relates to 2020*. https://www.nbcnews.com/news/us-news/racial-violence-pandemic -how-red-summer-1919-relates-2020-n1231499

Patitu, C. L., & Hinton, K. G. (2003). The experiences of African American women faculty and administrators in higher education: Has anything changed? *New Directions for Student Services*, 2003(104), 79–93. 10.1002/ss.109

Paulise, L. (2023). How can women overcome the pet to threat phenomenon in 7 tips. *Forbes*. https://www.forbes.com/sites/lucianapaulise/2023/02/23/how-black -women-can-overcome-the-pet-to-threat-phenomenon-in-7-steps/

Pauls, E. (2024, June 12). Assimilation. *Encyclopedia Britannica*. https://www .britannica.com/topic/assimilation-society

Pedulla. (2020). Diversity and Inclusion efforts that Really work. https://hbr.org/ 2020/05/diversity-and-inclusion-efforts-that-really-work

Peet, A., & Robbins, E. R. (Writer) & Longino, G. D. (Director). (2021, August 20). The Faculty Party. (Season 1, Episode 2) [TV Series]. In Peet, A., Benioff, D., Weiss, B. D., Caufield, B., Longino, G. D., Oh, S., (Executive Producers), *The Chair*. Netflix.

Peet, A., & Wyman, J. A. (Writer) & Longino, G. D. (Director). (2021, August 20). The Town Hall. (Season 1, Episode 3) [TV Series]. In Peet, A., Benioff, D., Weiss, B. D., Caufield, B., Longino, G. D., Oh, S., (Executive Producers), *The Chair*. Netflix.

Peet, A., Benioff, D., Weiss, B. D., Caufield, B., Longino, G. D., Oh, S., (Executive Producers). (2021). *The Chair* [TV Series]. Netflix.

Pendell, R. (2022, September 22). Workplace equity: The "E" in DEI and why it matters. https://www.gallup.com/workplace/401573/workplace-equity-dei-why -matters.aspx

Pilgrim, D. (2008, August). *The sapphire caricature*. Jim Crow Museum. https:// jimcrowmuseum.ferris.edu/antiblack/sapphire.htm

Price, J. H., & Khubchandani, J. (2019). The Changing Characteristics of African-American Adolescent Suicides, 2001-2017. *Journal of Community Health*, 44(4), 756–763. 10.1007/s10900-019-00678-x31102116

Purdie-Vaughns, V., Steele, C. M., Davies, P. G., Ditlmann, R., & Crosby, J. R. (2008). Social identity contingencies: How diversity cues signal threat or safety for African Americans in mainstream institutions. *Journal of Personality and Social Psychology*, 94(4), 615–630. 10.1037/0022-3514.94.4.61518361675

Redstone, I. (2020, November 18). *This is why diversity programming doesn't work*. Forbes.

Rev.com. (n.d.). *Ai speech to text transcription service*. Retrieved from: https://www.rev.com/

Rhimes, S., Beers, B., D'Elia, B., Nowalk, P. (Executive Producers). (2014). *How to Get Away with Murder* [TV. Series]. Shondaland. NoWalk Entertainment. ABC Studios.

Robbins, E. R. (Writer) & Longino, G. D. (Director). (2021, August 20). Don't Kill Bill. (Season 1, Episode 4) [TV Series]. In Peet, A., Benioff, D., Weiss, B. D., Caufield, B., Longino, G. D., Oh, S., (Executive Producers), *The Chair*. Netflix.

Roberts, L. M., Mayo, A. J., & Thomas, D. A. (Eds.). (2019). *Race, work, and leadership: New perspectives on the Black experience*. Harvard Business Review Press.

Roebuck, J. B., & Murty, K. S. (1993). *Historically Black colleges and universities: Their place in American higher education*. Praeger.

Sáenz, V. B., Hurtado, S., Barrera, D., Wolf, D., & Yeung, F. (2007). First in my family: A profile of first-generation college students at four-year institutions since 1971. *Higher Education: Handbook of Theory and Research, 22*(1), 141–183.

Schuessler, J., Hartocollis, A., Levenson, M., & Blinder, A. (2024, January 2). *Harvard president resigns after mounting plagiarism accusations*. The New York Times. https://www.nytimes.com/2024/01/02/us/harvard-claudine-gay-resigns.html

Seggar, J. F., & Wheeler, P. (1973). World of work on tv: Ethnic and sex representation in tv drama. *Journal of Broadcasting*, 17(2), 201–214. 10.1080/08838157309363684

Seo, B.-I., & Hinton, D. (2009). How they see us, how we see them: Two women of color in higher education. *Race, Gender & Class (Towson, Md.)*, 16(3), 203–2017.

Shipp, K. (2023). Mental health looks different for everyone: The Black female perspective. *The Red & Black*. Retrieved from https://www.redandblack.com/

Shorter-Gooden, K. (2004). Shifting: The Double Lives of Black Women in America. *The Journal of Black Psychology*, 30(3), 333–335.

Smith, K. (2020). Hidden Heirlooms: Black Families and Their Stories of Continuity. *Journal of Narrative Politics*, 6(2).

Social Sciences Feminist Network Research Interest Group. (2017). The Burden of Invisible Work in Academia: Social Inequalities and Time Use in Five. *Humboldt Journal of Social Relations*, 2828–245.

Solomon, B. M. (1985). *In the company of educated women: A history of women and higher education in America*. Yale University Press.

Sombret, P. (2023, March 21). Workplace equity vs. equality: What's the difference? RSS. https://www.deskbird.com/blog/workplace-equity-vs-equality

Spates, K., Evans, N. L., & Jackson, C. E. (2020). Gendered racism and mental health among young adult US Black women: The moderating roles of gender identity and Africentric worldview. *Sex Roles*, 83(1-2), 47–57. 10.1007/s11199-019-01081-2

Spruill, I. J., Coleman, B. L., Powell-Young, Y. M., Williams, T. H., & Agwood, G. (2014). Non-biological (fictive kin and othermothers): Ebracing the need for a culturally appropriate pedigree nomenclature in African-American families. *Journal of the National Black Nurses' Association. Journal of National Black Nurses' Association*, 25(2), 23–30. https://www.ncbi.nlm.nih.gov/pmc/articles/PMC4847537/27134343

Stanford, T. N. (2018). African American grandmothers as the black matriarch : You don't live for yourself. (ThinkIR). The University of Louisville's Institutional Repository. https://ir.library.louisville.edu/etd/2944/

Stanley, C. A. (2009). Giving voice from the perspectives of African American women leaders. *Advances in Developing Human Resources*, 11(5), 551–561. 10.1177/1523422309351520

Stevenson, E. J. (2023). Impacts of the Sapphire stereotype seen on reality television in college-aged Black women [Senior Honors Thesis, Eastern Michigan University]. https://commons.emich.eduhonors/766

Stockstill, D., & Swafford, G. E. (Writer), & Foley, M. (Director). (2015, February 19). Mama's Here Now. (Season 1, Episode 13) [TV Series]. In Rhimes, S., Beers, B., D'Elia, B., Nowalk, P. (Executive Producers), How to Get Away with Murder. Shondaland. NoWalk Entertainment. ABC Studios.

Stone, E. (2008). *Black sheep and kissing cousins: How our family stories shape us*. Transaction Publisher.

Strayhorn, T. L., & Terrell, M. C. (2007). Mentoring and Satisfaction with College for Black Students. *Negro Educational Review*, 58, 69–83.

Sue, S. W., Rivera, D. P., Watkins, N. L., Kim, R. H., Kim, S., & Williams, C. D. (2011, July). Racial dialogues: Challenges faculty of color face in the classroom. *Cultural Diversity & Ethnic Minority Psychology*, 17(3), 331–340. 10.1037/a002419021787066

Sullivan, L. S. (2020). Trust, risk, and race in American Medicine. *The Hastings Center Report*, 50(1), 18–26. 10.1002/hast.108032068281

Swafford, G. E. (Writer), & Innes, L. (Director). (2014, October 16). Let's Get to Scooping. (Season 1, Episode 4) [TV Series]. In Rhimes, S., Beers, B., D'Elia, B., Nowalk, P. (Executive Producers), *How to Get Away with Murder*. Shondaland. NoWalk Entertainment. ABC Studios.

Szymanski, D. M., & Stewart, D. N. (2010). Racism and sexism as correlates of African American women's psychological distress. *Sex Roles*, 63(3-4), 226–238. 10.1007/s11199-010-9788-020352053

Templeton, J. (2000). *Pure unlimited love*. Templeton Foundation Press.

The Amplified Study Bible. (2016). Zondervan.

The Systemic Scarcity of Tenured Black Women. (2021, July 15). Inside Higher Education. Retrieved from https://www.insidehighered.com/advice/2021/07/16/black-women-face-many-obstaclestheir-efforts-win-tenure-opinion

Thomas, M. (2022). What does work-life balance even mean? *Forbes*. https://www.forbes.com/sites/maurathomas/2022/07/26/what-does-work-life-balance-even-mean/?sh=4450a28a2617

Thomas, T. D., & Hill, M. (2022). Reversing the dehumanization of black women. In *Black women and public health: strategies to name, locate, and change systems of power* (pp. 36-40). State University of New York Press, Albany 10.1515/9781438487335-003

Thomas, K. M., Johnson-Bailey, J., Phelps, R. E., Tran, N. M., & Johnson, L. N. (2013). Women of color at midcareer: Going from pet to threat. In Comas-Díaz, L., & Greene, B. (Eds.), *Psychological health of women of color: Intersections, challenges, and opportunities* (pp. 275–290). Praeger. 10.5040/9798216002536.ch-014

Toossi, M., & Joyner, L. (2018, February). *Blacks in the labor force*. U.S. Bureau of Labor Statistics. https://www.bls.gov/spotlight/2018/Blacks-in-the-labor-force/pdf/Blacks-in-the-labor-force.pdf

Travis, D. J., & Thorpe-Moscon, J. (2020). Day-to-day experiences of emotional tax among women and men of color in the workplace. *Catalyst : Feminism, Theory, Technoscience*.

Tulshyan, R. (2022). *Inclusion on purpose: An intersectional approach to creating a culture of belonging at work*. MIT Press. 10.7551/mitpress/14004.001.0001

Turman, L. (2024). *Emails surface from LU's VP of Student Affairs sent the day she died by suicide*. KRCG13.https://krcgtv.com/news/local/emails-surface-from -lus-vp-of-student-affairs-sent-the-day-she-died-by-suicide

Turman, L. (n.d.). (2024). *Emails surface from Lu's VP of Student Affairs sent the day she died by suicide*. KRCG. https://krcgtv.com/news/local/emails-surface-from -lus-vp-of-student-affairs-sent-the-day-she-died-by-suicide

Turner, K., Myers, S., Creswell, J., Sherraden, M. S., Loke, V., & Smith, A. W. (2018). Women's career advancement: An examination of the influence of representation on women's pursuit of leadership roles. *Journal of Women & Aging*, 30(1), 3–18.29558298

Tynan, J. (2023). *Inclusive sponsorship a bold vision to advance women of color in the workplace*. Rowman & Littlefield.

Tyree, C. M. T., & Powell, A. (2022). African American women's representations on television. *Journal of African American Studies*, 26(3), 277–296. 10.1007/ s12111-022-09587-1

U.S. Bureau of Labor Statistics. (2018). U.S. Department of Labor. *Occupational Outlook Handbook*.

U.S. Census Bureau. (2011). *The Black population: 2010*. U.S. Department of Commerce. Economics and Statistics Administration. https://www.census.gov/prod/ cen2010/briefs/c2010br-06.pdf

Underwood, L. (2009). Compassionate love: A framework for research. In Fehr, B., Sprecher, S., & Underwood, L. (Eds.), *The science of compassionate love: Theory, research, and applications* (pp. 1–25). Blackwell Publishing Ltd.

United States Census Bureau. (2012, December 12). *U.S. Census Bureau*. Retrieved March 19, 2024, from Newsroom Archive: https://www.census.gov/newsroom/ releases/archives/population/cb12-243.html#:~:text=The%20U.S.%20is%20 projected%20to%20become%20a%20majority-minority,comprise%2057%20percent %20of%20the%20population%20in%202060

Va.gov: Veterans Affairs. Racial Trauma. (2021, August 16). Retrieved October 2, 2023, from https://www.ptsd.va.gov/understand/types/racial_trauma.asp

Vakalahi, H. F., & Starks, S. H. (2011). Health, well-being and women of color academics. *International Journal of Humanities and Social Science*, 1(2), 185–190.

Valandra, M.-E., Murphy-Erby, Y., Higgins, B. M., & Brown, L. M. (2019). African American Perspectives and Experiences of Domestic Violence in a Rural Community. *Journal of Interpersonal Violence*, 34(16), 3319–3343. 10.1177/0886260516 66954227659684

Wallace-Sanders, K. (2010). *Mammy: A century of race, gender and Southern memory*. University of Michigan Press.

Warren-Gordon, K., & Mencias McMillan, D. (2022). Analysis of Black Female Belizean Stereotypes in Visual Media: Jezebel, Mammy, Sapphire, and their Contributions to Violence against Women. *Journal of International Women's Studies*, 23(1), 248–262. https://doi.org/https://vc.bridgew.edu/jiws/vol23/iss1/23/

Watson, N. N., & Hunter, C. D. (2015). Anxiety and depression among African American women: The costs of strength and negative attitudes toward psychological help-seeking. *Cultural Diversity & Ethnic Minority Psychology*, 21(4), 604–612. 10.1037/cdp000001525602466

Webb, J. G. (2010). The evolution of women's roles within the university and workplace. In *Forum on Public Policy Online* (Vol. 2010, No. 5). Oxford Round Table.

Webster, L., & Mertova, P. (2007). *Using narrative inquiry as a research method: An introduction to using critical event narrative analysis in research on learning and teaching*. Routledge., 10.4324/9780203946268

West, C. M. (1995). Mammy, Sapphire, and Jezebel: Historical images of Black women and their implications for psychotherapy. *Psychotherapy (Chicago, Ill.)*, 32(3), 458–466. 10.1037/0033-3204.32.3.458

West, C., Donovan, R. A., & Daniel, B. (2020). The price of opportunity: Coping with gendered racial microaggressions as a Black woman senior leader. *Equality, Diversity and Inclusion*, 39(2), 175–194. 10.1108/EDI-11-2018-0218

What is posttraumatic stress disorder (PTSD)? (n.d.). Psychiatry.org - What is Posttraumatic Stress Disorder (PTSD)? https://www.psychiatry.org/patients-families/ ptsd/what-is-ptsd#:~:text=Posttraumatic%20stress%20disorder%20(PTSD)%20is ,events%20or%20set%20of%20circumstances

Whitfield, J. (2022). Systemic racism in communication sciences and disorders academic programs: A commentary on trends in racial representation. *American Journal of Speech-Language Pathology*, 32(1), 381–390. 10.1044/2022_AJSLP-22-0021036450159

Whitford, E. (2020, May 5). *Who Holds Professional Positions in Higher Ed, and Who Gets Paid?* Retrieved from Inside Higher Ed: https://www.insidehighered.com/news/2020/05/06/report-details-gaps-women-and-minority-professionals-higher-ed

Whitford, E. (2020, October 27). *There are so few that have made their way*. Retrieved from Inside Higher Ed: https://www.insidehighered.com/news/2020/10/28/black-administrators-are-too-rare-top-ranks-higher-education-it%E2%80%99s-not-just-pipeline

WHOQOL SRPB Group. (2006). A cross-cultural study of spirituality, religion, and personal beliefs as components of quality of life. *Social Science & Medicine*, 62(6), 1486–1497. 10.1016/j.socscimed.2005.08.00116168541

Will, M. (2022, May 17). "Brown v. Board" decimated the black educator pipeline. A scholar explains how. *Education Week.* https://www.edweek.org/teaching-learning/brown-v-board-decimated-the-black-educator-pipeline-a-scholar-explains-how/2022/05

Williams, D. R., & Mohammed, S. A. (2009). Discrimination and racial disparities in health: Evidence and needed research. *Journal of Behavioral Medicine*, 32(1), 20–47. 10.1007/s10865-008-9185-019030981

Williams, M. T., & Lewis, J. A. (2019). Gendered racial microaggressions, trauma, and mental health in African American women. *Journal of Feminist Family Therapy*, 31(3-4), 129–151. 10.1080/08952833.2019.1651090

Wilton, L. (2020). *Show don't tell: Diversity dishonesty harms racial/ethnic minorities at work.* Sage Journals. Show don't tell: Diversity dishonesty harms racial/ethnic minorities at work. Sage Journals.

Wolfe, B., & Fletcher, J. (2013). *Estimating Benefits from University-Level Diversity.* National Bureau of Economic Research. 10.3386/w18812

Woman of Color and the Wage Gap. (2023). Center for American Progress. Retrieved from: https://www.americanprogress.org/article/women-of-color-and-the-wage-gap/

Wong, A. (2024, January 16). *An HBCU administrator died by suicide. the school's president is now on leave.* USA Today. https://www.usatoday.com/story/news/education/2024/01/12/lincoln-university-president-leave-sudden-death/72205406007/

Woods-Giscombé, C. L. (2010). Superwoman schema: African American women's views on stress, strength, and health. *Qualitative Health Research*, 20(5), 668–683. 10.1177/1049732310361892201154298

Woyshner, C., & Schocker, J. B. (2015). Cultural parallax and content analysis: Images of Black women in high school history textbooks. *Theory and Research in Social Education*, 43(4), 441–468. 10.1080/00933104.2015.1099487

Zimmer, L. (1988). Tokenism and Women in the Workplace: The Limits of Gender-Neutral Theory. *Social Problems*, 64-77. Retrieved 6 11, 2023, from https://www .jstor.org/stable/800667

About the Contributors

Ashley N. Storman (she/her) is a Diversity, Equity, and Inclusion Scholar, Practitioner, Author, and Educator that identifies as a Christian, Wife, and Mother. Dr. Storman has over 15 years of higher education experience in the following: diversity, equity, & inclusion, recruitment, retention, coaching, leadership development, mentor programs, affinity groups, departmental and organization-wide program development, social justice curriculum development, consulting, teaching, and strategic collaboration to implement programs and strategies to assist marginalized communities, educate allies, and build inclusive environments. Dr. Storman was born and raised in Davenport, Iowa, and received her Bachelor of Arts degree in Criminology and her Master of Arts in Education with an emphasis in Post-Secondary Education: Student Affairs, both from the University of Northern Iowa. In 2019, Dr. Storman obtained her Doctor of Education (Ed.D) in Higher Education Leadership with a Teaching emphasis from Maryville University. In April of 2022, Dr. Storman decided to put her passion to work and launched The Storman Group LLC. to impact culture by cultivating inclusive work environments. Dr. Storman is also a published author with research that focuses on the leadership development of African American women who aspire to be leaders in the academy. Dr. Storman is a fellow of the St. Louis Business Diversity Initiative Leadership Program, a past Board Member of the NASPA Center for Women, Rides N' School Supply, and American Association of Advertising STL. Currently she serves as Board Member for Habitat for Humanity St. Louis, committee member for Girls Inc. of St. Louis, and a proud member of Alpha Kappa Alpha Sorority, Incorporated. Dr. Storman resides in St. Louis, MO with her husband, two sons, and dog. Dr. Storman is very passionate about DEI, women's empowerment, and addressing issues of equity that hinder those from marginalized backgrounds from having an equitable and fair opportunity.

Destiny Reddick is an educator, equity champion, and social justice influencer with 17+ years of experience in K-12 and higher education. Her track record of effectively leading and inspiring diverse students, teachers, and schools and advocating tirelessly to promote educational equity intentionally focuses on supporting traditionally underserved, under-resourced schools and communities. Reddick has served as a public school teacher, instructional specialist, district-level curriculum and instruction leader where she authored an instructional framework for teachers that incorporated social-emotional learning and anti-racism, Assistant Professor of education, and Assistant Dean of undergraduate and graduate education programs. She currently serves in a few roles, including the CEO/Founder of Redefine the Pipeline, LLC, which provides I.D.E.A. (Inclusion, Diversity, Equity, and Anti-Racism) consulting and coaching services for organizations, school systems, and universities, an associate and professional speaker for Solution Tree professional learning and educational publishing company, and an evaluator for Western Governors University's teacher education program. Reddick is a national presenter in education, assessment, and diversity and inclusion. She has participated in years of formal, site-based training in cultural and linguistic responsiveness and assessment literacy and has also achieved various state-endorsed educational certifications. Some of her most experienced areas include: sound assessment and grading practices, evaluation, culturally and linguistically responsive pedagogy, social-emotional learning, restorative practices, adult learning principles, professional development, instructional, course, and curriculum design, facilitating adult learning and strategic organizational support in diversity, equity, inclusion, and anti-racism in PK-12 and higher education settings. Reddick recently joined ForbesBLK, a platform, and community that amplifies the voices of Black entrepreneurs, professionals, leaders, and creators, and was inducted into the National Honor Society of Leadership & Success. Additional accolades include the President's Award for Strategic Leadership in Diversity and Inclusion (2019); Power 100 Honoree (2019), Who's Who Diversity in Color Honoree (2019); Teacher of the Year (2012); Outstanding Missouri Beginning Teacher (2007); Leona Korol Award for Professional Promise (2006). Reddick holds her doctorate in teacher leadership and a master's degree in early childhood education. She soon completes another master's, this time in educational leadership. Her bachelor's degree is in elementary education. In her spare time, Dr. Reddick serves on the Board of a nonprofit called A Red Circle that promotes community betterment in North St. Louis County through a racial equity lens and leads a Diversity, Equity, and Inclusion parent volunteer committee at her children's school (ages 10 and 6).

* * *

Asueleni Deloney is a graduate of Lincoln University of Jefferson City Mo. with a Bachelors in Journalism as well as a Lindenwood University graduate with a Masters of Art in Education. She has worked in education over a decade. This has allowed her to not only support students in their academics but also in their social emotional development, as she is trained in trauma informed awareness. In doing this work she not only works closely with students but their families, providing guidance and, teaching them how to advocate and become the primary voice for their child. Asueleni finds this work very rewarding as she believes, parents are their child's first teachers and when parents feel empowered and knowledgeable they are better able to parent and advocate for their child. As a Journalist for over 15 years she is passionate about telling the stories and capturing the moments that will impact and support change in her community. In doing this she is able to support important conversations and assist in igniting change in significant subject matter. The work she's doing in the area of Social Justice allows her to merge both of her skills sets as she brings to light this pervasive issue through education, and work to build awareness around it while uncovering the hidden agenda of traffickers and engaging the community so that protections can be built to support our most vulnerable demographic, young innocent girls and boys. Asueleni is currently nurturing a growing business Hand 'N Hand Coaching, she serves as the President on the Board of the a non for profit The Community Reach, She is the Local Recruiter for the Greater St. Louis Alumni Association of Lincoln University as well as a member, and a Proud Member of Alpha Kappa Alpha Sorority Incorporated severing in multiple capacities in her chapter.

Ty Jiles-Vaughn is an early childhood educator with expertise in community based childcare programs and teaching pre-service candidates with an emphasis on equity based learning. Currently, Dr. Jiles serves as the Dean of Career and Technical Education at Prairie State College. Most recently Dr. Jiles is currently studying the use of virtual stimulations in preparing pre-service teachers to work with adults and innovative curriculum for Hybrid and Electrical Vehicles. In addition to being a qualitative researcher Dr. Jiles is an early childhood advocate and higher education commissioner. She serves on several committees and works with organizations that support the advancement and welfare of teachers, young children, and their families.

Zinnia Marie Mack Lewis, Ed.D., is a catalyst for change and does so by guiding high school students on the post-high school journey. A school counselor, an educator, and an advocate for diversity, equity, inclusion, and belonging, Dr. Lewis embody the characteristics of a dedicated community member. She has over 20 years of experience in public school education and is employed with the St. Bernard Parish School System. Dr. Lewis plays an important role as a liaison between staff, parents, and students. She is an integral part of the landscape of the school and works alongside administrators in imparting knowledge and guidance to students. She has been selected to serve on a district-wide and school-wide committee to begin the implementation of new programs centered around emotional intelligence. She is a member of the National Sorority of Phi Delta Kappa, Inc., Delta Sigma Theta Sorority, Inc., the American Association for School Counselors, and the Louisiana School Counselor Association. Educational Background: Doctorate of Education – University of Holy Cross, 2021 Master of Education – University of Southern Mississippi, 2006 Bachelor of Science – Southern University at New Orleans, 1999.

Chenell Loudermill, PhD, CCC-SLP, is a Clinical Professor and Director of Clinical Education in Speech-Language Pathology in the Department of Speech, Language, and Hearing Sciences (SLHS) at Purdue University where she oversees and provides clinical education in speech-language pathology. She serves and the SLHS Chair for Diversity, Equity and Inclusion and Health and Human Sciences Dean's Fellow for Faculty Success and Empowerment. Chenell obtained her Master of Science and doctoral degree from the University of Arkansas for Medical Sciences (UAMS). She has over twenty years of experience, thirteen of which were obtained working as a speech-language pathologist in the public schools before moving to higher education. Chenell has expertise in assessment and treatment of language-based literacy disorders such as dyslexia as well as treating individuals with social interaction and communication difficulties such as Autism Spectrum Disorders (ASD). Other interests include leadership, administration and supervision in speech-language pathology, culturally responsive practices and pedagogy and interprofessional education and practice. Chenell teaches graduate and undergraduate courses in clinical practice and literacy. She also co-leads the Purdue Literacy Education and Practice Project (Purdue-LEaPP) and is the Project Director for an Office of Special Education Programs (OSEP) personnel development program grant. Chenell is also a member of several professional organizations such as the National Black Association for Speech, Language and Hearing (NBALSH) and the American Speech-Language Hearing Association (ASHA).

Megan Lyons is an Assistant Professor at North Carolina Central University and a former high school special education teacher. She earned a Bachelor's of Science in Communications Disorders and a Master's of Education in Special Education from Auburn University. She later earned a Specialist Degree in Educational Leadership from Columbus State University and holds a doctorate in Educational Leadership from Valdosta State University. Her research interests include social emotional learning and culturally responsive pedagogy.

Bri'Yana Nicole Merrill is an innovator and life-long learner. In 2023, she received her BS in Physics of Medicine and Bioethics with a Pre-MBA minor from Rockhurst University. She constantly strives to create environments centered around belonging, justice, and accessibility. In May of 2021, she was awarded "Outstanding Support for Diversity" on her campus. With previous internships ranging from the Federal Reserve Bank of St. Louis (2022) to BJC Healthcare (2023), and the American Society of Clinical Oncology (2024), she is intentional in diversifying her skillset while elevating her passion for DEI work. She's currently enrolled in an MPH program with a concentration in Health Equity & Social Justice at George Mason University and plans to graduate in May of 2025. Her mission is to impact and empower the generations that precede and follow her through her innovative thinking, creativity, and effective leadership. Her philosophy is that chasing her impact is far greater than chasing a title.

Lovis M. Nelson-Williams, MS, EdD, is the Deputy Project Director for Bronx Community Solutions (BCS), a project of the Center for Justice Innovation. BCS is an organization that provides diversion options for justice-involved individuals. She has developed a robust criminal justice experiential internship during her tenure at BCS. In this capacity, she connected with Monroe College in the Bronx and became an adjunct faculty member. This role inspired her to pursue and acquire a Doctorate in Education, which she achieved in 2023.

Eboni Sterling, Ph.D., is a creative at the intersection of the arts and data evaluation, where storytelling meets research. Weaving tales through the lens of her camera, she documents life for the sole purpose of legacy. Beyond the realm of creativity, Dr. Sterling wears the responsibility of a researcher, firmly convinced that life itself is the richest well of data. In May 2022, Dr. Sterling became a Doctor of Philosophy in Higher Education with an emphasis in Social Justice from the University of Missouri-St. Louis (UMSL). In her academic pursuits, Dr. Sterling is a dedicated advocate for women's leadership, virtue ethics, African American studies, storytelling functions, and emancipatory knowing. She served the fields of Education and Human Services in various roles, from Program Director at Girls Inc. St. Louis to the Center of Character and Citizenship Post-Doctoral Fellow, Multicultural Student Services' Academic Coach, and Academic Advisor for the UMSL College of Education. A three-time graduate of UMSL, she currently serves as a Director of Research and Evaluation. Dr. Sterling seamlessly transitions between her gifts as a nurturer, speaker, artist, and researcher. For Dr. Sterling, family and soul-care take precedence. She spends her days and nights tending to her family of origin, her family of choice, and her garden.

Chinyere Turner (she/her) hails from Okinawa, Japan – Kadena Air Force Base. Moving from Okinawa to St. Louis, she attended Maryville University, graduating in 2017 with a Bachelor's degree in History and English and a minor in Secondary Education. Turner has continued her education by receiving a Master's degree in Higher Education Administration from the University of Missouri, St. Louis. As many higher education professionals deem themselves, Turner is also a "life-long learner" and has started the journey of pursuing a doctoral degree at the University of West Georgia. Having now served at multiple institutions, her previous roles have allowed her to focus on the retention of students of color through assessment and data collection, programming that cultivate student identities, and teach courses and give presentations that assist with students' knowledge of social justice issues. Currently, Turner serves as the Associate Director of the Cultural & Community Centers at Kennesaw State University. While navigating the higher education space, Turner has always had black women support her in her educational and professional goals, and therefore she wants to reach back and do the same for the next generation. As Issa Rae once stated, "I'm rooting for everybody black". Turner works in the DEI field because this work is important for the empowerment of marginalized communities and she understands that all of our liberation is tied together. Turner's personal mission is to strive to always be a source of support for people of color and all underrepresented populations. Turner is also co-founder of "Partners In Justice LLC" a social justice education company whose mission is to spread knowledge of cultural competency through workshops and presentation facilitation around diversity, equity, and inclusion frameworks.

Taylor C. J. Wynne (she/her/hers) is a first year Ph.D. student at The Ohio State University in the department of Educational Studies. Taylor earned her Master of Education in Higher Education Student Affairs from the University of Florida and her Bachelor of Arts in English Literature from the University of Toledo. Taylor's research agenda centers three main foci: (1) the identity development and intersectional experiences of Black undergraduate women, (2) Black Girlhood Studies, and (3) Anti-Blackness in education. Through qualitative research methodologies, Taylor's aim is to create safe, holistic, and healthy educational environments conducive to the development of Black girls and women.

Index

A

Academia 65, 68, 70, 71, 74, 79, 81, 83, 86, 87, 88, 91, 92, 93, 102, 125, 127, 150, 159, 163, 167, 170, 171, 172, 180, 219, 224, 232, 237, 238, 239, 240, 242, 245, 246, 247, 253, 254, 266
Affinity Organization 118, 121
Aftershock 106, 114, 115, 116, 121
Authentic Leadership 52, 251, 255, 259, 261, 262, 267, 268, 270, 272, 274

B

BIPOC 85, 91, 93, 94, 95, 97, 98, 99, 101
Black Feminist Theory 1, 15
Black Feminist Thought 15, 58, 79, 129, 154, 164, 173, 194, 251, 252, 255, 256, 267, 268, 273
Black Women Educators 177, 178, 181, 182, 191, 192, 199, 210, 251, 252, 253, 254, 257, 261, 269, 270, 272
Black Women Faculty 64, 65, 66, 67, 68, 69, 70, 71, 72, 75, 76, 77, 78, 104, 159, 160, 163, 164, 171, 172
Black Women Graduate Students 63, 67, 69, 77, 78

C

Communication Sciences and Disorders 91, 92, 104
Cultural Betrayal 1
Culturally Responsive Mentorship 63, 67, 71
Culture Shock 107, 121

D

Dehumanize 122, 171, 178, 180
Diaspora 109, 121, 188
Diversity Dishonesty 197, 204, 206, 209, 213

Diversity Programs 201, 207, 210, 212, 213

E

Educational Leadership 1, 3, 4, 5, 6, 7, 13, 14, 22, 23, 35, 36, 37, 38, 43, 45, 46, 47, 54, 57, 59, 155
Emancipatory Knowing 129, 130, 134, 135
Emotions 9, 55, 84, 85, 86, 101, 110, 114, 116, 117, 133, 168, 198, 205, 255, 262
Empowerment 6, 23, 47, 48, 49, 51, 53, 58, 79, 109, 118, 128, 129, 140, 142, 146, 150, 154, 161, 171, 194, 240, 252, 268, 270, 273
Entrepreneurship 240, 266, 271
Equality 61, 111, 119, 197, 201, 202, 207, 209, 213, 217, 241, 242, 243, 246
Equity 20, 21, 48, 49, 50, 53, 57, 58, 76, 77, 78, 98, 126, 154, 197, 201, 204, 209, 212, 213, 220, 226, 228, 229, 231, 232, 251, 252, 268, 272

F

Faculty of Color 91, 104, 156, 224

H

Heat Map 204, 213
Higher Education 13, 26, 63, 64, 65, 66, 67, 68, 74, 75, 76, 77, 78, 79, 81, 82, 86, 87, 88, 89, 91, 92, 99, 105, 114, 125, 126, 127, 128, 135, 138, 142, 143, 145, 146, 148, 152, 153, 155, 156, 159, 160, 163, 173, 194, 207, 217, 218, 220, 222, 223, 224, 225, 227, 228, 229, 230, 231, 232, 234, 235, 236, 237, 238, 239, 240, 241, 244, 245, 246, 247, 248, 249, 251, 252, 256, 258, 260, 261, 266, 270, 273, 274

I

Identity Negotiation 1, 4, 6, 7, 13, 14, 22, 24, 25, 26, 28, 36, 37, 53, 54, 57

L

Limited Resources 82, 86
Love Ethic 146, 148, 149

M

Mainstream Media 159, 160, 162
Matrix of Domination 1, 7, 8, 48, 58, 173
Mental Health 15, 25, 48, 51, 53, 54, 60,
61, 67, 71, 75, 102, 107, 112, 117,
180, 208, 212, 218, 229, 231, 253,
254, 268, 270, 272
Mentorship 28, 43, 44, 49, 50, 63, 65, 67,
68, 69, 70, 71, 72, 73, 76, 77, 78, 93,
127, 153, 177, 185, 186, 187, 191,
192, 235, 240, 241, 242, 243, 244, 247,
255, 258, 259, 260, 261, 268, 270, 271
Microaggressions 7, 8, 9, 24, 29, 33, 35, 59,
61, 85, 91, 96, 97, 99, 102, 104, 126,
135, 150, 204, 214, 218, 225, 229, 233
Misogynoir 75, 92, 222, 229, 231, 234, 271

N

Nurturing 10, 65, 152, 178, 180, 186, 187,
188, 190, 191, 192, 241, 245, 269

P

Pet to Threat 60, 211, 213, 214
Psychological Safety 4, 6, 23, 24, 48, 197,
202, 203, 208, 212, 214
PWI 82, 91, 94, 95, 97, 98, 107, 113,
122, 218

R

Racism 3, 4, 8, 14, 20, 59, 60, 66, 69, 82,
84, 89, 92, 93, 94, 96, 97, 99, 102,
104, 114, 115, 121, 127, 137, 178,
186, 187, 190, 198, 204, 207, 208,
222, 226, 229, 234, 253, 254

Retrospective Family Storytelling 125,
127, 128, 130, 135

S

Sapphire 10, 61, 177, 178, 183, 184, 185,
187, 191, 192, 194, 195
Self-Care 51, 66, 71, 105, 112, 116, 117,
118, 152, 268
Servant Leadership 150, 151, 154
Social Identity 60, 68, 177, 221, 225,
233, 234
Solidarity 52, 68, 80, 111, 206, 210, 214
Stereotypes 6, 7, 8, 9, 10, 11, 12, 14, 22,
23, 25, 26, 27, 28, 31, 32, 36, 37, 38,
41, 43, 44, 45, 46, 47, 51, 54, 58, 59,
67, 74, 86, 106, 161, 162, 164, 177,
178, 191, 192, 195, 214, 218, 219, 221,
223, 225, 226, 229, 235, 238, 239, 240,
241, 245, 246, 247, 268
Storytelling 125, 126, 127, 128, 129, 130,
135, 140, 153, 154, 155, 156, 236
Strong Black Woman 9, 41, 58, 81, 174
Student Leader 38, 105, 106, 107, 108,
109, 116, 122, 224
Systematic Scarcity 67

T

Tokenism 8, 38, 159, 217, 218, 219, 220,
221, 222, 223, 224, 226, 227, 228,
229, 230, 231, 232, 233
Transparency 16, 116, 147, 259, 260, 267,
270, 271, 272

U

Unconscious Bias 208, 214

W

Work Pet to Work Threat 7, 8, 9, 206

Publishing Tomorrow's Research Today

Uncover Current Insights and Future Trends in
Education
with IGI Global's Cutting-Edge Recommended Books

Print Only, E-Book Only, or Print + E-Book.
Order direct through IGI Global's Online Bookstore at **www.igi-global.com** or through your preferred provider.

ISBN: 9781668493007
© 2023; 234 pp.
List Price: US$ 215

ISBN: 9798369300749
© 2024; 383 pp.
List Price: US$ 230

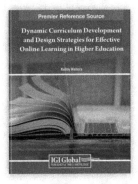

ISBN: 9781668486467
© 2023; 471 pp.
List Price: US$ 215

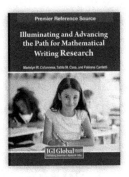

ISBN: 9781668465387
© 2024; 389 pp.
List Price: US$ 215

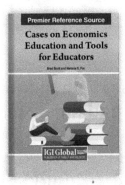

ISBN: 9781668475836
© 2024; 359 pp.
List Price: US$ 215

ISBN: 9781668444238
© 2023; 334 pp.
List Price: US$ 240

Do you want to stay current on the latest research trends, product announcements, news, and special offers?
Join IGI Global's mailing list to receive customized recommendations, exclusive discounts, and more.
Sign up at: www.igi-global.com/newsletters.

Scan the QR Code here to view more related titles in Education.

www.igi-global.com | Sign up at www.igi-global.com/newsletters | facebook.com/igiglobal | twitter.com/igiglobal | linkedin.com/igiglobal

Ensure Quality Research is Introduced to the Academic Community

Become a Reviewer for IGI Global Authored Book Projects

  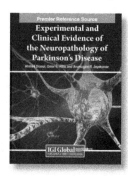 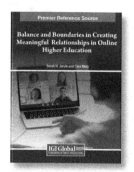

The overall success of an authored book project is dependent on quality and timely manuscript evaluations.

Applications and Inquiries may be sent to:
development@igi-global.com

Applicants must have a doctorate (or equivalent degree) as well as publishing, research, and reviewing experience. Authored Book Evaluators are appointed for one-year terms and are expected to complete at least three evaluations per term. Upon successful completion of this term, evaluators can be considered for an additional term.

If you have a colleague that may be interested in this opportunity, we encourage you to share this information with them.

Are You Ready to Publish Your Research

IGI Global offers book authorship and editorship opportunities across three major subject areas, including Business, STM, and Education.

Benefits of Publishing with IGI Global:

- Free one-on-one editorial and promotional support.
- Expedited publishing timelines that can take your book from start to finish in less than one (1) year.
- Choose from a variety of formats, including Edited and Authored References, Handbooks of Research, Encyclopedias, and Research Insights.
- Utilize IGI Global's eEditorial Discovery® submission system in support of conducting the submission and double-blind peer review process.
- IGI Global maintains a strict adherence to ethical practices due in part to our full membership with the Committee on Publication Ethics (COPE).
- Indexing potential in prestigious indices such as Scopus®, Web of Science™, PsycINFO®, and ERIC – Education Resources Information Center.
- Ability to connect your ORCID iD to your IGI Global publications.
- Earn honorariums and royalties on your full book publications as well as complimentary content and exclusive discounts.

Join Your Colleagues from Prestigious Institutions, Including:

Learn More at: www.igi-global.com/publish
or by Contacting the Acquisitions Department at: acquisition@igi-global.com

Individual Article & Chapter Downloads
US$ 37.50/each

Easily Identify, Acquire, and Utilize Published Peer-Reviewed Findings in Support of Your Current Research

- Browse Over **170,000+ Articles & Chapters**
- **Accurate & Advanced** Search
- Affordably Acquire **International Research**
- **Instantly Access** Your Content
- Benefit from the **InfoSci® Platform Features**

" *It really provides an excellent entry into the research literature of the field. It presents a manageable number of highly relevant sources on topics of interest to a wide range of researchers. The sources are scholarly, but also accessible to 'practitioners'.* "

- Ms. Lisa Stimatz, MLS, University of North Carolina at Chapel Hill, USA

Printed in the USA
CPSIA information can be obtained
at www.ICGtesting.com
LVHW081756041124
795688LV00005B/608